CASEBOOK FOR
THE FOUNDATION:
A GREAT AMERICAN SECRET

CASEBOOK FOR

THE

FOUNDATION

A GREAT AMERICAN SECRET

JOEL L. FLEISHMAN,

J. SCOTT KOHLER, AND

STEVEN SCHINDLER

PublicAffairs

New York

Library of Congress Cataloging-in-Publication Data
Fleishman, Joel L.
    Casebook for The Foundation : a great American secret / Joel L. Fleishman, J. Scott Kohler, and
Steven Schindler. — 1st ed.
        p. cm.
    ISBN-13: 978-1-58648-488-0
    ISBN-10: 1-58648-488-5

    1. Charities—United States—Case studies. 2. Endowments—United States—Case studies.
3. Associations, institutions, etc.—United States—Case studies. I. Kohler, J. Scott, 1982–
II. Schindler, Steven, 1980–   III. Fleishman, Joel L. Foundation. IV. Title.

HV97.A3F538   2007
361.7'6320973—dc22

                                                                                    2006034660

First Edition
10 9 8 7 6 5 4 3 2 1

CONTENTS

INTRODUCTION

This book of cases was originally intended to be an appendix to Joel L. Fleishman, *The Foundation: A Great American Secret, How Private Wealth is Changing the World* (New York: PublicAffairs, 2007), and many of them are referred to in that volume's discussion. That book, ISBN 1-58648-411-7, can be ordered via www.publicaffairsbooks.com or through customer service at 1-800-343-4499. The cases that follow were written by either J. Scott Kohler or Steven Schindler, under the direction of Joel Fleishman, for analysis in that book.

A few words would be in order about how these particular cases were identified and how they were developed.

No single book could possibly do justice to all that America's foundations have done or are trying to do. There are a few excellent works on foundations, most of which are included in the Selected Bibliography of *The Foundation*, although only a tiny handful of those attempt any assessment of foundation impact.[1] My intention in assembling the cases in this volume was to be selective and illustrative rather than fully representative or comprehensive, neither of which would have been possible in any single volume. The initiatives documented and analyzed here represent my personal choices, informed by my professional and scholarly experience with foundations, stretching across some forty-five years of seeking support from foundations, preparing program strategy papers for foundations, evaluating foundation initiatives of a variety of kinds, assessing the effectiveness of foundation governance and evaluation mechanisms, chairing the board of a foundation, serving as head of the United States program staff for a large foundation,[2] serving as president of a small foundation, raising money for universities and other grant-receiving organizations, and teaching for some twenty years about foundations and the not-for-profit sector. This book is also informed by two years of concentrated research in the existing literature on foundations, and more than a hundred interviews with observers of and participants in America's foundation world, especially the systematically philanthropic, a list of whom can be found in the Appendix I to *The Foundation*.

The selection of foundation initiatives represented here, however, is not entirely subjective. Virtually all of the longest-existing American foundations are dealt with in one way or another, and one or more of their senior officers or trustees have been interviewed. Most of the wealthiest American foundations, irrespective of their age, are also included within the scope of this study, but almost none of those established or preponderantly endowed after 1990 are included, primarily because they have had too little time since their founding to achieve measurable impact comparable to longer-existing foundations. This is most certainly not to slight these foundations. On the contrary, there is every reason to believe that they will, in years to come, change the world profoundly—to the enormous benefit of us all. In addition, a few mid-sized private foundations and a small sample of community foundations, which have earned the admiration of others in the foundation community, were also interviewed.

Those interviewed, too, are a personal rather than either a random or representative selection. Most of them are widely known and admired, expert nonprofit practitioners or scholars whom I have had the good fortune to come to know over the years. Some of them I sought out without any prior relationship because the institutions with which they are involved seemed, to me, responsible for foundation initiatives which I had come to believe had resulted in significant social impact. Some lead, or are trustees of, foundations, while others are the chief executives of grant-receiving organizations that depend in part on foundation support. It seemed essential to be able to triangulate the impact assessments by comparing the views of foundation-related individuals with the views of those who are both expert in substantive fields and who also are usually in the position of petitioning foundations for support. All of them, in my view, are persons of integrity, have judgment of high quality, and are capable of making objective judgments about foundation successes and failures. None of them pulled any punches or allowed their self-interest or involvement in initiatives to undermine their objectivity.

It is important to underscore that this study, therefore, is not what the purest of social scientists would regard as a scientifically valid one, although ethnographers, who employ the so-called snowball sample, might well find the results of my sampling persuasive. The choice of interviewees and foundations covered is a personal, subjective one, but the initiatives included are supported by such objective data as are available and have been carefully examined with as objective a lens as could be brought to bear.

A word now about the structure of the cases.

They are divided for clarity's sake into sections—background, strategy, outcomes, and impact (outcomes and impact are collapsed into a single section in one-third of the cases). Certainly, I do not suppose that any of these four is wholly extricable from the others. In particular, it is often difficult to draw a line between outcomes—which I view as the more or less measurable results associated with a particular foundation intervention—and impact, an amorphous heading under which is discussed the bigger picture significance of the intervention; a third of the cases do not attempt this line. Moreover, I wish to refer readers back to the discussion in *The Foundation* of the terms "strategy" and "tactic." The two are not coextensive, but the distinction between them (often a hazy one) does not generally find expression in the case studies herein, which assay only to provide an accurate and concise, not exhaustive, description of what foundations and their partners in each case were doing and what they achieved.

As mentioned above, in rare instances, researchers have produced thorough and insightful accounts of particular foundation programs and their impact on society. In those instances, the cases here rely heavily on those accounts. A majority of these cases, however, are attempts to piece together thin published records and firsthand accounts from interviews (when readily obtainable) into a comprehensible story about a foundation's impact on society through a particular program. Part of the premise of my book was that too little is known about the extent to which foundations have shaped and improved society. These cases were intended to inform my analysis in *The Foundation*, but I hope they also provide the public with a more complete picture of specific instances when foundations have acted to affect substantial change in our society. If they also promote further research into these and other cases of foundation impact, all the better.

JOEL L. FLEISHMAN

ROCKEFELLER UNIVERSITY

(Formerly the Rockefeller Institute for Medical Research), 1901

SCOTT KOHLER

Background. In the final years of the nineteenth century, John D. Rockefeller began seriously to discuss, with his philanthropic advisor Frederick T. Gates, and his son, John D. Rockefeller Jr., the possibility of funding a new institution of medical research. Over the next three years, Rockefeller's attorney, Starr Murphy, met with leading medical professionals in an effort better to understand the needs of the field. After Rockefeller Sr.'s three-year-old grandson, John Rockefeller McCormick, died in 1901 of scarlet fever, Gates and John D. Rockefeller Jr. persuaded him to create the Rockefeller Institute of Medical Research. Rockefeller Jr. later said of Gates, ". . . the institute was conceived in his own mind; it was the child of his own brain."[1] And along the same lines, he recalled, "Gates was the brilliant dreamer and orator. I was the salesman—the go-between with Father at the opportune moment."[2]

Strategy. In 1901, Rockefeller committed $200,000 over the next ten years for construction of the Institute. Committed to assembling the best possible researchers, Rockefeller, and the Institute's first board chairman, William H. Welch—himself a noted pathologist and the first dean of the Johns Hopkins School of Medicine—recruited Simon Flexner to run the Institute. With Flexner on board, Rockefeller supplemented his initial donation in June 1902 with an additional $1 million, also to be distributed over the next ten years.[3] The Institute grew slowly at first: a deliberate move by Rockefeller, who was not eager to repeat the difficulties caused by the University of Chicago's rapid growth a few years earlier. To encourage Flexner and the rest of the RIMR's staff to work hard, Rockefeller remained deliberately vague as to how much future support the Institute could expect from him.[4]

The Rockefeller Institute for Medical Research was the first institute of biomedical research in the United States. Its truest predecessors were such celebrated European research facilities as the Koch and Pasteur Institutes of Germany and France, respectively.[5] Recalling a letter he had sent encouraging Rockefeller Sr. to create the Institute, Gates reflected:

> I enumerated [to Rockefeller] the infectious diseases and pointed out how few of the germs had yet been discovered and how great the field of discovery, how few specifics had yet been found and how appalling was the unremedied suffering. I pointed to the Koch Institute in Berlin and at greater length to the

Pasteur Institute in Paris. . . . I pointed out, as I remember the fact, that the results in dollars or francs of Pasteur's discoveries about anthrax and on the diseases of fermentation has saved for the French nation a sum far in excess of the entire cost of the Franco-German war.[6]

The Institute was organized around several distinct laboratories, each one run by a distinguished leader in his field of medical research. In his classic biography of Rockefeller Sr., Ron Chernow writes:

That Rockefeller placed scientists, not lay trustees, in charge of the expenditures was thought revolutionary. This was the Institute's secret formula: gather great minds, liberate them from petty cares, and let them chase intellectual chimeras without pressure or meddling.

The Institute's first public triumph came in 1907, when its researchers—led by Dr. Flexner—developed a serum to cure cerebrospinal meningitis, which was just then sweeping through the streets of New York. The serum—which the RIMR distributed free of charge until the New York Board of Health took over the task in 1911—saved hundreds, if not thousands, of lives, and earned the Institute wide acclaim. In recognition of its success, Rockefeller donated to it an additional $2.6 million, which he then followed, later that year, with $8 million for the construction of Rockefeller Hospital, "the first center for clinical research in the United States."[7] The Hospital enabled RIMR researchers "to bridge the gap between science and the bedside, studying diseases both in the laboratory and as they manifested in patients."[8]

Outcomes. By the mid-1950s, the Institute's approach to research was widely emulated, and, seeking continually to stay ahead of the curve, it "expanded its mission to include education, admitting its first class of graduate students."[9] In 1965, the RIMR formally changed its name to Rockefeller University, a graduate institution pairing a well-funded, highly distinguished faculty with a very small, select cadre of graduate researchers. Since the early 1970s, Rockefeller University has also forged partnerships with several hospitals in New York, including Cornell University Medical College, the Sloan-Kettering Institute, and the Aaron Diamond AIDS Research Center.[10]

Very soon after its creation, the Rockefeller Institute of Medical Research joined the ranks of the world's elite centers of biomedical research. Today, Rockefeller University remains at the leading edge of progress in a wide range of medical areas. Its seventy-four laboratories study such conditions as addiction, Alzheimer's, diabetes, heart disease, and many others.[11] The first

RIMR scientist to be awarded the Nobel Prize was Alexis Carrel, who in 1912 became the first American ever to receive the prize for medicine. Since then, Rockefeller University has been directly associated with twenty-three Nobel laureates and nineteen recipients of the prestigious Lasker Award.[12] Its current faculty includes five MacArthur Fellows; twelve winners of the National Medal of Science, the most important award given in the United States for Science; and thirty-three elected members of the National Academy of Sciences.[13] Among the many significant breakthroughs achieved by these and other distinguished Rockefeller researchers are the following:[14]

- The discovery of new ways to freeze blood, which led during World War I to the creation of the first blood bank

- The discovery that DNA double-helixes are the building blocks of heredity

- Proving the connection between cholesterol and heart disease

- The invention of drugs to treat sleeping sickness

- The introduction of methadone as a tool to help manage heroin addiction

And this is only a small sample.

Impact. According to Chernow, "[n]one of the titan [Rockefeller]'s other philanthropies was perhaps such an unqualified success."[15] And for Winston Churchill, the creation of the Rockefeller Institute was John D. Rockefeller's crowning benefaction. Shortly before Rockefeller died, Churchill praised him, saying:

> When history passes its final verdict on John D. Rockefeller, it may well be that his endowment of research will be recognized as a milestone in the progress of the race. For the first time, science was given its head; longer term experiment on a large scale has been made practicable, and those who undertake it are freed from the shadow of financial disaster. Science today owes as much to the rich men of generosity and discernment as the art of the Renaissance owes to the patronage of Popes and Princes. Of these rich men, John D. Rockefeller is the supreme type.[16]

Even today—more than a century after its founding—Rockefeller University continues to study, to innovate, and to "make practicable" the great experiment set in motion by Rockefeller and his far-seeing advisers.

Case 2

General Education Board Support for Public High Schools

Rockefeller Foundation, General Education Board, 1902

Steven Schindler

Background. John D. Rockefeller's philanthropic tendencies were well developed long before his success in business enabled him to amass a personal fortune to act on those tendencies. His own personal religious devotion, which left an indelible mark on his giving, has been well noted, but the influences of his family's interests also led to some of his specific philanthropic tendencies. Southern Negro education, for instance, was an interest he inherited from his grandparents, who supported a Baptist seminary for African American women in Atlanta, renamed Spelman College in their honor.

When Rockefeller's son, John D. Rockefeller Jr., completed college, he joined his father's office, where he was assigned to work with his father's advisor Frederick Gates in the administration of the family's charitable activities. The younger Rockefeller also inherited the family interests in philanthropic activity. In 1901, he joined a trip to attend a conference on African American education in the South and to visit significant African American education sites, including the Tuskegee Institute in Alabama. Later, he would call the trip "one of the outstanding events in my life."[17]

At the conference, Henry St. George Tucker, president of Washington and Lee University, gave perhaps the most influential address. Mindful of the poor state of rural education for whites in the South and the likely racial backlash that would result if whites perceived their educational opportunities to be inferior to those available to African Americans, Tucker cautioned against focusing exclusively on the problem of African American education. Instead, Tucker advocated, philanthropists from the North would do better to devote their resources to improving education for all in the South. "You must lift up the 'poor white' and the Negro together if you would approach success," Tucker cautioned.[18]

Strategy. Rockefeller Jr., inspired by the conference and Tucker's remarks, convened a group of experienced educators and leaders to consider possible approaches to improving education in the South. The group was constituted in 1902 as the General Education Board (GEB) with a million-dollar pledge from Rockefeller Senior and with the express purpose of "the promotion of education within the United States without distinction of race, sex, or creed."[19] While Rockefeller hoped to prompt other philanthropists to support the organization in part by leaving his name off of the Board's name, no other philanthropists opted to support a Rockefeller philanthropy.[20]

One of the Board's first objectives was to help develop a system of public secondary education in the South, in hopes of increasing the rate of attendance for both primary and secondary education.[21] At the turn of the century, most high schools in the South were private academies catering to wealthy planters; those without the means or the social standing necessary for entrance into these academies had little hope for attaining a high school education. Aiding elementary schools, the GEB's first initiative, was limited in its effectiveness by a lack of teachers adequately trained to staff the schools. Consequently, aid to primary schools was linked to high school aid, and that, in turn, required increased support for college and university education to produce high school teachers.[22]

Promoters of secondary education in the South faced a number of obstacles. There was considerable opposition to public high schools in the South. Public opinion opposed the high costs of creating public schools. Because, in contrast to the northern states, the South was relatively rural and much poorer, the tax base for financing public education was much lower. Southern states would have to charge relatively high tax rates to fund public education. Further, private academies feared the prospect of tuition-free competition. In some states, such as Georgia, state law actually prohibited public funding of secondary education.[23]

In response to this political environment, the GEB adopted the strategy of supporting a "specialist" in each southern state, trained in secondary education, linked to a state university, and subordinate to the state superintendent of schools. Each state specialist would have a set of requirements for advocating to the state legislature for public high school support; typically, the state specialist was also permitted to teach at a state university, an attractive benefit for the state university, if those requirements were first met.[24]

The GEB first employed its strategy of funding a specialist in Virginia in 1905, at a cost of $3,000-per-year. Later that year, specialists were funded in North Carolina, Georgia, Alabama, and Tennessee. By 1910, twelve states had such specialists cultivating support for public secondary schools were there were none before. These specialists submitted monthly reports to their state universities and to the GEB, writing of the seemingly insurmountable obstacles, either of perceptions that public schools resembled institutions for the poor or of perceptions that public schools would be unnecessarily duplicative of the private schools.[25]

One of the requisite, if undeveloped, skills of the specialists was lobbying on behalf of legislation permitting local taxation in support of public high schools. Virginia's specialist attained the votes necessary for the legislation by securing pledges of state legislators that they supported public high schools and then threatening to publish the pledges in the legislators' home newspapers if they backed down from their commitments. North Carolina's specialist mobilized the state Federation of Women's Clubs against the governor's opposition to public secondary schools and won passage of his legislation without opposition. In 1910, Georgia's specialist finally convinced the state legislature to amend the constitution to allow local support of public secondary schools.[26] Upon securing state enabling legislation, the specialists then engaged in local campaigns supporting bond proposals to build the local high schools. Once the schools were built, the specialists' task then turned to lengthening the school year, improving curriculum, and recruiting students to the schools.[27]

In addition to advocating to public officials for publicly funded high schools, the GEB pursued a complementary strategy for building support for high schools by strengthening the tax base. The GEB conducted a series of agricultural demonstration projects throughout the South intended to improve agricultural methods in the region, increase agricultural output, and build the South's capacity to fund public education.[28]

In almost all of the GEB's grants, Rockefeller's own philosophy of helping recipients help themselves resulted in a familiar strategy in other Rockefeller philanthropies of conditional giving, or of requiring grantees to match the Rockefeller grants with funding from other sources. In the case of promoting public support for secondary education, the GEB would often make imposition of local school taxation a condition of receiving its support.[29]

Impact. By 1912, state specialists could be credited with the passage of state enabling laws in twelve southern states, allowing state specialists to then build support at the local level for tax levies in support of the creation public schools.[30] By 1914, four years after the constitutional amendment enabled the state specialist in Georgia to campaign for local bond issues to create high schools, he had secured support for more than 200 new schools.[31] Across the south, the state specialists turned immediately from lobbying state legislators to campaigning in local districts; they, acting on behalf of the GEB, directly facilitated the creation of 800 public high schools. This strategy successfully turned public opinion in the South from detesting publicly financed education to expecting local government provisions for public secondary education.[32]

Case 3

The Transformation of American Medical Education: The Flexner Report

Carnegie Foundation for the Advancement of Teaching, 1906

Steven Schindler

Background. In 1905, Andrew Carnegie established the Carnegie Foundation for the Advancement of Teaching (CFAT) as a vehicle for providing financial security and well-being for college faculty members and their families. He tapped Henry Pritchett, president of MIT and a recent acquaintance of Carnegie's, to lead the new foundation.[33] Rather than restrict the trustees of the new foundation to his own strategies and objectives, however, Carnegie gave the trustees the flexibility to determine their own course by which to advance the teaching profession.

Carnegie's personal interest in medicine and medical education was not particularly strong. In "The Best Fields for Philanthropy," the sequel to his famous "Gospel of Wealth," both of which appeared in the *North American Review* in 1889, "the founding or extension of hospitals, medical colleges, laboratories, and other institutions connected with the alleviation of human suffering" appeared third on Carnegie's list of worthy philanthropic causes.[34] Consistent with the views he articulated in "Wealth," Carnegie gave priority to those causes aimed at the prevention of illness over those aimed at finding cures. He also praised Vanderbilt's gift to Columbia College for its chemical laboratory. Laboratories, Carnegie thought, were an essential part of any medical college.[35]

Carnegie's early philanthropy, however, largely neglected the professional education of doctors, focusing instead on the support of college educators and public library construction. Carnegie found the proprietary character of medical education distasteful. His relationship with Henry Pritchett, fifteen years after first articulating his philanthropic priorities, was the real beginning of Carnegie's imprint on medical education.[36]

Carnegie was not the first philanthropist to operate in the field of medical education. Johns Hopkins, an institution established by the bequest of a Quaker merchant in Baltimore, quickly became a model of academic medical education. Its first president, D.C. Gilman, developed a medical school that rejected the prevalent model of education-by-practitioners in favor of a school that replicated typical university conditions: professors fully dedicated to academic pursuits and a centralized governing hierarchy.[37] Two of the school's first faculty members, William Welch and William Osler, would become profoundly influential in medical education reform. Osler's *Principles of Medicine* inspired Rockefeller philanthropic confidant Frederick Gates to promote medical education as a primary object of Rockefeller financial support.[38]

Strategy. Pritchett, sharing Carnegie's conviction about the great potential of higher education to benefit society, understood well the urgent need for standardization and reform in order to remedy outmoded practices in American colleges and universities.[39] Accordingly, he led CFAT to commission a series of studies of the then-current state of many individual parts of higher education and the necessary course of action for reform in each.[40] Some critics to education reform suggested that using CFAT funds for endeavors outside the pension provision realm Carnegie articulated. In response, one of the trustees of CFAT wrote a letter to the editor of the *New York Times* in which he explained the rationale for studying education:

> Mr. Carnegie intrusted [sic] the administration of the fund to men who were themselves necessarily students, as well as administrators, of education, and that their habit of mind led them to look beneath the surface and to face at once the problems on whose wise solution the proper administration of their trust must depend.[41]

The trustee went on to note the particular need for a study of medical education, given the central importance of adequately trained physicians to the nation.

Medical education reform of the style that would soon be championed by a CFAT study found its earliest prominent champion in the Council on Medical Education of the American Medical Association, a group of five academic physicians. This group strongly advocated high academic standards in medical education, and consequently more full-time medical faculty and fewer practitioner-professors. In 1906, the Council conducted its own survey of the medical schools in the United States. Fearing that the impact of its own study might be limited by bias accusations stemming from the fact that a medical organization produced it, the Council chose not to publish its study and instead approached Pritchett and CFAT to propose that it engage in its own study and to offer consulting support.[42]

In 1906, Abraham Flexner approached CFAT for employment. Flexner had just returned from Europe, where he wrote a critique of American higher education in which he favorably quoted Pritchett. Flexner was able to secure a personal meeting with Pritchett about employment prospects; when nothing materialized at the first meeting, he secured a second. At the second meeting, Pritchett suggested, in accordance with the proposal by the Council on Medical Education, that Flexner undertake a comprehensive evaluation and prepare a report on the state of medical education in the United States and Canada on behalf of the Foundation. In the report, Pritchett noted, Flexner was to identify the best practices of various institutions and to highlight the areas of greatest need and potential for reform. Flexner noted that he had no expertise in the field of medical education, but Pritchett insisted that both his educational expertise and his objective and neutral perspective with respect to medical education made him ideal for the project, as his conclusions would be immune from attack for bias. Flexner agreed to conduct the study, which involved visiting more than 150 medical schools and institutions throughout North America. Flexner also enjoyed the promised cooperation of the Council on Medical Education of the AMA, particularly the advice of two of its members, throughout the study.[43]

Flexner's first report, *Bulletin Number 4: Medical Education in the United States and Canada*, set off an explosion of unprecedented controversy, protest, and reform in the institutions of medical education.[44] In that report, Flexner first outlined the current state of medical education and identified the best characteristics of a medical education institution, and then he provided an assessment, often harshly critical, of each medical school in the U.S. and Canada.[45]

Some institutions responded immediately and drastically. Washington University in St. Louis was the subject of some of Flexner's harshest criticisms. Robert Brookings, a wealthy merchant who had recently come to dominate the management of Washington University, requested an immediate audience with Flexner and Pritchett and a subsequent tour of the campus in St. Louis with Flexner. Brookings became convinced of the accuracy of Flexner's criticisms. Shortly after Brookings's second inspection of the medical school, the trustees adopted a plan of reconstruction that required the resignation of every member of the medical school faculty and replacement with faculty members with academic training.[46] Other medical schools also responded to Flexner's report favorably and with comparable action. The Yale Corporation, for example, approved changes exactly in line with Flexner's suggestions. Many schools, however, reacted negatively and with forceful resistance to criticisms of their programs.[47]

Flexner followed his initial study with a review of the systems of medical education in Germany, Austria, France, England, and Scotland. In *Bulletin Number 6: Medical Education in Europe*, he analyzed the effectiveness of the distinguishing aspects of those systems, and he promoted without reservation the English system of clinical education. He insisted on "a noncommercial relationship between medical school, hospital, laboratory, and university" in the American institutions.[48]

Ironically, Flexner's report had the effect of deterring Carnegie from focusing his own philanthropic resources on reform of medical education. After learning of the report's findings, Carnegie told Flexner, "[y]ou have proved that medical education is a business. I will not endow any other man's business."[49] Until Carnegie's death, virtually no support for medical education reform came from Carnegie philanthropies.[50]

Those leading the Rockefeller philanthropic endeavors, however, most notably Rockefeller advisor Frederick Gates, reacted quite differently to Flexner's studies. In 1913, Rockefeller's General Education Board (GEB), of which Gates was the chairman, hired Flexner to deploy its resources to catalyze the changes he urged in his bulletins.[51] From his grantmaking post at the GEB, Flexner set to work to raise the standards of medical education dramatically. More specifically, Flexner sought to replicate nationally the model of medical education developed at Johns Hopkins, where the medical faculty devoted themselves "full-time" to clinical work at the university and its affiliated teaching hospital rather than splitting their time between university work and their own private clinical practices.[52] To that end, the GEB systematically funded the reorganization of select medical schools, including, initially, the medical schools at Washington University in St. Louis, Yale, the University of Chicago, and Vanderbilt University.[53] In 1923, the GEB decided, over strong protest by Gates, to expand its mission of medical education reform to public universities in order to allow geographic expansion to the West and the South, including medical schools at the Universities of Iowa, Colorado, Oregon, Virginia, and Georgia.[54] The Rockefeller Foundation gave a $45 million grant to the General Education Board to fund its medical education reform efforts.[55] Funding from other private sources for medical education reform followed.[56]

Impact. CFAT's impact in the realm of medical education through the Flexner reports were at least two-fold. First, the bulletins collected and disseminated on a national basis the latest thinking on what modern medical education could be at its best. Changes at such institutions as Washington University and Yale attest to the immediate impact directly attributable to the study. At a minimum, the Flexner reports served as a catalyst for immediate change that would probably have been achieved over a longer period of time.[57] Second, by providing Flexner with early resources to establish his expertise that the GEB would later harness to bring about widespread reform, CFAT positioned Flexner as an individual with the empirical knowledge, organizational skills, and reputation necessary to lead a movement of significant reform.[58] Without CFAT's original support of the Flexner reports, there may have been no Flexner—no central figure of leadership—to drive a national revolution in medical education. Flexner's signal achievement, first in highlighting the universally poor state of medical education and then in marshalling Rockefeller's philanthropic resources to focus on the improvement of medical education, helped to elevate medical education as well as medical research in America to a position of dominant international leadership, from which it has not fallen.[59]

Curing and Preventing Disease and Promoting Public Health

Rockefeller Foundation, 1909

Steven Schindler

Background. By the 1890s, John D. Rockefeller's personal wealth from his oil business was burgeoning. Rockefeller had long been committed to charitable work due in large part to his lifelong religious devotion. This charitable impulse, however, prompted numerous charitable requests, and these requests eventually began to overwhelm his capacity to examine each request and to maintain his business enterprises. In 1892, Rockefeller appointed Frederick T. Gates, a former Baptist minister and administrator of the American Baptist Education Society, to advise and direct his philanthropic activities.[60]

Rockefeller first became acquainted with Gates when he assisted in Rockefeller's creation of the University of Chicago. Education, however, would not be the central area toward which Gates would steer Rockefeller's charity. On a summer holiday in 1897, Gates read William Osler's *Principles and Practices of Medicine* and was so profoundly influenced by the prospects for medical advances and the consequential alleviation of suffering that he persuaded Rockefeller to make medicine the top priority of his philanthropic endeavors.[61] His first inspiration, a center for research in medicine, was the Rockefeller Institute for Medical Research, later renamed Rockefeller University.

Through the work of another Rockefeller philanthropic organization, the General Education Board, Gates was introduced to the Dr. Charles Stiles, a zoologist and public health official. Stiles strongly advocated for action to combat the hookworm disease in the American South, an affliction by which victims are infected when small worms entered the bloodstream by boring through the victims' bare feet. The primary symptom was loss of strength and chronic pain; the disease was thought to be a major impediment to increased productivity in the rural South. While difficult to treat, Stiles found that hookworm was easily preventable with the use of sanitary latrines and wearing of shoes. The major challenge to combating the disease was the lack of awareness in the South of the disease's existence.

Strategy. Gates was immediately drawn to the challenge and excited about the possibility of devoting Rockefeller's resources to eradicating the disease.[62] In October 1909, Gates, Rockefeller's son John D. Rockefeller Jr., and twenty others formed the Rockefeller Sanitary Commission, chaired by Gates, for the Eradication of Hookworm Disease in the South. Rockefeller granted $1 million over five years to the new commission.[63]

Between 1909 and 1913, the Sanitary Commission, under the administrative leadership of Dr. Wickliffe Rose, a professor of philosophy at Peabody College in Nashville, mounted an assault on hookworm disease in the South. Despite having to overcome the regional bitterness between the North and the South that was still pervasive in that period ("laziness," for instance, was emphasized in Northern newspapers as a symptom of the disease and as a broader characteristic of the South), Rose built relationships with eleven state departments of health to combat the hookworm problem and dramatically raised the level of public awareness regarding hookworm disease and methods for its prevention.[64]

In May, 1913, near the end of the five-year Sanitary Commission grant, the trustees of the newly incorporated Rockefeller Foundation held their first meeting. Enthusiasm over the progress of the Sanitary Commission prompted the trustees to affirm a recommendation by Gates to pursue public health as the primary focus of the new foundation's grantmaking. In particular, the trustees, learning from Rose that the eradication of hookworm required action beyond U.S. borders to other countries where hookworm persisted, asked Rose to prepare a plan of operation for the Foundation to undertake such action. A month later, the Foundation established the International Health Commission (later renamed the International Health Board and then the International Health Division), with Rose as director, to pursue the eradication of hookworm abroad and, more broadly, the promotion of public health and sanitation. At the same time, the Sanitary Commission was merged with the new Commission.[65] The International Health Commission operated as a division of the Rockefeller Foundation until 1951.[66]

Rose developed a strategy for combating hookworm in the United States that became a template for controlling the same disease, as well as other dis-

eases, throughout the world. First, a campaign under the auspices of the Sanitary Commission and later the International Health Commission undertook a comprehensive survey to understand the geographic reach of the
disease as well as the rate of infection. The next step consisted of a broad
publicity campaign to express to the public, and to medical practitioners in
an area, the extent to which the disease was hindering the community's prosperity, as well as the relative ease with which treatment and preventive measures could control the disease. For hookworm control in the South, each
state was assigned a director of sanitation as well as a staff of sanitation in-
spectors and microscopists to conduct free traveling clinics at which attendees could be treated and could receive literature on improving public
sanitation. Central to Rose's strategy was that the International Health Commission would work behind the scenes, empowering local governments to
authorize and direct all action.[67]

Rose's early ambitions included the eradication of diseases, beginning with
hookworm. His ambition for total eradication of disease made its way into
the Rockefeller Foundation's early annual reports and was reported in the
news.[68] Indeed, the Rockefeller Foundation celebrated successful elimination
of various diseases in specific countries in which the International Health
Commission worked, almost invariably attributing the success to the Rockefeller Foundation.[69] In Rose's work with the Sanitary Commission, however,
he learned that prompt eradication of hookworm was impractical. Accordingly, the objective became control of the disease rather than eradication.[70]

In developing and administrating a plan of attack against hookworm,
Rose began to think of public health in terms broader than any particular
disease. In his mind, the campaign against hookworm could be a demonstration project for disease control and public health.[71] The International Health
Board later applied this model to malaria, tuberculosis, and yellow fever.

Furthermore, controlling any specific disease was complementary to
spreading Rose's broader philosophy that governments should take responsibility to equip themselves with adequate pubic health organizations that
would undertake future campaigns to control diseases. Determining that the
county was the optimal unit of organization for public health efforts in the
United States, the International Health Commission began in 1916 making
grants of seed money to start county offices of public health, a strategy Rose
called "pump priming."[72] International Health Commission campaigns
against hookworm in Mexico and Ceylon similarly instilled in the public the
expectation of public health offices and an increased interest in public
health.[73]

Impact. Some have made efforts to quantify the impact of Rockefeller
philanthropic efforts toward disease eradication, such as in terms of the rise

in school enrollment immediately following hookworm campaigns in the South, as well as the enhanced development of human capital in the South and, later, in developing tropical countries.[74] More generally, the $94 million spent by the International Health Commission of the Rockefeller Foundation and the Rockefeller Sanitary Commission between 1909 and 1951, in grants for public health worldwide, created the concept of public health in this nation and around the world, and the Rockefeller Foundation's efforts have widely been credited with major public health advances in the first half of the twentieth century.[75]

The Rockefeller Foundation's success in combating yellow fever has been particularly well documented. In 1938, a *New York Times* editorial noted that "[t]he more recent history of yellow fever is largely the history of the Rockefeller Foundation's support of research and preventative tropical medicine."[76] The following year, International Health Division research Max Theiler discovered a vaccine for the disease, which the Foundation then mass produced for distribution during World War II.[77] The discovery earned Theiler the 1951 Nobel Prize in Medicine and the nickname "conqueror of yellow fever" among his colleagues.[78]

Case 5

CARNEGIE PUBLIC LIBRARIES FOR AMERICA'S COMMUNITIES

Carnegie Corporation of New York, 1911

STEVEN SCHINDLER

Background. Andrew Carnegie's personal interest in libraries stemmed from his father's involvement in the creation of a small library in Scotland and his own boyhood experiences at a private library in Pittsburgh. His father, a weaver, organized a group of fellow weavers to pool resources in order to purchase books they could read to one another as they worked. The collection of books became the first circulating library in Dunfermline, Scotland, Carnegie's boyhood home.[79] While Carnegie was still a boy, his family moved to the United States and settled in Allegheny, Pennsylvania. Almost on arrival, Carnegie sought and was granted access to a private library established for working men in the town. He was infatuated with the library, and he later confessed that the joy he took from his afternoon visits to the library inspired him to resolve that, should he ever accumulate wealth, he would devote some of it to extending library access to other young boys.[80] The first recipient of a library grant in the United States was his hometown of Allegheny, in 1886.[81]

Carnegie's library-giving may have also been inspired by earlier philanthropists whose gifts established libraries. Ezra Cornell gave funds to establish a library in Ithaca, New York, and Enoch Pratt built a million-dollar library in Baltimore. Carnegie particularly appreciated the wisdom of the structure of Pratt's gift: Pratt stipulated that the city must pay 5 percent of the initial gift annually for the maintenance of the library and the purchase of books.[82]

For Carnegie, the library was the manifestation of one central theme in his philanthropic philosophy: self-betterment.[83] He was known to enjoy elite company, but he devoted much of his philanthropy to building ladders for individuals to lift themselves in the world. Libraries provided opportunity for social improvement, and Carnegie structured his gifts to avoid pauperization of recipient communities so as not to hinder that improvement. Carnegie, like Pratt, required a commitment by recipient municipalities to provide annual funding for book purchases and maintenance, and he required the municipality to provide the site for each library building.[84] These philosophical underpinnings and the gift structure adopted from Pratt would propel Carnegie's library program from meager beginnings to a grand scale.

Strategy. Early in his philanthropic career, Carnegie funded a public library in Dunfermline, Scotland. He then sponsored the construction of combination library-and-community centers in Pennsylvania towns, including Allegheny, where his steel plants were located. Without issuing any apparent formal request for proposals from other communities, Carnegie received and granted a few additional requests for local libraries in other cities. As word spread of Carnegie's gifts, large numbers of requests for library construction began to pour in.

Between 1886 and 1896, Carnegie gave over $1.8 million to construct fourteen library buildings in six Pennsylvania communities, all of which were home to Carnegie's industrial facilities. In 1897, James Bertram became Carnegie's personal secretary, and it became his duty to administer the library building grants. For the most part, Bertram's procedure for issuing Carnegie library grants was mechanical—he sent the list of prerequisites to all who inquired about obtaining a library grant, and if the recipient town's official, usually the mayor, agreed to the terms of the grant (provision of a favorable space on which to build the library and a commitment of an annual 10 percent of capital contribution for the operating expenses of the library), then Bertram approved the grant.

Carnegie's deepening involvement in philanthropic activities led him to establish the Carnegie Corporation of New York in 1911 to administer his wide array of giving. Carnegie himself filled the post of president, but Bertram became secretary of the Corporation, and he continued to run the library building program. The parameters of the program itself did not significantly change when the Corporation took over; by the founding of the Corporation, Carnegie had already given almost $30 million from his personal accounts to establish libraries in the United States.[85] The Corporation continued funding library construction with the same requirements that the municipality provide the building site and commit 10 percent of the gift per year for upkeep. From 1898 to 1919, Carnegie's library gifts surpassed $39 million.[86]

In one of the earliest efforts to evaluate foundation programs, the Corporation began to distribute a survey in 1915, in response to a number of complaints about library management. The survey asked recipients of library grants questions about the status of the local library, including spending on books, salary expenditures, numbers of library card holders, and amount of money spent toward the construction of the building by other sources.[87] On the basis of the results of the survey, the Corporation suspended grants to nine communities that had abnormally high rates of default in contribution pledges, pending a reaffirmation by the default communities to fund the promised contributions.[88]

In November 1915, the foundation decided to pursue a more exhaustive and intensive evaluation effort by hiring Alvin Johnson, economics professor at Cornell University, to conduct a nationwide assessment of the Carnegie Library program.[89] Johnson undertook a ten-week study of about one hundred Carnegie libraries throughout the United States.

Johnson considered public library funding a particularly fruitful example of foundation spending because libraries were appreciated by the public only on a general level but not enough to prompt the public to compel local officials to build a library. In his general assessment of public opinion, however, Johnson identified nuances between states such as California, which built libraries with only supplementary capital grants, and Texas, which benefited from fewer, more comprehensive gifts of buildings, as well as book and overhead provisions, that led to a wider acceptance of public libraries. In light of these differences, Johnson noted that a more flexible approach to the grant prerequisites might be a wiser policy.[90]

In his report, Johnson made a number of recommendations for modification of the library program. Johnson's primary recommendations to the Corporation included hiring field agents to evaluate in person each community requesting a library grant, supporting trained librarians to help establish effective organization and service at new libraries, and providing scholarships for students attending library schools to increase the number of available trained librarians.[91] Johnson also recommended that the Corporation narrow its grantmaking in the South, the region least receptive to public library service, to the support of a few model libraries to assume leadership roles in promoting effective and widespread library service.[92]

Rather than adopt Johnson's recommendations, the Corporation, on the urging of James Bertram, rejected Johnson's report. Less than two years after the report, with a resolution adopted on November 7, 1917, the Corporation discontinued the library grant program and refused any grant inquiries received after that date. Though none of Johnson's recommendations would directly influence the process of issuing library grants, the Corporation eventually pursued some of Johnson's proposals, including support of model libraries, funding of library education, and support of the American Library Association.[93]

Impact. In addition to Carnegie's personal expenditures, the Carnegie Corporation granted a total of $13 million to its library building program between 1911 and the conclusion of the program—7 percent of its total grant amount during the Corporation's first thirty years.[94] These grants, in addition to Carnegie's personal disbursements of $29 million, helped to build 1,679 libraries in 1,406 communities in the United States, with multiple branches in some cities. Including libraries established outside the United States, Carnegie was responsible for the construction of a total of 2,509 libraries.[95]

The vast new network of Carnegie libraries appeared at a time when support for publicly funded libraries was growing. In the mid-nineteenth century, many States enacted laws enabling municipalities to raise funds to support public libraries, beginning with Massachusetts in 1848. By 1887, twenty states had public library enabling laws on the books, and a total of 649 public libraries had already been constructed.[96]

Carnegie's library gifts clearly sparked public interest in the concept of public libraries. The opportunity to obtain a Carnegie library grant provided an incentive for communities to utilize the power of the state enabling laws and to rally behind a library grant request. In addition, Carnegie's contributions, along with his suggestion in his famous essay, "The Gospel of Wealth," that libraries should be the second highest priority for philanthropic resources, prompted a flow of private resources into public libraries. In the 1890s, $10 million went from private donors to public libraries; that number more than doubled between 1900 and 1906. Finally, the condition that the recipient municipalities provide 10 percent of the total grant in yearly funding for donated libraries pressured municipal bodies to take on the responsibility of providing local libraries, and Carnegie libraries were sufficiently widespread, that the public came to hold municipalities accountable for providing local libraries.[97]

Case 6

LEARNING TO UNDERSTAND THE PROBLEMS FACED BY CLEVELAND: AMERICA'S FIRST COMMUNITY FOUNDATION

The Cleveland Foundation, 1915

STEVEN SCHINDLER

Background. As president of the Cleveland Trust Company in the early 1910s, Frederick Goff was intrigued by the prospect of providing to the community a means by which individuals could commit their wealth to charitable purposes upon their deaths. He thought such a means would be good both for revenues and for public relations. Devising a community trust as an entity to be shepherded by community leaders (initially bank directors), Goff envisioned a fund to which benefactors could leave their wealth for the improvement of the community. Aiming toward that objective, Goff created The Cleveland Foundation on January 2, 1914—the first community foundation in America.[98]

Strategy and Impact. The Cleveland Foundation's initial purpose was to alleviate the social ills facing Cleveland, beginning with poverty. Its strategy would be to study the city in detail and to gain a deeper understanding of the problems it faced. Within six weeks of the creation of The Cleveland Foundation, Frederick Goff expressed his intention that the Foundation conduct "a great social and economic survey of Cleveland, to uncover the causes of poverty and crime and point out the cure." Goff envisioned a comprehensive survey modeled after an earlier Russell Sage Foundation survey of living and working conditions in Pittsburgh.[99] The Foundation created a five-member Survey Committee to oversee research administered by the Foundation's Distribution Committee. While the Foundation received numerous requests for surveys regarding a wide variety of problems facing Cleveland, it focused on a few specific areas to be funded primarily by Goff, his associates, and his company.[100]

In 1915, the Foundation undertook a major study of the Cleveland public schools, forecast to cost $50,000. In agreeing with the appropriateness of studying the school system, Goff underscored the Foundation's unique capacity to undertake such a study: "the schools are the very thing we ought to tackle. Nobody else dares do it." Goff hired Leonard P. Ayres, the education director of the Russell Sage Foundation and a former school superintendent, to lead the study.[101]

Ayers announced the Foundation's study in April 1915, and he and his staff began researching and presenting findings in the fall at public meetings. He proposed more than 100 recommended changes to the school system in the public presentations and in twenty-five public reports, including special education for the gifted, handicapped, foreign-born, and "the incorrigible;" expanded vocational training; the introduction of general science teaching and civics; free textbooks; and compulsory attendance.[102]

The elected school board relied on Ayers's assistance in selecting a new school administrator to be appointed by January 1917. Over the next six years, nine-of-eleven school board seats were filled with candidates friendly to Ayers's recommendations; a follow-up investigation by the Foundation determined that three-quarters of the recommendations had been implemented. By then, the widespread interest in the education system in Cleveland sparked by the Foundation survey led to the passage of five school-bond issues.[103]

For decades thereafter, the Cleveland school system was considered a model system, and about 100,000 volumes of the Ayers reports were sold to members of the community as well as to those interested in education reform throughout the world.[104]

Propelled by the wide publicity and positive reception and impact of the education survey, the Survey Committee of the Cleveland Foundation decided to undertake a survey on recreation in Cleveland in late 1916. Recreation opportunities were thought to be too few in Cleveland and their scarcity was believed to increase both the attractiveness of billiard parlors and the propensity of young people to populate the streets.[105]

The survey consisted of an inventory of current offerings in the city as well as an assessment of the recreational needs of youth and adults. Of six contemplated reports, only three were completed before World War I brought the study to a halt.[106]

Raymond Moley, then a young professor at Western Reserve University who would later become a member of President Franklin Roosevelt's brain trust and assistant secretary of state, approached the Distribution Committee of the Cleveland Foundation about the possibility of working on the unfinished recreation survey. Moley was hired in May 1919 to direct the study to completion; he completed the survey in late 1919 at a total cost of approximately $35,000.[107]

The recreation survey called for Cleveland to consolidate operation of the city's playgrounds into a single city office, to increased funding from the Cleveland Board of Education for recreational programming, and to create city-sponsored sports leagues. Most notably, the survey articulated the need for a new coordinating body to promote "wholesome sparetime activities."[108]

The recommended coordinating body was established in 1920 as the Cleveland Recreation Council under the auspices of the Welfare Federation. The Council immediately pushed for passage of a special tax levy to raise revenues to purchase green tracts on the edge of Cleveland's outlying districts for the creation of parks. The levy passed, and the park board used the new revenues in creating Cleveland's "Emerald Necklace" of parks which encircle Cleveland to this day.[109]

Case 7

THE DEVELOPMENT OF INSULIN TO TREAT DIABETES

Carnegie Corporation of New York, 1916

STEVEN SCHINDLER

Background. The discovery of insulin and its capability of restoring extremely ill diabetic patients to virtually normal health was a miracle of modern medicine in the early 1920s. Prior to that discovery, diabetic patients suffered under radical dietary restrictions and treatment regimes with little hope for recovery. Today, insulin can be taken for granted, but in the early part of the twentieth century, this lifegiving substance had yet to be developed.[110]

Strategy. In 1916, the Carnegie Corporation of New York, still in its infancy, received a project proposal by Dr. Nathaniel Potter for a study of the treatment of diabetes. Dr. Potter noted in his proposal that diabetes had no known cure and could be managed only through strict dietary regimes. Unless a patient had means to receive ongoing treatment from a diabetes clinic, the patient would have to be taught to observe strict dietary rules that, in combination with the effect of the disease, often left the patient emaciated.[111]

The essence of Dr. Potter's proposal was that research should be conducted at a laboratory of high quality near a clinic with diabetic patients. The Corporation trustees agreed to grant Dr. Potter $7,500 annually, conditioned on his raising an additional $20,000 himself in external funding.[112]

Potter began his research at the French Hospital in New York, but after a year, his own illness compelled him to move to a milder climate. He moved to Santa Barbara, California, where he believed he could continue effective research of diabetes. There, Cottage Hospital, whose trustees recognized the importance of Potter's research, funded the construction of a $50,000 research laboratory adjoining the hospital. The Carnegie Corporation subsequently agreed to allow its grant to be redirected to the Cottage Hospital facility. After conducting research and treating diabetic patients for a short time, Potter died in 1919.[113] Dr. William D. Sansum, a recognized metabolic researcher from Wisconsin, was recruited by the trustees of Cottage Hospital and the Potter Metabolic Clinic from his post at the University of Chicago to become Potter's successor as the Director of the Clinic. He agreed and promptly took up Potter's diabetes research.[114]

During this same period, Frederick G. Banting, a twenty-nine-year-old junior faculty member at the University of Western Ontario, also endeavored to discover more effective diabetes treatments. He conceived of his idea to extract insulin from the pancreas of dogs in 1920. While quite a bit of research on diabetes and its connection with the pancreas had already been published, the discovery of insulin remained elusive.[115] Earlier in 1920, Dr. Moses Barron of the University of Minnesota published an article addressing the problem of extracting the insulin hormone without its first being destroyed by the stronger digestive hormone products of the pancreas, a problem that had long plagued researchers. Banting read that article and imagined his solution.[116]

Banting's colleagues encouraged him to seek research support and guidance from Dr. J.J.R. Macleod at the University of Toronto, a renowned researcher in the field of diabetes and metabolism. Banting traveled to Toronto in the fall and again over the Christmas holidays to ask Dr. Macleod for research space and assistance; he was rejected flatly each time. Finally, upon learning that Macleod would be vacationing in Scotland for the summer of 1921, Banting traveled to Toronto a third time to ask for use of the vacant research laboratory; this time, Macleod allowed Banting eight weeks of laboratory use.[117] On July 30, Banting and his assistant, Charles Best, injected the first insulin extract into a diabetic dog and observed as the dog showed signs of recovery.[118] Over the next two months, they discovered progressively improved methods for extracting insulin from dogs and then cattle and calf fetuses. In January 1922, at the Toronto General hospital, a diabetic child patient of the research team was restored to health using insulin injections, the first use of insulin in the treatment of humans.[119]

During the time Banting and Best worked to improve their insulin extraction methods, Dr. Sansum corresponded with the Toronto researchers about one of their early publications. They sent news of developments to Dr. Sansum in hope that his research team would cooperate in seeking to improve the extraction process.[120] Dr. Sansum's researchers were also successful in insulin extraction; they administered the first doses of insulin produced in the United States to an adult patient, the first U.S. recipient, in May 1922. The patient, a fifty-one-year-old man terminally ill with diabetes, lived to age ninety with insulin treatments.[121] Within two months, the Santa Barbara researchers had developed enough of the substance to use on nine patients at the hospital.[122] Sansum continued to develop insulin, communicate results, and ask questions of the researchers in Toronto.[123]

Also in 1922, the Carnegie Corporation granted $8,000 to Macleod's laboratory at the University of Toronto for further research in the treatment of diabetes.[124] In a dispute between Banting and Macleod involving control over and credit for the insulin research in the summer of 1922—that would eventually drive the two apart—the Corporation's grant provided Banting with the means to continue his research at the University of Toronto independent of Macleod.[125]

Impact. The Corporation found particularly heartening the notion that two grantees in the same field were coordinating their efforts to advance knowledge and understanding. The Report of the President expressed this sentiment:

> Not the least pleasing feature of this investigation lies in the admirable attitude in which two sets of investigators, each of whom has received modest help from the Carnegie Corporation, have cooperated toward a common end. . . . This [sharing of research] is in entire consonance with the spirit and the purpose of true scientific research.[126]

By virtue of Sansum's connection with the Toronto researchers, the laboratory and clinic under his direction was one of the first to manufacture and use insulin in human patients. The Corporation supported this research with an additional $15,000 grant in October 1922. Dr. Sansum's successes in insulin use in humans as well as in diet-based treatment of diabetes were published in various medical journals and contributed to the early understanding of insulin's effects on the diabetic patient.[127] The Toronto researchers also enjoyed continued support from the Corporation. In conjunction with the Toronto researchers, the Connaught Laboratories (affiliated with the University of Torono) and Eli Lilly Company of Indianapolis, both working in conjunction with the Toronto researchers, began developing large-scale production methods of insulin in 1922. By late 1923, insulin began to appear in drug stores.[128] Hundreds of thousands of patients near death from diabetes, like the first U.S. patient in Santa Barbara, subsequently recovered relatively rapidly with the insulin treatment.

Case 8

PROVIDING SCIENTIFIC KNOWLEDGE TO SOLVE PUBLIC PROBLEMS: NATIONAL RESEARCH COUNCIL

Carnegie Corporation of New York, 1917

STEVEN SCHINDLER

Background. In 1863, Congress chartered the National Academy of Sciences as a means by which the government could obtain the advice of scientists about matters of national interest, particularly relating to the country's needs in the midst of war. After the Civil War, however, the Academy became relatively inactive, as the government rarely sought its services.[129] In 1913, George Ellery Hale, renowned astronomer and foreign secretary of the Academy, was displeased with the lack of participation of the Academy in matters of growing national importance.[130] Hale proposed sweeping reforms to make the Academy more relevant to social and government needs and more active as a scientific authority in the United States. His plans included opening membership to younger scientists and constructing a new home to suit the Academy's new purpose. Initially, his proposals met with little favor among other Academy members. Undeterred, in 1914, Hale sought a grant from the Carnegie Corporation for $950,000 to build the new headquarters he envisioned for the Academy, but the Corporation rejected his request.[131]

The same year, war broke out in Europe. Responding to an appeal by Thomas Edison following the 1915 sinking of the *Lusitania*, the Navy constituted a Navy Consulting Board to assist in the development of viable military technology to ready the United States for potential future involvement in World War I. Notably to Hale, none of the Academy's members were asked to serve on the Consulting Board. Rallying a group of fellow scientists, Hale secured from the Academy an offer to provide President Woodrow Wilson with such scientific counsel as the country might need in case national crisis or war arose. A group led by Hale personally delivered the Academy's offer to the president, who accepted the offer under a condition of confidentiality.

Two months later, in a reorganization intended to strengthen its capacity for scientific coordination and research, the Academy created the National Research Council (NRC). Next, Hale convinced the Council of National Defense, created by Congress, to rely on the National Research Council for advice on any scientific matters.[132] Throughout World War I, the NRC operated by matching particular needs of the military services with civilian scientists who had expertise in the relevant research area.[133]

The National Research Council found early financial support for its work in the Engineering Foundation, the Carnegie Corporation (its largest supporter during the war), the Rockefeller Foundation, and the federal government.[134]

Strategy. The Carnegie Corporation, only a few years old, provided an ideal source of funds for promoting coordinated scientific expertise to the government. Hale first approached Elihu Root and Henry Pritchett, a fellow astronomer, to enlist their support for reforms. Pritchett was less than confident in Hale's vision for the Academy, but Root became a strong supporter. Despite the Corporation's initial disapproval of Hale's objectives and proposals, Root remained confident in the eventual success of reform. The establishment of the NRC, which opened its membership to more active, younger, more broadly representative scientists than those in the Academy, apparently diffused the Corporation's initial disapproval of Hale's proposals. The U.S. involvement in war also raised the stature of the NRC to national importance. Root secured Corporation grants for the Academy and the NRC channeled through the Carnegie Institute of Washington $50,000 in 1917 and $100,000 in 1918.[135]

Following the war, President Wilson, pleased with the work of the NRC in national crisis, decided that the NRC should be maintained in peacetime. With Executive Order No. 2859 of May 11, 1918, President Wilson recognized the contributions of the NRC and extended it as an organization in perpetuity.[136] This action gave the NRC a stronger basis from which it could secure more significant funding. Root demonstrated his support of Carnegie funding in a speech entitled "The Need for Organization in Scientific Research," in which he cited successful research coordination efforts in Europe alongside those of the National Research Council. The National Research Council tended to be more favored than other efforts in part because it was private and independent of government.[137] In March 1919, The Carnegie

Corporation gave $5 million to the National Academy of Sciences and National Research Council for endowment and new building construction.[138]

Impact. During World War I, the technological developments coordinated by the National Research Council include "listening devices to detect submarines, range finders for airplanes, and intelligence tests to classify army recruits."[139] More broadly, the NRC is now the primary source, for Congress and agencies of the Executive Branch, of objective scientific assessments of major problems facing the American public.

Case 9

PENSIONS FOR AMERICA'S EDUCATORS: TIAA-CREF, ONE OF THE WEALTHIEST PENSION FUNDS IN THE WORLD

Carnegie Foundation for the Advancement of Teaching, 1918

STEVEN SCHINDLER

Background. The early part of the twentieth century occasioned rigorous arguments in North America and Europe over the nature of the state and the responsibilities of states to their citizens. The established system of poor relief in Great Britain and the United States came into question, and a movement soon arose to replace poor relief with a system of social insurance and pensions. Germany first began to institute national social insurance programs in the 1880s.[140] Great Britain enacted old age pension insurance legislation in 1908, preceding passage in the United States of the Social Security Act in 1935 by twenty-eight years. A few states began their own minimal social insurance programs in the 1920s.[141]

Andrew Carnegie weighed in on the debate with his wallet on behalf of college and university teachers. Carnegie's involvement began with a private pension list he kept of faculty and other individuals whose contributions to the public he deemed worthy of lifetime financial security; Carnegie would make regular pension payments out of his pocket to those on his list.[142]

After meeting Henry Pritchett and sharing his ideas for a more substantial pension program for college faculty, Carnegie created the Carnegie Foundation for the Advancement of Teaching in 1905. The Foundation was given the primary charge of securing financial independence for higher education faculty members. In his Letter of Gift, Carnegie wrote that he "had reached the conclusion that the least rewarded of all the professions is that of the teacher in our higher education institutions.[143] The Foundation's first objective would be to remedy the disparity between the great value conferred on society by higher education faculty and the miserly financial benefit society gave faculty in return. In addition, however, Carnegie hoped that the Foundation would promote efficiency in higher education more broadly. He noted that, at the front end, potential faculty members chose other, more lucrative professions, and at career end, professors no longer really able to teach effectively were forced to continue to work because they were financially strained.[144] The President of Bowdoin College, in line with Carnegie's likely intention, predicted that the pensions would expedite faculty retirement and improve recruitment at the same time.[145]

Strategy. To govern the Foundation and carry out his intentions, Carnegie appointed a board of twenty-five individuals, twenty-two of whom were higher education administrators. He empowered the trustees to interpret his purposes and to change the direction of the Foundation as they determined appropriate.[146] Carnegie's Letter of Gift indicated that sectarian schools would be excluded from his Foundation's pensioning, a gesture aimed at prompting higher education institutions with exclusive religious associations to become more inclusive. Carnegie also stipulated that tax-supported state schools should not participate, although his exclusion of state school involvement was less absolute. This exclusion was apparently prompted by Pritchett, who then sought to reinforce the exclusion by the Foundation trustees in a three-year dispute with state-supported higher education institutions. In *Pensions for Professors*, Theron Schlabach argues that the policy of excluding state schools from the pension system, changed in 1908 with an additional gift from Carnegie to the Foundation to fund state school pensions, was a campaign by Pritchett to ensure the dominance of private universities in the Northeast even though the policy was clearly inconsistent with Carnegie's previous giving precedents and philosophies.[147]

In 1907, Carnegie suggested to Pritchett that the Foundation provide life insurance for faculty members, but he learned that the Foundation was not properly incorporated to issue life insurance policies. Over the next few years, the Foundation studied pension and life insurance systems and considered the optimal configuration for such a system. Erroneous forecasts of pension costs and age spans prompted Pritchett and the Foundation to begin considering alternatives to its non-contributory pension system. In the Foundation's Annual Report in 1912, Pritchett discussed the merits and deficiencies of different types of contributory and non-contributory pensions. In 1916, he included in the report an essay entitled "Fundamentals of a Pension System."[148] Finally, the Foundation created the Teachers Insurance and Annuity Association of America (TIAA), which was incorporated in the State of New York as a stock company in 1918, and funded by a $1 million grant from the Carnegie Corporation.[149] TIAA would receive more than $7 million in grants from the Corporation over the next twenty-four years.[150] In addition, higher education institutions made financial contributions to TIAA for the privilege of becoming members.[151]

Impact. Initially, with the feeling that securities investments were risky and therefore inappropriate investments for insurance company assets, TIAA limited its investments to government and railroad bonds. This strategy proved fortuitous during the stock market crash of 1929 and the Great Depression of the 1930s, as assets grew from $10 million in 1929 to $100 million in 1939. During the 1940s however, inflation emerged as a new risk to the company's assets, and the S&P 500 stock market index more than doubled during the 1940s. TIAA commissioned a risk analysis study of investment classes between 1890 and 1950, and the study concluded that a blend of stocks and bonds would provide the optimum investment mix in reducing the risks of inflation and securities devaluation. To implement these proposals, in 1952 TIAA created the College Retirement Equities Fund (CREF), the world's first variable annuity. Since then, TIAA-CREF has created additional variable annuities, including funds focusing on international investment and real estate.[152]

In 2004, TIAA-CREF had a total of over $343 billion in assets under management. It was second on *Fortune*'s list of the largest U.S. mutual life and health insurers. More than three million individuals and 15,000 member institutions have been served by TIAA-CREF.[153]

Case 10

BUILDING SCHOOLS FOR RURAL AFRICAN AMERICANS

Julius Rosenwald Fund, 1920

STEVEN SCHINDLER

Background. Julius Rosenwald amassed his fortune through the success of his clothing business and during his tenure as president of Sears, Roebuck & Co. Rosenwald's religious beliefs motivated him to use his fortune toward charitable ends.[154] Among the beneficiaries of his philanthropy were Hull

House, Hebrew University in Jerusalem, and various entities aimed at the betterment of educational opportunities for African Americans. Rosenwald's interest in African American education was inspired by *An American Citizen, the Life of William H. Baldwin* as well as the writings of Booker T. Washington. Through his contributions to a number of YMCA and YWCA buildings dedicated to African Americans, Rosenwald developed a relationship with Washington that further fueled his interest in African American education.

On his fiftieth birthday in 1912, Rosenwald gave $650,000 in gifts to a number of charitable causes, including $25,000 to Washington to support the expansion of the Tuskegee Institute. Washington, after using less than the full $25,000 grant for offshoot campuses of Tuskegee, contemplated different uses for the remaining $2,100. After deciding he would like to build six small, rural schoolhouses for African American pupils, Washington asked Rosenwald to approve this use. Upon Rosenwald's agreement, Washington built the six schools with the unused $2,100 of Rosenwald's Tuskegee gift.

Strategy. Washington prepared a glowing report of the dedication of the six new schools, particularly noting large numbers of both black and white attendees at dedication ceremonies. Rosenwald, pleased with Washington's report, contributed an additional $30,000 to Tuskegee to build 100 similar schools throughout rural Alabama. State agents of African American education in other Southern States, distressed with the condition of African American education in their own states, asked Rosenwald to expand the building program to other states in the South, but Rosenwald declined to expand the building program until the degree of success of the schools in Alabama could first be ascertained.

Tuskegee administered the building program with Rosenwald funding from 1913 until 1920.[155] For the duration of what would become a massive school-building program, Rosenwald annually reviewed the budget of the program, and he took great interest in the design and quality of the school buildings, even prompting an effort to modernize the designs midway through the program.

Rosenwald generally structured his philanthropic gifts in a way that attracted greater philanthropic and public financial support for his causes. He often provided less than 50 percent of the costs of various enterprises and challenged the recipients to raise the remaining funds from other sources.[156]

In 1917, while Rosenwald was in Washington to advise President Woodrow Wilson on financial matters related to World War I, he made an appearance at a conference on education to report on the school-building program. State education agents and officials in other Southern states urged Rosenwald to support similar building programs throughout the South, and Rosenwald finally agreed to do so. In October of 1917, Rosenwald incorporated a foundation, the Julius Rosenwald Fund, to administer his philanthropic endeavors. Because the school-building program had outgrown Tuskegee's administrative capacity, Rosenwald established a Southern Office of the Fund in Nashville in 1920 to take control of the rural school-building program, enlisting S.L. Smith, a former state agent of African American education in Tennessee, to serve the office as director. In the program's first year, 1920–21, the budget exceeded $500,000.

Impact. In *The Emergence of the New South*, historian George Brown Tindall calls the rural school-building program of the Rosenwald Fund "one of the most effective stratagems to outflank the prejudice and apathy that hobbled Negro education."[157] Julius Rosenwald's building program overhauled the educational infrastructure of African American education in the rural South. By the school-building program's termination in 1932 (the year of Rosenwald's death), the Fund had facilitated the construction of 4,977 rural schools throughout the South with an additional 380 homes and shops to complement the schools. Many of the schools operated continuously until desegregation, as ordered by *Brown v. Board of Education* in 1954, was slowly enforced in the communities in which Rosenwald schools were operating. In 1928, Rosenwald schools accounted for one out of every five African American schools in the South, and these schools enrolled one of every three Southern African American pupils.[158]

Rosenwald schools were noted for their modern architectural designs. In some communities, the Rosenwald schools surpassed the quality of the local white schools, prompting renovations or new building projects for white pupils. The Rosenwald school-building program served as a countervailing force in a public environment that often sought to undermine African American education in the South. At a time when Jim Crow laws and pervasive racism made large-scale public support of African American education highly unlikely, Rosenwald's program circumvented popular negative sentiment and sparked public financing for widely underfunded African American schools.

The final Rosenwald School was built in Warm Springs, Georgia in 1937, after the termination of the program, at the special request of President Franklin Roosevelt. When Roosevelt was governor of New York, he sought funding from the Rosenwald Fund for an African American school in his summer retreat home of Warm Springs, noting "[i]t must be a Rosenwald School because of the influence these schools have on the officials and communities." For five years, the Rosenwald Fund did not take up the Warm Springs school, in part because the building program's termination coincided approximately with Roosevelt's initial request. In 1937, however, President Roosevelt renewed his request that the Rosenwald Fund build a school in Warm Springs. The Fund's board granted approval of special funding to build the school, and President Roosevelt personally dedicated the building.[159]

Tindall notes that the larger impact of the Rosenwald Fund's school-building program was the spark it ignited in providing public financial support for African American schools "while neutralizing the opposition of white taxpayers."[160] The Fund's contribution to the total cost of the program totaled only 15 percent of the overall building cost, but the program ignited local public funding of a majority of the building costs and almost all of the operating expenses of the rural schools.

Case 11

ECONOMIC POLICY RESEARCH OF THE HIGHEST QUALITY: NATIONAL BUREAU OF ECONOMIC RESEARCH

Carnegie Corporation of New York, 1921

STEVEN SCHINDLER

Background. For most of the 1910s, a debate ensued about philanthropic funding in the field of economics, particularly among Rockefeller Foundation officials and observers. One side, led by Theodore Vail of AT&T and joined by John D. Rockefeller, Jr. and Rockefeller Foundation advisor Frederick Gates, argued that the public lacked a basic understanding of economics and that the promulgation of economic knowledge, coordinated by what Vail called a "publicity bureau," would best resolve the class dispute many capitalists and philanthropists sought to address.[161] Countering this sentiment, many, including economists Edwin F. Gay of Harvard and Wesley C. Mitchell of Columbia, as well as Jerome Greene of the Rockefeller Institute for Medical Research, felt that this approach sidestepped the most significant national need: more and better basic economic research.[162]

Mitchell believed that economics research held the same promise for social policy that scientific research held for medicine. Gates, wholly committed to devoting the maximum possible proportion of Rockefeller philanthropy to the development of medicine, rejected this analogy.[163] The Rockefeller Foundation's interest in pursuing economics funding at all, however, was thwarted when the implication of the Foundation in managing the public perception of the "Ludlow massacre" turned the Foundation against social science research for more than a decade.[164]

Strategy. The Carnegie Corporation of New York first became interested in supporting economics research in 1916, when Henry Pritchett, president of the Carnegie Foundation for the Advancement of Teaching and trustee of the Carnegie Corporation, supported the idea. Pritchett's proposal, funding an effort to spread basic understanding of economics, was more in tune with Vail and Gates than with the economists. The spark behind Pritchett's proposal was what he perceived as the promulgation of inaccurate information by newspapers and labor organizers for commercial and political gain. In particular, Pritchett criticized the reports of the Committee on Industrial Relations, which to some degree shared the same interest in publishing its views regarding labor-related problems facing the nation's economy. Accordingly, the brunt of his proposal entailed the purchase and endowment of a newspaper with the mandate to print truthful information.[165] After it became clear that the costs of purchasing a newspaper would be too great for the Corporation, the discussion about economics funding was altogether dropped.[166]

Parallel to Pritchett's initiative, the economists initially involved in the Rockefeller discussions were independently pursuing their vision of an economics research institute devoted to basic research. Gay and Mitchell, together with acquaintance Malcolm Rorty through work on the nation's Committee on Industrial Relations, believed that much disagreement about national economic policy was rooted less in differing economic interests than in disagreement about basic economic facts.[167] Gay's role as director of the Central Bureau of Planning and Statistics during World War I instilled in him a commitment to pursue a federal program of gathering economic statistics. Woodrow Wilson disagreed, however, with Gay's assessment of the value of peacetime statistics coordination, and so the Central Bureau was closed after the war.[168] In January 1920, Gay and Mitchell joined Rorty to charter the National Bureau of Economics Research (NBER).[169] In an effort to provide credibility and faithfulness to the mission of pursuing pure economic research, the NBER organizers placed control in the hands of a board of directors of a politically diverse group of economists, businessmen, and individuals linked to labor and economic associations.[170]

The Commonwealth Fund was one of the earliest supporters of NBER, granting $20,000 to the Bureau for its first year's operations, but, in accordance with the Fund's decision to limit its focus to medicine, it ceased its support of NBER with a second grant of $15,000. The general director of the Fund at the time, a Yale historian named Max Farrand, wrote to new Carnegie Corporation president James Angell in November 1920 to seek

Corporation support of NBER.[171] The secretary of NBER then wrote to the Corporation in December requesting $45,000 in grant support, which the Corporation granted a month later after attaching a matching requirement of $20,000.[172]

Pritchett's disagreement with the objectives of NBER, as they conflicted with his preference for widespread economics educational efforts over basic research, was likely overwhelmed by his desire to support Angell in his efforts to centralize decision-making power and to wrest control away from the Corporation's secretary and treasurer, James Bertram.[173] When Angell left the Corporation after only one year as president, NBER appealed to Pritchett in 1921 for further support. By this time, Secretary of Commerce Herbert Hoover was seeking a credible private research entity to conduct studies on unemployment and to propose actions to combat unemployment.[174] In support of NBER funding, Hoover contacted the Russell Sage Foundation, the Commonwealth Fund, and the Carnegie Corporation, writing to Pritchett on November 18, 1921. Although the first two declined to support NBER to the degree Hoover sought, the Corporation responded to Hoover's request in February 1922 with a $50,000 grant, which the Corporation allowed NBER to use to satisfy the Corporation's own matching grant requirement that it had attached to the first grant.[175]

The Carnegie Corporation also supported a number of other economics research entities in the early 1920s, and, as with the NBER, it adopted a policy of disclaiming any adherence to the findings or positions of the economic research it funded.[176]

Impact. Little of NBER's substantive work can be attributed directly to Carnegie Corporation support, but the Corporation grants played a significant role in launching NBER. Carnegie can therefore be credited, to some degree, with NBER's prominence. Among NBER's earliest publications include studies determining national income and unemployment levels. Today, the Bureau continues its work as a "private, nonprofit, nonpartisan research organization dedicated to promoting a greater understanding of how the economy works." The NBER is the premier research organizational framework in which some 600 economists of high quality, who focus on public policy, work together on a variety of projects while remaining based at their home academic institutions. While the only official action taken in the name of the NBER itself is the declaration of the beginning and ending of national recessions, the NBER is the nation's leading nonprofit economic research organization. Of the thirty-one American winners of the Nobel Prize in Economics, twelve of them have been researchers for the Bureau.[177]

Case 12

REFORMING THE LEGAL PROFESSION THROUGH EDUCATION AND PRACTICE

Carnegie Foundation for the Advancement of Teaching, 1921

STEVEN SCHINDLER

Background. In the first few decades of the twentieth century, the leaders of the legal profession, particularly the leadership of the American Bar Association, were concerned about the path of their profession. For one, the sheer number of practitioners exploded, as the number of law schools rose nearly 50 percent and the number of law students nearly doubled between 1900 and 1920. The number of young lawyers was not as disconcerting to many in the legal profession as was the influx of immigrants. Because many of these new entrants into the field did not have access to the requisite educational background to be admitted to the prestigious university-associated law schools, they came to the practice of law through proprietary night schools and other schools with virtually no selective admission policies. To reform-minded legal scholars, raising the academic standards of legal education was a means of limiting access to the legal field.

Another concern of the legal profession's leadership was the widespread belief that the volume of case law and legal literature in the various jurisdictions of the United States was growing at an unmanageable rate and needed to be addressed in a systematic fashion.[178] Corporate lawyers representing wealthy corporations complained that the unwieldy state of case law left them unable to advise their clients with any confidence as to which behavioral paths would be clear of legal threats.[179] A group of representatives from the legal profession argued that they, and not outside reformers, should be responsible for addressing these.[180] Elihu Root, a trustee of the Carnegie Corporation and a lawyer himself, advocated a solution of self-regulation so as to avoid outside interference and meddling in the profession's course.[181]

Strategy. In light of Abraham Flexner's influential report on the status of medical education that included a recommendation of higher admissions standards and standardization of the profession, these legal reformers thought that the Carnegie Foundation for the Advancement of Teaching (CFAT), the sponsor of Flexner's report, could fund another study to repeat the process in the legal profession and thereby address the first objective: raising the bar of entry into the profession.[182] The Committee on Legal

Education of the American Bar Association asked CFAT to conduct a study of legal education. Pritchett commissioned two studies to that end: Joseph Redlich's *The Common Law and the Case Method in American University Law Schools* in 1914 and Alfred S. Reed's *Training for the Public Profession of the Law* in 1921, published after Reed's eight-year study of the field.[183]

While Redlich's report had relatively little influence in legal education, Reed's report was quite controversial. Reed did not share the desire to restrict access to the field of law that motivated those prompting his report. In *The Public Profession of the Law*, his conclusion was instead that the public nature of the legal profession demanded diversity in training styles in order to prepare a diverse corps of lawyers for the legal practice. Committed to maintaining the "poor boy's" access to the legal profession, Reed rejected the push for standardization that the Legal Committee of the ABA desired in favor of wider access to the profession.[184] The report took issue most directly with the unified nature of the bar, especially in its inadequacy in serving the diversity of practice areas within the legal profession.

Prior to the report's publication, CFAT provided advance copies to the ABA Section on Legal Education and Admission to the Bar. The Section, chaired by Elihu Root, was disheartened by the report's findings. In order to prevent the report from enjoying the same influence as did Flexner's report on medical education, the Section quickly offered its public endorsement of a competing proposal by the Amerian Association of Law Schools to raise academic standards.[185]

Ironically, this rejection of legal education standardization led to where the reform-minded legal scholars had hoped. Reed's acknowledgement that the part-time and night schools were the entryways for immigrants into the legal profession prompted the ABA to adopt the Legal Committee's position on increased academic standards for all legal education as a prerequisite to admission to the bar.[186] The ABA's prominence enabled its leadership to institute its own recommendations and to raise academic standards while dismissing Reed's recommendations.

Following Reed's report, CFAT began publishing The Annual Review of Legal Education, written from the premise that a balance was needed between maintaining high bar admission standards and providing access to careers as lawyers for individuals of all socio-economic backgrounds.[187] The report noted that the thirteen states that empowered their high courts to control bar admission generally administered the most advanced rules and best standards.

While CFAT continued to monitor legal education, the Carnegie Corporation took aim at the profession's second concern—reform of the system that produced vast and growing amounts of case law and scholarship. In 1914 two speeches to the Association of American Law Schools (AALS), delivered by Wesley Newcomb Hohfeld and Joseph H. Beale, prompted the creation of a committee, chaired by Elihu Root, to pursue the establishment of a center for legal reform. A committee formed in 1915, but it was inactive until after World War I.[188]

One of the early motivations for legal reform, as for reform of legal education standards, was the tremendous immigration boom from Eastern and Southern Europe. Practicing lawyers in particular were fearful that immigrants from dictatorial or anarchical countries would be incapable of showing respect for the rule of law in the United States.[189] This xenophobic response to perceived threats, which brought together the ABA and the AALS, were shared by leading trustees of the Carnegie Corporation. In addition to Root's warnings of lawless traditions being transferred to the United States through immigration, Henry Pritchett sought an investigation to verify his perception that immigrants learned more slowly the legal traditions unique to America.[190]

In pursuit of his desire to bring about a stronger, more uniformly well-qualified legal profession, Root formed an alliance with the legal academics at the AALS, and he secured critical funds from the Carnegie Corporation to fund the endeavor that became the American Law Institute (ALI).[191] In 1922, the Carnegie Corporation granted $25,000 to a committee, chaired by Root, on the establishment of a permanent organization for the improvement of the law. At a meeting in Washington, D.C. in February 1923, Root delivered the address that preceded the motion to establish the American Law Institute. On April 17, 1923, a grant of $1,075,000 followed the initial $25,000, this time to provide the ALI with sufficient financial support to render it independent of financial concerns for its first decade.[192] The corporation authorized a third grant of $1,020,196 in 1933 for continued support of the ALI in developing restatements of the law.[193]

Impact. In its eighty years of existence, the ALI has become the authoritative body for compiling and publishing restatements of the law in all major fields and in developing and recommending, in conjunction with the National Conference of Commissioners on Uniform State Laws, the Uniform Commercial Code, now adopted in forty-nine states and the District of Columbia, and several other model laws which have also been adopted by many states.[194]

Case 13

THE RURAL HOSPITALS PROGRAM

The Commonwealth Fund, 1927

SCOTT KOHLER

Background. In 1926, health care in the rural United States lagged far behind what was then routinely available in cities. Less well-known than the health risks associated with urban over-crowding and industrialization was the virtual unavailability of health care to much of the country. At the time, Dr. Hermann Biggs, the New York Commissioner of Health, documented the inadequacy of rural healthcare in his state:[195]

- Over 250 incorporated villages in New York State "were without the services of a physician"

- eleven New York counties were without any hospital

New York was not alone in this problem. In fact, over half of the 3,027 counties in the United States had no hospital.[196] And, even when there was a local doctor or hospital, the quality of rural medical care was very low.

Dr. Biggs "convinced [the Commonwealth Fund's general director] Barry Smith that the Commonwealth Fund could do no greater service than to meet the need for hospitals for rural communities and for areas in which the black population predominated."[197] As it happened, Edward S. Harkness, the Fund's president and co-founder, was already sympathetic to the need for more hospitals, having wondered, in a 1919 report, "[m]ight it not be that the Commonwealth Fund could better confine itself to giving money to help build new hospitals. . . [in which] each patient pay[s] what he is able to. . . ."[198]

Strategy. The first Commonwealth hospital was "a pilot endeavor; if it succeeded, Smith proposed to establish a Division of Rural Hospitals, which would erect one or two fifty-bed hospitals a year. . . ." Several conditions were imposed. The Fund chose to leverage its grants by requiring communities to raise one third of the construction costs and to defray all future hospital expenses—similar to what Andrew Carnegie required in the construction of the libraries he financed. Furthermore, each hospital must provide care "without considering race, color, creed, or economic status." Still, applications for Commonwealth funding came from far more communities than the Fund could possibly support. So two criteria were used in the selection process: (1) a community's need, and (2) its willingness and ability to operate and maintain the hospital, without further Commonwealth assistance, once it had been built.

Outcomes. The first Commonwealth-funded rural facility, the Southside Community Hospital, in Farmville, VA, cost $180,000 to build and opened on November 9, 1927. Between 1926 and 1948, the Commonwealth Fund supported the construction of fifteen rural hospitals. And all told, in its twenty-seven years of operation (1925–1952), the Fund's Division of Rural Hospitals gave out a total of $6.84 million.[199]

By 1930, the first six Commonwealth hospitals combined were serving some 410,000 people. During the subsequent five years, new construction stopped, as the hardships of the Great Depression made it difficult for local communities to support new hospitals. The Fund meanwhile concentrated its efforts on shoring up the six existing hospitals, and, as a result, although fewer and fewer people could afford to pay for their medical treatments, none of the six stopped operating for a single day during the Depression.

Impact. By 1931, Barry Smith could assert that "[n]o project undertaken by the Fund has aroused more interest and favorable comment, none has presented greater difficulties, and none has shown more marked results in a period of equal length."[200] The fifteen hospitals built through the program have provided medical care to millions of people, many of whom could not otherwise have afforded the services they received. All of these hospitals are still operating today.[201] A single one of them, for example—the Southside Community Hospital, in Farmville—had revenues of over $37 million in FY 2003 and net assets worth over $11.4 million.[202] This hospital was founded in 1927 thanks to a $120,000 donation by the Fund, or $1.27 million in 2003 dollars.

By far the most significant impact of the Rural Hospitals Program was in serving as a blueprint and a spur for the Hill-Burton Act, which passed Congress in 1946. Hill-Burton, properly known as the Hospital Survey and Construction Act, directed federal funds to follow the foundation's lead on a massive scale. Before Hill-Burton was written, The American Hospital Association and the United States Public Health Service—with financial support from Commonwealth and several other foundations—formed in 1942 the Commission of Hospital Care, which made the formal recommendations to Congress upon which the Act was based.[203] Following the example of the Commonwealth Fund, Congress required, for instance, that each local community raise a portion of its hospital's construction costs[204] and maintain the hospital without further assistance. Congress also required the hospitals "to provide free or reduced charge medical services to persons unable to pay."[205] Since 1946, Hill-Burton has provided over $4.6 billion in grants and $1.5 billion in loans for the construction of hospitals in communities that lack them.

Case 14

MOUNT PALOMAR "HALE" TELESCOPE

Rockefeller Foundation, 1928

SCOTT KOHLER

Background. George Ellery Hale remains today among the greatest astronomers of all time. He made groundbreaking discoveries of his own, and organized many scientific projects of enormous significance. Among these are the founding of *The Astrophysical Journal,* and the establishment of several cutting edge observatories.[206] But Hale's greatest triumph may be one he did not live to see completed. In April 1928, Hale wrote an article in *Harper's Magazine* arguing that a massive new telescope would be a worthy investment in scientific progress. Later that month, Hale followed up on his argument by sending a letter making his case to the International Education Board[207] of the Rockefeller Foundation. Hale contended:

> No method of advancing science is so productive as the development of new and more powerful instruments and methods of research. A larger telescope would not only furnish the necessary gain in light space-penetration and photographic resolving power, but permit the application of ideas and devices derived chiefly from the recent fundamental advances in physics and chemistry.[208]

Strategy. Hale's request was approved, and the Foundation committed $6 million[209] for a new 200-inch telescope, which would be the largest by far in the world. At the time, the record-holder was the 100-inch telescope of the Mt. Wilson Observatory, which George Hale had also helped to build, and of which he served as director until 1923. Many different locations were tested out as possible sites for the new telescope, and in 1934, Mount Palomar, California was chosen for its ideal atmospheric conditions.

Outcomes. Construction of the new telescope took twenty years from the time Hale's funding request was granted to the day the telescope began operation: June 3, 1948. During those years, it had had been "easily the most famous scientific undertaking of the 1930s."[210] Although George Hale had died in 1938, the new colossus was named the Hale Telescope, after the man who had conceived it and worked to make it a reality. Once it was ready, the Hale Telescope could see a billion light years away—twice as far as any other telescope in the world. It gathers four times as much light as the Mt. Wilson Telescope, and enables scientists to photograph and resolve objects 40,000,000 times dimmer, from Earth, than anything visible to the naked eye.

Impact. The Hale Telescope was not built for "practical" uses. Rather it is an instrument of discovery for discovery's own sake. As a 1948 article in *The New York Times* reminds us, "[l]ife was not made any easier or business more profitable after Galileo added to the known universe 500,000 stars which had never been seen before he turned his little telescope on the celestial vault."[211] Yet we honor Galileo all the same. Furthermore, "scientific research at Palomar Observatory since 1948 has been remarkably productive."[212] In 1963, for example, Maarten Schmidt—looking through the Hale Telescope—became the first human ever to observe quasars, "quasi-stellar objects," billions of light years away, that have bewildered astronomers and astrophysicists ever since.[213] The Telescope remains a powerful means of exploration. It is owned and operated by the California Institute of Technology, and has been pointed skyward almost every clear night since June 1948. It is no longer the largest telescope in the world, but its Pyrex reflective mirror, cast in 1936, is still as advanced as any in the world.[214] Certainly, the Hale Telescope stands as a monument to the man whose name it bears. But the exploration, research, and discovery that it has enabled certainly owe something as well to the Rockefeller Foundation, which brought it forth from Hale's imagination onto the slopes of Mount Palomar.

Case 15

THE DEVELOPMENT OF MOLECULAR BIOLOGY AND THE DISCOVERY OF THE STRUCTURE OF DNA

Rockefeller Foundation, 1933

STEVEN SCHINDLER

Background. In 1928, after a review of the activity of four different Rockefeller-endowed philanthropies, the trustees of each of the boards agreed that all activities "relating to the advance of human knowledge" would be absorbed by the Rockefeller Foundation. Among the program areas taken over by the Foundation was grantmaking in the natural sciences formerly administered by the International Education Board and the General Education Board. The Foundation organized these activities under a single division of

Natural Sciences. After a brief period of organization of the Natural Sciences division, the Foundation recruited Warren Weaver, professor of mathematics at the University of Wisconsin, to become director of the new division. This newly-created division of the Rockefeller Foundation, and its newly recruited leader, would come to have a profound impact on the development of the sciences for many decades, and this impact would become one of the quintessential and widely discussed examples of foundation impact.[215]

Strategy. Weaver's first endeavor was to determine the area of science to which the Foundation might best apply its financial support to maximize the advancement of knowledge to benefit the welfare of mankind. He determined that the life sciences offered the greatest such opportunity, and in 1933, the board of trustees of the Foundation agreed to make experimental biology the field of primary interest for the Natural Sciences division. This was a relatively new course for the Foundation. The Foundation made grants in the early 1920s supporting the spread of knowledge in the biological sciences, but Foundation support of biology was far from systematic. Medical research, however, had been the Foundation's primary focus, and biology as a field was actually an outgrowth of the Foundation's prior work in that area. Weaver was able to draw broadly from the Foundation's experiences in medical research funding.[216]

Weaver's own intuition and expertise led him to emphasize the application of quantitative techniques of mathematics, physics, and chemistry to the field of biology, or the borders of biology with other research disciplines. While Weaver did not initiate collaboration between biologists and physical scientists, the Natural Sciences division made a large number of grants to individuals designed to promote such collaboration.[217] In addition to individual grants to scientists, the Rockefeller Foundation supported the development of molecular biology on an institutional level, funding programs to elite universities to support research programs in molecular biology, most notably among them the California Institute of Technology.[218]

The funding approach of the Foundation in the field of molecular biology was nimble and highly supportive of the grantee scientists. George Beadle, recipient of the 1958 Nobel Prize in Medicine, recounted approaching the Rockefeller Foundation as a young professor at Stanford in the early 1940s for a grant to support the genetics research for which he would be awarded the Nobel Prize. At the time, however, he and his team of researchers at Stanford had been working for only three years on a ten-year grant from the Foundation; one of the conditions of the grant was that the team could not reapply for additional funds for the ten-year period. Beadle was rightly undeterred when it became clear to him that his research should be accelerated and that more funding was needed. He met with an officer of the Foundation who promptly made the additional grant needed. Beadle labeled this story an "example of foundation flexibility and speed of decision."[219]

Impact. The precise role of Warren Weaver in the creation or development of the field of molecular biology during his long tenure at the Rockefeller Foundation has been the source of substantial debate.[220] Still, few deny that Weaver's influence, and the influence of the Rockefeller Foundation, during the period in which molecular biology first began to shed light on the genetic makeup of life. Indeed, Weaver himself has been credited with coining the term "molecular biology."

Among the Natural Sciences division's early grants was a fellowship for biochemistry research to Hans Adolph Krebs to enable him to go to Cambridge from the University of Freiberg, which he was forced to leave for political reasons. While at Cambridge, Krebs discovered the Krebs Cycle, a description of the respiration process in human beings.[221] While the discovery would land Krebs a prominent and enduring place in life science textbooks, it was merely a precursor of the important scientific discovery financed by Weaver's Natural Sciences division.

In 1953, the culmination of a number of lines of research converged in Cambridge, England, where James Watson and Francis Crick, two young scientists, discovered the double helical structure of DNA. Watson and Crick were able to make their discovery with the aid of a number of lines of cutting edge research, virtually all supported by private foundations. At King's College, London, a group led by Maurice Wilkins was advancing X-ray diffraction imaging research. At Columbia University, Erwin Chargaff discovered the relative proportions of the four nucleotides in DNA. Both of these researchers were aided by Rockefeller Foundation grants.[222] As for the Cambridge Medical Research Council Laboratory of Molecular Biology, the laboratory from which Watson and Crick worked, laboratory researcher Max F. Perutz suggested that the entire unit owed its existence to the Rockefeller Foundation.[223] Rockefeller Foundation grants funded foreign researchers at the lab who would not have been able to study in England without the Foundation's assistance. Grants also made possible the purchase of X-ray diffraction equipment, critical to the discovery of DNA. Knowledge of the structure of DNA rapidly opened the way for genetic research and a better understanding of cell replication and mutation, and their discovery earned Watson and Crick a Nobel Prize.

Case 16

PREDECESSOR TO BLUE CROSS AND BLUE SHIELD OF NORTH CAROLINA

The Duke Endowment, 1935

STEVEN SCHINDLER

Background. Concern about the extreme costs of hospitalization and the severe economic effects extended hospital stays would have on families was of increasing concern in North Carolina in the 1920s. Lack of access to adequate health care was also a major concern in the state, which ranked forty-second out of forty-eight states in doctors per capita and forty-eighth in hospital beds per capita.[224] The concern over rising costs of medical care and hospitals was a broader concern, one that the Committee on the Costs of Medical Care, a national body formed and funded by several foundations to address the problem in 1927, studied for five years.[225]

In the late 1920s, no public, organized, voluntary health service prepayment plan existed. Wilburt Davison, founding dean of the Duke University School of Medicine, was intrigued by the problem and began thinking about possible solutions to funding medical care. Through his studies in England as a Rhodes Scholar, Davison was exposed to voluntary, community-based prepayment plans for hospitalization. In the late 1920s, Davison, along with prominent Durham banker and philanthropist George Watts Hill, formed the Durham Hospital Care Association.[226] The stock market crash of 1929 followed shortly thereafter, and the Association was forced to close.[227]

A plan similar to that imagined by Davison and Hill was implemented in 1929 at Baylor University Medical School in Dallas, Texas.[228] That plan would become the first Blue Cross agency nationwide. Two years later, a citywide prepayment plan was established in Minneapolis-St. Paul, and a county-wide plan followed shortly thereafter in Newark, New Jersey.[229] In 1932, the national Committee on the Costs of Health Care produced a majority report recommending "universal (if not compulsory) health insurance," despite the relatively few group hospital prepayment or health insurance plans that had yet been brought into existence.[230]

There remained no such plan in North Carolina in the early 1930s, so Davison and Hill made another attempt.[231] In 1933, two men incorporated the Hospital Care Association (HCA) in North Carolina as a nonprofit corporation. Hill provided the capital for a cash operating fund. Additional funding came from the Duke and Watts Hospitals. [232] Their attempt was unique, even threatening to the political establishment; Davison and Hill were regarded as socialists for their efforts. [233]

Strategy. For the following two years, Graham L. Davis of The Duke Endowment, which had been established by James B. Duke in 1924, organized a group of leaders representing hospitals, medical professionals, and the public to study hospital prepayment service plans, particularly for the poor. The Duke Endowment, which was already making payments to hospitals in North Carolina for treatment of charity patients, had a special interest in prepayment programs for low-wage people to decrease the number of patients without either insurance or the financial capacity to pay their hospital bills. [234] The study included trips by Davis and I. H. Manning, charter member of the HCA Board of Trustees and former dean of the UNC School of Medicine, to Europe to study prepayment plans. The group also studied the plans in Dallas, Minneapolis, and Newark. [235]

As a result of this study, in March 1935, the Hospital Saving Association came into being as a non-profit corporation "for the purpose of providing a prepayment plan for hospital service to people of the entire state," in part to compete with the Hospital Care Association. [236] The Duke Endowment provided the first and only capital in the amount of $25,000 to fund the newly chartered HSA. [237]

Impact. Only a few years after HSA was chartered, the American Hospital Association established its first set of guidelines and standards for nonprofit prepayment health care plans. The Hospital Saving Association appeared among its list of thirty-nine approved plans nationwide. [238]

For the next several years, the two organizations competed statewide for members of their health insurance plans. Until 1962, Hospital Saving Association was the only Blue Shield-approved prepayment plan in the state; Hospital Care Association was a Blue Cross organization. That year, HCA became Blue Shield certified, and the two organizations began to work together more closely. Five years later, after careful study, the boards of the two organizations voted to merge into Blue Cross and Blue Shield of North Carolina, Inc. [239] Today, Blue Cross and Blue Shield of North Carolina, with its origins owning in part to the Duke Endowment, is the market leader in the North Carolina health care industry, serving approximately 2.9 million members. [240]

Case 17

TRANSFORMING AMERICA'S PERCEPTIONS OF RELATIONS AMONG ITS RACES: KARL GUNNAR MYRDAL'S *AN AMERICAN DILEMMA*

Carnegie Corporation of New York, 1936

STEVEN SCHINDLER

Background. In its first few decades, the Carnegie Corporation of New York was largely occupied with meeting its financial commitments to other Carnegie philanthropic organizations. In the mid-1930s, when the Corporation began to catch up with those obligations, then-president Frederick Keppel began to contemplate new strategies for the Corporation's discretionary income.[241]

A member of the Carnegie Corporation's board of trustees, Newton D. Baker, first suggested at a board meeting in 1935 that the Corporation consider "the general questions of *negro education and negro problems.*"[242] Baker grew up in the South and was suffused with Confederate tradition. The motivation behind his suggestion was clearly conditioned by his racist attitudes; Baker believed that racism was based on biological distinctions, and he suggested "an infant race like the black people in this country" would enjoy greater benefit from education if they were forced to work for it.[243]

Keppel traveled to Cleveland in 1936 to visit with Baker about a possible Corporation project embodying Baker's suggestion. In following Baker's advice, Keppel settled on a comprehensive study of race in America as an appropriate endeavor for the Corporation.

Strategy. Influenced by the 1936 study on race published by the Rosenwald Fund, which was written by a Dutch scholar, Keppel sought a European to conduct the study, understanding that the study should be perceived as objective and unbiased by domestic racial attitudes.[244] Keppel collected a list of nominations from a variety of advisors of potential European scholars to conduct the Carnegie study on race in America. Karl Gunnar Myrdal, a Swedish economist, was one of twenty-five nominations, submitted by former assistant to a previous Corporation president, Beardsley Ruml. Myrdal had been a Rockefeller Foundation Fellow, along with his wife, in 1929–30, and his interaction with the Rockefeller philanthropies caused his path to cross Ruml's. In August 1937, Keppel asked Myrdal to lead the Corporation study. Myrdal first declined, but then accepted in a telegram from Stockholm. Baker, when he learned of Keppel's decision, expressed his satisfaction that the European professor was a better choice than any American.[245]

Myrdal came to the United States in 1938 to deliver the Godkin Lectures at Harvard and to meet with Keppel about the proposed study. Myrdal then returned to Sweden while Keppel arranged a two-month tour through the South upon his return, to be guided by Jackson Davis, associate director of Rockefeller's General Education Board.[246]

Upon completion of this tour, Myrdal submitted an initial report to the Corporation on how he intended to conduct his study. In Keppel's response to this report, he demonstrated a concern that the approach might be too broad and that he hoped Myrdal's study would focus more directly on opportunities for Corporation grantmaking in the area of "Negro" education.[247] Aside from this request, Keppel never directly ordered any particular approach nor wavered from steadfast support for Myrdal's independence, despite what became growing criticism of Myrdal and his work. In assessing the relationship between Keppel and Myrdal, Ellen Condliffe Lagemann writes, in her history of the Carnegie Corporation, that Keppel's "willingness to help [Myrdal] by making suggestions, combined with his insistence upon regard for Myrdal's autonomy as a scholar, were vital to the inquiry from beginning to end."[248]

After submitting his initial plans to Keppel, fifty-one individuals reviewed Myrdal's plans for proceeding. In April 1939, a group of scholars met at a week-long conference to refine and finalize his plans. Myrdal then commissioned forty research memoranda from scholars on race-related issues across the country.[249]

From the research memoranda and his own observations, Myrdal compiled and drafted the two-volume *An American Dilemma*, a vast study containing the commissioned studies of particular facets of the race problem as well as Myrdal's own analysis stemming from his interpretation of these reports and his experiences on the Southern tour. The Carnegie Corporation published *An American Dilemma* in 1944.[250]

Impact. According to Lagemann, *An American Dilemma* "had a lasting impact on public opinion and public policy."[251] In his assessment of the role of Myrdal's study in American public policy, David Southern compared the impact of *An American Dilemma* in the civil rights field to George Kennan's influence in the field of foreign policy through his famous "X" article in *Foreign Affairs*.[252] The Supreme Court decision in *Brown v. Board of Education* in 1954 rested its reasoning in part on Myrdal's conclusions and those of other social scientists in part because it found history "inconclusive."[253] Myrdal's study has been cited by the Supreme Court in at least five different opinions.[254] *An American Dilemma* served as supplemental proof to anecdotal evidence, from the service of blacks in World War II, that racial discrimination had no foundation in natural inferiority. It was a critical element of the persuasive case the early builders of the civil rights movement pieced together to combat institutional racism.[255]

John Stanfield, in *Philanthropy and Jim Crow in American Social Science*, takes a more skeptical view of the impact of *An American Dilemma*, at least of its intrinsic value. He declares that the Myrdal study "has been viewed as a seminal work because it is too big for most people to read and because at least through the early 1980s no other agency or foundation has successfully attempted such a comprehensive analysis about blacks."[256] In deriding the study for providing a paradigm that essentially distracted liberals with false hopes for racial integration in lieu of the more efficacious means of solving racial problems through power and pluralism, Stanfield notes that *An American Dilemma* stood as a formidable weapon for liberals in discourse on race on account of its origins and association with what he calls, with some sarcasm, "a great democratic organization." Despite Stanfield's reservations about popular and intellectual reverence accorded to the Carnegie Corporation, the credibility Myrdal's study was afforded in social matters cannot be denied, and Stanfield's own critique demonstrates the value and forcefulness that the study gained, aside from financial support, from the study's association with a foundation such as the Carnegie Corporation.[257]

Despite its broad use outside the Carnegie Corporation, and despite Keppel's request that the study offer the Corporation guidance in its grantmaking, the Corporation found little of practical use in *An American Dilemma*. No significant shift in its funding strategies can be detected. Only in the 1960s did the Corporation first begin to celebrate its role in providing intellectual stimulus to the civil rights movement in Myrdal's study.[258]

Case 18

SUPPORT FOR THE DEVELOPMENT OF THE PAP SMEAR TEST

The Commonwealth Fund, 1941

SCOTT KOHLER

Background. In 1913, a physician named George Papanicolaou moved from Greece to the United States and began to study chromosomes and sex determination at Cornell Medical College, in New York.[259] Dr. Papanicolaou proved that the vaginal smear technique was effective in observing the human sex cycle, and by 1928, he was convinced that observing vaginal smear samples under a microscope enabled him to differentiate between normal and cancerous cells, a claim that was vigorously contested by the medical establishment. Pathologists were not convinced that it was possible to detect cancer by observing individual cells, and, in any case, they argued that the existing technique for diagnosing uterine cancers—biopsy—was effective and accurate enough. Discouraged, Dr. Papanicolaou abandoned his cancer research, focusing instead on such fields as ovulation. At the time, cervical cancer was the deadliest of all forms of cancer among women.

Strategy. Ten years later—in 1939—however, Dr. Papanicolaou returned to the study of cellular irregularities, using exfoliative cytology,[260] when he began to collaborate with a gynecologist named Herbert Traut. At first, the pair had great difficulty obtaining funding. Papanicolaou's techniques had still not won acceptance, and traditional funders of cancer research declined to offer them support. In 1941, however, the Commonwealth Fund took a chance on Papanicolaou, offering him an $1,800 research grant that was considered "highly speculative."[261]

Outcomes. Using smears obtained from Dr. Traut's patients, Papanicolaou was able to establish definitively that exfoliative cytology revealed cellular irregularities—even before they had become cancerous—far earlier than biopsy could. In 1943, the Commonwealth Fund published Papanicolaou's now-classic monograph, *Diagnosis of Uterine Cancer by the Vaginal Smear*, which demonstrated his findings conclusively.

Its effect was tremendous. As soon thereafter as 1960, the American Cancer Society estimated that over 6 million American women had received Pap Tests (named for Dr. Papanicolaou), and that deaths from uterine cancer had been reduced—by Dr. Papanicolaou's work—to half of what they would otherwise have been.[262] Today, the Pap Smear Test is a routine part of every gynecological checkup. It is still "the most effective screening test for cervical cancer."[263] Exfoliative cytology was also subsequently applied by Dr. Papanicolaou to detect respiratory, gastrointestinal, urinary, and other types of tumors.[264]

Impact. According to Quest Diagnostics' online Patient Health Library, Pap Tests, when performed regularly, "almost always detect cervical cell changes before the changes become cancerous."[265] This is critical, since cervical cancer, like virtually all cancers, is far less deadly when it is detected early. As a result, "the use of the Pap Test as a screening tool for cervical cancer has dramatically increased cure rates."[266] It is no exaggeration to say that Dr. Papanicolaou's work has saved millions of women's lives over the past half century.

Dr. Papanicolaou, himself, believed that the support of the Commonwealth Fund—which provided him with over $120,000 between 1941 and 1951[267]—was of critical importance in allowing him to develop the Pap Test and prove its efficacy. As he wrote in 1953 to Roderick Heffron, the Commonwealth program officer who had, at the time, been in charge of medical research:[268]

> At this moment as I am writing what is possibly my last report to you, my thoughts return to the time some eleven and one-half years ago when our first application for financial support was submitted to the Commonwealth Fund. *That was one of the most critical periods in my scientific career as it was then that I found myself totally deprived of funds for the continuation of my research.* . . . Both projects [I had tried to undertake] were rejected by every one of the societies supporting cancer research to which I turned for help.
>
> It was then, at a moment when every hope had almost vanished, that the Commonwealth Fund, a society not primarily devoted to cancer research stepped in. . .
>
> As I write these lines my eyes are moist from the memory of those critical days. It is with a feeling of deep gratitude that I want to express my appreciation to the Commonwealth Fund for having extended to me since that time the financial and moral support which made possible the continuation of my scientific studies. . . .What appeared to be a speculative project eleven years ago is now a recognized and well founded contribution to the biological and medical sciences. *This could never have been realized without the inspiration and help which came from the Commonwealth Fund.* . . [emphasis added]

Case 19

SUPPORT OF THE NATIONAL INSTITUTES OF HEALTH

Albert and Mary Lasker Foundation, 1942

SCOTT KOHLER

Background. Born in 1900, Mary Woodard had already achieved success as a businesswoman and art collector by the time she married advertising executive Albert Lasker in 1940. It was soon after that marriage, however, that

Mrs. Lasker entered the medical research field—in which she would ultimately realize her greatest achievements. Motivated by her own childhood frailty, the early deaths of both her parents, and the loss of several other friends to disease, Mary Lasker turned her own outrage at the slow pace of medical research into the driving force behind a tremendously significant advocacy campaign, and behind the subsequent grant-making of the Albert and Mary Lasker Foundation.

The Lasker Foundation was created in 1942, "with a mission that was novel at the time: to encourage federal financial support for biomedical research in the United States."[269] At the time, such research was funded almost entirely by private interests, in particular such private philanthropies as the Rockefeller Foundation, the Markle Foundation, and the Commonwealth Fund.[270] Mary Lasker, who herself had no background—or aptitude, she used to joke—as a scientist, felt that the support of basic research into the causes of disease and disability was the key to finding cures. Deciding that the federal government was the only possible source of funds large enough to fund adequately the level of research she envisioned, Mary Lasker, as president of the Lasker Foundation, set out on an advocacy campaign that would last for the rest of her long life.

Strategy. Led by Mrs. Lasker, the Foundation served as "catalyst and conduit" for the increase of federal funding for medical research. Mrs. Lasker began by making use of her and her husband's social and political connections to encourage members of Congress, as well as White House officials, to support increased appropriations for the study of disease. Mrs. Lasker was a tireless advocate and lobbyist who often put doctors and researchers in touch with the policymakers with the power to make available federal research grants. The primary beneficiary of Lasker's work was the National Institutes of Health (NIH). Although it already existed in 1945, NIH was a tiny operation with funding of only $2.4 million.[271] In Mary Lasker's own words, she "would ask Congress to establish new branches such as the one for mental health and I got people to testify that the cancer institute needed money."[272] It was a simple strategy, but it proved hugely effective.

Part of Mrs. Lasker's effectiveness certainly flowed from her wealth and social skills. But most important was her tenacity. In addition to the many relationships she forged with congressmen, Mrs. Lasker had direct access to virtually every U.S. president from Franklin Roosevelt onward, and she was never afraid to lobby one directly. Though she was particularly close to President Lyndon Johnson, Mrs. Lasker was effective in her national lobbying across eleven administrations—both Republican and Democrat. The expenditures of the Foundation were very modest, with small appropriations going for direct research, and more going to support the prestigious Lasker Awards and an urban beautification program. But, by serving as a vehicle for Mary Lasker to pursue her extensive education and advocacy efforts, and as a convener for other medical research supporters from across the health research fields, the Foundation achieved outcomes vastly greater than the value of its inputs.

Outcomes. By continually encouraging Congress and the White House of the need for further research dollars, Mrs. Lasker became the primary advocate behind a massive increase of federal research dollars. In 1945, appropriations to NIH had totaled about $2.4 million.[273] By 1985, this amount had skyrocketed to $5.5 billion,[274] and in 2004, the NIH budget topped $27.8 billion.[275] Much of this increase was owing to the rise of such federal programs as Medicare and Medicaid, but much of it—including the creation of a multitude of new research centers focused on specific illnesses—was brought about by the campaigning of Mary Lasker, the Lasker Foundation, and such collaborators as Florence Mahoney, and Drs. Sidney Farber and Michael DeBakey.

Impact. The contributions of these private advocates, and in particular of Mrs. Lasker, have been widely acknowledged. In 1969, Mrs. Lasker received the Presidential Medal of Freedom, the nation's highest civilian honor. And in 1989, she was honored with the Congressional Gold Medal. At the time of her death in 1993, Mrs. Lasker—dubbed "the fairy godmother of medical research" by *Business Week* magazine—was still president of the Lasker Foundation, honorary president of the American Cancer Society, and vice-chairman of the board of trustees of the United Cerebral Palsy Research and Education Foundation.[276]

Mrs. Lasker credited her effectiveness in working for the immense growth of public funding for medical research to the Foundation. In late 1985, she wrote, ". . . for 40 years, all of us at the [Lasker] Foundation have been dedicated to education and motivating Congress to support the idea of more funds and a higher priority for medical research on the major causes of death and disability."[277] According to Johnson White House aide Lawrence F. O'Brien, Mary Lasker and Florence Mahoney "played a significant role" in the creation of the Medicare program in 1965.[278] But the two were especially well known for their work campaigning on behalf of the National Institutes of Health. John Gardner, the former Secretary of Health, Education, and Welfare, described NIH—now a massive agency with over 18,000 employees—as "practically a monument" to their efforts, and President Truman described the pair as "the most tireless, consistent, and effective crusaders" he had ever known.[279]

Case 20

THE GREEN REVOLUTION

Rockefeller Foundation, 1943

SCOTT KOHLER

Background.

> For the last five years, we've had more people starving and hungry. But something has happened. Pakistan is self-sufficient in wheat and rice, and India is moving towards it. It wasn't a red, bloody revolution as predicted. It was a green revolution.

Norman Borlaug recalls William Gaud speaking these words at a small meeting in 1968.[280] Gaud, who, at the time, administered the United States Agency for International Development (USAID), was describing an almost unbelievable surge in food output then being achieved by a number of Asian nations that had seemed, until very recently, to be on the brink of disaster. The two nations cited by Gaud were especially worrisome. Neither Pakistan, a country of 115 million people, nor India, whose population already exceeded half a billion, had been producing enough food to meet the growing need of its rapidly expanding population. Famine, and its attendant turmoil, seemed inevitable. But Gaud was right. Something *had* happened. Within a few years, food production in India, Pakistan, and many of their neighbors, would outstrip population growth. The threat of mass starvation would loom less ominously over the land, and Borlaug, an agronomist working for the Rockefeller Foundation, would be a Nobel laureate credited with saving more lives than any person in human history.

Despite all appearances, this "green revolution" did not occur overnight. Its roots go back several decades earlier. In 1940, the Vice President-elect, Henry Wallace, traveled to Mexico. He was "appalled" by the conditions there. Masses of people were eking out an existence on meager quantities of food. At the time, Mexico was forced to import over half its wheat, and a significant portion of its maize.[281] Wallace met with an official of the Rockefeller Foundation, and, soon after, with the Foundation's president, Raymond Fosdick. He described the plight of the Mexican poor, emphasizing to Fosdick "that the all important thing was to expand the means of subsistence."[282] Fosdick and his colleagues at the Rockefeller Foundation were agreeable to the idea. The Foundation had a long history of combating disease in poverty-stricken regions, and there was a feeling among its officers that hunger and malnutrition were closely related to many of the world's health care problems. So, in 1943, when the Mexican government requested the Foundation's assistance in an effort to improve that nation's agricultural productivity, its trustees agreed, seeing the new project "as a natural outgrowth of [the Foundation's] interest in public health and the biological sciences. . . ."[283] With an initial outlay of $20,000 for a survey in 1943, followed, in 1944, by $192,800 for construction costs and equipment, the Rockefeller Foundation embarked, with the Mexican Ministry of Agriculture, upon the Mexican Agricultural Project (MAP).

Strategy. From the start, the Foundation was deeply involved in the programmatic aspects of the operation. A team of Rockefeller scientists was sent to Chapingo, outside Mexico City, where they established an Office of Special Studies (OSS). Led by George Harrar (who, in 1961, would become the Foundation's president), the group included Borlaug and four other agricultural specialists. For almost two decades, this team employed a three-part strategy to "improve the yields of the basic food crops" in Mexico.[284]

The first element of the strategy was to engage in ongoing research in an effort to produce ever-better varieties of corn, wheat, potatoes, and other crops, and to develop ever better methods of growing these crops. As soon as a new variety or technique was developed, it was put to use. "Research from the outset was production-oriented and restricted to that which was relevant to increasing wheat production. Researches in pursuit of irrelevant academic butterflies were discouraged. . . ."[285] The second element of the strategy employed was a persistent outreach effort with two goals. First, the American scientists and their Mexican colleagues sought to teach Mexican farmers about their latest advances in agricultural science. And second, they worked to convince farmers to take advantage of these new breakthroughs, whether by planting a new type of seed or by fertilizing or irrigating their fields in new ways. The third element of the strategy adopted was to help train a corps of agronomists, plant protectionists, and other professionals, who would ultimately be able to assume primary responsibility for the well-being of agriculture in Mexico. This was accomplished by Foundation-sponsored fellowships and scholarships enabling hundreds of Mexican students to study at American universities on the cutting edge of agricultural sciences. Moreover, an intern program was incorporated into the Foundation's activities in Chapingo.

The goals of the Mexican Agricultural Project were simple. Gordon Conway, the former president of the Rockefeller Foundation, writes that the Foundation wanted to "improve the yields of the basic food crops, maize, wheat, and beans."[286] Crop yields in Mexico were "low and static . . . soils were impoverished and chemical fertilizer virtually unknown."[287] But the

Foundation did not want Mexican agriculture to become dependent on its involvement. Rather, as Borlaug describes, "the philosophy of the Rockefeller Foundation was to 'help Mexico help itself' in solving its food production problems, and in the process work itself out of a job."[288] And the Foundation was already thinking big. Conway writes that "[a] conscious objective of the Green Revolution from the beginning was to produce varieties that could be grown in a wide range of conditions throughout the developing world."[289]

Outcomes. "Officials at the Mexican Ministry of Agriculture," writes Deborah Fitzgerald, Professor of the History of Technology at MIT, "were pleased to have not only a revitalization of agricultural science, but also the input of Rockefeller dollars."[290] But progress on maize started out slowly. Fitzgerald suggests that this was because of systemic differences between the primarily subsistence-oriented corn farming in Mexico and its more commercial counterpart in the U.S. The farming techniques advocated by the Rockefeller team were not cheap, and few small farmers could afford the initial investment.[291]

Progress with wheat (which was Dr. Borlaug's division) was much faster. Mexican wheat farms were, in general, larger than local corn farms, and were more commercial than subsistence-oriented. In this way, they more closely resembled American farms. The scientists at Chapingo had developed wheat varieties resistant to stem rust, and these were distributed widely throughout the country. By 1956, Mexico was self-sufficient in its production of wheat, and it has remained so ever since. Furthermore, between 1954 and 1961, Borlaug had worked to produce a disease resistant, high-yield, photo-insensitive[292] dwarf wheat. He succeeded at this by crossing indigenous Mexican varieties with a Japanese dwarf wheat that had been cultivated centuries ago.[293] When the first seeds of the new dwarf hybrid were distributed in 1961, yields-per-hectare became even more impressive. Between 1948 and 1970, Mexican wheat yields rose from 750 kilos-per-hectare to almost 3,000—a four-fold increase in productivity.

In 1943, there had not been a single trained plant protectionist in Mexico. Local agriculture was outdated. Twenty years later, the Rockefeller Foundation had contributed, by providing funding, hands-on experience, and often both, to the training of over seven hundred Mexican scientists in fields of agriculture.

The success of the Foundation's efforts in Mexico led many of that country's neighbors to request similar assistance. To that end, the Foundation set up a similar program in Colombia in 1950. Other countries soon followed, and the benefits of Rockefeller-sponsored research were spread throughout Latin America. The Foundation's 1968 report proclaims that "it had been clearly demonstrated . . . that, with organized assistance, a food-deficit nation could rapidly modernize its agriculture."

But Mexico had not been caught on a global wave of agricultural progress; the report continues: "Still, in most developing nations, efforts to increase production of major agricultural commodities were relatively ineffective [over the same period of time]." Several major factors had helped Mexico turn the corner. Certainly, the initiative of its government was one. But it was widely recognized that foundation-sponsored technological advances and the relentless labors of foundation scientists had been others.

Programs in Mexico, Colombia, and Chile had proven successful and had demonstrated the enormous potential for improvement in the food output of many developing nations. As the Rockefeller Foundation "worked itself out of a job," national governments began to assume primary responsibility for the existing programs, and the Rockefeller Foundation looked for the best way to apply the lessons of the past twenty years to other hunger-ravaged nations around the world.

And many nations were, indeed, being desolated by hunger. By the mid-1960s, India, already the world's second most populous nation, consumed fully a quarter of all U.S. food aid each year.[294] Explosive population growth in much of Asia was making it less and less plausible that nations like India, Pakistan, and the Philippines would ever be able to feed themselves. In *Famine—1975! America's Decision: Who Will Survive?* William and Paul Paddock argued that a Time of Famines would soon lay waste the developing world. "The famines are inevitable," they warned. And "riding alongside [them] will surely be riots and other civil tensions which the central government[s] will be too weak to control." The Paddocks derided the naïve hope that "[s]omething [would] turn up" to forestall this doom.[295] The Paddocks were not alone in their assessment. Stanford biologist Paul Ehrlich, for example, argued that *Famine—1975!* "may be remembered as one of the most important books of our age."

The Rockefeller Foundation shared these men's sense of urgency. But, rather than advocate a triage system (as the Paddocks did), in which the worst-off nations would be denied assistance and left to their Darwinian fate, the Foundation looked for new ways to attack the problem. The Foundation had first extended its agriculture programs to India in 1956, at the request of the Indian national government. In the ensuing years, Rockefeller partnered with USAID and the U.S. Department of Agriculture (USDA). Together, they "helped establish five state agriculture universities in India."[296] These universities collaborated with their American counterparts on research and training. As it had in Mexico, the Foundation thereby contributed to the development, in India, of a community of home-grown agriculturalists with access to the most advanced technologies in the world.

But their training would take time. And in India, as in many of its neighboring countries, time was of the essence, as Dr. Borlaug describes in his Nobel Lecture:

> So great is the food shortage in many underdeveloped and emerging countries that there is not enough time to develop an adequate corps of scientists before attacking food production problems. A shortcut and organizational change had to be invented to meet the needs. And so was born the first truly international research and training institute, the International Rice Research Institute (IRRI) at Los Banos, the Philippines, in 1960, to work exclusively on the regionally all-important but too-long-neglected rice crop."[297]

In 1959, the Rockefeller Foundation was joined in its food production efforts by the Ford Foundation, which paid $7.15 million to build the International Rice Research Institute and contributed an additional $750,000, for research and training, over the Institute's first three years of operation. The land upon which the Institute was built was provided by the Filipino government, and the Rockefeller Foundation assumed primary responsibility for staffing and operating IRRI, which proved to be the first of four major international centers for agricultural research and training on which Rockefeller and Ford collaborated.

International Rice Research Institute (IRRI)
Los Banos, Philippines   1961

International Center for Maize and Wheat Improvement (CIMMYT)
Chapingo, Mexico   1966

International Institute for Tropical Agriculture (IITA)
Lagos, Nigeria   1968

International Center for Tropical Agriculture (CIAT)*
Bogota, Colombia   1968

* CIAT was supported by the W. K. Kellogg Foundation as well as Rockefeller and Ford.

These international centers served as focal points for the global battle against hunger. No longer was the Foundation restricted to tackling, one at a time, the problems of individual nations. Scientists from around the world brought home from these centers the most up-to-date agricultural advances, and new high-yield crop varieties could be exported from these institutes out to a multitude of food-deprived nations.

Meanwhile, the Rockefeller and Ford Foundations remained directly involved in India and Pakistan respectively. From 1963–65, Dr. Borlaug worked in India and Pakistan to convince local farmers of the merits of Mexican dwarf wheat varieties and other recent advances. By 1965, food shortages on the subcontinent had gotten so bad that these nations' governments began to import large quantities of seed from CIMMYT and IRRI, especially after strong monsoons in 1966 and 1967 ravaged crop yields, leading to an increase in the global price of wheat and a greater acceptance, in those nations, that new techniques needed to be tried if widespread famine was to be averted.[298] In India, Rockefeller staff members "serve[d] as co-leaders of the national rice, wheat, and sorghum schemes. Leadership of the national coordinated maize program was provided by the Foundation for the first eight years," before it was assumed by an Indian scientist.[299]

Progress throughout Asia was dramatic. The first time Borlaug and his associates (mostly scientists he had trained in Mexico with Rockefeller Foundation funds) planted on the Indian subcontinent, they often worked "in sight of artillery flashes.[300] Sowed late, that [first wheat] crop germinated poorly, yet yields still rose 70 percent . . . the next harvest was . . . a 98 percent improvement."[301] At IRRI, researchers developed IR8, widely hailed as "miracle rice" for its high yields. By 1967, just five years after IRRI was completed, the Philippines achieved self-sufficiency in rice.[302] In the same year, the Turkish government imported dwarf wheat from CIMMYT for the first time. Yields on the farms using the wheat soared to double, often triple, their previous averages. In 1968, Pakistan, which by then had imported tens of thousands of tons of high-yield seed from the international centers, became self-sufficient in wheat. And by 1974, India, which Paul Ehrlich had labeled "so far behind in the population-food game that there is no hope that our food aid will see them through to self-sufficiency," was self-sufficient in the production of all cereals. It has remained so ever since. By the time Norman Borlaug accepted the Nobel Peace Prize[303] in 1970, it was apparent that food production in the famine imperiled nations of Southeast Asia had, for a time at least, surpassed the rate of population growth, something that had seemed impossible to many observers.

Impact. The impact of the Green Revolution was enormous. High-yield agriculture is credited with saving at least a billion lives since the mid-1960s.[304] Global cereal production more than tripled between 1950 and 2000.[305] Absent an adequate supply of food, political stability and economic prosperity cannot be achieved. This is why, in 1970, the Nobel Committee recognized Dr. Borlaug with its prize for peace.

But Borlaug did not work alone. In his Nobel Lecture, he explains, "I am but one member of a vast team made up of many organizations, officials, thousands of scientists, and millions of farmers—mostly small and humble—who for many years have been fighting a quiet, oftentimes losing war on the food production front." Certainly this is true. The Green Revolution could not have taken place without the collaboration of its many composite parts. And, as Borlaug, himself a Rockefeller scientist, makes clear, the Rockefeller Foundation was at the vanguard of the Revolution.

Certainly other organizations deserve credit. The governments of Mexico, Chile, Colombia, Thailand, India, Pakistan, and a host of others sought help from foundations, the U.N., and other governments. And they supported, within their own borders, the invigoration of agricultural sciences. But they were aware of the expertise that the Rockefeller staff had built up as one of the earliest coordinators of the modern attack on hunger, and they made the most of it. Foundation staffers were invited to direct national crop programs (as discussed earlier in the case of India) and, along with the international centers it helped to found, often administrated new efforts, as it did with Thailand's "network of eighteen experimental [rice breeding] stations" in the mid-1960s.[306]

Other foundations deserve credit as well. From 1959 onward, the Ford Foundation was a major participant in the spread of high-yield technologies, and the Kellogg Foundation soon added its support.

The United Nations and the U.S. government were also deeply involved. But early on, they had little success transferring "production technology from the industrialized temperate zones to the tropics and subtropics." This is why, according to Borlaug, the "Cooperative Mexican Government–Rockefeller Foundation" model "ultimately proved to be superior" to "public sector foreign technical assistance programs. . . ."[307] By the time the Green Revolution really took off, these national and supranational bodies had recognized the success of the Foundation-pioneered model and supported it, as demonstrated by USAID's commitment of funds to the international centers.[308]

The Green Revolution would not have been possible without earlier scientific breakthroughs. Dr. Borlaug estimates that fully 40 percent of the world's current population would not be alive today were it not for the Haber-Bosch ammonia-synthesizing process.[309] The spread of Mexican dwarf wheat and IR8 rice (and their continually improving offspring) would have been impossible without such breakthroughs in fertilizer technology. But that is the nature of progress. Scientific achievement is not diminished by its debt to the work of previous generations.

It has been argued that the Green Revolution produced negative side effects commensurate with its benefits. Critics point out that, in some parts of

the world, the greatest benefits of new seed varieties and agricultural technologies have flowed more to well-off, rather than poor, farmers. They also
claim that the irrigation needs of high-yield agriculture drain local water resources. And fertilizer use, essential if high-yield crops are to reach their full
potential, can lead to runoff that pollutes streams and rivers. Observers have
also worried that, by enabling the developing world to feed more and more
of its people, the Green Revolution has been a disincentive for them to get
serious about population control. But population growth historically levels
out in developed nations, and it is impossible to make the leap from developing to developed without an adequate supply of food. Advocates of high-
yield agriculture say that runoff and water table depletion are problems only
when planting techniques are misapplied. More education is obviously
needed.[310] Dr. Borlaug, yet again a convincing spokesman for the revolution
he helped to lead, explains that "[h]ad we tried to use the technology of 1950
to produce the harvest of 2000 it would have taken an additional 2.75 billion acres of land."[311] Environmentalists would agree with Borlaug that de-
forestation on such a massive scale would have been disastrous. Even more
disastrous would have been the mass starvations once predicted for much of
the developing world.

This is not to say that famine is not still a very real threat in many places.
It is. But thanks to the Green Revolution, in which the Rockefeller Foundation was a widely acknowledged leader, food production has essentially kept
up with population growth. If farmers, scientists, governments, and civil societies around the world continue to meet this challenge, and the challenges
of environmental stewardship and the equitable distribution of food, then it
may be possible to reach population equilibrium without anyone's worst
fears coming to pass.

Case 21

THE ROCHESTER REGIONAL
HOSPITAL COUNCIL

The Commonwealth Fund, 1946

SCOTT KOHLER

Background. By 1942, after seventeen years of involvement in rural hospital-
building, officers of the Commonwealth Fund had come to appreciate the

vast gap in quality between urban and rural medical care. The rise of special-ization in the practice of medicine had, by the early 1940s, yielded tremen-dous advances in medical technology. But the cost of treatment had also increased considerably. The escalating cost of medical care meant decreased access to it for much of the rural United States, where average incomes were significantly lower than in cities. In rural areas, access to medical care of high quality was such that "few communities [could] be self-sufficient and still maintain the average standard of living characteristic of industrial societies."[312]

Henry Southmayd, director of the Commonwealth Fund's Rural Hospi-tals Program, discovered that rural hospitals linked to personnel at larger, more advanced urban hospitals tended to offer far better care than did stand-alone rural hospitals. The Fund, inspired by its experience in rural hospital-building, was, at the time, searching for a model by which access to hospitals could be expanded nationwide. The organization of hospital systems along regional lines had been tried before: in Great Britain in 1920 and in Maine in 1931. And, in other places around the country, limited attempts to create bonds among hospitals were already underway. All of this convinced the Commonwealth Fund to support a demonstration project to investigate the efficacy of a regional hospital network. It was hoped that a successful demon-stration would show rural hospitals that regionalization could enhance their access to expert consultation services, clinical specialists, and other resources. In 1945, Rochester, NY, was chosen from among several options because it already had in place an active municipal hospital network (the Rochester Hospital Council, founded in 1939), an excellent school of medicine, and a "generally favorable level of economic and social development."[313]

Strategy. Representatives from the Commonwealth Fund held a series of conferences with health professionals in the region, and on February 18, 1946, the Regional Council of Rochester Hospitals was incorporated with a five-year grant from the Fund. Under the terms of that grant, $75,000 per year was allocated to education and administrative support. $200,000 per year was given for facility construction, and $25,000 was budgeted for spe-cial projects. In 1951, the Fund approved three years of supplemental grants, diminishing annually. All told, the Commonwealth Fund invested $1.51 million in the Rochester plan between 1946 and 1954.[314]

Each hospital in the seven-county Rochester region was given an equal seat on the Council, which was empowered to coordinate the joint plan-ning of new hospital construction and expansion, and the joint manage-ment of "certain institutional services."[315] By "pooling clinical, administrative, and technical" capabilities, the Council's members hoped to realize efficiency gains and, thereby, to expand access to high-quality hospital care. In addition, the Council (which, in 1951, combined with the Rochester Hospital Council to create the Rochester Regional Hospital Council) offered additional support to its members, such as consultation to help them pass inspections by the Joint Commission on Accreditation of Hospitals.

Outcomes. According to Dr. McGehee Harvey and Susan Abrams, of Johns Hopkins Medical School, "the region offered a kind of meeting ground for the medical school, the hospital planning group, and public health and medical care agencies."[316] As hoped, the smaller, rural hospitals in the region benefited the most from the new network. Services like X-ray consultation and specialist care became available to a clientele that would not otherwise have had access to them, and, as early bureaucratic obstacles were overcome by increased personal interaction, the average quality of medical care available throughout the region improved rapidly.[317]

The experiment in regionalization attracted the attention and support of the Rochester-based Eastman-Kodak company. In particular, an Eastman-Kodak executive named Marion Folsom emerged as a driving force behind the Council. Folsom initiated in Rochester the practice of issuing "certificates of need" to facilitate hospital improvements and then lobbied to get that process instituted statewide by the New York Legislature. This Rochester innovation became the model for the federal Planning Act of 1966,[318] and is now standard practice in most of the states.

Near the end of Commonwealth's initial five-year grant, the Council began supporting itself by assessing a per-bed fee from each of its member hospitals. As foundation support wound down, this fee increased steadily, reflecting the willingness of the hospitals to pay out of their own pockets to support the regional network, which by then had already become integral to the provision of care across the region.

Impact. In the creation of the Rochester Regional Hospital Council, the Commonwealth Fund stepped into a supporting role that other actors could not fill. As Harvey and Abrams noted, "[t]he Commonwealth Fund's important contribution was its initiative in supporting the early phases of the Rochester Regional Health Plan, a function that government agencies and even other private foundations would have found difficult."[319] Because the Fund took this initiative, this carefully developed and meticulously documented demonstration project laid the groundwork for what is now the norm in regional linkages connecting medical care providers by region.

Case 22

INSTITUTION BUILDING FOR EVIDENCE-BASED PUBLIC POLICY

Ford Foundation, 1948

SCOTT KOHLER

Background. When, in 1950, the Ford Foundation became the world's largest private philanthropy, it did not immediately begin to throw money into hands-on programming. Rather, the Foundation, quite often over the next three decades, preferred to fund studies and analysis, believing that thorough research could unlock the solution to many of society's most pressing concerns. Nowhere has this approach yielded higher returns, nor left such lasting monuments, than in the field of public policy research. Between 1950 and 1981, the Ford Foundation was the catalyst for building and strengthening a host of research institutions, operating in several different fields, to inject statistical and economic analysis into the policy-making process. In addition, the Foundation provided significant support for several existing policy research organizations, helping to build them into eminent centers of social science research and application.

Strategy. In *Think Tanks, Public Policy, and the Politics of Expertise*, Andrew Rich explains that the Ford Foundation "actively pursued a program supporting 'knowledge-creating' institutions . . . [and was] a principal source of support for many think tanks."[320] These institutions created or supported by the Foundation have many similarities, but each operates within its own niche of the policy-making process. Among the most significant[321] are the following:

- The RAND Corporation (which takes its name from a contraction of the term "research and development") began as a government sponsored program run by the Douglas Aircraft Company. Begun in 1945, the RAND Project grew out of an understanding, according to the Commanding General of the Army Air Force, that:

    During [WWII] the Army, Army Air Forces, and the Navy have made unprecedented use of scientific and industrial resources. . . . [But] we have not yet established the balance necessary to insure [sic] the continuance of teamwork among the military, other government agencies, industry, and the universities. Scientific planning must be years in advance of the actual research and development work.[322]

In order to conduct this planning, the RAND Project employed mathematicians, engineers, physicists, economist, psychologists, and a range of other professionals. By 1948, the Chief of Staff of the newly formed U.S. Air Force decided that RAND could better function as an independent nonprofit agency. The Ford Foundation at that point approved an interest-free loan of $1 million to fund the new RAND Corporation's early operations. In addition, Ford guaranteed RAND's credit, enabling it to qualify for private bank loans. According to the Corporation's website, "[t]his marked the beginning of the diversification of RAND's agenda [to non-military as well as military research] and was the first of many grants to RAND by the Ford Foundation to support important new research initiatives."[323]

- Resources for the Future was created in response to the release, in the early 1950s, of the final report of the President's Materials Policy Commission. The report pointed out that very little was known about the United States' reserves of such natural resources as oil, water, energy, and minerals. It went on to recommend the creation of a new organization to study the natural environment and make policy recommendations on the basis of its findings. The Eisenhower administration opposed the Commission's proposal, so the young Ford Foundation took it up. In 1952, the Foundation set up Resources for the Future (RFF) to "formulate a framework for analyzing resource conditions, show how to collect and use the relevant data, and develop the professional expertise that could do the job in the years to come."[324] Intended to collect data and analyze them in a way comprehensible to policymakers, RFF was staffed with economists and statisticians, rather than scientists and engineers.[325]

- The Urban Institute was created in 1968 on the initiative of President Lyndon Johnson. The President had handpicked a blue ribbon commission of leaders from government and the not-for-profit sector to study America's cities, and this group had included Robert S. McNamara, a Ford Foundation trustee. The Urban Institute (UI) was envisioned as a military-style think tank (similar to the RAND Corporation), except that it was not to be affiliated exclusively with any single government agency (as RAND had originally been with the Air Force). Instead, the Institute would conduct contract research for several government funders, as well as with the support of private foundations. Funded initially by grants from the Department of Housing and Urban Development (HUD), the Department of Transportation, and the Ford Foundation, the Urban Institute soon grew beyond its focus on urban centers into a policy research center focused on a number of issues, including housing, health, and income maintenance programs. In its first ten years, the Institute received $10.3 million from the Ford Foundation. This money was used to augment government project funds, and to enable UI to pursue research interests for which federal funds were not forthcoming. In this way, the Ford Foundation not only helped the Institute pursue its government contract research, but it also helped it survive financially by mitigating UI's exposure to the shifting political winds.

- The Center on Budget and Policy Priorities was founded in 1981 by economist Robert Greenstein to study budget and tax policies, especially their effects on low-income Americans. The Center's original start-up grant came from the Field Foundation, and Ford quickly joined in as the Center's largest underwriter. The Center analyzes proposed policy changes, disseminates broadly the results of its analyses, and makes policy proposals of its own. Founded in part "to [provide] an independent and critical analysis of the implications of the Reagan budget cuts for low-income people," the Center in the early 1990s expanded its work to the state level. Formed "in response to the devolution of responsibility over many areas of low-income policy to the state level," the Center's State Fiscal Project—funded primarily by the Ford, Casey, and Mott Foundations—now makes up almost half of its research and advocacy operation.

- The Brookings Institution began in 1916 as the Institute for Government Research, "the first private organization dedicated to analyzing public policy issues at the national level."[326] Robert Somers Brookings, a major benefactor of IGR, created in the early 1920s two supporting institutions, a graduate school and an economic research institute. In 1927, the three organizations merged to form the Brookings Institution. Throughout its long history, Brookings has conducted influential studies of various issues of political economy, and served as a prominent critic and evaluator of government policies. According to its current president, Strobe Talbott:

> Brookings has dedicated itself to improving the equity of the American democratic process, the performance of the economy, the health of society, the effectiveness of diplomacy and defense, the quality of

public discourse, and the workings of institutions—public and private, domestic and international.[327]

The Institution uses the tools of social science research and analysis, and an interdisciplinary approach, to respond to policy proposals and make suggestions of its own. In 1953, the Ford Foundation began to give Brookings programmatic and unrestricted financial support. Over the next fifteen years, Ford gave to Brookings seventy-three project grants for specific research and education initiatives. And in 1966, the Foundation made a grant of $14 million to provide Brookings with $10 million of endowment support, and $4 million in unrestricted funds. Thanks to the rising value of Ford stock (the form in which the gift had been made), this grant wound up yielding fully one quarter of all the Institution's unrestricted funding over the next thirteen years. In addition to Ford, the Rockefeller Foundation gave Brookings significant support. Together, the two foundations "put the Institution on a strong financial basis" at a time when Brookings was emerging as a center of academic study and practical expertise for influential policymakers.[328]

Outcomes. Each of these five policy research organizations has been enormously successful. Along with the conservative Heritage Foundation and American Enterprise Institute, the Brookings Institution and the Urban Institute constitute the so-called "big-four" think tanks.[329] The Urban Institute has done groundbreaking work in a number of fields, including by pioneering evaluation techniques and new statistical methodologies like the TRIM microsimulation model, which was adopted in the 1960s by the Congressional Budget Office and the Departments of Agriculture, Labor, and Treasury to analyze welfare and other income transfer proposals.[330] And Brookings, the oldest and largest of the four, remains at the cutting edge of policy analysis. A 1997 survey found Brookings to be considered—across all respondent groups, including both Republican and Democratic congressional staffers, journalists, and others—the most credible source of information among all think tanks.[331] Its many notable past successes include: "helping develop such ideas as unified budgeting for the federal government, the establishment of the Congressional Budget Office, and revenue sharing. . . ."[332]

The RAND Corporation has conducted path-breaking research and analysis, and its "early defense-related agenda [has] evolved—in concert with the nation's attention—to encompass such diverse subject areas as space; economic, social, and political affairs overseas; and the direct role of government

in social and economic problem-solving at home." RAND played a significant role in the initiation of America's space program, developed early com-
puters and computing networks, and has researched applications for game
theory, mathematical modeling and simulation, and systems analysis, which
"served as the methodological basis for social policy planning and analysis
across such disparate areas as urban decay, poverty, health care, education,
and the efficient operation of municipal services such as police protection
and fire fighting."[333] In the 1997 survey of think tanks' credibility noted
above, the RAND Corporation scored second, behind only Brookings.

The other two are no less impressive. A Ford Foundation review in 1996
concluded that "[a]fter twenty years of research and training RFF had filled
in many of the most glaring gaps in our knowledge about resource conditions in the United States and had developed a new generation of professionals to keep us up to date."[334] Jonathan Rauch, a *National Journal* columnist,
in 2002 praised Resources for the Future as "the most important think tank
you've never heard of."[335] RFF was among the first voices in the nascent environmental movement to advocate market-based solutions to problems like
pollution and global warming, and, according to Ford's 1976 review, "resource economics, urban economics, and environmental economics were
largely invented at RFF and were built into intellectually respectable disciplines by the efforts of a group of scholars centered around RFF."[336]

The Center on Budget and Policy Priorities has played a significant role in
major budget and economic policy debates at the state and federal levels. According to Michael Weinstein, an editorial writer for the *New York Times*,
"What makes [the Center] unique is the consistently high quality of [its] research and analysis."[337] This quality has been recognized by policymakers
from both political parties. A 1998 survey of members of Congress and
White House officials found that the Center on Budget and Policy Priorities
"was identified as the single most influential non-profit organization in
Washington on federal budget policy."[338] It took a lead role in the expansion
of Earned Income Tax Credit,[339] and now conducts major outreach programs
directed at the states to ensure that low-income families take advantage of
this and other government benefits for which they are eligible (such as the
Child Tax Credit and Medicaid-guaranteed children's health insurance).[340]
Over 6,000 not-for-profit organizations and government agencies currently
participate in these campaigns.[341]

Impact. Ford has played a different role in the creation and support of
each of these five institutions. Resources for the Future, for example, was
proposed by an outside agency but designed and funded by the Foundation.
Brookings, on the other hand, had been in existence for decades before the

Ford Foundation became a major philanthropy. But the Foundation has supported a host of Brookings projects, and by providing general operating support and major endowment funds, it helped the Institution become financially secure at a critical period in its development. In the case of the Urban Institute, the Foundation's support was dwarfed by the backing of the federal government. But even there, Ford provided crucial unrestricted support in the '60s and '70s, and gave the Institute $10 million to start its endowment in 1966. When federal funds dried up in the 1980s, Ford and other foundations helped the Institute survive.[342]

Ford's deliberate strategy of promoting social science research has enriched the policy-making process for decades. It has enabled these and other institutions to subject politicians' claims to rigorous fact-checking, and has helped point the way toward more promising solutions to problems of the environment, the economy, foreign relations, urban development, and more. One need not give foundations all the credit for the rise of evidence-based public policy, nor agree with the political inclinations of any particular think tank, to conclude that public policy studies, and public policy-making, would both be significantly worse off but for the work of these institutions, and the sustained involvement of the Ford Foundation.

Case 23

PREVENTING CRASHES ON AMERICA'S HIGHWAYS

Dorr Foundation, 1952

STEVEN SCHINDLER

Background. Dr. John V. N. Dorr was internationally known for his inventions and innovations in the field of metallurgical engineering. While still a teen, Dorr worked for Thomas Edison in his laboratory.[343] He later began an engineering firm that gradually brought him the wealth with which to establish a foundation in his name in 1940.[344] The indenture for the foundation specified scientific research, after-retirement utilization of the skills of professionals, special educational projects for youth, and support of charitable work of other organizations as focus areas for the foundation. Early grants from the foundation largely supported scholarships, research, and aid to service organizations. [345]

The Dorr Foundation was established with the initial purpose of supporting the fields of chemistry and metallurgy exclusively. Inspired by the complaints of his wife, however, Dr. Dorr steered the foundation's resources and his own efforts toward the traffic hazards of night-time and bad-weather driving. Mrs. Dorr complained that, in poor driving conditions, headlight glare from oncoming traffic led drivers to hug the center line or to swerve away from the center line and into the soft shoulder of the highway, resulting in a high frequency of accidents in both cases. [346] Dorr became convinced that a shoulder line marking the division between the road lane and the shoulder would significantly reduce such hazards. Such a line, he thought, could also increase the safety of pedestrians walking along the shoulders of roads by providing a clear demarcation. [347]

Strategy. Dorr's first response was to mail a letter to the Connecticut State Highway Commissioner suggesting his idea of a shoulder line in 1952, but the state took no action in response to his suggestion. [348] The next year, Dorr wrote a letter to his local newspaper, the *Westport Town Crier*, with an outline of his suggestion, a plan for a test site, and an offer to fund the test. [349] "If the white line were painted on the outer or right-hand side," Dorr wrote, "the driver's eyes would avoid meeting the headlight's glare." [350]

Dorr's advocacy this time led the Connecticut highway officials to conduct a field test on a portion of the Merritt Parkway. The position and driving behavior of 11,289 vehicles along this test strip demonstrated that the shoulder lines improved automobile position in the center of the lane, corrected speed differentials resulting from adverse driving conditions, and nullified the effects of distracting roadside features, particularly during the dawn and dusk hours. [351] These results supported the conclusions that shoulder striping would reduce same direction sideswipe accidents, would prevent the early destruction of paved shoulders, and would prevent accidents resulting from automobiles losing traction upon drifting onto the soft shoulders. [352] The results of this test prompted the state to stripe the entire length of the Parkway. [353] New York followed suit with a test of its own on the Hutchinson River Parkway, which is the continuation of the Merritt Parkway into New York State. In seven months prior to the application of white stripes along the parkway shoulders, 102 accidents resulting in forty-nine injuries occurred. In the seven months after the application of the white stripes in 1954, only forty-six accidents occurred with twenty-seven injuries, a 55 percent reduction from the pre-stripe period. [354] Credit for the reduction in accidents was blurred, however, because two additional motor-cycle police began to patrol the test strip after the application of the white stripes. This gave critics of the stripes an opportunity to challenge the validity attributed to the benefits of the shoulder stripes.[355]

Highway officials were reluctant to pursue Dorr's suggested course of action. The cost of shoulder striping, estimated as high as $150 per mile, as well as some skepticism both regarding the effectiveness of the stripes in decreasing accidents and arising from potential harmful effects of the stripes, were all obstacles to Dorr's campaign.[356] California officials even charged that motorists would mistake the right shoulder line for the center line and would drive to the right of the line, placing the driver and passengers at grave risk.[357]

In 1957, the shoulder line was still considered to be "highly controversial," but the controversy stemmed from ignorance of its effects rather than reasoned judgment and weighing of factors.[358] In New York, the State Traffic Commission deemed the shoulder lines unnecessary, speculating that the lines were effective only on roads with paved shoulders. Other states, particularly in the West, felt that lines were appropriate only on roads without paved shoulders. These conclusions justified not striping, as few New York roads had shoulders, and many roads in the Western states did.[359]

After the tests along the Hutchinson River Parkway, the Dorr Foundation encouraged further safety testing.[360] In response to the reservations among highway department officials about potential harmful consequences of the shoulder lines, the Dorr Foundation organized extensive studies in Rhode Island, New Jersey, Ohio, and Connecticut, overseen by the Highway Research Board of the National Academy of Sciences.[361]

In addition, public sentiment in Dorr's favor began to mount. Numerous newspaper editorials and letters to the editor, many citing Dorr's pioneering efforts, called for shoulder lines on highways for increased safety.[362] In a report to the Highway Research Board in 1958, the chief of research of the Bureau of Public Roads strongly urged the Board promptly to begin the testing urged by Dorr. "The Public is demanding it," the Chief of Research wrote, "and is now leading us in the matter of road-shoulder edge-lining of highways. . . . As highway engineers we've got to stop dragging our feet."[363]

The Ohio study was documented in 1960 in a research bulletin issued by the Highway Research Board.[364] In Ohio, researchers selected twelve lengths of two-lane state highways spread throughout the state to test the effects of the white shoulder lines (three of the sections turned out to be unusable for the study). Each strip was divided into two sections—a control section and a test section—and the researchers literally flipped coins to determine which section in each of the nine study-strips would be the test section along which shoulder lines would be drawn. All accidents in each section of highway were recorded during the year 1956 and again during the first full year after the application of the white lines in the test sections. A total of 132 accidents occurred in all of the control sections during the first period and 167 accidents occurred after shoulder lines were applied on the test sections (indicating an overall increase in all accidents, possibly resulting from increased traffic). In the test sections, 123 accidents occurred prior to the shoulder line application and 126 accidents occurred after the application. Using the control section to provide a forecast multiplier, the test sections could have expected 156 accidents. In other words, the number of accidents in the test sections would likely have been much higher without the white shoulder lines, and the slower growth of accidents in the test sections is attributable to the white shoulder lines.[365] There was an even more significant difference in the number of fatalities and injuries resulting from accidents between the test sections and the control sections. Generally, the study showed that a 19 percent decrease in accidents, a 35 percent decrease in night accidents, and a 37 percent decrease in fatalities and injuries were attributable to the white shoulder lines.[366]

Impact. The Dorr Foundation served as a clearing house for information on the white shoulder line. It issued bulletins in which it reported new tests, as well as new states and regions applying the white lines to road shoulders. The Foundation also reprinted and distributed copies of the early studies in Connecticut.[367] The Foundation, primarily through Dr. Dorr, also worked with a number of safety groups and state highway departments, including the President's Action Committee for Traffic Safety, the Highway Research Board of the National Academy of Sciences, and the Federal Bureau of Public Roads, to promote white shoulder lines.[368] A few years after Dorr began supporting his idea with his foundation's resources, the highway shoulder line, proven to be effective at reducing traffic accidents and fatalities, would gain universal acceptance and application.

Case 24

CURBING GLOBAL POPULATION GROWTH: ROCKEFELLER'S POPULATION COUNCIL

Rockefeller Foundation, 1952

STEVEN SCHINDLER

Background. Throughout the first half of the twentieth century, the Rockefeller Foundation had been a significant contributor to broad advances in medical research and efforts in worldwide disease eradication. In contemplating the work of the foundation his grandfather created, John D. Rockefeller III began to believe that a reduction in mortality resulting from his family's foundation efforts in medicine, without a corresponding decline in fertility rates, could contribute to unsustainable population growth, particularly in developing countries. In the late 1940s, a Rockefeller Foundation-sponsored team returning from Asia noted that an imminent worldwide surge in population growth demanded immediate action.[369] Rapid worldwide population growth was known to be taking place, but scholarship on population and demography lacked organization and coherence in part because of the complexity of the problem of population growth and because of the cultural and religious sensitivities implicated in fertility issues. Rockefeller, however, felt that the complexities of rising population growth and the sensitivities of birth control should not inhibit the needed focus of science and public policy.[370]

Strategy. In the early 1950s, Rockefeller's interest in the problems related to population growth led him to provide the financial support for a two-day conference, held under the auspices of the National Academy of Sciences, the president of which was also the president of the Rockefeller Institute for Medical Research.[371] When the Rockefeller Foundation declined to take up population growth as an issue of concern, Rockefeller formed the Population Council as an independent entity.[372] He provided an initial gift of $100,000 to enable the Council to begin its work.

The Council's charter members were Frank Notestein, demographer at Princeton University who urged attention be given to high fertility rates; Frederick Osborn, influential proponent of population research; Thomas Parran, dean of the Graduate School of Public Health at the University of Pittsburgh; and John D. Rockefeller, III.[373] Shortly after its formation, Rockefeller provided an additional grant of $1.25 million to the Council over five years. The Ford Foundation also made an early contribution to the Council, a grant of $600,000.[374] Later financial backers included the Rockefeller, Mellon, Hewlett, and Packard Foundations.[375]

Rather than develop and advocate public policy positions, the Council made grants to individuals and research institutes in various countries and regions to improve research on population growth that promoted a wider understanding of population issues worldwide.[376] Also, understanding the sensitivities across cultures regarding population control, particularly birth control, the Council sought to strengthen the indigenous capacity of researchers and governments in various countries throughout the world to address population issues in ways consistent with local cultural norms. One of the Council's earliest programs was the distribution of fellowship grants to students of population and demography.[377] In light of the dearth of scholarship in these fields, these fellows became the drivers of population control policies and demographic scholarship throughout the world over the next few decades. When public attention began to focus on population issues in the 1960s and 1970s, alumni of the Council's fellowship program were already placed and prepared to steer policy.[378] The United States, under the Kennedy administration, began to adopt foreign policy positions on global population reflecting Rockefeller's concerns articulated a decade earlier.[379]

At the same time, the Council strengthened its own in-house expertise in population-related science and policy issues. Because of the Council's early leadership on population issues, it became a source of crucial guidance to the United Nations as it began to take on responsibility for such issues around the world. After helping to fund the UN's first World Population Conference in 1954, the Council assisted the UN in establishing the first regional centers for demographic training and research in India, Chile, and Egypt.[380]

Impact. In the culturally sensitive field of birth control development and research, the Council played a significant role in the development, testing, establishment of local development, and distribution of the intrauterine device (IUD). Physicians had already begun developing IUDs thirty years before the Population Council became involved, but the Council helped to coordinate international efforts to develop a safe and effective IUD.[381] In 1962, the Council organized an international conference in New York for scientists to report on their usage of various forms of IUDs. Over the next two years, the Council made research grants in excess of $2 million to support IUD development. An innovation in the Council's approach to IUD development was the large-scale statistical monitoring and analysis of data regarding the IUD's safety and effectiveness from different physicians using the IUD with Council grants.[382]

In 1969, the U.S. Office of Economic Opportunity granted the Council

$2 million to support family planning for poor women in the United States.[383] The following year, responding to a report issued by a panel chaired by John D. Rockefeller III, the United Nations transformed its capacity to respond to countries requesting assistance in reducing rapid population growth.[384]

Since its founding, the Council has pioneered research and enhanced understanding in numerous arenas of population growth, including demographic research and tracking, contraception use, family planning service delivery, and AIDS tracking and prevention.[385] During the time of the Population Council's operation, rates of population growth have begun to slow, and fertility rates are falling, particularly in the developing world. Total fertility rates in developing countries have declined from 6.0 per woman in 1965 to 3.2 in 2000.[386]

Case 25

FACILITATING GLOBAL KNOWLEDGE CREATION: UNIVERSITY AREA STUDIES PROGRAMS

Ford Foundation, 1952

STEVEN SCHINDLER

Background. America's diplomatic experiences in World War II demonstrated significant gaps in its own policymakers' knowledge and understanding of international regions and cultures. While such gaps may have been inconsequential in a pre-World War II world, the nation's assumption of superpower status and international leadership in the aftermath of the war made filling these gaps imperative.[387] University international studies programs eventually would play a central role in foreign policy development in the 1960s, but they were anomalies in higher education immediately after the war, only twenty years earlier.[388] Large foundations, particularly Rockefeller, Carnegie, and Ford, recognized the discrepancy between American power in international affairs and American understanding of regions over which it exerted great influence. A Ford Foundation officer noted that "the abysmal lack of knowledge" in areas that would take on great diplomatic importance in the Cold War needed to be addressed by the Foundation.[389]

Strategy. In the years immediately following World War II, the Rockefeller Foundation and the Carnegie Corporation were the first to fund programs in area studies. Both funded the creation of large scale Russian centers; Columbia's center was funded by the Rockefeller Foundation and Harvard's by the Carnegie Corporation.[390]

Later, the Ford Foundation entered the arena. Its initial strategy was to create experts and knowledge through direct grants and fellowships to individual scholars and students. This strategy was an essential first step in building world-class centers of area studies—more widespread foreign area studies programs would need some basic knowledge from which to start and trained scholars to run them. Ford's fellowship program began in 1952 and continued after the conclusion of the area studies building programs.[391] From its beginning until 1977, the Foreign Area Fellowship program was responsible for $35.1 million of Ford disbursements.[392]

In 1960, Ford began the institution-building phase of its foreign area studies strategy with $15.1 million in long-term grants. Columbia received $5.5 million for expanded programs on the Soviet Union, East Europe, East Asia, and the Near and Middle East. Harvard received $5.6 million for building its programs on the Soviet Union, Middle East, and East Asia. Berkeley and UCLA together received $4 million. Smaller grants for experimental and specific research purposes went to Johns Hopkins, Michigan State, Syracuse, Texas A&M, Oregon, and Pittsburgh.[393] The next year, Ford disbursed $20.77 million for long-term institution building to Indiana, Northwestern, Princeton, Yale Universities, and the Universities of Chicago, Michigan, Notre Dame, Pennsylvania, and Washington.[394] The 1961 Annual Report of the Ford Foundation describes the objectives for these long-term grants: "The grants are designed to put studies dealing with Asia, Africa, the Near East, the Soviet Union, and East Europe on a competitive footing with other subject-matter fields. . . . The long-term grants, in contrast [to smaller Foundation grants intended for specific experimental or developmental purposes], provide support for up to ten years and may be used at the universities' own discretion for comprehensive development of their international interests."[395]

A Ford Foundation officer, in describing the Foundation's understanding of its purpose in the international studies field, indicated that the Foundation had recognized "the need to improve the capabilities of the United States in meeting its responsibilities in world affairs—more especially for maintaining the strength of the non-Communist nations and for assisting the social and economic development of the new emerging nations."[396]

Impact. In assessing the broader role that foundations played in the development of foreign policy, Edward Berman, in *Ideology of Philanthropy,* assesses the importance of the foreign area studies building efforts of Ford, and to a lesser extent, Carnegie and Rockefeller, essentially indicating that Ford achieved its articulated objectives: "These programs facilitated the scholarship that would shape American foreign policy."[397] As for the Ford Foundation in particular, he notes: "The Ford Foundation almost single-handedly established the major areas-studies programs in American universities."[398] The university recipients of Ford's long-term grants are, Berman indicates, the leading producers of scholars and the primary training facilities for corporate, political, and academic leaders in international arenas.[399] Early high profile individuals linked closely with foreign area studies programs such as W.W. Rostow, foreign policy advisor to Kennedy and Johnson, Secretary of State Henry Kissenger, and countless foreign policy diplomats and leaders since, demonstrate that these grants have had a direct impact on American foreign policy.[400]

Case 26

Howard Hughes Medical Institute

1953

Scott Kohler

Background. In 1925, the young Howard Hughes stipulated—in his newly written will—that his burgeoning fortune be used, upon the event of his death, to create an institution of medical research. A man of bold vision, Hughes demanded that this new institution would explore "the genesis of life itself."[401] In fact, the Howard Hughes Medical Institute (HHMI) was chartered in December 1953, some twenty-three years before Mr. Hughes' death.

But it was not until 1984 that the Institute began to realize its full potential. In that year, the Delaware Court of Chancery appointed to its Board eight "prominent citizens"[402] who soon began to guide the Institute through a period of tremendous expansion. In 1985, the trustees sold off the Hughes Aircraft Company, which had been owned entirely by the Institute. This sale provided HHMI with its sizeable present endowment. Along the way, the trustees reaffirmed the Institute's status as a medical research organization (MRO) under § 170(b) of the Internal Revenue Code.[403] So technically, the Howard Hughes Medical Institute is *not* a private foundation. In practice, however, it functions effectively as both an operating foundation and a private foundation, making grants and running programs of its own design. It is, therefore, an instructive case of scientific philanthropy on a massive scale. Like a foundation, the Howard Hughes Medical Institute is a stronghold of

American polyarchy, striving, in accordance with its donor's provisions and the best judgment of its trustees, to advance human understanding and redefine the boundaries of human possibility.

Strategy. The Howard Hughes Medical Institute has today an endowment of over $12.8 billion, making it one of the largest pools of philanthropic capital in the world. It supports an enormous range of activities, primarily in the fields of genetics, immunology, cell biology, and neurobiology, but also in the sciences more broadly. These activities can be divided into three programs.

- HHMI Investigators: The Institute has on its payroll over 300 HHMI investigators. These are scientists on the Institute's payroll, working at HHMI laboratories around the country while also serving as faculty members at 64 different universities and other research institutions. Each investigator is supported by a team of roughly 10–25 students, postdoctoral associates, and technicians. Investigators are given, by the Institute, the freedom to explore problems thoroughly, see projects through without the need to keep re-applying for grant support, and, when necessary, change directions and try something new. HHMI investigators are nominated by their home institutions and then selected in a nationwide competition for their "potential to make significant contributions to science."

- Grants Program: The Institute's Grants Program seeks to "[strengthen] science education and training, from elementary school through graduate and medical school."[404] To that end, HHMI makes research grants to individual scientists and science education grants to academic institutions at all levels.

- Janelia Farm Research Campus: HHMI is in the midst of spending a projected $500 million to build and outfit a new research facility where top scientists in a variety of fields will come together, for periods ranging from a few weeks to several years, to tackle a range of scientific questions. The institute plans to focus research at the 281-acre, state-of-the-art facility on the Potomac River near Leesburg, Virginia, on two primary areas: the "identification of general principles that govern how information is processed by neuronal circuits," and the "development of imaging technologies and computational methods for image analysis."[405] twenty to thirty such small teams will work in a "highly collaborative, interdisciplinary culture" at the Janelia Farm campus. Each will be led by a distinguished group leader, and both leaders and group members will be chosen from the fields of biology, chemistry, engineering, mathematics, physics, and computer science. In planning the Janelia Farm Research Campus, HHMI planners studied other for-profit and academic labs around the world that have been especially successful, such as AT&T's Bell Laboratories. One goal of Janelia is for the scientists who study there to go out, after their time at the campus, and serve as ambassadors, disseminating its cutting edge innovations among the wider research communities of their respective fields.

Outcomes. With an operating budget projected in 2005 to be $564 million,[406] the Howard Hughes Medical Institute is an enormous presence in the fields of biomedical research and science education. Among its investigators—past and present—are thirteen Nobel Prize winners, including Thomas R. Cech, a 1989 laureate in Chemistry, who now serves as the Institute's president. These investigators are at the top of their fields, and their relationships with HHMI not only provide them with the resources to do groundbreaking research, but also free their respective universities from the need to pay them while they are HHMI Investigators. The Institute's Grants Program has, since 1988, given out over $1.5 billion for research and education.[407] Among its many interesting activities has been a project identifying excellent teachers and paying them to teach other professors to be better educators.

Impact. HHMI Investigators and grantees have achieved many important breakthroughs. These include such discoveries as the genes responsible for cystic fibrosis and muscular dystrophy, a non-invasive test for colon cancer, a new drug to fight leukemia, and many others.[408] And the Janelia Farm Research Campus promises to house and foster some of the most exciting research of the coming years. As one of the world's largest philanthropies, the Howard Hughes Medical Institute is breaking new ground, literally and figuratively, in its quest to "probe the genesis of life itself."

Case 27

PROGRAM TO STRENGTHEN BUSINESS EDUCATION

Ford Foundation, 1954

SCOTT KOHLER

Background. In 1954, working through its Program in Economic Development and Administration, the Ford Foundation set out to reform business education in the United States. It was an ambitious goal, especially because undergraduate business departments and graduate schools of business were then enrolling one out of every seven students in all of higher education.

The Foundation undertook this initiative for several reasons. First among these was, according to a 1966 review by Ford consultant James E. Howell, "the urgency and magnitude of the problem."[409] Business programs enrolled too many under-qualified students, and their faculties were dominated by men of the old guard, who resisted the encroachment of economic analysis and the methodological advances that had proved so fruitful in the social sciences. Furthermore, neither the government, nor other foundations, nor "even universities themselves," were yet confronting the weaknesses of American business education. The project was consonant with Ford's statement of purpose for the EDA Program, and had the particular interest of several influential Ford officials.[410] It was also politically uncontroversial, which made it attractive to the Foundation, which had just endured a spate of attacks from members of Congress and the conservative press.[411]

Strategy. The program had three main goals: to make business education more academically sound, to orient business training more around "the needs of American management," and to increase the efficiency of business schools nationwide. The Foundation decided early on to focus, not on undergraduate business departments, but rather on full-blown schools, combining undergraduate and graduate studies, exclusively. According to Howell, "[t]he strategy . . . was simple: pour large sums of money into a few reasonably good or promising schools of business which would then be the instruments of change for the rest of the field." Seeking to create "centers of excellence," the Foundation was pursuing a tried-and-true philanthropic strategy.

More specifically, Ford provided $35 million over the next twelve years for institutional and research support, graduate fellowships, workshops, seminars, conferences, and new teaching materials. This was, in fact, a fairly modest expenditure for a Ford program carried out over so many years. Chief among the grant-receiving schools were Harvard, the Carnegie Institute of Technology,[412] Columbia, and the University of Chicago. At these four schools, and a handful of second-tier "centers," the Ford Foundation helped the recipient universities to train and hire new faculty, disseminate advocacy publications intended to promote a "New Look" in business education, and support reform movements within faculties. Beginning in 1956, the Foundation made "trickle-down" grants, to promote the spread of new advances from its centers of excellence to the rest of the nation's 200 business schools and 400 undergraduate departments of business.

Outcomes. Not all the initiatives Ford pursued were successful. It failed, for instance, to make the behavioral sciences take root in business education, and discovered that "[s]ignificant educational reform requires more pressure than is exerted by a foundation curriculum grant."[413] On the whole, however, the Foundation's efforts to strengthen business education achieved tremendous results. The $800,000 spent, for example, to promote the case study method, helped it to gain acceptance at the Harvard Business School, from whence it has spread around the country. The seminars, workshops, and conferences held as part of the "trickle-down" plan were highly successful; nearly a quarter of all business faculty members in the nation took part in one or more of them.[414]

Ford's greatest success flowed from commissioning the enormously influential Gordon-Howell report, which changed the face of business education not only at the centers, but nationwide. The report found:

> . . . That the business schools (and departments of business) need to move in the direction of a broader and more rigorous educational program, with higher standards of admission and student performance, with better informed and more scholarly faculties that are capable of carrying on more significant research, and with a greater appreciation of the contributions to be made to the development of business competence by both the underlying non-business disciplines and the judicious use of clinical materials and methods.[415]

According to Professor John Wheeler, the Gordon-Howell Report was "the single most important factor in determining the nature of curricula in schools of business administration in the United States today."[416] In a survey conducted in the mid-1960s by Professor Wheeler, the Report[417] was found to have been discussed in every curriculum review conducted after its release, and to have been mentioned by every single respondent as a critical jolt to the business education community.[418] In addition to funding the report, Ford had sent a copy of it to every business school faculty member or administrator in the county, as well as journalists, business leaders, and other interested parties.

Impact. Business education since the Ford Foundation launched its reform program has changed dramatically for the better. It has incorporated virtually all of Ford's recommendations, and its changes in the 1960s even "trickled out" to Europe, Latin America, and Asia. This was a development that the Foundation had not expected, and only serves to reinforce James Howell's contention that Ford's efforts to reform business education constituted its most successful project to date. According to Howell, "[m]easured against its own objectives, the Foundation effort was successful. It was the strategic force behind the reorientation of one of the largest sectors in American higher education; and it was by far the single most powerful force in bringing about that reorientation."[419]

Case 28

FINANCING HIGHER EDUCATION FOR AMERICA'S TALENTED STUDENTS: NATIONAL MERIT SCHOLARSHIP CORPORATION

Ford Foundation and Carnegie Corporation of New York, 1955

STEVEN SCHINDLER

Background. In the years after World War II, the number of students attending colleges and universities rose dramatically, and with that rise came an increase in the cost of higher education. By the mid-1950s, the rising cost of tuition was believed by many to be preventing many gifted students from pursuing a college degree and causing a great waste of the nation's intellectual talent.[420] During that time, a study by Dael Wolfle revealed that 38 percent of students in the top 2 percent of intelligence quotients were not pursuing a college education. In the midst of the Cold War, concerns mounted that the United States was being surpassed by the U.S.S.R. in education efforts, particularly in science and engineering disciplines. In 1955, the Carnegie Corporation funded M.I.T. studies of science and engineering education in the U.S.S.R.[421] Many in America perceived a need to promote college education among the nation's brightest students to match the Cold War adversary.

Strategy. After studying the college admissions and funding environment for more than a year, the Ford Foundation, with the cooperation of the Carnegie Corporation, established the National Merit Scholarship Corporation (NMSC).[422] In 1955, the Ford Foundation gave an initial grant of $20 million to NMSC. Of the $20 million, $8 million was a match to draw business and corporate contributions to a general scholarship fund, $1 million a year for ten years was for scholarship funding, and $2 million supported administrative expenses.[423] The Carnegie Corporation supplemented Ford's gift with a $500,000 grant to fund administrative costs for the first five years of NMSC's operation.[424] To ensure a smooth beginning, the NMSC tapped

John Stalnaker as its founding president. In the late 1940s, Stalnaker had been responsible for establishing and administering the Pepsi-Cola Scholarship Board at Stanford University, and he drew from his experience at Stanford as he coordinated the larger NMSC program.[425]

Since its inception, the objectives of the NMSC have remained the same: identify and honor high school students with great promise for collegiate success, stimulate increased financial support to help fund those students' educations, and provide administrative support to other scholarship organizations.[426]

Impact. The NMSC has enjoyed broad success in achieving its objectives. Its talent search began with a nation-wide scope, involving 25,000 high schools in the first year of the program. Out of the 60,000 students that participated, 525 students were named to the first class of National Merit Scholars and received a scholarship based on demonstrated need. Four years later, 80 percent of the first class of National Merit Scholars had graduated college, and three out of four were pursuing graduate or professional studies in their fifth year.[427] By the tenth year of the program, more than 11,000 scholarships had been awarded.[428] Since 1955, NMSC has provided scholarships to 300,000 students worth over $1.1 billion. Furthermore, the National Merit Scholarship awards have developed a brand for academic excellence widely acknowledged throughout the country's higher education institutions.[429] Many institutions compete for National Merit Scholars and pride themselves on the number of such students they enroll each year.[430]

One of the NMSC's great successes was its ability to attract corporate, institutional, and individual donations and sponsorships of the scholarships it offered. Corporations or other entities interested in offering scholarships but unwilling to conduct and administer a full-scale scholarship search could sponsor NMSC scholarships without the hassle or added cost of marketing a separate scholarship program and judging applications.[431] The Sears-Roebuck Foundation and Time, Inc. both acknowledged the benefits of sponsoring scholarships through NMSC and were charter contributors.[432] In 1957, Standard Oil and I.B.M. joined the NMSC as corporate sponsors.[433] The A.F.L.-C.I.O. sponsored six scholarships in 1959.[434] In 1965, the tenth year of the scholarship program, the NMSC attracted 270 sponsors.[435] By 2004, 273 business organizations sponsored almost 10 percent of the National Merit Scholarships in addition to more than 2,000 targeted scholarships provided through the NMSC to children of donor employees, students in the geographic area of the donor, or students whose particular course of study the donor wished to encourage.[436]

Case 29

VERA INSTITUTE OF JUSTICE: MANHATTAN BAIL PROJECT

Ford Foundation, 1962

SCOTT KOHLER

Background. The Vera Foundation began in late 1960 with a small experiment run by Herbert Sturz, a young journalist, and funded by Louis Schweitzer, a wealthy New York businessman. Introduced by a mutual friend, the "unlikely pair" shared one important belief: that the criminal justice system was not living up to the promise of the U.S. Constitution. A visit to a Manhattan prison had convinced the pair that far too many men and women were being locked up before their trials, simply because they could not afford bail. Pondering a system that claims to presume innocence until guilt is proven, they found this unacceptable.

Soon after their initial conversation, Schweitzer offered Sturz a one year salary to focus full-time on researching this issue and seeking a remedy for it. Sturz agreed, and set out to learn more. Interviews with judges and lawyers led Sturz first to support the idea of a charitable bail fund, and then to a revelation: why not simply release more of these "presumed innocent" defendants without any bail at all?

Strategy. By the summer of 1961, Sturz was ready to suggest a concrete plan of action to Schweitzer, who, in turn, took the idea directly to New York's mayor, Robert Wagner. Mayor Wagner liked the idea and arranged for Sturz to be given an office in the criminal court building. Still funded by Schweitzer, the Vera Foundation had begun its first program: the Manhattan Bail Project. The Project was to run for three years. Schweitzer contributed $95,000 in the first year and $25,000 in each of the subsequent two. In 1962, almost a year into the project, the Ford Foundation awarded Vera $115,000 for the program.

Sturz and his staff employed a simple strategy. They conducted objective inquiries into the backgrounds of thousand of defendants to assess whether the accused could be trusted to return for his or her trial without being required to purchase a bail bond. Factors such as employment history, local family ties, and prior criminal record were considered in determining the flight risk posed by each defendant. Whenever Vera staff determined (based on a points system of risk factors) that a defendant was not likely to skip or flee his or her court date, a recommendation was made to the presiding judge to release that defendant on his own recognizance. Vera staffers also made an effort to follow up on their recommendations, calling defendants to remind them of an impending court date, and, in some cases, even bringing them by taxi to the courthouse.

To measure precisely the program's impact, Vera conducted a controlled experiment in the project's first year. Accused persons considered eligible for a recommendation of release on recognizance were divided into two groups, an experimental and a control. Vera made recommendations for no bail for the experimental group, but let the judges decide, absent any Vera recommendation, what to do with the defendants in the control group.

Outcomes. Over the project's three years, 3,505 accused persons were released without any requirement of bail as a result of Vera recommendations. Only 1.6 percent of them failed to show up for their trials for reasons within their control.[437] The results of the randomized experiment were especially striking: 60 percent of the experimental group was released without bail, while only 14 percent of the control group was. Data also showed that those released before trial were 250 percent more likely to be acquitted in court.[438]

As the project progressed, Vera staffers became increasingly confident in their predictions, leading to more and more recommendations for no bail. And judges, seeing the high rate of accuracy of Vera recommendations, came to trust Vera more and more. When the program started, Vera recommendations were upheld about 55 percent of the time. By three years later, judges agreed to release 70 percent of those recommended for no bail by Vera.

By the end of 1963, the program's outstanding results had convinced the presiding justices of the first and second appellate departments that bail reform along the lines of the Vera project should be undertaken by the city and spread throughout the five boroughs of New York. Concerned about overcrowding in the city's jails, the Mayor agreed, and the Bail Project became a function of the probation department. And by 1964, the Manhattan Bail Project had attracted enough national attention that the U.S. Department of Justice organized, along with the Vera Foundation, a National Conference on Bail and Criminal Justice. In 1966, President Johnson signed the national Bail Reform Act. When he did, the President credited the Vera Foundation as the source of the legislation,[439] which assured that no defendant, rich or poor, would be "needlessly detained pending [his or her] appearance in court."[440] By 1970, bail reform had also been instituted by nearly every state, and in "scores of cities."[441]

Impact. The Ford Foundation provided critical early support of Vera's work. Its $115,000 grant was the first major outside support Vera received, and it gave the nascent organization legitimacy in seeking to persuade government agencies of the need for change.[442] Ford's continuing support enabled Vera to serve as a "national clearinghouse for information on the subject."[443]

In addition, the Foundation continued to fund other innovative programs undertaken by Vera, and, in 1966, McGeorge Bundy, the new president of the Ford Foundation, approved a five-year, $1.1 million grant to turn the Vera Foundation into the Vera Institute for Justice, a nonprofit institution that "works closely with leaders in government and civil society to improve the services people rely on for safety and justice."[444] The Vera Institute was no longer reliant on the largesse of one man: Louis Schweitzer, and was able to leverage Ford's commitment many times over in support from city and state agencies, and from the federal government.[445]

The Vera Foundation's Manhattan Bail Project pioneered the bail reform movement, proving, with convincing data, that thousands of people in Manhattan alone were spending unnecessary, unjustified weeks and months in jail. And over the years, the Vera Institute has dramatically expanded its operations. It now operates on a national scale, and has tested numerous other experiments. Some have been successful; some have not, but all have been instructive. The Institute now receives funding from a wide range of sources, including a modest endowment donated by Ford. It has had a tremendous impact through its many projects, not least of all from its very first.

Case 30

MEASURING AMERICAN EDUCATION REFORM: NATIONAL ASSESSMENT OF EDUCATIONAL PROGRESS

Carnegie Corporation of New York, 1964

STEVEN SCHINDLER

Background. In the early 1960s, educators and policy makers in the United States began to sense that the public's hunger for education and educational progress had outpaced factual knowledge about whether the education system was getting any more effective in educating young students. Without evidence, policy makers had no way to know if educational reforms were improving student performance or not. No assessment tool existed to monitor student performance in a comprehensive and consistent manner to provide that needed evidence.

Strategy. In 1964, in response to the sense of need for better evidence of the success or failure of education reforms, the Carnegie Corporation of New York allocated $112,500 for an internal study of the feasibility and need for a regular assessment of the progress of education in the United States and the formation of a committee to explore the possibilities of measuring educational progress.[446]

In 1965, the Carnegie Corporation made follow-up grants totaling $260,000 toward the development of educational assessment methods. The first grant funded the work of the newly formed exploratory committee, called the Committee on Assessing the Progress of Education. The Committee was composed of school superintendents, administrators, school board members, and others representing public and private institutions. Grants also funded a set of conferences to complement the work of the Committee in contemplating how the progress of education reform might be assessed. The Corporation also funded the development of tests to be administered for the purpose of educational assessment. The Corporation made clear that its aim was not to monitor individual student progress, but to study the progress of schools and systems.[447]

By 1967, the Committee decided to assess periodically the progress of the education system in ten areas of learning: reading, writing, science, mathematics, social studies, citizenship, music, literature, fine arts, and vocational education. The Committee remained determined to track learning among large groups of people rather than among individuals, schools, or school districts. That year the Corporation made a grant of $640,000, along with additional support from the Ford Foundation, to administer trials of the instruments developed for assessment among 256 specific subpopulations divided by gender, age, socioeconomic level, and population density.[448]

In June 1969, the Corporation made a final grant of $750,000 to the Committee on Assessing the Progress of Education to finalize the development of its assessment tools. The Corporation also made a $250,000 grant to the Education Commission of the States, to which administration and control of National Assessment of Educational Progress was transferred.[449]

Impact. The National Assessment of Educational Progress (NAEP), known today by the U.S. Department of Education as "the Nation's Report Card," was first administered in 1971. Participation in the evaluation was voluntary, and information about individual performance remains confidential.[450] The program was conducted on that basis until 1988, when the Federal Government established the National Assessment Governing Board to set policy for the administration of NAEP. NAEP was expanded to produce state level results in 1990. Responsibility for coordinating NAEP was shifted to the U.S. Commissioner of Education Statistics.[451]

Today, NAEP pursues two major objectives—measuring student achievement across jurisdictional boundaries and monitoring changes in achievement levels over time. It remains the only nationally representative and continuing assessment of the achievement levels and progress of students in American schools.[452] NAEP assessments are a primary source of education statistics for measuring the effects of education policies. It has tracked gaps in student performance between white students and their minority counterparts, enabling educators to study potential contributing factors to education gaps as well as potential solutions.[453] Its results have been cited in assessing whether President Bush's "No Child Left Behind" policy has had a positive impact on educational outcomes,[454] whether private schools offer any learning advantage over public schools,[455] and whether students in charter schools match the performance of their public school counterparts.[456]

Case 31

The Development of the Nurse Practitioner and Physician Assistant Professions

The Commonwealth Fund, Robert Wood Johnson Foundation, and Carnegie Corporation of New York, 1965

Scott Kohler

Background. In the years following World War II, the United States suffered from an acute shortage of doctors. As urban populations escalated and rural communities continued to rely on inadequate medical infrastructure, the demand for health care grew rapidly to outstrip supply. This, in turn, led to rising costs, which made health care inaccessible to many of the poorest Americans. Concentrated in inner cities and the rural countryside, these underserved populations were quite often those in the greatest need of medical attention. By the mid-1960s, however, there emerged two new classes of health care professionals: nurse practitioners and physician assistants.

Although their engagement did not reform entirely the inequities of American medicine, they did begin to play a significant and still-growing role in spreading access to health care services and holding down the costs of care. Enterprising health care professionals in academic medicine pioneered both professions. And starting with the Commonwealth Fund, but soon after to include other foundations, primarily the Robert Wood Johnson Foundation and the Carnegie Corporation of New York, private philanthropy also played a major role in helping the nurse practitioner and physician assistant professions get up and running, and then expand nationwide.

Strategy.

Nurse Practitioners:

The first nurse practitioner training program was conceived in 1965 at the University of Colorado by Loretta Ford, a nurse, and Henry Silver, a physician.[457] Its goal was to increase the supply of primary care providers, especially in underserved urban and rural areas. The program would train registered nurses in clinical care so that they could—by performing such tasks as testing, routine examination, and immunizations—free up physicians for those patients who really needed their attention.

The training program commenced in 1966, and was "principally supported" by a three-year, $253,998 grant from the Commonwealth Fund.[458] Although the traditional nursing establishment, led by nursing school deans, opposed the expansion of nurses' responsibilities, the program was successful and soon replicated. It started in Colorado with a focus of pediatrics, but the profession soon grew to include a range of general and specialist nurse practitioners. In 1970, the Commonwealth Fund gave $84,540, again to the University of Colorado (and, this time, to the Denver school system), to train school nurse practitioners that would improve the quality of care available to thousands of children.[459] In 1976, the Robert Wood Johnson Foundation funded an effort at the University of New Mexico to develop curriculum guidelines to improve and standardize the training of nurse practitioners. The product of this grant was the influential *Guidelines for Family Nurse Practitioner Care*.[460] The following year, RWJF sought to create a corps of outstanding teachers to help grow the profession by funding Nurse Practitioner Faculty Fellowships in Primary Care.[461]

Physician Assistants:

The physician assistant profession was born at Duke University. Faced in the 1950s with heightened patient volume, "and a shortage of all types of nursing and allied health personnel,"[462] the Duke Hospital sought a solution quite similar to that pursued in Colorado by Drs. Ford and Silver. Dr. Eugene Stead, chairman of Duke's Department of Medicine, made three unsuccessful attempts in the late '50s and early '60s to get a clinical nursing program accredited.[463] Each time, the National League of Nursing, which, as we have already seen, feared any change in the traditional nurse's role, blocked his efforts. Looking to the military medical corps as an example, Dr. Stead envisioned a mid-level class of health care providers who could play the part of nurse or physician, and would be trained in far less time than the latter.

Stead obtained initial funding from the National Heart Institute to begin training former military medical corps veterans in the sciences and clinical medicine.[464] In what amounted to an intense two-year abbreviated version of medical school, Stead's new physician assistants (as they were called) learned to perform much the same role as a doctor, while working under a licensed physician's direction. Soon after the NHI grant, Duke received a three-year grant from the Josiah Macy, Jr. Foundation. This, in turn, was soon followed by grants from the Carnegie Corporation, the Rockefeller Foundation, and the Commonwealth Fund.[465]

To support Stead's promising innovation, the Commonwealth Fund in 1967 began to fund the undergraduate training of physician assistants at the Alderson-Broaddus Medical College. In the mid-1970s, RWJF joined the

Commonwealth Fund in supporting the national model by funding Alderson-Broaddus.[466] Meanwhile, a number of academic health centers were requesting Dr. Stead's help in setting up physician assistant programs, so when Duke followed Alderson-Broaddus' lead, changing its post-graduate training to a baccalaureate program, the rest of the nation did as well.[467] The overwhelming majority of physician assistants were trained in this way until the mid-1980s, when a graduate degree, the Master of Health Science (MHS), was created for physician assistants.[468]

Outcomes.

Nurse Practitioners:

The Colorado program served as the model for the multitude of nurse practitioner training programs that quickly sprang up around the country.[469] Today there are over 200 such programs, and clinical training has become a valued asset within the nursing profession.[470] As of 2001, there were an estimated 78,000 nurse practitioners working, and the profession has received certification in all fifty states.[471]

The fears of nursing school deans have not come to pass. In fact, studies show that nurse practitioners can handle approximately 75 percent of the work that physicians handle, and provide care at a much lower cost to the consumer.[472] Nor has the rise of nurse practitioners exacerbated the shortage of registered nurses. On the contrary, it has eased it, as thousands of nurses, more satisfied in their professions, are staying in their jobs longer.[473]

The standards underwritten in the late '70s by the Robert Wood Johnson Foundation led, in 1980, to the creation of the National Organization of Nurse Practitioner Faculties. Foundation support—by fostering the profession's growth in the face of doubts that have since been disproved—opened the door to government support. To date, the federal government has spent over $100 million on the training and support of nurse practitioners.[474]

Physician Assistants:

The first class of physician assistants graduated from Duke on October 6, 1967. The Duke program relied on outside funds until 1982, when it became financially self-sustainable, something it remains to this day.[475] The profession's first pioneer, Duke has graduated well over 1,200 physician assistants. The larger profession, too, has won wide acceptance. Physician assistants enable clients in low-income and community health centers access to advanced healthcare services. Though they work under supervision, physician assistants extend the reach of modern medicine farther than M.D.s, still scarce in many areas, would alone be able to do. As of 2000, there were over 38,000 physician assistants working in the United States.[476] Their accreditation is nationally standardized, and they are board certified in forty-nine states. In 1971, President Nixon called for $15 million to train mid-level health care professionals. Congress responded in 1972 with the Comprehensive Health Manpower Act, which allocates federal funds for the training of physician assistants and other health providers.[477]

Impact. As McGehee Harvey and Susan Abrams write in *"For the Welfare of Mankind:" The Commonwealth Fund and American Medicine,* the Fund's early support of nurse practitioner training at the University of Colorado, "enabled Silver and his group to obtain grants . . . from the Carnegie Corporation, the Robert Wood Johnson Foundation, and [most significantly,] federal agencies."[478] Before the Commonwealth stepped in, the Colorado team had failed several times to raise the needed funds.[479] Likewise in the creation of the physician assistant, private foundations provided the crucial early support that enabled the profession to get up and running, and to disprove the arguments of its critics. Discussing the Robert Wood Johnson Foundation's later role in supporting these two innovations, former RWJF vice president Terrance Keenan credits the Commonwealth Fund and the Carnegie Corporation, "that had participated in the birth of the new professions, and in the face of considerable odds had nurtured them through their infancy."[480] Although it did not begin grant-making until 1972, the Robert Wood Johnson came also to play an important role in fostering both professions. According to McGehee and Abrams:

> For the nation's health-care system, the training of nurse practitioners has emerged as one of the most important developments of the past thirty years. The value of nurse practitioners is now widely recognized, and nurses are seen as a key group in meeting the need for well-trained professionals to provide primary care. By now, nurses have skills previously considered the exclusive province of physicians; accreditation of nurse practitioner programs and certification of qualified graduates have also contributed to an improved identity for nurses and acceptance of their expanded role by other health professionals and the public.[481]

Much of the same can be said of physician assistants. Taken together, the two groups have improved the availability and quality of care for millions of patients. Private foundations, most notably the Commonwealth Fund, but also the Robert Wood Johnson Foundation, the Carnegie Corporation of

New York, and others, have played a crucial role in providing startup capital, as well as helping the two professions evolve and gather additional funding to go to scale over the last forty years.

Case 32

AMERICA'S SYSTEM OF PUBLIC BROADCASTING AND PUBLIC RADIO

Carnegie Corporation of New York, 1965

STEVEN SCHINDLER

Background. In 1964, the U.S. Office of Education issued a grant to Educational Television Services to host the first national conference on the Long Range Financing of Educational Television Stations, to be held in December of 1964.[482] Ralph Lowell, a conference attendee who represented WGBH and was a prominent civic leader in Boston, was invited to deliver a statement.[483] Lowell enlisted the assistance of WGBH general manager Hartford Gunn and his assistant, David Ives.[484] Ives, a friend of Carnegie Corporation officer Arthur Singer, was familiar with the Carnegie Corporation's pivotal work in bringing objective voices to bear on other problems of national importance, particularly Flexner's report on medical education and Myrdal's study of race. Ives contacted Singer to inquire if Carnegie would be interested in directing a similar effort in the arena of educational television.

Singer, who thought that the Carnegie Corporation officers and board would embrace such an opportunity, made the case for the effort to Carnegie president John Gardner. On the spot, Gardner decided that Carnegie would commit resources to study educational television. Knowing well that the Ford Foundation had long dominated educational television funding, however, Gardner called Ford president Henry Heald to be sure that such a study would not be interpreted as an attempt to invade Ford's territory. Heald, on the contrary, expressed his belief that, given Ford's longstanding activity in the field, a Carnegie study would carry much more weight in public opinion as an objective and unbiased voice.[485]

At the 1964 conference, Ralph Lowell advocated the establishment of a public body of civic leaders to "collect information, listen to testimony, and recommend a national policy" regarding educational television in America.[486]

That conference produced eight mandates for the direction of educational television, the last and most important of which urged that "[i]mmediate attention . . . be given to the appointment of a Presidential Commission to make recommendations for educational television development, after intensive study of a year or more duration."[487]

In preparation for Carnegie's planned study, Singer contacted S. Douglass Cater, special assistant to President Lyndon Johnson for domestic policy issues, to ask for the president's reaction to Lowell's proposal. Cater noted that the first lady owned television properties in Texas and that he would not want to pursue a policy that would adversely affect those properties. Further, President Johnson himself expressed some unease about the potential political implications of initiating a presidential commission on educational television because of the possible appearance of self-dealing.[488] The president expressed no reservations, however, about a privately-funded committee, to be coordinated by the Carnegie Commission. Such a commission seemed likely to provide a politically insulated means by which educational television policy could advance.[489]

Gardner presented the proposal to the Board of the Carnegie Commission at a meeting on April 21, 1965; the proposal met with unanimous approval.[490] The Annual Report of the Carnegie Corporation for 1965 discusses the grant in optimistic terms: "Under a Carnegie grant the Carnegie Commission on Educational Television will examine the role of educational television broadcasting and recommend how educational television can be strengthened and financed so it will make the most effective contribution possible."[491]

Strategy. In November 1965, with President Lyndon Johnson's endorsement, the Carnegie Corporation established the Carnegie Commission on Educational Television. A grant of $500,000, spread over 1965 and 1966, funded the activities of the Commission.[492]

Singer, the Carnegie program officer with responsibility for the Commission, recruited Stephen White, a colleague from earlier projects and a documentary writer for CBS, to direct the Commission's activities. White and Singer had both worked at the Massachusetts Institute of Technology; when White suggested as Commission chairman Dr. James R. Killian, Jr., chairman of the corporation of M.I.T., Singer enthusiastically approved. Killian had been Science Advisor to President Eisenhower, and he also had a technology background. Killian, Singer, and White collaborated to identify and recruit the remainder of the commissioners.[493] Though the Carnegie Corporation officially controlled the selection of the commissioners, the White House recommended the appointment of two individuals, for the dual purposes of protecting Johnson's interests and of keeping the White House informed of the Commission's progress.[494] Other Commissioners included Harvard President James B. Conant, author Ralph Ellison, United Automobile Workers Vice-President Leonard Woodcock, Polaroid founder and President Edwin Land, and former North Carolina Governor Terry Sanford.[495] The Commission held its first of eight formal meetings in early 1966.[496] To help it understand the existing providers of public television, the Commission contacted all 124 educational television stations that were operating in 1965 and visited ninety-two of those stations. Its report on those television stations was the first collection of nationwide information on all educational television stations.[497]

From early in the process, the Commission staff planned, on release of the Commission's report, to recommend legislation enacting the proposals it would likely contain. Accordingly, White and Killian began to visit various congressmen in Washington, as well as the presidents of the three major television networks, to present briefings of the Commission's findings and to float legislative ideas. Cater similarly briefed others at the White House about the Commission's work.[498]

Impact. The Commission published its findings and twelve recommendations in January 1967.[499] The detail of the Commission's recommendations reflected two major goals—that federal support should be significantly increased and that a Corporation for Public Television should be established.[500] Near the conclusion of the Commission's work, the Commission staff hired a Washington law firm to draft legislation enacting the report's proposals in hopes that such legislation might win quick passage.

Shortly after the release of the report, the *New York Times* forecast its importance, with widely-admired columnist James "Scotty" Reston opining that its release "may be recognized as one of the transforming occasions in American life."[501] In January 1967, Johnson used his State of the Union address to urge the passage of the Public Broadcasting Act and the creation of the Corporation for Public Broadcasting, a direct recommendation from the Commission.[502]

The Public Broadcasting Act of 1967 passed the House of Representatives by a three-to-one margin.[503] While some witnesses before the Senate Committee considering the bill disagreed with particular aspects of the legislation, each witness supported the overall legislation's passage. Killian and Commissioner Edwin Land, president and founder of Polaroid, were the key witnesses on behalf of the Commission's report.[504]

Some recommendations were eventually rebuffed: the Commission recommended that funding for CPT come directly from an excise tax on television set sales, like that in existence in the United Kingdom, so as to create a dedicated tax and thereby insulate CPB from appropriation politics and possible political control of content, but that recommendation was rejected in Congress. Furthermore, despite the Commission's recommendation that only half of the Corporation trustees be political appointees, all were eventually to be appointed directly by the president.[505] Despite these changes in the legislation, the bill was reported to have been based "in large measure" on the report of the Carnegie Commission.[506]

The Congressional Reports of the Public Broadcasting Act of 1967 highlight the importance of the Carnegie Commission and the testimony of Dr. James Killian, its chair, in establishing the need for a Corporation for Public Broadcasting. The Report of the Department of Housing, Education, and Welfare to the Senate cited with approval Killian's testimony on the need for the Corporation to be insulated from political control and for the Corporation's control of interconnectivity among stations.[507] The House Report also referred favorably to Killian's testimony and the report produced by the Carnegie Commission, particularly the latter's findings and forecasts of the Corporation's costs.[508] Significant credit for the overwhelming support behind the Public Broadcasting Act can be partially attributed to "the deference given to the prestigious Carnegie Commission, chaired by MIT president James Killian."[509]

While the impact of the Corporation for Public Broadcasting on American life is widely understood to be significant, the Carnegie Commission on Public Television was responsible for more than merely the passage of the Public Broadcasting Act of 1967. The Commission's report, authored by Stephen White, articulated a vision of great potential for properly financed television in the public sphere. White was the first to transform the phrase "educational television" into "public television," thereby broadening the public understanding of the Commission's work beyond traditional classroom-extension use. In addition to establishing the infrastructure for public broadcasting, the Commission laid the groundwork for connecting the American public to informative, entertaining, and enlightening television and radio programming.

Case 33

BEDFORD-STUYVESANT AND THE RISE OF THE COMMUNITY DEVELOPMENT CORPORATION

Ford Foundation, 1966

SCOTT KOHLER

Background. By the early 1950s, it was readily apparent to anyone paying attention that American inner cities were descending into a state of crisis. Upper- and middle-class families were rapidly fleeing urban centers for the burgeoning suburbs, and masses of uneducated blacks fleeing the rural South for big cities were finding that America's traditional proving grounds for social advancement—its cities—were becoming havens of chronic poverty marked by declining social services and a rising tide of violence.

In 1950, the Ford Foundation became the largest private foundation anywhere in the world. Eager to take on projects of magnitude befitting its tremendous resources, the Foundation soon turned its attention to urban decay. Between 1964 and 1966, Ford committed millions of dollars to the "Gray Areas" program in an attempt to coordinate a strategy for reversing the spread of urban decay. This controversial program had mixed results. Under the leadership of Mitchell Sviridoff, its New Haven demonstration project was widely praised, and became the model on which the Johnson administration based its War on Poverty (although that federal program quickly ballooned into something largely unrecognizable).[510] But Gray Areas did not, as it turned out, show the way forward. Rather, it was the first major attempt, as Robert F. Kennedy used to say, to "grab the web [of urban poverty] whole." Because of the intense popular and media attention it attracted, "Gray Areas helped make poverty *visible* to America."[511] And it had a profound impact on the field of philanthropy. As Sviridoff recounts:

> In the period prior to Gray Areas, rarely did a major foundation venture forth in the wilderness of the inner-city ghetto with experimental and demonstration programs. Nor did many foundations recognize the overriding significance of the urban crisis, never mind the ticking time bomb of race. Gray Areas literally electrified these staid institutions and, for better or worse, life for this community has never been the same. Gray Areas broke the mold.[512]

A critical learning experience, Gray Areas set up directly the next leap forward in the fight against urban poverty. That leap would be made soon after, and its principal movers would be Senator Robert Kennedy, Franklin Thomas, and the Ford Foundation.

Kennedy, the junior Senator from New York and former Attorney General, had first worked to shore up failing urban communities in the early 1960s, when he served as Attorney General and chairman of the President's Committee on Juvenile Delinquency. In February 1966, Senator Kennedy was invited by community leaders from Brooklyn's run-down Bedford-Stuyvesant district to tour the neighborhood and discuss community development. Moved by the community's problems, Kennedy saw, in Bedford-Stuyvesant, an ideal place to attempt a major intervention bringing together the public and private sectors in support of the efforts of the community to improve its lot. At the time, the median income in Bedford-Stuyvesant was $1,500 below the city average;[513] it was the most overcrowded neighborhood in the entire United States; and more than half of the neighborhood's employed men held unskilled, low-wage jobs. Bedford-Stuyvesant's population was 80 percent black and 15 percent Hispanic, and was without any effective political support in the city or national government.[514]

Strategy. Kennedy hoped to emulate the best parts of the Gray Areas Program,[515] while learning from its mistakes and drawing in such broad support that true urban renewal—that elusive outcome Gray Areas had failed to produce—would be achieved, first in Bedford-Stuyvesant, then nationwide. In August 1966, testifying before the Subcommittee on Executive Reorganization of the Senate Committee on Government Operations (of which he was a member), Kennedy suggested, "the creation of Community Development Corporations, which would carry out the work of construction, the hiring and training of workers, the provision of services and encouragement of associated enterprises."[516]

The first such community development corporation (CDC) would operate in Kennedy's Brooklyn test site. In a single day, Kennedy secured the support of several major for-profit companies, including IBM, CBS, First National City Bank, and Equitable Life. He also convinced Mayor John Lindsay, Governor Nelson Rockefeller, and New York's senior senator, Jacob Javits, to support his plan. For philanthropic support, Kennedy approached the Ford Foundation. Many Ford officials were skeptical of Kennedy's "grab the web whole" approach, and, chastened by the difficulties encountered by Gray Areas, argued against supporting the new Bedford-Stuyvesant project. Paul Ylvisaker and McGeorge Bundy, however, the Foundation's vice president and president, respectively, were impressed. According to Eli Jacobs, who helped plan and run the project, Bundy (who had been national security advisor to the senator's brother) liked the inclusive, nonpartisan style of the program, and was willing to appropriate the requested funds "just to teach Robert Kennedy that businessmen didn't have horns."[517] Although they had hoped to raise more than the $750,000 initially granted, Jacobs and the rest of Kennedy's team "were grateful that [they] had [the Ford money]; there were no other sources of funding."[518]

The project would, in fact, be carried out by two newly created independent nonprofits. The Bedford-Stuyvesant Restoration Corporation[519] set the agenda and managed the various programs pursued in the neighborhood. The Bedford-Stuyvesant Development and Services Corporation (D & S), composed of a small staff and a board of powerful Manhattan business leaders, would advise the Restoration Corporation, and offer it technical assistance and a wealth of connections in the for-profit sector. D & S would also control the funds received and disbursed under the initiative, though the two organizations would apply for funding as partners. Franklin Thomas, deputy commissioner of the New York police department, an attorney and former strategic air command navigator, and himself a Bed-Stuy native, was recruited to direct the Restoration Corporation.

Like Gray Areas, the Bedford-Stuyvesant project "held itself out as a new, more effective delivery system for the best efforts of government, foundations, and corporate philanthropy."[520] While Robert Kennedy had supplied the vision and the early initiative, Franklin Thomas was the mastermind of the Restoration Corporation's strategy on the ground. Thomas believed in an incremental, block-by-block approach that rejected sweeping, macro solutions in favor of concrete improvements that neighborhood residents could take part in and see clearly in the short term. Thomas recognized that, despite its rampant poverty and crime, Bedford-Stuyvesant did have one advantage, compared to other poor neighborhoods in New York—its rates of home ownership were actually significantly higher, an indicator that residents might in fact be willing to commit strongly to the long-term improvement of the area.

To that end, Thomas pioneered the Community Home Improvement Program, which taught residents basic maintenance and repair skills, then funded external property improvements in exchange for a promise from each participant to fund, out of pocket, an equal amount of internal improvements to homes, offices, and retail space. The Program also took such visible measures as donating garbage cans (brightly marked with an "R" for "Restoration"), so that residents' trash did not spill out onto the streets while they waited for garbage pickup, which was notoriously unreliable in Brooklyn. These measures were sometimes criticized as being insubstantial band-aids, but for Bed-Stuy residents, they were concrete improvements in the quality of life, and investments in the neighborhood's ability to take care of itself.

The two Corporations worked to attract investment in the community, and helped residents start up their own businesses. Recognizing that big money would have to come from the public sector, they also lobbied the federal government for financial support. After Franklin Thomas joined the Restoration effort, the Ford Foundation began to feel that "[t]his was going to be something altogether new, something that had absorbed and profited from the lessons of the past—and would not, apparently, be doomed to repeat them." This enthusiasm was heightened in late 1966, when Mitchell Sviridoff, the former head of the New Haven Gray Areas project, left his post as commissioner of New York City's Human Resources Administration to join the Ford Foundation as vice president for national affairs. Ford approved another $1 million, and would continue to support and expand the Restoration.

Outcomes. Even after the assassination of Senator Kennedy in 1968, the Bedford-Stuyvesant Restoration Corporation achieved tremendous success in helping the residents of one of the nation's most blighted ghettos lift up their community. In late 1966, Senators Javits and Kennedy had spearheaded the passage of an amendment to the Economic Opportunity Act of 1964. That amendment enabled federal funding for community development projects aimed at reducing urban poverty, and was ultimately responsible for the disbursement of some $106 million for community development corporations nationwide in the 1960s and '70s. Thanks to its strong connections, Bedford-Stuyvesant received fully one third of these funds.[521] The incremental approach gave residents an almost immediate sense that progress was being made. This led more and more Bed-Stuy resdients to buy into the program, and so a cadre of community leaders gradually emerged. IBM opened a plant in Bedford-Stuyvesant, and, by 1968, residents had started up over twenty new businesses, all providing gainful employment in the neighborhood.[522] Both government and foundations continued to contribute. By the end of 1968, the Department of Labor had given $7.5 million, and philanthropies, mainly the Ford, Rockefeller, and Astor Foundations, had given an additional $3.7 million.[523] And, under Franklin Thomas' leadership, the Restoration Corporation "convinced 85 banks to establish a mortgage pool of $100 million" for the residents of Bedford-Stuyvesant.[524]

The Ford Foundation did more than support the Brooklyn project. Recognizing a model of community development that could achieve similarly impressive results around the country, Ford helped set up and support the expansion of the strategy pioneered at Bedford-Stuyvesant. The Foundation

made a series of grants—usually of several hundred thousand dollars each—
to nascent community development organizations, modeled after Bedford-
Stuyvesant, in cities around the country. During Mitchell Sviridoff's
thirteen-year tenure, the Foundation gave out over $100 million in grants
and program related investments (PRIs) to support the creation and growth
of community development corporations.[525] In order to demonstrate the
broad applicability of the CDC approach, Ford made the grants and PRIs in
a diverse range of communities—urban and rural, predominantly white,
black, and Hispanic alternately. In addition, the Foundation sought to
gather the support of policymakers and other foundations, regardless of political ideology.

Impact. And, indeed, CDCs have crossed political boundaries. Ford has
collaborated with the conservative Scaife Foundation to set up a CDC in
Pittsburgh, and the Bedford-Stuyvesant model, brought forth by Robert F.
Kennedy, has received major support from Republican and Democratic presidents alike. Writing near the end of his life, Mitchell Sviridoff described the
community development landscape:

> Today, community development corporations blanket the American land-
> scape. Various attempts to count or classify them have turned up different
> numbers, but estimates are in the thousands, and each year brings larger num-
> bers than the year before. They have produced hundreds of thousands of af-
> fordable houses and apartments, millions of square feet of retail and other
> commercial space, and drawn billions of dollars in private investment into
> neighborhoods once written off as lost.[526]

The Ford Foundation contributed, though its Gray Areas Program, to the
evolution of the community development corporation. And it provided crucial early funding of Senator Kennedy's vision. Kennedy, his staff, and the
political and business leaders they recruited, not only conceived the Bedford-
Stuyvesant project, but also made sure it was equipped to succeed. And none
of that would have mattered had the residents of Bedford-Stuyvesant not
worked with the Restoration Corporation to transform their community.
When the program was announced, there was a very high degree of "poverty
program despair" that left many Bed-Stuy residents skeptical of new interventions. But as Franklin Thomas said, "we . . . figured out that development
is really a process as much as a product." The importance of the process was
that it showed that members of a depressed and crime-ridden community
could, and would, reverse the trend of urban decline.

Thomas, himself, became Ford's president upon the retirement of McGeorge Bundy. He was there on a 1978 visit to a Ford-supported community

development project in Baltimore when Mitchell Sviridoff came up with the idea of LISC: the next great step forward in the field of community development.

Case 34

CHILDREN'S TELEVISION WORKSHOP AND *SESAME STREET*

Ford Foundation, Carnegie Corporation of New York, 1966

STEVEN SCHINDLER

Background. In the mid-1960s, children's television programming was hard to find, with *Captain Kangaroo* as the only weekday show directed at the pre-school audience. The Ford Foundation, the primary financial supporter of National Educational Television, was interested solely in adult "liberal educa-tion."[527] A couple of studies in the 1960s, however, would spark new ideas in the potential for television to educate mass audiences of children. One re-ported that it could cost as much as $2.75 billion to educate, in a traditional classroom setting, the country's twelve million three- to five-year-old chil-dren who, at the time, received no formal education.[528] Another, a Nielsen survey, noted that children under six watched an average of thirty hours of television a week.[529]

Strategy. The idea that led to the creation of Children's Television Work-shop arose at a conversation in 1966 at the home of Joan Ganz Cooney. Cooney hosted a dinner party at her Gramercy Park apartment to celebrate her first Emmy for a documentary entitled *Poverty, Anti-Poverty and the Poor*, to which she invited Carnegie Corporation of New York Vice President Lloyd Morrisett.[530]

Morrisett, who had long worked on the Corporation's efforts in child-hood development and was mindful of both the costs of preschool education and the prevalence of television among children, asked Cooney whether tele-vision could be used effectively to educate young children.[531] Cooney, in-trigued, thought through the prospects of children's educational television with Morrisett. Shortly after the party, the Carnegie Corporation agreed to fund a feasibility study that Cooney would conduct. She began the study in June 1966, interviewing twenty-six cognitive psychologists, educators, and pediatricians.[532]

Cooney presented the results of her study to the Carnegie Corporation in October. In it, she suggested that a full scale evaluation be conducted in light of the widespread viewing habits of young children.[533] The Corporation wanted to pursue the evaluation Cooney suggested, but the cost of the evaluation was higher than the Corporation could commit. Morrisett, forecasting the cost to be about $4–5 million, began to seek foundation partners to join with Carnegie in funding the proposal.[534]

For months, Morrisett's fundraising attempts with other foundations and other organizations came up dry. On June 30 of the following year, however, at a meeting in Washington with U.S. Commissioner of Education Harold Howe II, a friend of Morrisett's, Howe expressed great interest in the project and suggested that the U.S. Office of Education might provide substantial financial support for such an effort.[535] The Carnegie Corporation board, demonstrating its faith in the project in hopes of attracting other donors, approved a $1 million commitment in January 1968, which the Ford Foundation followed with a commitment of $250,000 three weeks later, along with a promise of additional funds if the program was successful in its early stages. Ford later contributed an additional $1 million. The Corporation for Public Broadcasting provided another $1 million in one of its earliest major grants. The U.S. Office of Education, true to Howe's pledge, contributed $4 million.[536]

The Children's Television Workshop (CTW), the name devised for the entity that would conduct the evaluation Cooney suggested, and *Sesame Street*, CTW's first program, were announced to the public in March 1968. Cooney was named CTW's executive director.[537] CTW was initially affiliated with National Educational Television for the legal and administrative services that organization could provide, but it became independent a year later.[538]

David D. Connell, former executive producer of *Captain Kangaroo*, became the executive producer of *Sesame Street*, giving the project substantial credibility. Connell was initially deterred from taking the post by the large team of academicians affiliated with the project and the fear that their presence would detract from the entertainment value of any resulting programs. When Cooney assured Connell that the program would not sacrifice entertainment for educational value, Connell agreed to join CTW.[539]

Part of *Sesame Street's* innovation was the comprehensive research effort that ensured the program would be both educational and would also sustain the attention of its young viewers. This research effort was coordinated in large part by the Educational Testing Service. Former CTW President David Britt noted at the twentieth anniversary of *Sesame Street's* debut that "research has been at the core of *Sesame Street*." Discussing the importance of research in ongoing CTW series development, Britt said that "research is there during preliminary development of shows, and continues during production, helping us create programs that children both like and understand."[540]

Impact. Sesame Street premiered on public television on November 10, 1969. Even considering the massive marketing campaign CTW undertook to promote a large audience for *Sesame Street's* first few episodes, particularly among minority and underprivileged children, its ratings far surpassed the expectations of its creators. [541] Almost 1.5 million television homes tuned in to *Sesame Street* during its first week.[542] Research efforts monitoring the learning progress of *Sesame Street* viewers demonstrated significant advances; quite simply, those children who watched the program demonstrated clear educational progress.[543]

CTW later drew some criticism for its "failure" to close the education gap between disadvantaged children and middle-class children. Early in the project, compensatory education was one of its objectives. Since many underprivileged children had access to television, the project, its early promoters thought, could help to close the education gap at an early age. The problem with such an objective was that its premise required that privileged children would not watch *Sesame Street*. Disadvantaged children who watched the program did surpass the children who did not watch, but in fact, almost all children, and their parents, were drawn to the program, neutralizing the potential for any compensatory effect.[544] A Russell Sage Foundation analysis of the initial ETS study even found that, since white children watched *Sesame Street* more than black children, the program exacerbated the education gap. CTW responded that it had dropped compensatory education as an objective for *Sesame Street*, focusing instead on maximizing the educational potential of television programming, an objective on which it exceeded all expectation.[545]

Despite any criticism levied against it, *Sesame Street* is widely understood to be one of the most successful television ventures ever. Today, *Sesame Street* is seen in more than 120 countries.[546] As of 2005, *Sesame Street's* Emmy wins total 101, the most for any television series.[547]

Case 35

FEDERAL COLLEGE SCHOLARSHIPS FOR AMERICA'S NEEDY STUDENTS

Carnegie Corporation of New York, 1967

STEVEN SCHINDLER

Background. In 1965, upon John Gardner's appointment by President Johnson to the post of Secretary of Housing, Education, and Welfare, Alan Pifer filled Gardner's vacancy as the president of the Carnegie Corporation of New York. Pifer's approach to philanthropy demonstrated his deeply rooted liberalism. The problems of poverty and unequal opportunity in America became primary targets of Pifer's Carnegie Corporation. The Carnegie Corporation focused on these issues prior to Pifer's leadership, but not with the degree of importance and urgency that Pifer brought to bear. That is partially because Pifer believed foundations to be well positioned to bring different stakeholders and constituencies together to seek to solve public policy questions.[548] Equal opportunity in education would be one of Pifer's early endeavors.

Strategy. In 1967, the Carnegie Corporation, employing its familiar strategy of convening and sponsoring a blue ribbon commission to solve major dilemmas, established the Carnegie Commission on Higher Education. The Commission was financed by the Carnegie Corporation and sponsored by the Carnegie Foundation for the Advancement of Teaching. Both foundations agreed that such a commission was needed to find ways to knock down the barriers that prevented some high-achieving students from pursuing higher education. Earlier, in 1966, a Corporation memo to Pifer maintained that the higher education system, particular the financing of higher education, was ripe for analysis and reform in light of the pressures simultaneously mounting in the 1960s. In December of 1966, Foundation representatives approached Clark Kerr, president of the University of California, to gauge whether he might serve as chairman of the commission. Shortly thereafter, when the Board of Regents of the University of California fired Kerr for his perceived leadership shortcomings during campus uprisings at Berkeley in the 1960s, Kerr agreed to chair the Commission. Fourteen members joined Kerr on the Commission to "study the future structure and financing of U.S. higher education."[549]

The Commission released its first report, *Quality and Equality: New Levels of Federal Responsibility for Higher Education*, in December 1968.[550] The report's recommendations included a Civilian Educational Bill of Rights, seeking to eliminate financial need as a barrier to higher education. The report called for dramatically increased federal aid to higher education, replacing federal student aid programs with educational opportunity grants, work-study programs, and loans. The Commission noted that the recommended educational opportunity grants would aid a high percentage of African American students, students who were otherwise significantly underrepresented at higher education institutions. It also noted that only 7 percent of the college-age students in the lowest quarter of income-earning families attended college, further justification for its need-based grant recommendation. Finally, the Commission expressed the hope that students with federal grants would attract recruiters for higher education interested in cashing in on the grants, which would in turn lead to an increase in educational quality.[551]

Impact. In 1969, Congressman Ogden R. Reid proposed a bill in the House of Representatives embodying much of what the Carnegie Commission on Higher Education recommended, but that bill was not immediately acted upon.[552] The following year, the Commission issued a second interim report focusing on the institutional hurdles blocking ethnic minorities and the economically disadvantaged from access to higher education.[553]

In 1971, the Nixon administration and Congress considered alternatives to the Commission proposal, with the administration proposing loan guarantees to students along with direct grants to institutions. Representative Edith Green proposed a bill giving grants to institutions on a per student basis, with the grants weighted in favor of smaller institutions whose financial challenges were more dire. Supporters of her bill criticized the Commission's plan for failing to provide adequate funding to the smaller institutions that could not attract students, but others noted that this built-in reward to institutions who could attract the most students was a virtuous characteristic of the plan.[554] A supporter of the Commission's plan in Congress, Representative John Brademas, noted that the Commission's plan both maximized a student's choice over which college to attend and rewarded colleges for attracting low-income students.[555] Meanwhile, in the Senate, Claiborne Pell sponsored legislation for higher education institutions that embodied the funding recommendation of the Carnegie Commission on Higher Education.[556] In August 1971, Pell's legislation passed the Senate, and in September, Green's legislation, which allocated only one-third of its funding in accordance with the Carnegie Commission's recommendation, passed the House of Representatives.[557] President Nixon's budget for 1973, however, included no funding for higher education.[558]

In June 1972, the House of Representatives approved the compromise that had already been passed by the Senate. The compromise legislation established the Basic Educational Opportunity Grant (BEOG), a federal scholarship program under which a student received an allowance for higher education reduced by parental capacity for contribution as determined by a formula. While the grant was a step in the direction of eliminating financial barriers for students as advocated by the Carnegie Commission, Congress initially failed to fund the scholarship program.[559] President Nixon included $959 million in funding for the program in his fiscal year 1974 budget.[560]

Case 36

SOCIAL MOVEMENTS AND CIVIL RIGHTS LITIGATION

Ford Foundation, 1967

STEVEN SCHINDLER

Background. The Ford Foundation, one of the more widely noted sources of foundation funding for the civil rights movement, was only one of many financial sources for the many civil rights organizations active in the 1960s and 1970s. Other foundations and other sources of private funding provided money for a variety of specific causes in the broader movement. In choosing their strategies, these other sources largely steered clear of funding litigation. Some funders may have thought that funding litigation would be too controversial, but in large part, their decisions stemmed from the widespread popular belief that any plaintiff, if injured, had complete access to the justice process to bring grievances to court.

The Ford Foundation, however, understood that many plaintiffs suffering from discrimination were too poor or too unfamiliar with the judicial system to know how they might bring a suit. Further, in the late 1960s, whether private foundations would even be permitted to fund litigation activity, in light of tax and spending regulations on private foundations, was unclear.[561]

Strategy. Prior to 1967, the Ford Foundation had spent very little money supporting the civil rights movement. That year, the Foundation elevated support for disadvantaged minorities to one of its top priorities. By 1970, grants in support of disadvantaged minorities constituted about 40 percent of Ford's annual giving.[562] Community development and civil rights advocacy efforts received the bulk of this funding. Other foundations were also funding community development and civil rights advocacy, but few were providing funding for the litigation strategy.[563]

From the late 1960s through the 1970s, however, the Ford Foundation would expand into the arena of civil rights litigation, appropriating about $18 million to civil rights litigation groups. In adopting this strategy, the Foundation included among its primary objectives the promotion of equal opportunity and fair treatment by the government. The first grants in civil rights litigation, appropriated in 1967, went to the NAACP Legal Defense and Education Fund (an independent organizational entity from the NAACP) and the Lawyers' Committee for Civil Rights Under Law.[564]

Seven additional organizations received crucial funding from the Ford Foundation, funding that helped these organizations get off the ground and that brought legitimacy to their efforts. Four of those organizations focused on the protection of civil rights for four disadvantaged subpopulations. These groups included the Mexican-American Legal Defense and Education Fund (MALDEF), the Native American Rights Fund (NARF), the Puerto Rican Legal Defense and Education Fund (PRLDEF), and the Women's Law Fund.[565]

While groups such as the NAACP Legal Defense and Education Fund were relatively well established at the time the Foundation began funding the group, the Foundation's support of MALDEF and NARF was critical to the creation, survival, and operation of those organizations.[566] In 1969, the Ford Foundation's $2.2 million grant established the Mexican-American Legal Defense and Education Fund.[567] By 1973, the Foundation's portion of MALDEF's budget had declined to a little less than 50 percent of the total.[568]

Similarly, in 1970, the foundation made a grant of $155,000 to California Indian Legal Services to start a national pilot project to bring litigation to protect Indian rights.[569] Shortly thereafter, the project was spun off to become the Native American Rights Fund, and the Foundation granted $95,000 to the new agency in 1971 followed by a three-year, $1.2 million grant in 1972.[570] The initial eighteen-month grant from the Foundation facilitated the development of a litigation organization on the model of the NAACP Legal Defense and Education Fund in advocating for civil rights and pursuing crucial test cases to combat systemic violations of civil rights with respect to specific populations.[571] Subsequently, the Puerto Rican Legal Defense and Education Fund—modeled after the NAACP Legal Defense Fund, MALDEF, and NARF—was formed in 1972 with the support of numerous donors, foundations and corporations alike, including early grants from the Foundation of $60,000 in 1973 and $150,000 in 1974.[572]

Impact. The litigation brought by these organizations is remarkable in the impact some of the cases have had on the rights of disadvantaged minority groups.[573] For example, NARF counts among its achievements securing the

rights of Alaskan Indians to tax oil operations on their land, obtaining federal recognition for a tribe that the government had refused to recognize, and
preventing the destruction of Pyramid Lake on behalf of the Paiute
Indians.[574]

PRLDEF has long been fighting for Latino rights, expanding from its original focus on Puerto Ricans to address the legal needs of all Hispanic populations. It filed lawsuits making New York City schools and the City University
of New York more accessible to Hispanic students, and its education division
has also helped assist Hispanic students in pursuit of legal careers.[575]

Perhaps more importantly, the Ford grantees in civil rights litigation have
become important facilitators of community action and advocacy on behalf
of sub-populations whose members have little understanding of the justice
and political systems. Ford's grantees have opened the courtroom doors to
individuals who might not otherwise have understood that their rights could
be vindicated.

Case 37

THE POLICE FOUNDATION

Ford Foundation, 1969

SCOTT KOHLER

Background. Throughout the 1960s, the Ford Foundation supported an array of projects in the field of criminal justice. Some of these efforts—in particular the establishment of the Vera Institute of Justice—produced
significant results. But they lacked cohesion. Furthermore, the urban riots of
the 1960s—many of which were touched off by encounters between police
officers and citizens—led to widespread recognition that police departments
needed to improve.[576] Several studies, including a Presidential Commission,
cited "the social isolation of urban police departments" as a major
problem.[577] In 1969, the Foundation commissioned Jon Newman (who later
became a U.S. appeals court judge) to undertake one of these studies on the
state of the police field and on funding opportunities for the Foundation.
Newman concluded that existing labor unions and most police departments
were resistant to change and insufficiently imaginative.[578] He recommended
the creation of a new institution as a vehicle through which Ford could support research and new ideas that might then spread through the field.

Strategy. Responding with enthusiasm, the Ford Foundation allocated $30 million over the next five years to create the Police Foundation. The new organization sought initially to provide resources to reform-minded police chiefs in five different cities. Two of these efforts produced notable successes. In Kansas City and San Diego, Police Foundation programs showed that random preventive patrol and two-officer motor patrol "had no measurable impact on crime." Later research projects have led to significant findings as well. For example, as Susan V. Berresford, the Ford Foundation's president describes it, Police Foundation research has shown "the capacity of female police officers to do police work, the value in reducing domestic violence recidivism of removing abusive husbands from their homes overnight[, and] effective measures for reducing excessive use by police of deadly force."[579]

From 1975 to 1993, Ford gave an additional $14 million, and, in 1993, Ford enabled the Police Foundation to become self-sustaining with a $10 million donation to its endowment fund.[580] In the ensuing years, the Police Foundation "made research and analysis in [the field] a legitimate and recognized undertaking."[581] As with many of the other important nonprofits it has started up over the years, the Ford Foundation not only underwrote the creation of the Police Foundation, it went on to provide core support, project-specific funding, and major endowment support.

Outcomes. The Police Foundation's initial results were mixed, and much of the first grant had been swallowed up by the time the Police Foundation found its footing. That happened in 1973, when Patrick Murphy was appointed the foundation's new director. Murphy, a former police chief who had worked in Rochester, D.C., Detroit, and New York, had extensive connections to many police chiefs, mayors, and other decision makers, and he was able to dampen the internal squabbling that had plagued the Police Foundation from the time of its founding. Recognizing this improvement, the Ford Foundation renewed its support, and enabled the Police Foundation to keep operating.

Relying on Ford funds, as well as limited support from the federal government and other funders, the Police Foundation became the pre-eminent voice for change and improvement in the field. It supported significant research—such as the Newark Foot Patrol project, which demonstrated that residents of neighbors with police foot patrols felt much safer than residents whose neighborhoods were patrolled only by car. This led to widespread reorganization of police patrols.[582] By means of research, communications, and Patrick Murphy's own networking abilities, the Police Foundation was able to open up dozens of police departments to change and point out many opportunities for improvement.

Impact. While plenty of its projects did not succeed, the Police Foundation, nonetheless, "must be ranked as one of the major domestic achievements of the Ford Foundation during the '70s."[583] According to Hubert Williams, the current president of the Police Foundation, "the police department has changed more than any other institution in our society since the urban riots of the 1960s. It's changed ethnically, tactically, and most importantly philosophically, with an openness to new ideas, new methods, new people and old-fashioned neighborhood involvement."[584] Among the most important engines of this change has been the Police Foundation, which, thanks to the Ford Foundation, has been able—both directly and indirectly—to improve the functioning of police departments around the country, and, in so doing, to improve relations between the American citizenry and those to whom the citizens look for protection.

Case 38

THE ROBERT WOOD JOHNSON CLINICAL SCHOLARS PROGRAM

Robert Wood Johnson Foundation, 1969

SCOTT KOHLER

Background. The Clinical Scholars Program was born out of a conversation among five senior professors of medicine and Margaret Mahoney, then a Carnegie Corporation program officer. The group was concerned that the education of future physicians was inadequate to meet the needs of society, and that the medical schools and medical establishment in general had an inadequate understanding of the need to respond to the societal changes that clearly required advances in medical care to meet the shifting needs of the population over time. Mahoney encouraged the professors to follow up on their conversation, and the Clinical Scholars Program (CSP) was initiated, in 1969, under the auspices of the Carnegie Corporation of New York and the Commonwealth Fund.

The program's aim was to create a corps of physicians, "with a strong grasp of the societal forces that impact health care, the quantitative and qualitative skills to assess both those forces and the health care system, and therefore the ability to effect change within the system."[585] It acknowledged that there were young physicians who wanted to improve medical care, not in the medical laboratory, but in work that could impact the policies that drive the system of medical care.

In 1972, the Robert Wood Johnson Foundation began to operate as a national philanthropy. Expanding tremendously its operations, the Foundation recruited Margaret Mahoney from Carnegie. With the three-year Clinical Scholars pilot program set to expire, Mahoney came to RWJF with the understanding that the Foundation would undertake support of the program over an unspecified period of time but with the understanding by the Foundation's trustees that it would require more support, over time, to build the number of physicians needed to have impact on the medical care system. The trustees bought that argument and the RWJF's initial contribution to the program, in 1972, was $5.9 million.

Strategy. Clinical Scholars was initiated as a national program, with sites at each of the universities at which the five professors taught (McGill, Case Western Reserve, Duke, Johns Hopkins, and Stanford). The sites have since changed in both number (expanding and contracting over the years) and location (none of the original sites has been in continuous operation since '69), and there is no central curriculum common to them all. A National Advisory Board was created to oversee the program and ensure that each branch is operating in line with the Foundation's general aims.

Two-year fellowships were offered to young doctors who had recently completed their residencies. The doctors were trained in economics, sociology, law, statistics, education, management, and epidemiology. The idea was to provide them the expertise to influence health care policy and medical care, and strengthen the nascent field of health services research. The scholars also continued to see patients throughout the fellowship.

Outcomes. Clinical Scholars is now RWJF's longest-running program and has served as a model for the Foundation's more recent human capital investment initiatives.[586] The program was managed internally, by RWJF program officer Annie Lea Schuster, until 1996, when the Foundation set up a National Program Office (administered by Schuster) at the University of Arkansas. That office has since moved to Stanford, and is now directed by Iris Litt, a distinguished pediatrician who is considered a pioneer in the development of Adolescent Medicine.[587] To date, the Foundation has allocated a total of $205.7 million to CSP.[588]

The program now has nearly a thousand alumni, who are active in all fifty states. As of 2003, they had served as hospital CEOs, foundation officers (including the president and some other senior execs of RWJF), academic faculty (at this writing, 162 full professors and twenty-five department chairs), in government (David Satcher, for example, former U.S. Surgeon General and Assistant Secretary of Health), and more.

Impact. The Foundation has periodically evaluated the program, in order to determine its impact and to assess its continued relevance and identify changes that would add value in the changing fields of health care and health policy. An internal assessment in 1981[589] of the Clinical Scholars Program documented the influence of the program on the universities with which it had been affiliated. Core curricula have, at some schools, been changed to include aspects of the program, and the field of health services research has been institutionalized and legitimated thanks to the long-term commitment of the Foundation and the continuing scholarship of the program's graduates. And an outside evaluation, conducted in 1992,[590] asserted that CSP had been a "tremendous success." The evaluators wrote that the program "had changed the intellectual climate of [the] institutions for the better." This was demonstrated by the fact that "host institutions consistently showed an interest in keeping Clinical Scholars on their faculty after they completed the program." More importantly, the evaluators concluded that the Foundation ". . . has molded a sorely-needed generation of scholars who would not exist without the Clinical Scholars Program." The many contributions of the CSP graduates are, without a doubt, the most significant impacts of the Foundation's investment.

The graduates have, by and large, served the role envisioned for them. As Dr. Halstead Holman, one of the original six who conceived the program has said, "[m]ost of the time, when we look at [CSP], only about 15 percent and maximum 20 percent of the scholars are off doing noninvestigative, nonleadership things in standard private practice. And even many of those are providing leadership in other ways in community medicine or something. So I think it's been an astonishingly successful program."[591] And a 2002 report,[592] by a team from UCSF, while discussing the many challenges faced by the program—among them the continued rise of subspecialization in medicine; the soaring costs of medical education, making fellowships unattractive to many young doctors; and the increasing competition for positions in academic medicine—also concluded that ". . . the Program continues to be productive and successful."

Case 39

ENVIRONMENTAL PUBLIC INTEREST LAW CENTERS

Ford Foundation, 1970

STEVEN SCHINDLER

Background. Beginning with its major reorganization into a national foundation in 1952, the Ford Foundation has had an interest in the environment and resource conservation. That year, the Foundation created a committee to offer guidance in determining if and how the Foundation might play a role in ensuring resource availability to sustain economic growth in the United States.[593] Members of this committee incorporated themselves as an organization named Resources for the Future, Inc.[594] The Foundation granted this newly-formed organization $150,000 in 1952 for its establishment and for its early work in determining the optimal strategy for larger foundation involvement.[595] The Foundation continued funding Resources for the Future as its mission expanded to include research coordination and education on resource availability and management, and by 1977, the Foundation's grants to the organization totaled $47.5 million.[596]

In 1962, the Ford Foundation trustees published a report indicating an interest in pursuing foundation activity "in the field of conservation, including its economic, ecological, cultural and aesthetic, leisure-time, and recreational aspects."[597] The same year, Rachel Carson's *Silent Spring* brought to public attention the potential dangers of widespread DDT use, and more broadly, the fragility and vulnerability of the ecological system under pressures of advancing technological development.[598] The use of DDT, however, was not dealt with in the public policy arena until 1966, when Victor Yannecone brought a suit first against the Suffolk County Mosquito Control Commission as well as subsequent suits in Long Island and in Michigan.[599] Yannecone and his colleagues in these suits established the Environmental Defense Fund (EDF, later Environmental Defense) in 1967 as an organization through which to carry out their efforts.[600] Yannecone's leadership style was not well suited to the organization, however, and he departed the organization a year after its founding. Shortly thereafter, the remaining scientists at EDF approached the Ford Foundation seeking funding for a legal staff to carry out subsequent environmental litigation. The Foundation initially declined to fund EDF, though it would later reconsider.[601]

Strategy. In the late 1960s, the Ford Foundation experimented with a new strategy to effect public policy change—funding public interest law centers.[602] The Foundation directed this strategy at environmental policy and resource conservation in 1970 when it gave a conditional grant to the newly incorporated Natural Resources Defense Council (NRDC) for $410,000 and later gave similar grants to EDF, the Sierra Club Legal Defense Fund, and the Southern California Center for Law in the Public Interest.[603]

By the time NRDC received its grant, Ford had already played a significant role in the organization's creation. For over a year prior to the final issuance of the grant, the Foundation had been in contact with a number of outstanding students from Yale Law School about their hopes of securing funding for their endeavors to solve environmental problems by creating a watchdog organization with the freedom to engage in public interest litigation. Upon graduation in June of 1969, six of the Yale students, as well as a recent graduate from Harvard, took temporary positions with hopes that their environmental public interest law organization would materialize.[604]

In the meantime, Stephen Duggan, a partner at a New York law firm, along with four other well-established lawyers incorporated Natural Resources Defense Council as a 501(c)3 organization in the State of New York. Duggan sought funding from the Foundation to host an organizing conference, but the Foundation rejected this request as preliminary, opting instead to monitor the organization's development.[605]

In March 1970, the Ford Foundation brought the group of recent law graduates together with the group of New York lawyers who incorporated the Natural Resources Defense Council, and Ford sought to facilitate a merger of purposes between the two parties. Over a period of two months, the two groups drafted a set of principles and strategies, and they together presented a grant proposal to the Ford Foundation.[606] In response, the Foundation granted $410,000 to the Natural Resources Defense Council as an initial grant for the Council's first few years of operation.[607] This grant was contingent, however, on a ruling by the IRS allowing tax-exempt organizations like the NRDC to engage in public interest litigation while maintaining their tax-exempt status.[608]

The initial IRS position on public interest lobbying organizations—that they could not be tax-exempt and therefore could not be funded by foundations—was a substantial barrier to the evolution of environmental public interest litigation.[609] The tax law changes in 1969 left unclear the tax exemption status of public interest law organizations that engage in litigation.[610] When the IRS temporarily halted consideration of tax-exempt applications for public interest law organizations, various stakeholders in the environmental movement mobilized, understanding the decision to be one of primary importance. Members of the board of NRDC contacted friends in the government, in the Republican Party, and editorial writers to attempt to influence the IRS decision.[611] In the fall of 1970, the *New York Times* and *The Washington Post* both editorialized on behalf of the public interest law organizations.[612] The IRS eventually decided to permit tax-exempt organizations to engage in public interest litigation, and the conditional grant from the Ford Foundation was cleared for use by the NRDC. The grants to other environmental public interest law activities followed.[613]

Impact. The NRDC and Environmental Defense are today among the most influential environmental organizations in the world. NRDC has a membership of more than 1 million. In 2004 alone, the organization participated in more than 200 lawsuits. The organization has appeared numerous times before the U.S. Supreme Court. In addition, NRDC staff members have advocated for environmental protection on virtually every public policy issue at the federal, state, and local level.[614] NRDC has been at least partially responsible for the passage of the Clean Water Act of 1971, the removal of lead from gasoline, and the increased energy efficiency of home appliances.[615] Environmental Defense, boasting 400,000 members, has done less of its work in the courtroom and more collaboration directly with businesses, government, and community groups in tackling environmental problems. McDonald's implemented Environmental Defense's recommendations by cutting down on its packaging waste, New York Governor George Pataki heeded Environmental Defense's encouragement in requiring that diesel-powered equipment involved in the World Trade Center site reconstruction use clean fuel technologies, and FedEx Express recently collaborated with Environmental Defense in rolling out a fleet of hybrid electric delivery trucks in Sacramento, California.[616]

Case 40

THE NATIONAL PRISON PROJECT OF THE AMERICAN CIVIL LIBERTIES UNION

Edna McConnell Clark Foundation, 1972

SCOTT KOHLER

Background. In the early 1970s, Aryeh Neier, then head of the American Civil Liberties Union (ACLU), decided to create a program to establish more expansive rights for prisoners incarcerated in the United States. Already, in the 1970s, it was apparent that overcrowding and a lack of adequate staff and services were making American prisons less humane and more violent places. Neier believed that an ongoing initiative focused on this specific area of civil and human rights would be more effective than the case-by-case interventions more commonly pursued by the ACLU.[617] He decided to combine two existing independent projects on prisoner's rights under the umbrella of the ACLU, and recruited Alvin J. Bronstein to direct the new ACLU National Prison Project (NPP). Bronstein was chosen because he "had the stature to unite the separate efforts," and for his skill and experience as a civil rights litigator.[618]

Strategy. The Project was funded, at its outset, by the Field Foundation, the Stern Family Fund, and the Playboy Foundation.[619] Very soon, it gained the support of the Edna McConnell Clark Foundation, which became by far its largest supporter. The NPP aims "to create constitutional conditions of confinement and strengthen prisoners' rights. . . ."[620] Its primary tactic is class action litigation which seeks to redress, in court, prison conditions and policies that violate the civil and human rights of inmates. The Project's four main priorities are to reduce overcrowding, improve medical care, eliminate violence and maltreatment, and minimize the United States' "reliance on incarceration as a criminal justice sanction."[621]

In addition to bringing lawsuits, NPP also publishes materials highlighting flaws and proposing reforms in America's prison system, holds training and education conferences, and "provides expert advice and technical assistance to local community groups and lawyers throughout the country."[622] During the time it worked in the prison reform area, the Edna McConnell Clark Foundation provided over 50 percent of the NPP's annual budget.[623]

Outcomes. The National Prison Project has, to date, won lawsuits on behalf of prisoners in more than twenty-five states.[624] In the Project's first major case, Bronstein, in 1975, argued for sweeping, broad reforms in the Alabama prison system. He won, and in January of 1976 the court, calling the Alabama prisons "barbaric and inhumane," ordered large-scale changes in response to the "overcrowding, violence, filth, and inadequate food, shelter, medical care and staff" of the state's prisons.[625]

Since then, the NPP has litigated successfully a great many significant cases. In 1987, for example, NPP, along with the Public Defender Service won a judgment declaring that Washington, D.C.'s juvenile detention facilities were characterized by unnecessary confinement and poor conditions. The court in that case ordered that half of D.C.'s youth offenders be released into shelters, foster homes, and drug rehabilitation facilities.[626] In 1988, the NPP won a case holding that no prisoner's political history could be used in determining his or her security status.[627] And in 1992, NPP lawyers argued a case before the Supreme Court of the United States in which was established the precedent that prison beatings can be "cruel and unusual," and therefore unconstitutional, even if the physical damage sustained is only superficial.[628]

Impact. All told, the lawyers of the National Prison Project have "successfully represented over 100,000 confined men, women, and children."[629] With years of Edna McConnell Clark Foundation support, the Project became an effective agent of major prison reform. The early support of the Field, Stern, and Playboy Foundations had enabled the ACLU to get its National Prison Project up and running. And the major funding provided soon after by the Edna McConnell Clark Foundation had underwritten much of its work for many years. In that time, the NPP did a great deal to improve conditions in America's prisons and preserve the rights of the confined. As the ACLU website declares, "[t]he great majority of offenders will return to their home communities; the public interest is ill-served if they return battered in body and spirit, schooled in crime and angry at their treatment by society."[630]

For most of its history, the NPP has been working against the grain. Although it has brought to light many of the injustices and inadequacies of the American prison system, the Project has been unable to convince many legislators that mandatory long-term incarceration, and the deprivation of needed resources, can, in fact, be counter-productive. The overall trend in Congress and many state houses has been toward mandatory minimum sentences and limits on the constitutional protections afforded prisoners.[631]

Despite this, some public officials have been willing to credit the National Prisoner Project for playing a major role in such prison reforms as have been achieved. In 1982, the head of the Federal Bureau of Prisons endorsed the NPP's strategy, saying, "I think the courts have done more to improve corrections in this country than any organization and individual. . . ." The National Prisoner Project of the ACLU is still the only program striving to protect in court the rights of the incarcerated, and its work was enabled—in large part—by the support of the Edna McConnell Clark and other foundations. It has been, and continues to be, absolutely vital work; it is work that defends the rights of a large class of Americans—now numbering over 3 million—who are not likely to be protected by anyone else.

Case 41

PROGRAMS TO ENHANCE THE RIGHTS AND OPPORTUNITIES OF WOMEN

Ford Foundation, 1972

SCOTT KOHLER

Background. In 1972, the Ford Foundation's president, McGeorge Bundy, convened an advisory committee of Foundation officials to make recommendations intended "to improve the representation of both women and minorities in the Foundation's ranks."[632] Later that year, Bundy also created a small, inter-divisional task force "to investigate grant-making possibilities in the area of women's rights and opportunities."[633] By executive order, the world's largest foundation had committed itself to equality of opportunity for women, both internally and in its relations to the outside world. At the time, women's rights to jobs, equal compensation, and a myriad of other opportunities—even in the United States—lagged far behind those of men. A host of laws, and far more deeply ingrained cultural bias, confined women to being caretakers of the home, disadvantaged in any attempt to assume responsibilities, professional or otherwise, historically reserved for men. Working women earned an average of sixty cents for every dollar earned by their male counterparts. And worldwide, especially in many less developed countries, gender inequality was—and still is—far more pronounced.

Strategy. In 1973, Bundy's task force recommended, to the Foundation's Board of Trustees, the creation of a new program to enhance the opportunities and protect the rights afforded to women around the world. This recommendation was accepted, and the Foundation's National Affairs and Education and Research Divisions quickly set aside $1 million each for grants on behalf of women's causes. Ford's International Division moved more cautiously into this new field. Members of the International staff were concerned that a focus on the problems of women alone might obscure the Foundation's broader development goals in the many third world countries, and that a foundation-sponsored attempt to impose gender equity would be seen abroad as a neo-colonial imposition of Western values. Nonetheless, the International Division soon adopted this new focus, and began funding programs to enhance the lot of women in a wide range of countries. Between 1972 and 1979, grant-making to enhance women's rights and opportunities accounted for 5.4 percent of Ford's total program budget.[634] In 1980, the

Foundation's trustees approved a special appropriation to double this amount, to over 10 percent of Ford's program expenditures.[635]

The Foundation's National Affairs division pursued a range of strategies to enhance gender equity in the United States. One primary focus was on "working for changes in the law and enforcement of women's legal rights."[636] To this end, Ford supported many organizations bringing women's rights litigation. These included the ACLU Women's Rights Project, the NAACP Legal Defense and Educational Fund's Minority Women's Employment Program, the Mexican American Legal Defense Fund (MALDF), and the Educational Fund's Chicana Rights Project.[637] Most significant among these was Ford's major support for the Women's Rights Project of the American Civil Liberties Union (ACLU). Founded and directed by Ruth Bader Ginsburg, the Project began to receive major support from the Ford Foundation in 1975. By that time, it had already successfully argued several influential cases before the Supreme Court.[638] However, according to the Women's Rights Project's website, Ford's major support "enabled us to develop a significant program to enforce women's statutory rights, including the right to equal employment opportunity guaranteed under Title VII and the Equal Pay Act."[639] The Foundation also spent over $3 million to improve access to day care facilities, and founded the Trade Union Women's Studies Program (TUWSP) in order "to train women for leadership in the workplace."[640] To build the knowledge base of the women's movement, Ford in 1975 also collaborated with the Urban Institute to start the Center for Policy Research on Women and Families.[641]

The Foundation's Education and Research division worked to pursue two primary strategies. On the one hand, it promoted improved access for women to education opportunities. This included support for the hiring and promotion of women within the field of education, where women had long worked but were rarely in positions of authority. It also included efforts to increase the educational opportunities available to disadvantaged girls. Ford's second main strategy in education was to support research on "the roles of women in diverse societies." The Foundation supported university women's studies programs and other research to examine gender stereotypes, and, in the mid-1970s, began funding increased advocacy to "[encourage] nonsexist educational practices."

Ford's International Division, as we have already seen, entered the field slowly. It began primarily by funding studies of women's issues and literature to raise awareness of women's many contributions to a range of diverse cultures. Active in a great many countries, the Foundation searched for promising women's advocacy groups, or other nonprofits headed by talented women, and offered them financial backing. As it became more comfortable working on women's issues abroad, the Foundation funded programs helping women find more stable and better paying livelihoods. This approach was supported by literature demonstrating that, as women's incomes rise in developing countries, family sizes and child poverty decline markedly. [642] The Foundation also supported family planning in the United States and abroad, including in countries with weak traditions of women's rights. The bulk of the Ford Foundation's international grant-making was bound by a common focus on women's economic security. This enabled field offices around the world to meet regularly to share lessons learned and discuss innovations in one country that might work well in others. After the special appropriation raised its budget in 1980, the Foundation's international women's programs began to support women's studies research centers around the developing world.

Outcomes. By 1986, the Ford Foundation had spent over $70 million on programs in support of women. Two-thirds of this was used in the United States, while about $23 million was given to international grantees. The full range of outcomes produced by Ford's many grantees dedicated to women's causes is beyond the scope of this case study. It is, however, certainly worth mentioning a few illustrative examples. Domestically, Ford's support either created or provided substantial funding to twenty women's studies research centers. The Foundation's grant to the Center for Women in Government (at Albany's State University of New York) funded research that served as the basis for a compromise between New York State and the Civil Service Employees Association that enabled thousands of women to move from support staff roles to professional positions. The Foundation also supported a series of meetings that grew into the National Conference on Women and the Law. This is now "the major national convention for lawyers and law students in the field."[643] Ford's international women's programs helped extend the women's movement around the globe, yet remained mindful of each local culture. And Ford-supported litigation "established critical principles and changed the lives of many women who won back pay, the right to compete for traditionally male jobs, and access to credit, health care, and educational and athletic programs." Even when such women's rights litigation was unsuccessful, it often raised the profile of the issue at stake. In one failed case, for example, public opinion shifted enough as a result of a high-profile case on the rights of pregnant women that Congress enacted legislation mandating exactly the protection that the courts had been unwilling to grant.[644]

As noted, the Foundation's support of the ACLU's influential Women's Rights Project produced especially significant results. Among the major victories won in Court by the ACLU with Ford's support are *Califano v. Gold-*

farb, which struck down discriminatory elements of Social Security, and *Craig v. Boren*, in which Ginsburg and the ACLU's quest to establish that gender discrimination is no different from discrimination by race culminated in the Court's adoption of a "heightened scrutiny" standard for evaluating sex discrimination claims. When President Clinton in 1993 nominated then-Judge Ginsburg to the Supreme Court, he praised her, pointing out that "[m]any admirers of her work say that she is to the women's movement what former Supreme Court Justice Thurgood Marshall was to the movement for the rights of African-Americans."[645] By then, it was widely accepted that the Women's Rights Project had, in the 1970s, served as "the spokesperson of women's interests" in the Supreme Court.[646]

The Foundation's progressive internal reforms changed the culture of the Ford Foundation, and made it a place far better suited to make good on its commitment to enhancing women's rights and opportunities. Between 1972 and 1986, the percentage of professional staff positions occupied by women within the Foundation increased from 22.9 to 53.2.[647] At the same time, the percentage of women composing the Foundation's support staff dropped, while the percentage of it Trustee positions held by women rose.[648]

Impact. At a critical time, when the women's movement stood on the brink of important steps forward, the Ford Foundation played an important role, first by realigning its internal commitment to gender equity, and then soon after, by extending that commitment to all aspects of its enormous grant portfolio. In so doing the Ford Foundation, by its major ongoing commitment to enhancing women's opportunities and protecting women's rights, created a bulwark of support for women's movements in the United States and around the world.

Case 42

THE EMERGENCY MEDICAL SERVICES PROGRAM OF THE ROBERT WOOD JOHNSON FOUNDATION

Robert Wood Johnson Foundation, 1973

SCOTT KOHLER

Background. By 1972, it was evident that emergency medical response mechanisms in most of the United States were severely lacking. Victims of accidental trauma were, in most cases, unsure which telephone number, if any, to dial in case of an emergency. Instead, they were forced to choose between different options, depending upon whether the emergency was a fire, car accident, violent crime, or some other occurrence. In the metropolitan Kansas City area, for example, there were no fewer than seventy-eight different emergency phone numbers from among which to choose![649]

And even when the caller had a phone book available, or knew a number to call, ambulance service was a far cry from what it is today. In the early 1970s, roughly "half of the country's ambulance services were provided by 12,000 morticians, primarily because in their areas they owned the only vehicle that could accommodate a patient on a stretcher."[650] Ambulances were intended only to transport accident victims to the nearest hospital. This had several disadvantages. First, trauma patients rarely received medical attention before arriving at the hospital, a delay that often cost lives and exacerbated any medical condition. In fact, fewer than half of all rescue personnel had medical training at the Red Cross level of advanced first aid.[651] Second, in bringing victims to the *nearest* hospital, ambulance drivers did not always get their passengers to the *right* hospital. Not all hospitals are equally well-equipped to treat all types of injuries or other medical emergencies. So, for example, a burn victim might be taken to a hospital lacking a burn clinic, while he or she would have been better served somewhere else nearby. Another part of the problem was that ambulance drivers almost never had any way to communicate with hospital personnel while on the road. When a victim arrived at the emergency room, doctors and nurses were often not ready and had no way, in advance, of knowing what kind of treatment an incoming patient might require. In addition to the lack of communications equipment, ambulance drivers were hindered in their work by complex jurisdictional problems. First responders were often delayed by debates over in which ambulance service's territory an accident had occurred. Looking back, Blair Sadler, who, in the early 1970s, was co-director of the trauma program at the Yale University School of Medicine, recalled that, ". . . in Connecticut, we had ambulance personnel literally fighting over patients."[652]

These many shortcomings were particularly significant because the first hour of medical treatment in trauma cases—often called the "Golden Hour"—is tremendously important in determining a patient's fate. Delays in emergency medical response cost lives. In a 1972 report, the National Academy of Sciences estimated that 1.5 million people each year were injured in accidents, and 115,000 of them were killed. Worst of all—the report claimed that 90,000 of these fatalities each year might have been prevented by better emergency treatment.[653]

By the early 1970s, public awareness of these flaws was on the rise. It did not hurt that a popular television show, beginning in 1972, focused attention on the work of first responders. *Emergency!* told the story of a team of Los Angeles paramedics, and its popularity helped to increase awareness of the importance of society's emergency response mechanisms. In the same year, the Department of Health, Education, and Welfare began to fund emergency medical systems (EMS) demonstration programs in Arkansas, Illinois, and several cities. Five years earlier, "the President's Commission on Law Enforcement and Administration of Justice had recommended the institution of a single nationwide telephone number for reporting emergencies." The first 911 test call was made in February of 1968 by Representative Rankin Fite of Alabama, but over the next few years, the idea was slow to take off.

The Robert Wood Johnson Foundation first operated as a national philanthropy in 1972. The foundation's creator, General Robert Wood Johnson, had, upon his death, endowed it with over $1 billion in shares of the Johnson & Johnson Company, of which he had been CEO.[654] That gift made the Robert Wood Johnson Foundation instantly the second largest private foundation in the United States.

Strategy. From the beginning, the Foundation's exclusive focus was on health and health care, and it quickly turned its attention to the ramshackle American non-systems of emergency response. In April of 1973, the Foundation announced a $15 million grant program to assist the development of regionalized emergency medical services. The Foundation's president, David Rogers, was an early proponent of EMS reform. Robert Blendon, who, in the early '70s, was a senior vice president of the Foundation, recalls that "[David Rogers] believed that there was something wrong in America if people who could benefit from the best of medicine never got to the hospital before it was too late, or they got to the wrong place."[655] Rogers initiated a partnership between the Foundation and the National Academy of Sciences, which would "set up a screening process for grant proposals, monitor the projects, and evaluate the impact of the program."[656] Meanwhile, Robert Blendon sought out experts in EMS, including Blair Sadler and others, to help the Foundation determine how best to increase the quality and reach of regional emergency response systems.

Ultimately, the $15 million were distributed to forty-four emergency response organizations in thirty-two states. Those forty-four were selected from 251 applicants, and the average grant was $350,000, while the largest was about $400,000. As Digby Diehl writes in his report on the program for the Robert Wood Johnson Foundation Anthology, "[t]he Foundation

actively recruited prospective grantees." In particular, grant-seekers were encouraged to form coalitions with other local agencies operating in the field of
emergency medical response.

According to Sadler, there were three main components of the Foundation's program.[657] The first of these was to increase access to technology. In
practice, this primarily meant equipping ambulances with radios that would
allow them to communicate with dispatchers and hospital personnel. The
second element of the strategy was training, both of ambulance drivers and
of central dispatchers, who would answer emergency phone calls and initiate
a response. The third component of the program was the promotion and facilitation of interagency coordination. This, Sadler recalls, "was perhaps the
most difficult [element] of all." Competition between, for example, police
and firefighters, or between rival ambulance companies, was fierce; and complex, sometimes overlapping fields of jurisdiction impeded cooperation.

The Foundation was very clear in telling grantees exactly what they
needed to do in order to receive the money. Funding was conditioned upon
the fulfillment of seven requirements.[658] Grantees were expected to:

- ensure "central and immediate citizen access to the emergency medical
  system"

- establish "central control of EMS communications"

- guarantee a prompt response to emergency calls for help

- employ "adequately trained dispatch and ambulance personnel"

- develop "emergency system capacity"

- ensure that all their emergency personnel would have access to open
  phone lines and radio channels, and

- provide "assurance that the program could become self-sufficient after
  a two-year period"

It was not, however, a thoroughly rigid strategy. As Blair Sadler, who was
hired as an assistant vice president of the Foundation for the Emergency Medical Services program, describes, the Foundation, an advocate of coalitions in
each region, did not care "who the lead [grant-receiving] agency was, as long
as that entity had the ability to bring all the key EMS players to the table."[659]
Diehl describes the Foundation's role as that of "a funnel for EMS information, bringing knowledge of hardware and procedures to grant recipients."[660]

The Foundation believed that emergency responses had to be coordinated
regionally. But this meant centralization, although on a regional level, as

Foundation dollars supported central dispatchers, uniform standards of medical training for ambulance drivers, and one central phone number (usually, although not always, 911) that people in a given region could call in the event of an emergency.

Outcomes. Progress in the emergency response capabilities of the forty-four grant recipients was considerable. One of the most visible developments associated with the program was the expansion of the 911 emergency system. In 1973, only 11 percent of people in the areas supported by the Johnson Foundation program had access to 911, or some equivalent emergency phone number. By the program's end, in 1977, 95 percent of them did. These outcomes were not mirrored in the nation as a whole. In 1979, only 25 percent of the U.S. population was covered by 911 or its like. Even today, the 911 system is available to only 85 percent of the population.[661] But progress in the Foundation's forty-four grant areas did serve as a model of the emergency phone number's effectiveness. In this way, Foundation dollars were the spur that encouraged subsequent federal support.

Interagency cooperation in the grant-supported areas was also improved. As Diehl explains, "[b]efore the program began, none of the grantees had any linkage between the central emergency dispatcher [when there was one] and the police and fire departments; by 1977, however 86 percent of them did."[662] In 1973, none of the Foundation-supported organizations communicated with their counterparts in other regions, even those nearest-by. By 1977, 61 percent of the forty-four had established such links, facilitating the resolution of jurisdictional uncertainties in cases on or near a border.

Ambulance service was also enhanced. In 1973, there were 6,000 emergency medical technicians (EMTs) and 240 of the more highly-trained paramedics in the forty-four areas. By 1977, those same regions were served by 26,000 EMTs and over 3,200 paramedics.[663] This more qualified pool of ambulance personnel also had better technology at its disposal. By 1977, 91 percent of all ambulance services in the program areas had radios installed in at least half their ambulances. In 1973, that percentage had stood at twenty-five.[664]

From the program's conception, the Foundation planned to evaluate its success. This was done in two outside evaluations: one by the Rand Corporation and one by the National Academy of Sciences. The Rand Corporation's evaluation was, according to Diehl, "lukewarm at best." It examined a sample of seven grantees from among the forty-four, but was frustrated by the grant-recipients' limited ability to produce empirical evidence of their progress. This "shortage of data" led the Rand evaluators to exclude three of their seven subjects. David Rogers acknowledged the problematic lack of data, and believed that the Foundation had "looked too soon . . . to obtain solid answers to the questions of most compelling interest to us."[665] The National Academy of Science's evaluation, on the other hand, was overwhelmingly positive. It cited the increased access to a 911 dispatch system, the rapid proliferation of EMTs and paramedics, and the expansion of ambulance-hospital communication as evidence of the program's success. While these data are valid, it must still be noted, as Diehl warns, that the Academy could not help but have a "built in bias in favor of the program, as its staff had actively participated in administering the grants."

Impact. When the Robert Wood Johnson Foundation got involved, EMS reform was an idea for which the time had obviously come. Otherwise, the Foundation would not have been able to tackle the inefficiencies of every region in the nation. Nor did every good idea originate at the RWJF headquarters. The idea of the 911 number, linked to central dispatch systems, went back to the 1960s, and the regionalization of emergency medicine had already been endorsed by such leading institutions as the Yale School of Medicine.[666] But the Foundation advanced the spread of both ideas by using funding as a lever to get these and other response mechanisms tested in thirty-two states. In addition to the benefits conferred on the citizens served by the Foundation grantees, the success of these mechanisms led to their implementation on a larger scale.

That larger implementation required federal support, and the government soon recognized the excellence of the Robert Wood Johnson Foundation's work. David Boyd, a member of the Foundation's advisory committee, was hired to coordinate the federal government's EMS program. According to Sadler, this "ensured that the feds would be supportive of [the Foundation's] effort."[667] And, indeed, Boyd recalled that the government "picked up the Robert Wood Johnson effort in the federal program in every one of those forty-four projects." Where the Johnson Foundation had enticed EMS providers with grant money, "Boyd's Division of Emergency Medical Services made regionalization a prerequisite for [any federal] funding."[668] By 1977, the U.S. Congress had appropriated over $454 million for the enhancement of emergency response services.[669]

Clearly the Foundation was not alone in its efforts. Federal involvement was important, as was the involvement of other organizations, including the National Academy of Sciences. Enterprising individuals within the emergency services field have also contributed mightily. Progress does not occur in a vacuum. The Foundation brought in outside voices, collaborated with interested organizations in the public and private sector, and, ultimately, used its funds to make a point, encouraging the federal government to use its own vast resources in a way that the Foundation had shown could strengthen the safety net beneath American citizens. Robert Merkel, president of the

Louisiana Hospital Association believes that "[w]e continue to see the fruits of the [RWJF Emergency Medical Services] program every day, and people still remember where it came from. The program was sorely needed at the time, and it pushed everyone to upgrade the level of care."[670]

Case 43

HOSPICE CARE MOVEMENT

The Commonwealth Fund, 1974

SCOTT KOHLER

Background. The concept of hospice care is not a new one. In fact, it has been around for centuries, if not millennia. The term "hospice" now refers to a method or place of treatment for the dying, focused on "the desire to provide some form of support—emotional, physical, or spiritual—for patients and families during terminal illness." But hospice care once embraced a more general definition of relief. During the Crusades, for example, hospices were way stations where road-weary travelers could rest and recover. Over time, however, hospice—whether or not it was explicitly named as such—came to refer primarily to the care of terminally ill patients on the brink of death.

For centuries before they were exported to the Americas, hospices—run primarily by religious orders and existing independently of governmental authorities—were scattered around Europe, and especially the United Kingdom. Around the turn of the twentieth century, Christian clergy members in the United States began operating hospices where the sickest of patients could seek relief from pain and peace with God. These places remained over the years unaffiliated with the larger healthcare community and uninterested in the advances of modern medicine. Perhaps unsurprisingly then, they were few and far between, and by the 1930s, it was becoming more and more common for sick patients to die in hospitals and nursing homes.

As the so-called "death with dignity movement" gathered steam in the 1950s and '60s, health care professionals around the United States began increasingly to doubt the wisdom of the conventional approach to dying: seek always to stave it off at any cost. Across the Atlantic, Dr. Cicely Saunders founded St. Christopher's Hospice in London in 1967. Offering inpatient and home care, bereavement support for families, and a range of other services, St. Christopher's was the most advanced example of European hospice care, and would soon become the model for the American hospice movement.

Strategy. A year before St. Christopher opened its doors, Dr. Saunders and Dr. Elizabeth Kubler-Ross, the psychiatrist who theorized the six psychic stages of dying, visited the Yale University Hospital as advocates for the death with dignity movement. The two impressed Florence Wald, dean of Yale's Nursing School, who soon became an enthusiastic supporter of hospice care. Along with colleagues from Yale's schools of Medicine and Divinity, Wald conducted a two-year study of existing facilities in the United States to care for the dying. During this time, Wald gathered and presided in 1967 over the landmark first meeting of the Yale Study Group, an assembly of health care professionals, religious leaders, and not-for-profit representatives that met to consider society's response to terminal illness. As Cathy Siebold describes in *The Hospice Movement: Easing Death's Pains*, the Group came together "to talk, even gripe, about the way terminally ill patients received aggressive treatment until they died."[671] The YSG saw a better approach in hospice care.

In the subsequent months, Florence Wald "proceeded to contact people around the country who were interested in terminal care to see if they would like to participate in a group whose goal was to develop modern hospice programs nationally." This new approach was controversial, and Yale University found it difficult to become too deeply involved in the work of the YSG and its successor, the International Work Group on Death, Dying, and Bereavement (IWG). However, according to McGehee Harvey and Susan Abrams, "[t]he deans of the medical, divinity, and nursing schools were very supportive of the project, as indeed was Yale's president, Kingman E. Brewster. . . ."[672] So, too, were the Commonwealth Fund and other private foundations. In 1973, the Fund gave Wald and her colleagues a small grant to study the feasibility of establishing in the United States a modern hospice along the lines of St. Christopher's.

In 1974, the Group's work researching models of terminal care and gathering support for the hospice model culminated in the opening of Hospice Inc., the first modern hospice in the United States. Modeled after St. Christopher's, Hospice Inc. was incorporated in Branford, Connecticut, although its services, both outpatient and at the physical hospice, would be available to Connecticut residents around the state. Hospice Inc. would also serve as a clearinghouse for information on hospice care and a center for the growth of the hospice movement. As Hospice Inc. took shape, the Commonwealth Fund, the Van Ameringen Foundation, and the Ittleson Family Foundation gave $100,000; $100,000; and $50,000 respectively for planning and the assembly of a complete home-care staff.[673] Also in 1974, program staff of the Commonwealth Fund helped Hospice Inc. secure a $1.5 million grant from the National Cancer Institute. Two grants of $1 million each from the

National Institutes of Health and the State of Connecticut defrayed the construction costs of Hospice Inc.'s inpatient facility.

According to Siebold, "[w]hile Saunders and Kubler-Ross were the charismatic leaders of the hospice movement, Florence Wald was its organizer."[674] Wald, who had resigned from the deanship of the Yale Nursing School to support and grow the hospice model nationwide, led the way in publicizing the work of Hospice Inc. and supporting the establishment of similar institutions around the United States.

Outcomes. The hospice model of care—with its emphasis on relieving pain and offering emotional, physical, and spiritual support to dying patients and their grieving families—spread rapidly in the years after Hospice Inc. first opened. In 1975, Hospice Inc. hosted the first National Hospice Symposium, and, in the following year alone, Hospice Inc. received thirty-six separate requests for help in launching new hospices. In 1977, Hospice Inc. became a charter member of the National Hospice Organization (NHO). Prior to NHO's founding, Wald's Connecticut hospice actually had trademark rights to the term "hospice" in the United States, but it voluntarily released those rights to the new umbrella organization. In 1978, Hospice Inc. "became the first program approved for insurance reimbursement as a hospice home care service."[675] Unlike the old church-run hospices, the modern hospice movement embraced the medical establishment, even if its enthusiasm was not always returned. Although much of the medical community supports the hospice movement, many health care professionals still find it hard to accept a model of care predicated on the death of its patients. But hospice care has spread nationwide all the same. The death with dignity movement came into the spotlight when the Karen Anne Quinlan case became national news in the mid-1970s.[676] And by the end of that decade, "the hospice movement had achieved national renown."[677] Today, there are an estimated 3,200 operating in the United States.[678] These centers of care at the end of life are reimbursable by Medicare, Medicaid, and private insurance agencies.

Impact. The work of Florence Wald and her colleagues from the Yale Study Group was instrumental in founding Hospice Inc. and then in promoting its replication. According to Harvey and Abrams, "[t]he pioneering New Haven Hospice Program is still considered the model for the inpatient and home care of terminally ill patients."[679] The support of the Commonwealth Fund was crucial in enabling this model to cross the Atlantic. Credit should be given to the staff of the Fund for supporting the transnational dialogue that connected the Yale Group to St. Christopher's in London. Recognizing a void in the American healthcare landscape, foundation officials searched for the right model, and, upon finding it abroad, provided crucial funding and encouragement to see it tried and proven in the United States. This, in turn, brought credibility to the hospice care movement. As Florence Wald recalls, "[o]nce the solid and prestigious foundations lent their support other ones felt more comfortable in following suit." Wald also reflects upon the decision to create Hospice Inc. as an independent entity, saying, "the then Deans of Divinity, Medicine, and Nursing [at Yale] were in agreement with the decision—but it did take the trust of Commonwealth!"[680]

The rise of hospice care has significantly altered the American health care landscape, and is the most visible achievement of the death with dignity movement. The extraordinary advance of medical technology and practice over the last hundred years has given enormous momentum to the natural impulse that every disease should be treated as aggressively as possible, since a cure may be just around the corner. As Cathy Siebold points out, "[l]imited exposure to natural disaster and increased life expectancy has fostered a belief among many Americans that technology can overcome everything, including death."[681] Alas, this belief is mistaken, and hospice care manifests an admission—still uncomfortable for most, and certainly in contrast to the prevailing trend—of our own mortality. As its spread throughout the United States clearly shows, however, it is an alternative which many people in their last days appreciate being offered.

Case 44

THE TROPICAL DISEASE PROGRAM

Edna McConnell Clark Foundation, 1974

SCOTT KOHLER

Background. The Edna McConnell Clark Foundation first became interested in international grant-making in the early 1970s. The Foundation searched for a niche in which it could leverage a modest commitment of funds for the achievement of maximum impact.[682] Health care seemed too broad a field, but the senior staff (including Jim Henry, the Foundation's president) felt that tropical disease research could be just such a niche. To that end, EMCF convened a workshop of practitioners to identify which disease(s) should be targeted. According to Donald Hoffman the officer in charge of exploring international grant-making opportunities, "we chose schistosomiasis for several reasons. It was not so distant a goal as to be hopeless. . . . [And limited]

Research was already underway . . . so there was already a good cadre of researchers who were the nucleus."[683]

The Foundation did not become involved in trachoma and onchocerciasis ("oncho") research until several years later. Following the Board's decision, in 1981, gradually to phase out of "schisto" research, a series of exploratory grants were made to identify new funding niches for the Foundation in the field of Tropical Disease Research. Two infectious causes of blindness—Trachoma and "oncho"—were selected, because they were consistent with the Foundation's previous work, did not appear intractable, but were not, at the time, receiving significant support from other funders.

Strategy.

Schistosomiasis

Between 1974 and 1994, EMCF invested $32.4 million in schistosomiasis research. The Foundation's initial goal was the development of a vaccine,[684] but its schisto program had three main components: immunology and vaccine development, epidemiology and control, and biochemistry and drug development. In following these three paths, EMCF acted as a catalyst for increased research, funding scientists and conducting workshops with governments, international organizations, and the scientific community.

As the Foundation's Retrospective Report explains, EMCF chose not to "seek to use communication systematically to develop a more committed public constituency for schisto research, or for bringing down the price of [available treatments]."[685] This decision reflected a belief among the Foundation's trustees that high-quality research would speak for itself. Over time, however, experience convinced the Foundation—and helped demonstrate for later funders—that effective outreach was a necessary component of health research, and, as a result, EMCF's later work on trachoma included extensive communications efforts.

Onchocerciasis

Between 1985 and 1998, the EMCF invested $21.5 million in onchocerciasis research. Again, the primary focus was on developing a vaccine. To that end, the Foundation employed a "tight rifle shot" approach in antigen screening. It was recognized, at the time, that this approach carried a "greater risk of failure than a broader one."[686] In addition, however, the Foundation—as it had with schistosomiasis—funded the development of a cadre of researchers focusing specifically on oncho and related conditions.

Trachoma

Between 1983 and 1999, the EMCF invested $21.8 million in trachoma research. EMCF's strategy for trachoma was "heavily guided by the staff's experience" with schistosomiasis. This enabled the Foundation to employ lessons learned in designing and carrying out this new research. As noted above, for example, EMCF employed a far more active communications strategy this time around, funding the creation and distribution of publications describing trachoma, its risks, and what could be done to prevent it. In December 1996, the EMCF and other interested organizations gathered to form the WHO Alliance for the Global Elimination of Trachoma. The group adopted a WHO-proposed strategy for treating trachoma. That strategy— SAFE (**S**urgery, **A**ntibiotics, **F**ace-Washing, **E**nvironment)—targeted individual communities, where it has been seen as tremendously successful. The groundwork for this development had been laid by a number of actors. Among these was the Clark Foundation, which "had earlier supported risk factor studies" to establish and field test the efficacy of each of these four measures.[687]

Originally, the Foundation worked on epidemiology and control of the disease. In particular, EMCF funded studies to demonstrate that a Pfizer drug, Zithromax, was effective in treating trachoma—far more effective, in fact, than the existing antibiotic ointment remedy.[688] The Foundation, with its own resources and with support from the National Institutes of Health, collaborated with Pfizer, stimulating the company's interest in trachoma.[689] Noting the positive impact that Merck's drug donations had had on onchocerciasis (see next page), the Foundation worked to convince Pfizer to donate Zithromax for the treatment of trachoma.[690] A 1992 Program Update explained that EMCF hoped "to capture Pfizer's interest and good will and [capacity for] humanitarian benefit. . . ."[691]

By 1994, the EMC staff had concluded that an independent research center, supported by donations from private funders, could most effectively navigate the various hurdles impeding the eradication of trachoma. Such an institution would also become the primary locus of a critical mass of trachoma research that would be more likely to sustain itself without major support from the Edna McConnell Clark Foundation. To that end, the EMCF moved away from epidemiology and control, and, instead, began to focus on attracting new funders and drawing attention to the cause.[692]

Outcomes.

Schistosomiasis

The Edna McConnell Clark Foundation provided one-third of all schisto-somiasis research funding between '74 and '94. While the Foundation did increase scientific and governmental engagement with the disease, it did not achieve its primary goal of developing a vaccine, despite twenty years of involvement. Nonetheless, it laid the ground for future schisto research, such as that now being funded by the Gates Foundation.

Onchocerciasis

The EMCF recognizes that its "tight rifle approach" to oncho research carried several high opportunity costs. One of these was that it led the Foundation to decline to collaborate with Merck in distributing that company's oncho treatment, Mectizan. "In 1987, a major treatment breakthrough occurred when Merck decided to donate . . . Mectizan, which made it possible to treat onchocerciasis safely, effectively and with a single dose."[693] The Foundation's efforts to develop a vaccine did not ultimately prove successful, and in 1994, the Foundation decided to shift its oncho research "to support for program facilitation rather than direct research. . . ."[694] In 1998, the Foundation gave out its last oncho grants.

The Foundation felt that the increased number of oncho researchers, the "rich publication legacy,"[695] and the forward movement in the direction of a vaccine (at some point in the future) were positive outcomes. Just as significantly, the Foundation did leave behind some self-sufficient R & D infrastructure—probably more so than with schistosomiasis. The European Union, for example, has committed funds to oncho research, as have several other international organizations.

Trachoma

In 1998, the Clark Foundation partnered with Pfizer to found the International Trachoma Initiative, an independent organization dedicated to advancing the SAFE strategy in five countries, and, in particular, to forming partnerships among international agencies, governmental and non-governmental organizations. ITI has expanded its operation steadily, and is now active in sixteen African countries. Furthermore, its success has attracted new funders, including the Gates, Rockefeller, and Starr Foundations. Pfizer has contributed some $266 million to the Initiative, which is on its way to self-sufficiency.[696]

Impact. Throughout the 1970s, '80s, and '90s, the Edna McConnell Clark Foundation—in an effort to eradicate schistosomiasis, onchocerciasis, and trachoma—provided major research and development support. During these years the Foundation was the dominant funder of efforts to prevent and control these diseases. EMCF collaborated extensively with the National Institute of Allergy and Infectious Diseases (a division of NIH) and the World Health Organization, but the Foundation's own appropriations for this work were always at least twice those of the WHO. A significant body of research was produced, a cadre of scientists was recruited to the field, and progress toward vaccines was advanced.

However, the Foundation did not meet its primary goal in either schisto or oncho research: the development of a vaccine. Inspired by advances like the Salk vaccine for polio, the Foundation underestimated the difficulty of developing a vaccine. As Dr. Joseph Cook, who worked on the schistosomiasis program, commented, "[w]e had very definite goals and expectations to do certain things by a certain time. Not all were successful. . . . Immunologists would tell us that a vaccine was about five years away. The problem was, they told us that every five years."[697] It seems likely that, at times, the narrow focus on vaccine development caused the Foundation to miss other opportunities along the way.

To its credit, however, EMCF learned from past mistakes and continually refined its strategy. And in the case of trachoma research, the Foundation adjusted its focus away from vaccine research when it realized that it could make more of an impact working with Pfizer and the WHO to eliminate trachoma. The SAFE strategy has proven highly effective. And while no one organization can take full credit for its development, EMCF was certainly a lead contributor.[698] And the ITI—which EMCF spun off as an independent entity when the Foundation adopted a new strategic focus on Youth Development—has unquestionably been effective in implementing SAFE. Less than three years after the ITI got involved in Morocco, for example, that nation's rate of trachoma infection had fallen from 28 percent of the population to 6.5 percent. The goal laid out at the WHO conference in 1996 was to eliminate trachoma completely by 2020. Currently, the ITI is on track to succeed ahead of schedule. The lessons learned by the EMCF in its first two decades of tropical disease research appear to be paying off mightily. And with schistosomiasis and onchocerciasis, the research and training supported by the Edna McConnell Clark Foundation have paved the road for the efforts still underway to find similarly effective solutions.

Case 45

MANPOWER DEMONSTRATION RESEARCH CORPORATION

Ford Foundation, 1974

SCOTT KOHLER

Background. The Great Society reforms of the 1960s tackled such social ills as poverty and homelessness head on. In so doing, President Lyndon Johnson's programs strengthened dramatically the social safety net in the United States, but their efficacy was difficult to establish. Liberals tended to exaggerate their usefulness, while conservatives derided them as reckless giveaways that caused more harm than good. In 1974, the Ford Foundation, in partnership with six government agencies, created an intermediary institution intended to enhance social innovation in the U.S. by designing experiments, and, more importantly, measuring and documenting meticulously the results achieved by new efforts to improve the lot of the American underclass.

Strategy. The Manpower Demonstration Research Corporation (MDRC) would use foundation as well as government dollars to test new social assistance programs. One of the earliest of these was, for example, an expansion of the promising Wildcat project of the Vera Institute of Justice, another Ford creation, and the subject of a separate case study in this volume. Wildcat was a training program that sought to rehabilitate former drug offenders into the workforce. Its results over a two-year period in New York City had shown potential, and MDRC evaluated it in thirteen different communities around the nation. Using sophisticated measurement techniques, MDRC was to document whether the program was really scalable, or whether it was just another entitlement program into which the government could sink tax dollars. Similarly, MDRC in the early 1980s conducted a major study of the Carter administration's $240 million Youth Incentive Entitlement Project, a government-subsidized job creation pilot program. The value added by MDRC was in the evaluation and documentation of impact. MDRC also tested out its own demonstrations, such as a project in 1984 working with recent high school dropouts to encourage them to continue their education. The program employed two different strategies at four sites, in an attempt "to find out which model [worked] more effectively with hard-to-reach youth."[699] The Ford Foundation provided ongoing financial and technical support to MDRC, both for general operating expenses and specific initiatives.

Outcomes. With this investment, MDRC was able to leverage major support from federal, state, and local governments. The U.S. Department of Housing and Urban Development, for instance, committed $20.2 million in 1979 "for [the] development of tenant managed public housing in response to a $600,000 commitment by the Ford Foundation.[700] As the federal government shifted much of the impetus for public assistance to the states in the early 1980s, more and more states created site-specific welfare to work projects with the help of MDRC. In 1982, for example, the Ford Foundation gave the Corporation over $2 million for the purpose of conducting such demonstrations.

These experiments did not all work as their proponents had intended. By 1980, it was apparent that the National Supported Work Demonstration project, which had been "one of [the] most extensive social experiments ever conducted in the U.S.," had shown only "limited success."[701] But MDRC could establish its credibility to point out worthy social investments only if it was also able to discredit flawed attempts. By introducing controlled, scientific data collection into social relief and reform efforts, MDRC helped the good programs to stand out all the more clearly. Indeed, the effective programs have been aided by MDRC's commitment to spreading the knowledge it gathers to the public and to relevant policymakers.[702] The Family Support Act of 1988 passed Congress on the strength of MDRC's "evaluations of the state efforts."[703]

The range of projects MDRC has pioneered or studied in its thirty-year history is too great for all to be considered here. It continues to apply rigorous evaluation techniques to innovative programs at the local, state, and federal level. Some half million people have participated directly in MDRC research over the years. The Ford Foundation continues to support its creation, and many other foundations have joined in. Today, MDRC has an annual budget of approximately $32 million, about 39 percent of which comes from foundations and corporations.

Impact. Over seventy foundations have given funds to MDRC. But it would never have come into being without the Ford Foundation, which recognizes that its support of the Corporation has been well invested. The development of the Manpower Demonstration Research Corporation is an example of Ford creating an institution from the ground up, with both core and project support, followed up by endowment support to secure the institution's future. According to Susan Berresford, the Foundation's president, "[s]ometimes we are privileged to be part of something that succeeds beyond our wildest dreams. MDRC, a widely respected and effective social policy research organization, is one of these special success stories."[704]

Case 46

CONSERVATIVE LEGAL ADVOCACY

John M. Olin Foundation, 1975

STEVEN SCHINDLER

Background. The John M. Olin Foundation, beginning with its emergence in 1973 as a major contributor on the philanthropic scene, was perhaps the premier philanthropic institution supporting conservative causes during its existence. Its founder, John M. Olin, built his fortune by growing a munitions firm his father started into a large chemical corporation. In the 1970s, when the Foundation transformed from a vehicle for personal giving into a philanthropic institution, Olin was deeply concerned about the future of the capitalist system; he wanted his foundation to counter what he perceived as a wave of political sentiment against American capitalism fueled substantially by liberal philanthropies. Olin found in like-minded Treasury Secretary William Simon someone to lead the charge as president of the Olin Foundation.

Simon understood that the Foundation would be most effective by funding the development of conservative ideas, by supporting what he called a "counterintellegentsia" of conservative-minded scholars whose influence would grow out of their ideas. Consistent with that approach, the Foundation funded scholarship favoring "limited government, individual responsibility, and free society."

Strategy. The Olin Foundation was particularly concerned with the direction of legal education. The Foundation was fearful that liberals controlled most law schools and directed the brightest students toward careers supporting liberal ideas in public interest law firms.[705] One of the Foundation's early grantees, the Institute for Educational Affairs, was recruited to help identify high impact conservative projects; it agreed with this assessment.

Understanding the direct concerns of the Foundation in the field of law, the Institute recognized early promise in a group of conservative law students in the early 1980s. These students were acutely aware of their minority status as conservatives at elite law schools, particularly after realizing that so few of their colleagues had supported Ronald Reagan in 1980.[706] Despite the increasing success of the conservative law and economics movement, a movement with substantial financial support from the Foundation, these students felt more could be done to give conservative perspectives on legal and political issues a more prominent platform in law schools. In particular, the group wanted to bring to their law schools leaders of conservative thought to engage in dialogue on conservative issues, which they thought were woefully underrepresented. Early members of the group, which eventually formed as the Federalist Society, included Spencer Abraham, future senator and secretary of energy, and David McIntosh, future member of the U.S. House of Representatives.[707] The Foundation made grants to sponsor the Society's first major event, a conference, which helped to jump start the organization's visibility and recruitment capabilities.[708]

Over the next two decades, the Olin Foundation contributed more than $2 million to the Federalist Society. The Society now counts among its members more than 5,000 law students at approximately 180 law schools and more than 20,000 practicing attorneys.[709] The Society's longtime executive director, Eugene B. Meyer, suggests that the Federalist Society might not exist had it not been for Olin's early, sustained support.[710]

In addition to supporting dialogue on conservative policy through the Federalist Society, Olin provided support for organizations that litigate on behalf of conservative causes in the same manner adopted by the public interest law firm grantees of the Ford Foundation. For example, the Olin Foundation has contributed over $2 million to the Washington Legal Foundation, $1.3 million to the Center for Individual Rights (CIR), and $1 million to support the Pacific Legal Foundation.[711] While these organizations have played an important role supporting conservative causes through litigation, they also serve as employers that enable intelligent, conservative-minded law students to direct their legal educations to advance conservative ideas and policies.

Impact. The Federalist Society's impact has stretched beyond the imagination of its early donors. Some credit the Society with effectively counterbalancing what the Federalist Society calls a shift to the left of the American Bar Association. In particular, many say the Federalist Society enabled the Bush administration to cease the traditional practice of asking the ABA for evaluations of judicial nominees, a practice many conservatives considered detrimental to the confirmation of conservative judges.[712] Furthermore, the Society has enabled conservative law students to develop networks that are maintained as they attain increasing public responsibilities in their careers. Three of President George W. Bush's cabinet members in his first term, as well as Bush's solicitor general and staff members in the White House counsel's office, were members of the Federalist Society. In addition, members of the Federalist Society are reported to have played central roles on President Bush's committee to propose nominees for judicial appointments.[713] The Federalist Society's importance in advancing conservative ideas in the law became a matter of common understanding during the confirmation process of

Chief Justice John Roberts; the appearance of his name on a leadership roster for the Society was a point of contention between Democratic senators and the White House.[714]

Olin's public interest law organization grantees have also enjoyed tremendous success. The Washington Legal Foundation has successfully opposed various government regulations, particularly regulations proposed by the FDA that the WLF believes are overreaching.[715] CIR has successfully litigated on behalf of professors accused of sexual harassment, for religious organizations seeking to participate in publicly funded activity, for constitutional limits on federal legislation of gender violence, and against racial preferences in higher education.[716] The Pacific Legal Foundation has been an ardent advocate for private property rights and limited government in the courts as well as the media.[717]

Case 47

Grameen Bank

Ford Foundation, 1976

Scott Kohler

Background. When Bangladesh gained its independence from Pakistan in 1971, Secretary of State Henry Kissinger called it "an international basket case."[718] With a weak economy, overcrowded cities, and a high exposure to catastrophic weather, Bangladesh has remained one of the least developed countries (LDCs) in the world, and has received more than $30 billion in international assistance over the past three decades.[719] However, Bangladesh is also the birthplace of the Grameen Bank, one of the great success stories in third world development.

Strategy. The Grameen Bank was created by Professor Muhammad Yunus, a Bangladeshi economics professor who, during the famine of 1974, felt compelled to reach out to the Bangladeshi poor in an effort to understand why they were unable to achieve economic success. Over the next two years, Professor Yunus studied the poor, landless underclass of Jobra, a village near his home in Chittagong. He concluded that the poor were poor not because they were inherently unable to support themselves, but rather because they lacked access to capital, a structural flaw that could be remedied. Yunus began by making small loans, of about $25 each, to forty-three villagers in Jobra. His largesse soon grew into the world's first experiment in microfinance.

Using these small amounts of money, Yunus' borrowers were able to generate a steady stream of income, with which they not only paid off their debts but also improved the economic lot of their families.

Between 1976 and 1979, these micro-loans "successfully changed the lives of around 500 borrowers."[720] Working at first with only his graduate economics students, then later through the branch offices of several state-run banks, Yunus eventually decided to quit his academic post and incorporate the Grameen (meaning "rural" or "countryside") Bank in 1983. The bank makes small loans (averaging about $376[721]) to clients, who are required to be members of a five-person team of borrowers. Teams are responsible for encouraging, as well as helping, each other to repay loans. A loan is made first to one member of the group. If the member successfully repays it, a loan is made to someone else in the group. So each borrower's access to credit is dependent upon the team's repayment of all loans made. This "peer group lending" uses a mixture of peer pressure and peer support to achieve a rate of repayment significantly higher than that enjoyed by even the most successful American banks.[722] Groups of five are organized into local centres, which are associations of eight-to-ten groups that act as a regional support net. Committed to transparency in a nation that has been plagued by corruption, the Grameen Bank makes all its loans publicly at the centre meetings.[723] In addition, Grameen required its borrowers to pledge to maintain certain social principles, such as educating female children, not giving dowry, and helping to build schools in their communities. As a result, the bank achieves leverage beyond the scope of its financial benefits.

The loans must be used to generate income. Borrowers use the loans to become self-employed, whether by purchasing dairy cows, honey bees, or bamboo to make furniture that can be sold.[724]

To finance its early lending,[725] the Grameen Bank received grants and loans (market rate and concessionary) from banks (in Bangladesh and around the world) governments (such as those of Bangladesh and Canada), international aid agencies (like the International Fund for Agricultural Development), and foundations.[726] Most notable among the latter group has been the Ford Foundation, which supported Yunus from his earliest efforts, while he was still an economics professor studying the causes of poverty in rural Bangladesh. In the mid-1970s, the Foundation gave Professor Yunus a $12,000 grant for his poverty research, which was then followed up by consistent support.[727] The Foundation has contributed to the Bank's resources for lending, and, according to Yunus, an early $800,000 grant from Ford was the critical guarantee fund that enabled him to attract the support of skeptical commercial banks.[728]

Outcomes. The Grameen Bank has grown dramatically, and its results have been extraordinary. The Grameen Bank now turns a profit and has deposits worth $324 million.[729] Since its inception, the bank has made over $4.57 billion in loans. Its rate of recovery is 98.85 percent, despite the fact that the Grameen Bank refuses to make loans to anyone except the poorest members of Bangladeshi society. The bank now has over 4 million members (clients) in 48,000 villages serviced by over 1,300 Grameen branch offices.[730] The Bank also makes housing loans that have enabled the Bangladeshi poor to construct over 600,000 new homes. The Grameen Bank has also empowered women in a society where they have traditionally been subservient to men. Ninety-five percent of all borrowers from the Grameen Bank are women. This is no accident. Professor Yunus realized early on that women are more likely to repay a first-time loan than men, and that female borrowers were far more likely than male to use the profits generated from a loan to support and uplift their families, rather than on personal consumption. So the Bank has also been an engine of social change.[731]

Impact. Microfinance was a true innovation. Its success flies in the face of traditional banking theory, which holds that destitute residents of third-world villages, often lacking any property of their own at all, do not make reliable borrowers. And the methods of the Grameen Bank have been emulated around the world. According to the United Nations, some 67 million people had access to micro-credit in 2003.[732] Institutions modeled after the Grameen Bank have sprung up in seventy countries; there are over 500 such organizations in the United States alone![733] The Ford Foundation has supported the spread of the Grameen model. In the late 1980s, the Foundation funded an exchange program between American development workers and the Bank.[734] According to Anwarul K. Chowdhury, the United Nations Under-Secretary-General and High Representative for the Least Developed Countries, "[m]icrocredit is an inducer, a catalyst for economic activity of the poor people" and leads "to the empowerment of women. . . ."[735]

The tremendous impact of Professor Yunus's foundation-supported experiment was recognized in October 2006 by the Norwegian Nobel Committee, which awarded the 2006 Nobel Peace Prize jointly to Yunus and the Grameen Bank. Announcing its decision, the Nobel Committee observed that, not so long ago, "[l]oans to poor people without any financial security had appeared to be an impossible idea."[736] Thanks to Yunus and Grameen, they no longer do. As the Nobel Committee recognized:

> Every single individual on earth has both the potential and the right to live a decent life. Across cultures and civilizations, Yunus and Grameen Bank have shown that even the poorest of the poor can work to bring about their own development.[737]

Case 48

MONTEREY BAY AQUARIUM AND RESEARCH INSTITUTE

David and Lucile Packard Foundation, 1977

SCOTT KOHLER

Background. The Monterey Bay Aquarium was first dreamed up one night by four young marine biologists who were concerned that increasing numbers of tourists would soon threaten the northern California bay, a treasure chest of marine biodiversity. The group, which soon grew to include a fifth member, thought that "a modest aquarium" might work as an anchor for research and protection efforts in the region. Their idea got a lot more serious when two of the five—Julie and Nancy Packard—took the idea to their father David, the billionaire electronics pioneer who, with his business partner Bill Hewlett, had established Silicon Valley as the epicenter of the twentieth century technology boom. David Packard, who had grown up fishing the waters of Monterey Bay, challenged his daughters to be practical, but also to think big.[738] A feasibility study was commissioned, and when the Packard Foundation agreed to fund the aquarium's construction, the project's cost was estimated to be $7 million.[739]

Strategy. In fact, the aquarium cost $54 million over seven years. The Packard Foundation paid all of this, and David Packard himself was deeply involved in designing the aquarium. He worked with architects and exhibit specialists, and designed the Aquarium's state-of-the-art wave machines personally.[740] When it opened in October 1984, the Monterey Bay Aquarium was the largest in the nation, and began to quickly attract hundreds of thousands of visitors.

From the start, "the Aquarium sought to apply the most current technology to further its purpose."[741] More than a tourist attraction, it housed extensive research, both of the Monterey Bay ecosystem and the oceans beyond. Increasingly interested in marine research, Packard in 1986 convened a blue-ribbon panel of oceanographers to consider the development of a full-scale research institute. The panel recommended that the new institution should fill "a mostly vacant niche of importance." In 1987, the Monterey Bay Aquarium Research Institute (MBARI) was incorporated, independently of the Aquarium, "with a broad mandate for cutting-edge research and development in oceanography." In contrast to traditional marine science, which seeks to answer questions to the best ability of the available technologies, the MBARI challenges scientists to formulate the questions, its engineers to make them answerable, and its operations staff to carry out the experimentation. The Institute is also committed to disseminating widely the findings of its research.[742] Again the Packard Foundation bore all the costs, and David Packard was determined that the traditional constraints of foundation support would not impede scientific progress. He told Bruce Robison, the Institute's former director, "I don't want you to waste your time writing grant proposals. I want you to do science and take risks."[743]

Outcomes. Today the Monterey Bay Aquarium draws almost 2 million visitors per year.[744] It is supported entirely by admissions fees, visitor donations, and the revenues of its gift shop and restaurant.[745] The MBARI now has assets of more than $120 million.[746] Its annual budget of $40 million is still supported largely by the Foundation,[747] helping to make MBARI "one of only two privately funded oceanographic research centers in the country. . . ."[748] By the year 2000, MBARI's four submersible research vessels had already carried out a total of more than 4,000 dives, discovering a number of previously unknown marine species along the way.[749] The Institute conducts a range of research projects, from a multi-year study of variations in coastal surface waters to investigations of the biological consequences of deep-sea geologic processes, such as underwater volcanic eruptions and tectonic movements.

Impact. In creating and continuing to support the Monterey Bay Aquarium and Research Institute, the Packard Foundation has performed two distinct services. It has given to the public a huge and state of the art attraction that, in addition to its recreational value, is a center of marine education. And the Research Institute—one of the world's premier centers for the study of the oceans and marine life—serves as a hub of cutting-edge science, exploring the seas for discovery's own sake, and adding volumes to human understanding of those vast regions of our planet which lie underwater. As federal funding for basic research in the field has declined, MBARI's mission has become all the more important. And thanks to the support of the Packard Foundation, it is able to carry out an ambitious research agenda, charting for human understanding places, species, and phenomena that would otherwise go unexplored.

Case 49

HUMAN RIGHTS AND THE INTERNATIONAL CRIMINAL COURT

John D. and Catherine T. MacArthur Foundation, Open Society Institute, and Ford Foundation, 1978

SCOTT KOHLER

Background. The idea of a permanent judicial body to punish the worst offenses of international law—genocide, war crimes, and crimes against humanity—harks back at least to the late nineteeth century, when Gustav Moynier, one of the founders of the International Committee of the Red Cross, proposed such an institution in the aftermath of the Franco-Prussian War.[750] More than seventy years later, the Nuremberg trials set a precedent that men, not abstract polities, commit atrocities. "Never Again" was the promise of Nuremberg, but that promise was soon lost in the realities of the Cold War. It was not until the mid-1990s that the idea of a permanent international court would gain real traction. That it finally did so is owing to a great many factors. Among the most important of these was a vigorous assault on the status quo of global diplomacy spearheaded by a coalition of NGOs. Foundations played an important role in supporting the work of this movement to build a constituency for universally enforceable international law.

In fact, the creation of the International Criminal Court is the result of a larger worldwide effort, stretching back at least sixty years, to codify and maintain a set of human rights to which even the Earth's most destitute and grief-stricken peoples are entitled. Supported largely in the civic sector, the human rights movement has been growing stronger at least since 1948, when the United Nations General Assembly passed the Universal Declaration of Human Rights. And with the creation, first, of several ad hoc international tribunals to investigate and adjudicate allegations of human rights abuses in the former Yugoslavia, in Rwanda, and elsewhere, and, more recently, of the International Criminal Court, the human rights movement is stronger than ever. Among this movement's oldest, most consistent supporters have been a number of private foundations. In this case study, three major philanthropies—the MacArthur and Ford Foundations and the Open Society Institute—are examined. These three are the largest foundation supporters of human rights support, and each has played an important role in bringing human rights monitoring and enforcement along to where they are today.

Strategy.

John D. and Catherine T. MacArthur Foundation

The MacArthur Foundation is a major funder of human rights work around the globe. Its grants have not only supported the development of the field as a whole, but have also played a significant part in a critical chapter in the history of human rights—the creation of the International Criminal Court. The Foundation's work in the field began in 1978 with a $50,000 grant to Amnesty International.[751] As the field of human rights protection has grown, so too has MacArthur's support of it. The Foundation has made grants to over 350 human rights organizations. In 1992, the Foundation initiated a major new focus on the protection of human rights. Since then, the Foundation has given out over $38 million. A very high proportion of the Foundation's grants to these organizations has been for general operating support "to allow for flexibility to address pressing issues, expand geographical reach, and move to new fields of inquiry."[752]

The Foundation has also leveraged significant impact from its support of the International Criminal Court. Human Rights Watch—to which the Foundation has given over $22 million over the last twenty-five years—as well as other MacArthur grantees, have been major supporters of the ICC, thanks, in part, to programmatic and general support from MacArthur. The Foundation also made grants to the World Federalist Movement[753] and other organizations central to the Coalition for the International Criminal Court, the network of NGOs that worked to bring about the Court. This money helped the coalition prepare for and execute a radical strategy that culminated, in the summer of 1998, at the Rome Conference where a draft statute for the ICC was adopted. In what David Davenport, a fellow at the Hoover Institute, calls "New Diplomacy," the coalition disregarded the existing work of the U.N. International Law Commission toward the development of a world court and used a range of tactics—not least among which was shame[754]—to force the hand of the 148 nations participating in negotiations.[755] Working with a group of like-minded states, the un-elected group of nonprofits controlled the proceedings to keep the draft statute on track, even over the objection of the U.S. delegation.[756]

Open Society Institute

An enormous portion of the Open Society Institute's work relates directly or indirectly to advancing the spread of human rights. The Institute's Justice

Initiative, for example, is an OSI-operated effort that "pursues law reform activities grounded in the protection of human rights. . . ."⁷⁵⁷ The initiative "combines litigation, legal advocacy, technical assistance, and the dissemination of knowledge. . . ." Among a range of activities, the Open Society Justice Initiative has supported the development of the International Criminal Court, and is now working to convince states to ratify the treaty that grew out of the Rome Statute, and to help states considering ratification amend their domestic laws to enable ratification. The Justice Initiative focuses these efforts on countries "not already addressed by existing organizations and where OSI has particular strengths."⁷⁵⁸ In addition to supporting the development of the ICC, the Justice Initiative works extensively with the ad hoc tribunals created by the United Nations to adjudicate the Rwandan genocide and the human rights abuses committed during Sierra Leone's years of strife, and the despotic reign of the Khmer Rouge in Cambodia. The Initiative is deeply involved with these tribunals, offering "advice and recommendations on prosecution, investigation, indictment, brief-writing, trial, and appeal strategies."⁷⁵⁹ The Justice Initiative also collaborates with local NGOs, building cases that may at some point be forwarded to the ICC prosecutor.

Ford Foundation

The Ford Foundation began to focus explicitly on the defense of human rights in the mid-1970s, when it made grants to advance such causes as ending apartheid in South Africa and promoting freedom of expression behind the Iron Curtain. Over the past three decades, human rights support has become a major grant-making area for the Foundation, which, in its human rights work, focuses primarily on the rights of "women, migrants, refugees, marginalized racial and ethnic groups, and international human rights efforts."⁷⁶⁰ In the latter field, the Foundation has funded a wide array of activities, such as the ad-hoc tribunals, the International Criminal Court and rights organizations working within the United States. In 1998, for example, the Foundation made grants to the World Federalist Movement to ensure NGO participation in the Rome Conference.⁷⁶¹ Ford is a sponsor of the Coalition for the International Criminal Court, and has substantial funding—$1.7 million over the last three years, and millions more over a longer period—to the Lawyers Committee for Human Rights, an international NGO committed to encouraging compliance with international human rights standards and strongly supportive of the ICC. As with MacArthur and OSI, it is worth remembering, however, that this is but one part of Ford's tremendous human rights portfolio. Last year, the Foundation made some 200 grants in the field.

Outcomes. The development of international law and human rights enforcement has been dramatic in recent years. The Rome Statute was approved by 120 of the 148 nations at the conference. As of November 2004, ninety-seven countries had ratified the Statute.[762] The threshold for entry into force was only sixty ratifications, so a nascent ICC now exists and is in the process of initiating its first proceedings. The pace of negotiation, adoption, and ratification has been incredibly fast. As at the Conference to Ban Landmines, this "new diplomacy" has shaken up the traditional model of foreign relations, which works in a far more deliberate and secretive manner. The support of a number of NGOs—most, if not all, funded by these three foundations—has been the key. These organizations have not only facilitated discussions before, during, and after the Rome Conference, but have also worked to gather evidence for the first two ICC trials, promulgate judicial standards, and support ratification in the nations party to the Rome Statute.

Impact. Foundations have by no means been the only significant nongovernmental actors in the process. But, by their targeted deployment of funds, and by their long history of building the field, these and other foundations have helped to create an institution that is now the most prominent fixture in the landscape of international law. This case has focused primarily on that story, but the context around it—the growth of the international human rights movement and the strengthening norms of international law—is an even larger development, and one in which foundations have consistently been leaders. Unlike many NGOs, most human rights organizations do not accept government funding. This makes foundations all the more important to their survival. Ford, MacArthur, and the Open Society Institute have given hundreds of millions of dollars, perhaps more, to protect the most basic rights, shared by every person on Earth. By 1988, the Annual Report of the Ford Foundation could rightly note the existence of "a powerful worldwide movement to protect fundamental civil and political liberties and to ensure the social and economic rights of disadvantaged people."[763] Even today, the human rights movement continues to gather steam. As Jonathan Fanton, the MacArthur Foundation's president, has said, "[a]lthough serious human rights abuses persist in many places, the direction of history is clear: There is a worldwide movement to prevent those abuses and bring perpetrators to justice."[764] Although ratification of the International Criminal Court has aroused serious controversy in the United

States, and although the Court's success is still far from assured, the direction to which Fanton alludes is one for which even the most ardent isolationist can be thankful.

Case 50

THE NURSE-FAMILY PARTNERSHIP

Robert Wood Johnson Foundation, 1978

SCOTT KOHLER

Background. Children born to low-income, first-time mothers are at increased risk for a number of problems, including low birth weight, abuse, neglect, and juvenile crime.[765] With this in mind, the Nurse Home Visitation program was conceived by Dr. David Olds, who, in 1978, approached the Robert Wood Johnson Foundation for help in funding a study to determine whether the risks associated with low-income, first-time pregnancies could be mitigated by partnering nurses with at-risk pregnant women. Although Olds was, at the time, "an unknown assistant professor," program officers at the RWJF were "impressed with both the scientific design of the experiment and the fact that the program had sound theoretical underpinnings."[766] The Foundation gave Dr. Olds an initial grant to set up a demonstration project in Elmira, New York.

Strategy. For over twenty-five years, the Robert Wood Johnson Foundation has provided ongoing support to the Nurse Home Visitation program (later renamed the Nurse-Family Partnership). The Foundation has supported research—especially controlled, randomized trials—in order to measure specifically the effectiveness of nurse home visitation. RWJF has also funded the program's replication at sites across the United States.

The Nurse-Family Partnership curriculum is, for the most part, uniform from one site to another.[767] Trained nurses—each with a caseload of no more than twenty-five women—pay weekly or biweekly visits to at-risk expectant mothers.[768] These visits continue for two years after the mother gives birth. Nurses are trained to help new mothers develop parenting skills and to monitor the health of the child.

The Elmira program was followed, in 1990, by a pilot program in Memphis. Because it was situated in a larger, more urban environment, in which external conditions were less subject to control, the Memphis study was intended to simulate more accurately the results—positive and negative—that could be expected in any large-scale implementation of the program.

In 1999, the RWJF contributed $10 million over three years to help spread the nurse home visitation curriculum. This grant helped establish the Prevention Research Center for Family and Child Policy (PRC) at the University of Colorado. Headed by Dr. Olds, the Center helped found the National Center for Children, Families, and Communities, which works to make available the tested and proven model of nurse home visitation to communities around the country. Continuing to refine the program's methods, the PRC also launched, in 1994, a third test site, in Denver.

Outcomes. Nurse-Family Partnership programs are now active in over 150 communities nationwide.[769] The most striking results were shown in a follow-up study of the Elmira project, fifteen years after the mothers had graduated from the program. The study showed:

- A 79 percent reduction in child abuse and neglect from birth to the first child's fifteenth birthday
- A 30-month reduction in welfare dependency by the first child's fifteenth birthday
- A 44 percent reduction in behavioral problems among mothers due to alcohol and/or drug abuse
- A 69 percent reduction in arrests among the mothers over fifteen years following birth of their first child
- A 51 percent reduction in alcohol consumption among adolescents by their fifteenth birthday
- A 54 percent reduction in arrests among adolescents by their fifteenth birthday
- A 56 percent reduction in emergency room visits for injuries and ingestions by child's second birthday[770]

In addition, mothers who participated in the program were significantly less likely to smoke cigarettes while pregnant, thus mitigating the health costs of prenatal smoking.[771] They also had fewer repeat pregnancies.[772]

The beneficial effects of the Memphis and Denver projects have, so far, been smaller than those in Elmira were at the same stage. However, all three studies have shown statistically significant results "on [the program's] targeted outcome domains (women's prenatal health, infant health and development, maternal life-course). . . ."[773]

Government officials have begun to take notice of its success. Hawaii, Oklahoma, and Colorado have each implemented statewide nurse home visitation programs, assisted by Dr. Olds and the RWJF. And in March 2004, a bipartisan group of U.S. Senators co-hosted, along with the RWJF, the first Nurse-Family Partnership National Forum, in Washington, D.C.

Impact. The home visitation model employed by the Nurse-Family Partnership costs about $2,800-$3,200 per family per year.[774] A RAND Corporation study estimates that for every dollar spent, the program yields four dollars of social benefit.[775] So Colorado, for example, which projects its 2008 budget for nurse home visitation at $17 million, could potentially achieve social benefits worth $68 million from that year's investment in the program.

The Nurse-Family Partnership's strong commitment to demonstrating impact has helped it attract additional support. The Partnership has received grants from many sources, including the Packard, Ford, and Grant Foundations, the Commonwealth Fund, the Edna McConnell Clark Foundation, the Carnegie Corporation of New York and the U.S. Departments of Justice and Health and Human Services. In particular, the Robert Wood Johnson Foundation's substantial investment was the seed money that enabled Dr. Olds to develop and refine his methods, and to measure and prove their effectiveness. There are a number of other, less effective home visitation programs aimed at high-risk mothers and children. The Nurse-Family Partnership is unique in its ability to achieve significant impact among geographically and ethnically diverse groups. Its results have been impressive, but even they are eclipsed by the enormous good it may yet achieve as it continues going to scale in the coming years.

Case 51

REVOLUTIONIZING LEGAL DISCOURSE: LAW AND ECONOMICS

John M. Olin Foundation, 1978

STEVEN SCHINDLER

Background. John Olin, founder of the Olin Foundation, accumulated his fortune through the success of a firearm munitions firm that his father started and that he grew into a large chemical corporation. He was a well-known outdoors enthusiast. He was also deeply committed to American capitalism and conservative ideals. [776]

The Olin Foundation was created in 1953, but until 1973, it served primarily as a vehicle for Olin's own personal charitable giving, primarily to a local PBS station, Cornell University (his alma mater), and the Episcopal Church.[777] In 1973, Olin recruited a staff for his foundation and expressed his desire that his fortune be used to help preserve the capitalist economic system which made the accumulation of his fortune possible.[778] The Foundation staff met with other conservative foundation leaders, researched pro-market academic scholarship, and drafted a memo to Olin outlining proposals for pursuing Olin's charge. [779]

Olin's philanthropic approach was influenced significantly by Henry Ford II's resignation from the Ford Foundation Board of Trustees in the 1970s in protest of Foundation activity Ford considered subversive to capitalism. William Simon, Treasury Secretary under Gerald Ford and a neighbor of John Olin, was also influenced by Henry Ford's resignation from the Ford Foundation. Upon his retirement, Simon published a book, *A Time for Truth*, in which he called on corporations and the broader national community to embrace a more laissez-faire economic system.[780] In the book, Simon pledged to convince the business community, particularly business philanthropies, to stop supporting liberal institutions which, as he saw it, were undermining American capitalism. "Most businessmen have been financing their own destruction," Simon stated in a *New York Times* article.[781]

In 1977, Olin recruited Simon to direct his foundation's activities.[782] Simon's strategy was to fund the development of a "counterintelligentsia" trained to combat the assumptions and change the direction of American life by advocating a broad set of guiding conservative principles.[783] The Olin Foundation concentrated its grantmaking in the mid-1970s on supporting "scholarship in the philosophy of a free society and the economics of a free market."[784]

Strategy. The law and economics movement began prior to Olin's involvement; many mark its birth at the University of Chicago in the 1950s, when Aaron Director, an economist, served as a professor at Chicago's law school. Ronald Coase, another University of Chicago economist, is credited for advancing the movement by authoring in 1961 his widely esteemed article "The Problem of Social Cost." Henry Manne, another Chicago alumnus, also played a leading role in incorporating law and economics into corporate law scholarship. Richard Posner, another member of the University of Chicago law school and now chief judge of the Seventh Circuit Court of Appeals, authored what is still considered the bible of law and economics, *Economic Analysis of Law*, in 1973.[785]

Staff members at the Olin Foundation noted that lawyers tend to play influential leadership roles in various segments of society. The Foundation consequently provided substantial funding to shape the intellectual climate in the legal realm to embrace free market insights through the study of economic implications of law.[786] According to the Foundation, law and economics was an accepted paradigm in legal scholarship in the 1970s, but its use was limited. The Foundation perceived an opportunity to spread its adoption in legal scholarship and among current and prospective legal practitioners.[787]

Among its early initiatives in Simon's tenure was the funding of a center of law and economics at the University of Miami as well as centers for economic study of the law at the University of Chicago and U.C.L.A.[788] The Foundation then pursued a strategy of making grants to outstanding law schools (including Harvard, Yale, Chicago, Georgetown, Stanford, USC, Virginia, Michigan, Columbia, Toronto, and Cornell) to establish law and economics programs on those campuses. The Foundation thought, correctly, that other schools would be compelled to follow these leading institutions in adopting law and economics programs. Foundation grants to establish law and economics programs at law schools totaled $50 million.

Later grants established John M. Olin fellowships that went to students in the top quarter of their class in order to provide them with an economic perspective of law. The Foundation also provided grants to universities to establish fellowships both for junior faculty members, who had not yet received tenure or established themselves as prominent scholars, as well as endowed chairs for senior scholars.[789]

Perhaps most controversially, the Foundation has supported a program of the Law and Economics Center at George Mason University to educate current members of the bench on law and economics through weeklong institutes and other seminars. The Foundation's giving to the LEC totaled more than $2 million. By 2002, the John M. Olin Foundation had given more than $68 million to support the law and economics movement.

Impact. As a measure of the success of the movement, the Foundation notes that numerous early advocates of law and economics have become prestigious members of the bench, including Robert Bork, Stephen Breyer, Guido Calabresi, Frank Easterbrook, Richard Posner, and Antonin Scalia.[790] An article in the ABA Journal considering the career of Richard Posner, widely considered something of a godfather of the law and economics movement, assesses the impact of the movement:

> Although criticism of law and economics has been abundant, most of it contending that it is inhumane to apply a cost-benefit analysis to conflicts and

issues of human behavior, particularly when it leaves out the role of human emotion, the approach has become entrenched in both academia and jurisprudence.

By 2002, more than 600 federal judges had participated in the LEC institutes supported by the Olin Foundation. The LEC survived legislative attempts by Senators Russ Feingold and John Kerry in 2000 to prevent it from providing free seminars to judges, but, in part because of the lobbying support of numerous federal judges, including Chief Justice William Rehnquist, the legislation did not pass. Associate Justice Ruth Bader Ginsburg, in fact, sent a letter of appreciation for the work the center had done in "lifting the veil on regression analysis" for members of the bench.[791] Law and economics has become an analytical tool that increasingly appears in judicial opinions.

Perhaps most significantly, law and economics have served as tools that support conservative ideals of limited government and regulation and that political opponents have failed to counter. Some consider the law and economics movement as one of a few factors that have fostered the rise of conservative politics in the United States.[792]

Case 52

LOCAL INITIATIVES SUPPORT CORPORATION (LISC)

Ford Foundation, 1979

SCOTT KOHLER

Background. As long as there have been cities, there have been slums. High crime rates, unsanitary conditions, and inadequate housing have been characteristics shared for centuries by underprivileged communities around the world. In the United States, urban decay became particularly acute in the years following the end of World War II, as upper- and middle-class whites fled the inner cities in favor of burgeoning suburbs. In dozens of cities, urban neighborhoods were left with predominantly black populations. Often marked by poverty, many such neighborhoods were beset by gang violence and a pervasive lack of opportunity. As early as the late 1940s, government officials at every level had come to recognize deteriorating communities as a major problem.

Efforts to improve conditions have, however, been disappointing. Too often, in the '50s, '60s, and '70s, many politicians' idea of community revitalization was to uproot working class communities to make way for glittering development projects that did more to enrich real estate interests than the urban poor. And as programs like Model Cities and the War on Poverty foundered, it became apparent that "Three decades of federal programs had done little to rescue the slum."[793]

In the 1960s, two projects, in particular, helped the Ford Foundation develop a reputation for involvement in the community development movement. The first was the foundation's Gray Area program, which contributed directly to the evolution of the community development corporation (CDC), which, in turn, would become one of the primary vehicles of community renewal in the ensuing decades.[794] The second was the Bedford-Stuyvesant Restoration project, which was led by Ford and Robert Kennedy, and aimed to revitalize a six-square-mile area of Brooklyn.

It was not until 1980, however, that the Ford Foundation would make its most significant contribution to-date to the fight against community decay. As it became apparent that the incoming Reagan administration planned to "drastically cut back the amount of money the federal government provided for social services and urban programs,"[795] Ford, as well as other institutions active in community development efforts, became worried about the fate of that often-frustrated movement. Alexander Von Hoffman, of Harvard's Joint Center for Housing Studies, argues, in his book *House by House, Block by Block: The Rebirth of America's Urban Neighborhoods*, that churches, foundations, and even civic minded for-profit corporations, were "spurred to some extent by Reagan's budget cutbacks" to find new ways to support embattled community development groups.

Strategy. The idea for the Local Initiatives Support Corporation (LISC) was born in 1979, when a group of Ford Foundation trustees and officials visited community development projects in Baltimore. On their way back to New York, James Ellis, a Foundation trustee, "asked [Foundation vice president] Mitchell Sviridoff what he would do if he had $25 million to spend on helping declining cities." Sviridoff responded with an idea that Franklin Thomas, another of the Foundation's trustees, had recently suggested: identify competent leaders in 50 to 100 communities around the nation and give them as much money and support as possible.[796]

In a way, it was an unremarkable idea. After all, giving money and support to worthy grantees is a large part of what foundations have always done. But Sviridoff and Thomas understood that in the case of community development, there were a host of people, residents of deteriorating neighborhoods, who were already passionate about turning things around. At the same time, there was an enormous amount of money available, from organizations cutting across all sectors of American society, for the same purpose. What needed to be done was to connect the two, and, in so doing, to enable the most innovative and capable community leaders to more effectively pursue their goals. For years, private financial institutions had refused to fund community development activities. The reason they gave for this unwillingness was that they could not reliably ascertain the credit-worthiness of borrowers in the field. Sviridoff perceived that the Ford Foundation could fill a critical niche by determining which would-be borrowers for community development could be relied upon to repay their loans.

The Ford Foundation understood that the for-profit sector could be a major resource in community development efforts. So, the following year, it joined with six corporations to found the Local Initiatives Support Corporation.[797] LISC was to be an intermediate organization, "[helping] community organizations attract new private and public support for their work. . . ."[798] Ford's initial contribution to LISC was $4.75 million to match the combined donations of its six partners. In addition, Mitchell Sviridoff left the Foundation to serve as LISC's first president. LISC was a completely new and autonomous organization. It had its own governing board, staff, and headquarters in New York. It has continued to receive support from the Ford Foundation, but today it is also supported by a multitude of other foundations, for-profit companies, and public agencies at all levels of government.

Active in both rural and urban areas, the Local Initiatives Support Corporation employs a three part strategy. First, LISC uses its own resources to provide CDCs with access to capital. It does this by offering grants and low-interest loans. Second, LISC acts as a go-between for the various stakeholders in local communities. This means collaborating with concerned community leaders, CDCs, local government, foundations, and businesses. LISC gives community organizations access to the pools of funding available through the latter three institutions. Third, LISC works to create a climate in government that is favorable to the community development industry. It lobbies Congress, for example, on behalf of legislation that supports rural and urban renewal.[799]

LISC does not try to solve the problems of every community in which it is involved. Rather, it marshals resources on behalf of those who would uplift their own communities, allowing local leaders and groups to test out their ideas. As Mitchell Sviridoff explained in 1984, LISC is "a finder for good social investments."[800] This is a nimble, case-specific approach. It keeps LISC from over-generalizing the problems faced by communities, and it leaves autonomy in the hands of leaders on the front lines. LISC itself is a national organization, but each of its projects is coordinated by a Local Advisory

Committee (LAC), composed of volunteers from local foundations corporations, and government. According to Robert Rubin and Michael Rubinger, the current board chairman and president of LISC, respectively, the LACs "bring local perspective, insight, and direction to a national model."[801] This structure also enables LISC to be active nationwide, while limiting its administrative costs to less than 14 percent of its total budget.

From the outset, the Ford Foundation saw the big picture. No one group or sector would, by itself, be able to make a significant dent in the spread of community deterioration. What was needed was a multi-sector collaboration, and so Ford set up LISC to remove barriers to collective action. As its predictions of credit-worthiness were borne out, LISC developed credibility among private lenders and government agencies. With their primary objection to investment in community development removed, financial institutions and, most importantly, the federal government, have become more and more willing to fund such efforts. And as an operating nonprofit, LISC is also able to do something the Ford Foundation could not. Ford, a private foundation, is precluded, by the Internal Revenue Code, from engaging in the sort of public advocacy and lobbying that is one of LISC's three primary tactics.

Outcomes. Within a year of its founding, LISC was engaged in forty ventures in eighteen cities. It was already working with twenty-five major corporate funders, with another twenty-five, in Sviridoff's words, "waiting on the back burner."[802] Three years after that, LISC had received more than $60 million in corporation and foundation support, over $16 million of it from the Ford Foundation.[803] And, by 1986, LISC had made 700 grants or loans to over 400 community organizations, totaling $43 million. And once LISC had turned the spigot, private and public funds poured in. So the real impact of this money was that it had served as the leverage that allowed these receiving organizations, with LISC's assistance, to attract more than $360 million from other funders. This was "more than four times what it had expected to achieve by 1986."[804] It was enough that LISC was "already the country's largest nonprofit community development organization."[805] Even though it had been joined by many partners, the Ford Foundation continued vigorously to support its brain child. In 1986, for example, the foundation committed $7.1 million to enable LISC to continue taking its model to scale. LISC has continued to grow rapidly, as any visitor to its website will readily perceive:

> Since 1980, LISC has marshaled more than $5.7 billion from 3,100 investors, lenders, and donors. In over 300 urban and rural communities nationwide,

LISC has helped 2,400 CDCs build or rehabilitate more than 147,000 affordable homes and almost 22 million square feet of retail, community, and educational space totaling almost $13 billion in development. As a result, hundreds of thousands of people have better lives and brighter futures.[806]

Impact. These claims are not mere hype. The measurable impacts, directly attributable to the Local Initiatives Support Corporation, total many billions of dollars. As for the latter part of LISC's self-assessment, its full impact is impossible to quantify. Officials on the front lines of the battle to rebuild decaying communities around the country have praised LISC for its role in the fight. In 1986, Harold Washington, who was then the mayor of Chicago, described LISC as "a shot of adrenalin."[807] On the same day, Mayor Wilson Goode of Philadelphia expanded on this, declaring, "What LISC has done has brought forth new resources, created hundreds of jobs and made real impact. . . ." And in the eighteen years since then, LISC has only expanded its reach and deepened its involvement.

It has not been alone in the effort. Nor could it function if it were. The entire objective of LISC is to enable others more effectively to pursue their visions of community development. It has collaborated with similar organizations, such as the Enterprise Foundation, often to great effect. And LISC has, from the start, been animated by an understanding that its role is to harness the resources and expertise of America's multi-sector society in the service of local inspiration.

It is now clear, however, that LISC has been, and continues to be, a major participant in the revitalization and development of literally thousands of urban and rural communities across the country. As Von Hoffman writes, "[i]n the waning years of the twentieth century, [many] developments—the non-profit community groups, the new wave of immigration, and gentrification—had converged. And lo and behold, the neighborhoods of the inner cities at last began to show visible improvements—in crime statistics, employment rolls, and physical appearance."[808] Regardless of its many other contributions to this renewal, the Ford Foundation deserves credit for imagining, nurturing, and bringing to fruition an organization that has amplified the voices of progressive leaders, enabling hundreds, if not thousands, of them to realize their dreams.

Case 53

Support of Democratization and Civil Societies in Central and Eastern Europe

Open Society Institute and Soros Foundation Network, 1980

Scott Kohler

Background. George Soros earned billions of dollars as a currency speculator, and has spent the last twenty-five years giving away his fortune at an astonishing rate. Preferring to underwrite his foundations' budgets each year, Soros has not endowed large philanthropies like Rockefeller and Carnegie. Last year, his Open Society Institute paid out slightly more than $110 million, ranking it twenty-sixth in giving among American foundations.[809] Yet even this high figure understates dramatically the extent of Soros' philanthropy. OSI serves today as the hub of the Soros network of foundations, which is comprised of thirty-three distinct private foundations, operating in more than sixty countries around the world.[810] In fact, George Soros' annual giving has for much of the last twenty years rivaled that of the Ford Foundation, which last year had assets worth $10 billion and made grants of $432 million.[811]

This case study seeks to document the efforts of Soros, his network of foundations, and the grantees they have funded, to aid dissident movements behind the Iron Curtain in the 1980s, and later to help support throughout Central and Eastern Europe the transition to democracy and the rise of civil societies. Soros, who is Hungarian by birth, grew up in the shadow of occupation: first by the Nazis and later by the Soviets. So it is perhaps not surprising that, as his wealth grew, Soros in the late 1970s and early 1980s became increasingly active in supporting dissident causes around Europe. What is sure, however, is that Soros has acted on a scale larger than most governments. Some of his greatest success stories, such as the support of Russian science in the crucial period after Communism's collapse, and his creation of Central European University, are not told here. But this case should stand on its own as an account of one philanthropist's part in weakening Communism's grip on Europe, and in promoting transformation and progress, both before and after the Berlin Wall fell.

There is no comprehensive record of Soros' philanthropy in Central and Eastern Europe. The Open Society Institute, which now monitors and oversees the vast network of Soros foundations, did not become fully operational until 1995. As a result, much of Soros' early philanthropy—that given out of pocket and that invested through one of his many private foundations—is difficult to trace, even for Soros himself. Furthermore, the Soros Foundations have not typically required, as a prerequisite for their grant-making, extensive documentation or analysis of problems to be solved and the specific uses to which donations have been put.

This was particularly true in the early years, when a portion of Soros' philanthropy was targeted at groups and causes seeking to undermine their own repressive governments. For example, Michael Kauffman writes that, in the early 1980s, "Soros suppressed his curiosity and showed the tactful discretion of an experienced conspirator"[812] in not demanding to be told where all gifts had gone. It was enough for Soros to know that his gifts had been passed on discreetly to dissident movements bubbling just under the surface in Poland, Czechoslovakia, and other oppressed nations where Communist regimes were struggling to maintain their increasingly tenuous hold on power. The lack of a paper trail was not, however, a function solely of the clandestine nature of certain grantees. George Soros himself has said, "I don't believe in being able to calculate these things too closely, and we haven't made any profound needs assessment studies. We just recognize the need is there. We'll do the best we can."[813]

Whatever the cause, any description of the Soros network's support of democratization and the rise of civil societies in the former Soviet Union and elsewhere will be unavoidably incomplete. The limitations of time and space will make this case study particularly so, but we hope the reader will gain some sense of the breadth and depth of Soros' massive philanthropy in the region, will come to understand certain broad themes in his giving, and will appreciate that, while the impact of Soros' efforts may be impossible to quantify, it can be reasonably said that his philanthropy was—for many years—a crucial lifeline to a region profoundly challenged. It may be an exaggeration to say—as some have—that George Soros was "a one man Marshall Plan."[814] But just how much of an exaggeration will be up to the reader to decide.

Strategy. In the early 1980s, Soros began quietly and gradually to support dissident movements in Czechoslovakia, Poland, and Hungary. By 1987, he was pouring funds into these countries and, especially, the Soviet Union, where Gorbachev's reforms had convinced him it might be possible to crack the veneer of state control, enabling long-strangled values like openness, tolerance, and economic liberalization to grow. And in the late '80s and early '90s, as European Communism crumbled, Soros offered millions upon millions of dollars to put in place the building blocks of what his mentor Karl Popper termed "the open society." Characterized by freedom of speech and the press, freedom of association, and other democratic values, the opening

of closed societies has been the guiding light of all George Soros' philanthropic endeavors. As the *New York Times* editorial page explained in a piece
honoring his achievements: "Mr. Soros recognized that a healthy democracy
required more than just a plurality of political parties and an uncensored
press. The institute also sponsored cultural activities and projects promoting
financial accountability, more adequate health care and prisoner's rights."[815]
At times, Soros foundations have supported innovative demonstration projects, as one of their American counterparts might do. Often, however, they
have served a quasi-governmental role, providing critical social services and
democratic infrastructure that states have been simply unable to offer. Into
the 1990s, and even past the turn of the millennium, Soros has sought to repair the damage caused by years of Communist rule, whether by reforming
primary education, retraining former military officers for civilian life, or
seeking to limit the destruction caused by ethnic violence.

Outcomes. Here then, is a brief sample of the activities undertaken by
George Soros and his network of foundations to introduce behind the Iron
Curtain the elements of open society, and later to relieve suffering and to
promote modernization and economic development in Central and Eastern
Europe.

Poland

Soros began in 1981 to send money to the Polish opposition movement.
Among his earliest philanthropic efforts there was the funding of a network
of unauthorized publishers in an attempt to make available some of Western
literature and scholarship that had been banned by the Communist authorities. According to Kaufman, Soros understood that the Solidarity movement
represented one of the most promising developments among the Warsaw
Pact countries, and he supported it steadily and discreetly. Later, after the fall
of the Berlin Wall, Soros helped Poland along the path to economic liberalization by sponsoring the renowned economist Jeffrey Sachs to help plan a
set of rapid market reforms (the so-called "shock therapy" approach). Soros
himself also consulted with the Polish economist who helped craft the highly
successful economic conversion plan implemented by Polish Finance Minister Leszek Balcerowicz.

Hungary

In 1984, Soros—who was born in Budapest—created in Hungary the first
of his philanthropic foundations. This very act was in and of itself a major
challenge to the status quo in Soros' native country. Soros insisted on auton-

omy for the new foundation, and convinced the government not only to allow ostensibly "forbidden" dissidents to benefit from his largesse, but also to permit the Foundation to publish freely the names of all its grantees. This was just the sort of openness of which the Hungarian regime had long been wary. The negotiations to bring this freedom about were tense, and it took the personal involvement of Soros, including on several occasions the bare threat to cancel the enterprise outright, to convince the Hungarian government to concede to the Hungarian Academy of Science/George Soros Foundation the privileges it enjoyed.

The Foundation's earliest donation was given to import some 50,000 previously unavailable books to Hungarian libraries. Like Soros' support of publishers in Poland, this donation increased the access of Hungarian citizens to democratic ideals they had long been denied. Both grants flowed from Soros' belief that Communist regimes could not withstand their citizens' knowing how deprived they were. The success of the book donation convinced Soros to purchase for Hungarian universities and libraries 200 Xerox copiers. Prior to that gift, access to such machines was strictly controlled. Researchers were required to submit an application to photocopy anything, and then wait several weeks while the application was considered. For Soros, the rapid and free spread of information enabled by these 200 copiers was analogous to the spread of openness, tolerance, and modernization he hoped to help enable throughout the region.[816] Soros' initial commitment to the Hungary foundation was for $1 million per year. This was soon increased to $3 million, and in the mid-1990s, it would peak with donations from Soros of $22 million in a single year.[817] The full range of the Foundation's activities—as with the other philanthropies Soros went on to create—was larger, however, than just supporting the spread of information. Like a major American foundation, the Soros Foundation in Hungary supported an array of philanthropic endeavors. All of these, however, were unified by a commitment to help the country develop into a modern democracy with all the building blocks of a fully open society more firmly in place.

Czechoslovakia

In the early 1970s, George Soros began sending money to the dissident group Charta 77, which was led by the playwright and activist Vaclav Havel. As he became more interested in philanthropy, and also more committed to supporting reform in the Communist-controlled nations of Eastern and Central Europe, Soros became Charta 77's largest single backer.[818] In December 1989, as Charta 77 became the Civic Forum, an embryonic political party, Soros flew to Prague and set up a new foundation to

support media outlets, cultural organizations, and other causes long neglected under Communist rule. While there, he also met with Marian Calfa,
the acting Czechoslovakian president. In a discussion of the nation's future,
Soros urged Calfa to support Havel for the presidency. Later, when Czechoslovakia split into two states, Soros opened another foundation in
Bratislava to do in Slovakia what his Prague foundation would continue
doing in the new Czech Republic.

The Soviet Union

By far the grandest of Soros' philanthropic efforts was in the Soviet
Union, and, later, the republics that succeeded it. While his Moscow Foundation remained the largest, Soros in the early '90s created independent
grant-making foundations in Ukraine, Belarus, Moldova, Georgia, Kazakhstan, Uzbekistan, Kyrgyzstan, and Tajikistan. Between 1987 and 2003,
Soros spent over $1 billion, first to pry open Soviet society, and then to help
many of its millions of citizens enjoy the fruits of democracy, or, more often,
to at least survive the upheaval it brought. Soros spent $100 million on the
Transformation of the Humanities Program, which published new works,
and funded the translation and distribution of dozens of previously unavailable titles by scholars such as Hayek and Popper. The program also contributed greatly to the modernization of Russian scholarship by introducing the
concept of peer review to such fields as history, political science, economics,
and art analysis. In the mid-1990s, Soros also funded a project to link all
thirty-three of Russia's regional universities to the Internet. His foundation
promoted independent media outlets and helped re-train mid-level military
officers for life as civilian entrepreneurs.[819] It also worked to reform nursery
school education and to equipe hospitals for more humane and more med-
ically sound childbirth services. And in late 1997, Soros pledged a donation
of $500 million to be made over three years.[820] With that gift, which was dis-
tributed among a range of causes, including $100 million for public health
projects, Soros, for a time, outspent the United States government, which
was then giving about $95 million per year for reconstruction and democra-
tization in Russia.

Yugoslavia

After the breakup of Yugoslavia, Soros created foundations in Croatia,
Slovenia, Bosnia, and Macedonia. Without a doubt, the most notable grant
made by any of these foundations was the $50 million Soros gave in Decem-
ber 1992 to alleviate the suffering of the Bosnian people. Although Soros

considers it a failure any time his foundations are forced to resort to such last ditch efforts against a backdrop of violence, this grant funded a number of remarkable projects. In addition to supporting an independent newspaper, several radio networks, art exhibits, and academic journals, this grant funded the work of an American named Fred Cuny. A maverick by any standard, Cuny organized ambitious projects in Sarajevo, amid constant violence, that included a grassroots seed production campaign by which citizens could feed themselves, and an engineering project to restore power to much of the city, including the critical plasma unit serving all of Sarajevo's operating rooms. Cuny organized 15,000 Sarajevans for a project to tap safely into the city's damaged natural gas line, enabling the people to cook their food, and, most remarkably of all, he conceived and oversaw the construction of a water purification plant within the city limits. This last project was completely unprecedented; it spared residents the need to travel to the city's scarce drinking wells (a favorite target of snipers), and by August 1994 had restored running water to Sarajevo's 275,000 remaining residents.

Impact. The sheer scale of the Soros network's operations in Central and Eastern Russia is impressive. But it is important to remember that hundreds of millions, even billions, of dollars can be squandered without any noticeable result, particularly on problems of the magnitude that Soros and his associates faced down. Certainly, some of Soros' donations have suffered this fate. In Russia, for example, Soros was often forced to rely upon well-connected members of the old status quo, some of whom appear to have abused and even stolen the funds entrusted to them. Other times, the Soros foundations have simply fallen short of their goals. As Soros says of his giving: "When I got into this business of philanthropy it was definitely a process of trial and error. From '79 to '84 was a period of painful experimentation. I didn't know what the hell I was doing, and I made some wrong steps."[821]

At other times, however, he and his associates have succeeded brilliantly. The Xerox machines project, for example, leveraged a relatively small grant to change the landscape of Hungarian academia. According to Kaufman, "[q]uite suddenly, without any announcement, people in intellectual or university environments were able to copy whatever they wanted. . . ." This and other Soros initiatives made it far harder for the authorities to stem the flow of information. And in Sarajevo, the grants overseen by Fred Cuny achieved remarkable things under extremely difficult circumstances. While problems of counterfactuality are of course unavoidable in such instances as trying to assign one man credit for weakening global Communism, they are less so in the case of the Bosnian relief projects. Without OSI support, Fred Cuny would quite simply not have been in a position to restore power and running water to the people of Sarajevo. Soros says of Cuny: "Truly, I think that Fred probably did save Sarajevo. You know, water, gas, the seeds and gardening, running in the electric cable and the blood plasma unit. He really did it, and that, you know, is something."[822]

Some OSI projects in the region are still too young to be accurately judged. Step by Step, for example, is an early education program similar to America's Head Start. Although it has been adopted by approximately thirty countries already, Aryeh Neier, the president of the Open Society Institute, feels that it will likely lead to only "a Rolls Royce early childhood for a relatively small number of children."[823] Others within the network, however, say that it is the best money Soros has ever spent.

Still, it is widely recognized that Soros has been a major player in the transformation of the entire region. Certainly, the various nations of Central and Eastern Europe still face a host of challenges, and they cannot be looked at as one bloc. As early as 1995, for example, OSI was fielding requests from the Poland foundation for public advocacy support for the rights of the disabled, while the Georgia foundation was buying generators to keep schools warm during the long winter.[824]

In aggregate, it is fair to say that Soros has probably made many grants that have had virtually no lasting impact. But he has also funded projects with enormous reach and of major consequence. Many prominent Russians, including Mikhail Gorbachev, have nominated Soros for the Nobel Peace Prize. As the editorial page of the *New York Times* stated in 2003:

> Mr. Soros' bold ambition was to nurture a broader base for democratic transformation. To a remarkable extent, he succeeded. . . . For the most part, he has spent his money wisely and generously. Russia and the other Eastern and Central European countries he has helped toward democracy owe him their appreciation.[825]

Case 54

MacArthur Fellows Program

John D. and Catherine T. MacArthur Foundation, 1981

Scott Kohler

Background. At one of the very first board meetings of the John D. and Catherine T. MacArthur Foundation, William T. Kirby, a trustee of the young Foundation, brought up an article that would have a major influence on the Foundations' subsequent charitable grantmaking. The article, written by Kirby's doctor, George Burch, argued that philanthropic organizations should allocate funds to free creative people from constraints on their ability to be innovative. Burch insisted, "[t]here is a need for granting agencies to seek out investigators who are genuinely interested in research and exploration of the unknown to advance knowledge for the sake of knowledge." This article was the jumping off point that led the MacArthur trustees to establish, as one of the Foundation's first endeavors, the MacArthur Fellows Program, which has been giving five-year unrestricted grants to talented and promising individuals every year since 1981.

Strategy. The fellowships, dubbed "genius awards" by the press, are intended to give "maximum freedom and flexibility,"[826] so that recipients can follow their own lights, free of virtually all outside constraints. The actual award is a five-year stipend, currently set at $500,000. As the Foundation's website proclaims: "There are no restrictions on how the money can be spent, and we impose no reporting obligations." The grants are not intended as rewards for past accomplishment; one criterion for selection is "promise for important future advances based on a record of significant accomplishment."[827] The other two prerequisites are "exceptional creativity" and "potential for the fellowship to facilitate subsequent creative work."[828] Rather, the fellowships are seen, by the Foundation, as investments in people. MacArthur fellows are chosen through an extensive process of nomination, evaluation, and determination that is carried out under a strict veil of confidentiality.[829] Those invited by the Foundation to serve as nominators are drawn from a wide range of fields, including business, the arts, academia, and the not-for-profit sector. They are asked to consider for nomination the most creative people they know of in their respective fields. Nominations proceed to a selection committee which, after a period of review, makes a recommendation to the president and board of the Foundation, which ultimately makes all final offers. The period of review can be as short as six or eight months, or as long as several years. Applications for support are not accepted,[830] and quite often, fellows are astonished to discover they have been chosen.

Outcomes. Since 1981, the Foundation has given 682 fellowships. About twenty to thirty are usually given each year, although there are no limits on the maximum or minimum number of awards. MacArthur fellows have come from virtually all walks of life. Among their number are poets, musicians, scientists, community activists and educators.[831] Some have used the award to finance travel or research, and some have donated it to their favorite charities; still others have used it to put their children through school. The physicist Jon Schwarz, who received a fellowship in 1987, did pioneering work on the so-called "theory of everything." He put his grant toward the purchase of "a nice house."[832] Each is free to choose for him or herself, and need not report back to MacArthur on progress supported by the grant.

Impact. Not surprisingly, this makes the program's effectiveness difficult to judge. There are no control groups and no benchmarks. The fellowship's effect is different on each recipient. And it is nearly impossible to determine the role of a five-year grant in a person's life's work. Doubtless, many fellows would have gone on to great things regardless. Perhaps some who have received the grants would have been better off without them.[833] There is no way to be sure. But there are plenty of stories attesting to the value of the grants. Video artist Bill Viola called his award "a tremendous boost," and said, "I'm like a sprinter who's been tied at the ankles for a decade, and finally they've let me go."[834] And Richard Muller, a physics professor and 1982 fellow, believes that "every dollar received from MacArthur, unencumbered by grant requirements, was worth ten times as much as a dollar you would get by writing a proposal."[835] Certainly the accomplishments of the fellows as a group are tremendously impressive. The fellowships are "regarded as one of the country's most prestigious honors."[836] Though each MacArthur fellowship is a risk, the return on which is impossible to determine, the enormous prestige of the awards, combined with the diverse achievements of hundreds of past recipients, suggests that in the aggregate, they are an investment well-made.

Case 55

THE ENTERPRISE FOUNDATION

Surdna Foundation, 1982

SCOTT KOHLER

Background. James Rouse, a successful real estate developer "who sought not just to make profits but to transform the landscape and the quality of civic life,"[837] got his first taste of community development work in 1972, when he assisted three women from his church in a venture to purchase and renovate a low-income housing complex in the Adams Morgan neighborhood near DuPont Circle in Washington, D.C. That project led Rouse and his wife Patty to become board members of the women's nonprofit, Jubilee Housing, where his involvement with the struggle of low-income Americans to find decent housing deepened.[838] In 1982, the Rouses founded the organization that James would later call "by far the most important work" of his life.[839]

Strategy. The Enterprise Foundation was conceived as an intermediary organization that would harness private and government capital to help build affordable housing for the poor. It would offer grants, low-interest loans, and equity investments, and would not shy away from the hardest cases: people with dim financial prospects and neighborhoods with histories of violence and poverty.

Today, the Enterprise Foundation works in thirteen cities, as well as the upstate New York area. It also has a program for Native American communities, and an office dedicated to public policy advocacy.[840] Over the last twenty-three years, the Foundation has spun off a number of nonprofit and for-profit affiliates. All of these are driven by social conscience, and they include such organizations as a not-for-profit lending firm and a "socially motivated for-profit subsidiary"[841] that collaborates with developers and other investors to support real estate projects that qualify under federal law for Low Income Housing Tax Credits. The work of the Enterprise Foundation is similar to that of the Local Initiatives Support Corporation (LISC), another intermediary organization started by the Ford Foundation to help secure funds for community development. Enterprise, however, is very "social welfare oriented," and has, therefore, maintained a firm commitment to taking on the most difficult cases.[842]

The Surdna Foundation has been a consistent supporter of the Enterprise Foundation, making a number of grants for infrastructure development, including strategic planning, new program development, fund-raising capacity building, and more. Since 1990, Surdna has given to Enterprise grants worth $1.07 million for this sort of institution building. The Surdna Foundation has also given $6 million to Living Cities: The National Community Development Initiative, which is co-managed by the Enterprise Foundation.

Outcomes. Since 1982, the Enterprise Foundation has wrought enormous change on the community development landscape. It has raised and invested over $5 billion from private funders and especially from the federal government. This money has gone to support affordable housing construction and renovation, childcare facilities, school improvements, job creation, and anti-crime programs.[843] In 2003 alone, the Enterprise Foundation invested over $550 million in community improvements around the nation. It also built or rehabilitated more than 14,000 homes for low-income buyers; helped 1,000 people get entry-level jobs; gave 400 children access to child care; and trained over 150 community residents to patrol their communities through neighborhood watch programs.[844] All told, the Enterprise Foundation's efforts since

1982 have helped provide more than 160,000 new affordable homes for the poor and 40,000 jobs to the unemployed.[845]

Impact. The Enterprise Foundation is one of the leading intermediary institutions working to strengthen the community development movement. In addition to economic development and housing, key features of community renewal, to be sure, Enterprise is distinguished by its strong focus on social service provision for the most disadvantaged Americans. This is an especially difficult niche to fill effectively, and Enterprise has been helped enormously by the steady aid of the Surdna Foundation. The kind of support Surdna has given Enterprise, for infrastructure development, is particularly important and notoriously hard for nonprofits to find. According to Ed Skloot, the Surdna Foundation's president, Surdna has made it clear to Bart Harvey, Enterprise's Chairman and Chief Executive, that Surdna cares deeply about Enterprise's organizational health, and will be receptive to requests for this kind of support. Bart Harvey and Enterprise's Board of Trustees have stayed true to James Rouses' difficult agenda. With the support of the Surdna Foundation and others, they continue to justify Mr. Rouse's conviction "that what ought to be, can be, with the will to make it so."[846]

Case 56

SELF-HELP

Ford Foundation et al, 1984

SCOTT KOHLER

Background. The original headquarters of the North Carolina-based Center for Community Self-Help consisted of a typewriter and some file boxes in the back of an old VW Beetle owned by Martin Eakes, Self-Help's founder. But though Eakes' offices were modest, his goals certainly were not. Eakes wanted to advance the civil and women's rights movements beyond the struggle for political and social equality toward a distant goal—economic equality. Eakes believed that low-income Americans were often unfairly denied opportunities to build wealth, and, along with Bonnie Wright (to whom he is now married), he set out in 1980 to assist disadvantaged families and entrepreneurs improve their prospects.

Strategy. With a grant from the Mary Reynolds Babcock Foundation, Eakes was able to hire a small staff in Durham, North Carolina, to assist him in offering technical assistance to low-income workers seeking to start their own businesses. The mixed record of his early efforts convinced Eakes that knowledge was not, in fact, the main barrier to success for the people he was trying to help. The main problem was access to capital.[847]

In 1984, with $77 raised in a bake sale, Eakes started the Self-Help Credit Union, which would use deposits to finance community development loans, primarily to women and minority borrowers, for the purchase of a home or the capitalization of a small business. The credit union, which started out offering slightly below-market returns to its depositors,[848] also worked with local banks to convince them to offer loans to low-income borrowers with poor credit or no credit, often by buying up those loans to show banks that they had overestimated the risk of lending to low-income clients. In the same year, the Self-Help Ventures Fund was started to receive program related investments from grant-making not-for-profits and market rate investments from banks. Because it was not subject to the same federal regulations as the Credit Union, the Self-Help Ventures Fund was able to assume a higher degree of risk, and to be more aggressive in supporting those whom conventional wisdom insisted were unworthy of credit.

In 1984, Self-Help received its first grant from the Ford Foundation: a grant for two years of general operating support. Ford continued its support over the next ten years, covering about half of Self-Help's operating expenses over that period of time. This flexible, continuing assistance enabled Self-Help to grow steadily.

Outcomes. By 1994, Self-Help had made loans totaling over $40 million and had been called upon to testify before the Banking subcommittee of the House of Representatives as an acknowledged expert in community development banking.[849] But there were hard times along the way. One year, for example, Self-Help used a $90,000 capital grant from the Ford Foundation to invest in a number of small North Carolina businesses, all of which promptly failed. Mary Mountcastle, of Self-Help, credits Ford and other foundations for not giving up when Self-Help tried things that didn't work.[850] In fact, Self-Help has benefited from consistent support from many funders, including the Ford and Babcock Foundations, as well also the Z. Smith Reynolds, Annie E. Casey, and John D. and Catherine T. MacArthur foundations. Self-Help has also received funds from socially responsible investors (in the Credit Union) and many churches. In 1996, Martin Eakes received a MacArthur Foundation fellowship. According to Catharine Stimpson, director of the program, MacArthur's "genius award" nominators "were impressed by the fact that Martin has made a difference in the lives of other people, and that he did it by giving a hand up instead of a handout."[851]

In 1998, Self-Help partnered with the Ford Foundation and Fannie Mae in an effort to provide affordable mortgages to 35,000 low-income families nationwide. The partnership was a major expansion of Self-Help's Home Loan Secondary Market Program, in which Self-Help convinces banks to make unusual loans to low-income clients by offering to buy the loans from the banks. The program reflects Self-Help's focus on changing behavior, rather than providing direct services.[852] Having assumed the risk of the loans, Self-Help shows the banks that low-income homebuyers are, in fact, worthy of capital. This, in turn, convinces the banks to offer more such loans.[853]

Under the terms of the new partnership, Ford gave Self-Help $50 million over five years to serve as risk capital, allowing Self-Help to increase dramatically its loan-buying. Fannie Mae agreed to purchase the mortgages from Self-Help, which was then free to keep buying loans from banks.[854] The "Self-Help Initiative," as the partnership was known, had an ambitious goal: to leverage $2 billion worth of mortgages[855] over its five-year lifespan.[856] By the time its five years were up, the Initiative had exceeded that target by over $200 million. Encouraged by this success, Fannie Mae committed in 2003 to buying an additional $2.5 billion in loans from Self-Help over the next five years.[857]

Self-Help, an "H-elector" under the Internal Revenue Code (signaling its intent to lobby),[858] has worked in policy advocacy as well. By the mid-1990s, Self-Help had become concerned that much of the good it was doing in promoting access to capital among low-income families and entrepreneurs was being undone by predatory lenders, who exploit their clients' need by offering them credit under outrageously unfair terms. To stop abusive lending from undermining its mission, Self-Help led "a coalition of private lenders and consumer groups" that successfully pushed for the enactment, in 1999 in North Carolina, of the nation's first bill outlawing predatory mortgage lending.[859] In its first year, this law saved North Carolinians an estimated $100 million.[860] Self-Help has since consulted with groups in other states seeking to outlaw such practices. And in 2002, Self-Help created another supporting organization, the Center for Responsible Lending, which works "to stop these financial abuses through legislative and policy advocacy, coalition-building, litigation, and industry research."[861] The Center is funded by a consortium of donors, including the Ford, MacArthur, Sandler, and Casey Foundations, as well as the Open Society Institute.[862]

Impact. Since its creation, Self-Help has provided total financing of over $3.6 billion to over 42,000 low-income borrowers. Its emphasis has been on extending access to women and minority-headed households, two groups that are chronically underserved by traditional financial markets. It provides direct assistance in North Carolina and leverages the resources of for-profit lenders around the nation. Self-Help's partnership with Ford and Fannie

Mae has been a resounding success. Overall foreclosure rates for the borrowers have been less than 1 percent, significantly below projections. The Initiative has enabled even the poorest lenders—those who could not otherwise have qualified even for a housing subsidy from HUD—to develop significant personal assets. As Susan V. Berresford, the Ford Foundation's president, describes:

> The median annual appreciation rate in the value of the homes financed in this demonstration whose mortgages are still outstanding is 5.3 percent, a rate which exceeds both the average annual increases in the Dow Jones Industrial Average and the average six month CD rate for the period between 1998 and 2002. Significantly, less than 1 percent of the homes decreased in value. This growth in the value of the homes means that household wealth—the single largest component of financial assets for low-income people—also has increased.[863]

And Self-Help now works to achieve policy change to protect low-income borrowers.

From almost the beginning, Self-Help has received significant support from many foundations, big and small. These foundations have provided it with the flexible support that has made it possible for Self-Help to continually try new things, discard what proves ineffective, and take to scale that which works. Self-Help has done its part by achieving results and always being willing to take a cold hard look at the financial viability of its plans. The foundations have done theirs by providing start-up funds for new ventures, general support for continuing progress, and major risk capital for the achievement of big goals. It has been a fruitful collaboration—one that continues to achieve major impact on many levels of American society.

Case 57

CONFLICT RESOLUTION PROGRAM

William and Flora Hewlett Foundation, 1984

STEVEN SCHINDLER

Background. In the early 1980s, officers and directors at the William and Flora Hewlett Foundation perceived an unfavorable trend in America: an alarming growth of conflicts and disputes, both domestic and international, which society was ill-equipped to handle. In particular, the Foundation felt increased litigation was exerting substantial pressure on the judicial system and the lack of viable alternatives to judicial resolution of conflict was a serious threat. The Foundation, named for one of Silicone Valley's first great technological entrepreneurs and his wife, may have been especially attuned to the potential for such conflict to impede technological and economic growth. William Hewlett, founding chairman of the Foundation, and Roger Heyns, the Foundation's first president, both shared an interest in dispute resolution, and both understood as early as 1977 that the Foundation's work would pursue that common interest.[864] The Foundation supported conflict resolution programs on a small scale in its first few years, but in 1984, the Foundation established a full-scale conflict resolution funding program.[865]

Strategy. One of the Foundation's early strategic decisions, before adopting conflict resolution as a major program, was to focus on institution-building rather than support of individual projects, the more common approach among foundations.[866] Much of the Foundation's grantmaking, across its program areas, had been in the form of large grants over multi-year periods.[867]

This focus was particularly well suited to the conflict resolution program. Conflict resolution, or alternative dispute resolution, was still relatively immature when the Foundation first began funding grantees in the field. Little in the way of conflict resolution theory had yet been developed, and the practice of alternative dispute resolution had not yet been attempted on a wide scale.[868] Accordingly, the field needed a solid base from which to grow.

The Foundation adopted a three-pronged "field-building" strategy in its conflict resolution program.[869] The program initially emphasized general support given to a few grantees with three objectives: building alternative dispute resolution theory, promoting organizations practicing alternative dispute resolution, and advancing the infrastructure of organizations promoting conflict resolution as a field.[870]

Early grants funded centers of academic theory of conflict resolution.[871] Beginning with a grant of $500,000 to Harvard in 1984, the Foundation helped to create eighteen "Hewlett Theory Centers," many at elite universities, to develop literature and scholarship in the field.[872] These centers developed the underlying knowledge essential to effective conflict resolution practice. Foundation grants had the effect of drawing brain power to the field, often promoting otherwise unlikely interdisciplinary dialogue among academics at these centers and advancing the discipline rapidly.[873]

Second, the Foundation supported a number of organizations engaged in conflict resolution practice in particular industries or communities; early grantees were engaged in the practice of family, neighborhood community, and environmental conflict resolution.[874] The Foundation's strategy was that leading successful practitioner organizations in these areas would attract attention from other areas where conflict resolution might be effective.

Third, the Foundation provided crucial funding to the major membership organizations in the field, including the Society for Professionals in Dispute Resolution, the National Conference on Peacemaking and Conflict Resolution, and the Academy of Family Mediators, which served as the infrastructure to maintain momentum.[875] Eventually, in the interest of minimizing duplication, increasing efficiency, and expanding capacity, the Foundation supported the merger of three major membership organizations into the Association of Conflict Resolutions (ACR).[876]

Impact. With the Hewlett Foundation's constant support, the conflict resolution field has grown dramatically. In 1998, the Alternative Dispute Resolution Act required every federal district court to adopt an alternative dispute resolution program. Thirty-two states have either mandatory or discretionary alternative dispute resolution in some cases, such as divorce, landlord/tenant, and small claims. The federal government also employs a variety of forms of conflict resolution in employment discrimination and disability claims. Informal estimates suggest that there are 20,000 private practitioners of alternative dispute resolution. In March 2001, the Supreme Court upheld employer efforts to mandate binding arbitration for employee grievances, ensuring that conflict resolution has become a mainstream alternative to courtroom litigation.[877]

Case 58

THE HEALTH CARE FOR THE HOMELESS PROGRAM

Robert Wood Johnson Foundation and Pew Charitable Trusts, 1985

SCOTT KOHLER

Background. By many indicators, the U.S. economy was strong in the mid-1980s. However, the problem of homelessness in American cities was acute, and it was growing rapidly. Estimates as to the number of homeless people in the U.S. ranged from 350,000 (according to HUD) to over 3 million (according to the National Coalition for the Homeless).[878] Unfortunately, the federal government did not seek to coordinate any substantial response to this growing crisis.

Of specific concern to the Robert Wood Johnson Foundation and the Pew Charitable Trusts was the widespread lack of health care options for the American homeless. Pew and RWJF teamed up for a four-year effort to try out new methods in reaching out to the homeless, specifically in offering them access to medical care. The two foundations aimed to achieve several goals through the program:[879]

- demonstrating new ways to deliver health and social services
- demonstrating better ways to link people with public benefits
- encouraging community agencies and organizations to work together to solve problems [of homelessness]
- providing an opportunity for learning which may lead to further action
- making a difference for the homeless people served

Strategy. Pew and RWJF committed a total of $25 million over five years to create the Health Care for the Homeless Program (HCHP). The initiative started out in five cities, but had expanded to nineteen by the time the foundations' involvement ended. The national program was overseen, for both RWJF and Pew, by Dr. Philip Brickner, but each regional HCH office had the flexibility to determine which combination of tactics would be most effective in connecting the homeless to local healthcare systems. In Philadelphia, for example, HCHP linked hospitals to homeless shelters, allowing the homeless to receive both inpatient care and outpatient "respite" care. In New York, on the other hand, the program focused on offering health care services at soup kitchens. All HCH programs emphasized "aggressive street outreach"[880] in targeting the homeless. Throughout the program, the foundations kept "meticulous records and reports [which] explained how to develop and conduct such programs."[881]

Outcomes. The nineteen pilot programs reached hundreds of thousands of homeless people, many of whom had previously been receiving virtually no medical attention.[882] Between 1985 and 1988, the foundations proved (1) that America's homeless were, on average, far more susceptible to health problems than average citizens, and (2) that the homeless "can be reached by emphasizing outreach and offering targeted, flexible services in locations [such as shelters] where homeless people can be found."[883]

Impact. Most of the program's impact was as a demonstration project that both spurred the federal government to action and blazed the trail for future efforts. It represents yet another example of a foundation initiative that almost certainly led to federal legislation. The careful record-keeping and self-evaluation done over the course of the program allowed homeless advocates to make a persuasive case to Congress in support of federal assistance for the homeless. In 1987, Congress passed the Stewart B. McKinney Homeless Assistance Act, "the first federal attempt to address the problems of homeless people."[884] Included in the McKinney Act was the authorization of a governmental Health Care for the Homeless Program, which picked up right where the foundations were leaving off.

The sections of the bill dealing with healthcare were "adopted nearly verbatim" from the two foundations' HCHP research materials.[885] In fact, the U.S. Department of Health and Human Services, which now oversees government funding of the HCHP, asserts on its website that "[t]he HCH Program was modeled after [the] successful four-year demonstration program operated in nineteen cities by the Robert Wood Johnson Foundation and the Pew Charitable Trust." The foundations' HCH Program probably did not cause the McKinney Act, but it certainly helped to shape it, and indeed made possible its effectiveness in providing health care. In particular, it illuminated the need for a health care appropriation to be included in the bill, and showed the government a proven way to attack effectively the problem at hand.

The Health Care for the Homeless Program now has over 130 local offices, active in all fifty states, the District of Columbia, and Puerto Rico.[886] The McKinney Act (now known as the McKinney-Vento Homeless Assistance Act) was reauthorized by Congress in 2002, and to date has contributed well over $1 billion to the HCH Program.[887]

Case 59

CERTIFYING AMERICA'S TEACHERS' COMPETENCE IN THE SUBJECTS THEY TEACH: NATIONAL BOARD FOR PROFESSIONAL TEACHING STANDARDS

Carnegie Corporation of New York, 1985

STEVEN SCHINDLER

Background. In 1983, the President's Commission on Excellence in Education published a landmark report, "A Nation at Risk: The Imperative for Education Reform," criticizing the education system as inadequate to address the changing economic and social needs of the country. The report sparked widespread discussion, and in some cases alarm, about the need for educational reform.[888]

Strategy. Also in 1983, a group of individuals assembled at the Carnegie Corporation under joint chairmanship of former North Carolina Governor Jim Hunt and Corporation President David Hamburg to discuss the educational needs of the country. In January 1985, the Corporation created the Carnegie Forum on Education and the Economy and allocated $100,000 to administer the Forum and continue the discussion.[889]

One year later, in 1986, the Corporation allocated $600,000 to the Forum to convene annual conferences on educational policy and to coordinate task force studies as well as smaller meetings on education-related topics.[890] In May, the Forum's Task Force on Teaching as a Profession presented a report titled "A Nation Prepared: Teachers for the Twenty-First Century."[891] A primary recommendation of the Task Force report was that a profession of better-educated teachers be developed to satisfy the growing need for more, as well as better-qualified, classroom teachers. The Task Force also recommended the creation of the National Board of Professional Teaching Standards which would establish teaching standards in course content areas and certify teachers who met its standards.[892]

The Corporation allocated $910,000 for operation of the Carnegie Forum, and of that sum, $140,000 was designated for implementation of the Task Force recommendations.[893] The Corporation made an additional allocation of $250,000 in 1987 for the special purpose of furthering implementation of the report's recommendations.[894]

Governor Hunt led a group of educational leaders in asking the Carnegie Corporation specifically to fund the National Board of Professional Teaching Standards recommended in "A Nation Prepared." A thirty-three-member planning committee drafted the bylaws and articles of incorporation for the NBPTS, and its first meeting was held in October 1987.[895] The Corporation granted $1,000,000 to NBPTS to aid its creation, and it continued to make annual $1,000,000 grants to support the NBPTS through 1998.[896] Soon, the NBPTS attracted other donors, and the U.S. Congress began supporting NBPTS in 1990 with a $5,000,000 appropriation.[897]

The NBPTS focuses education reform efforts on improving the quality of teaching in the classroom.[898] It issues National Board Certificates to outstanding teachers, as judged by peers, as a supplement to state certification and as a mark of excellence. Certification standards are the same nationwide. For the first time in U.S. history, a certification to teach in the public schools is fully portable throughout the country. Certification through the NBPTS has facilitated, therefore, also for the first time, a national market for public school teachers.

Impact. NBPTS Certification is voluntary, but all fifty states and hundreds of local school districts recognize National Board Certification, and many provide incentives for certified teachers.[899] Educators consider the NBPTS to be the "single most powerful merit pay system in public education," with some certified teachers receiving annual premiums of $5,000.[900] The benefits of NBPTS Certification, though, are not confined only to those students or colleagues of a certified teacher. The tough and time-consuming standards adopted by the Board have influenced state policies for initial licensing of all teachers.[901] Its work has served as the foundation not only for state policies but also for other education commissions making policy recommendations on improving the education system.[902] By 2005, more than 40,000 teachers had been certified by the NBPTS.[903]

Case 60

CLEANING UP BOSTON'S HARBOR AND WATERFRONT

The Boston Foundation, 1986

SCOTT KOHLER

Background. The city of Boston has long relied upon its harbor as an engine of economic growth. And the beaches surrounding Boston have, for many people, distinguished the city from other great metropolises of the United States. But for most of the twentieth century, Boston's geographic and economic growth far outstripped the development of its sewage and water treatment capabilities. Consequently, as Harvard law professor Charles M. Haar recounts:

> Boston's harbor was [by the early 1980s] the most degraded in the United States, with twelve billion gallons of raw or partially treated sewage going directly into its waters each year. . . . [This pollution] demonstrated beyond any doubt that the state's inability to meet its sewage disposal obligations jeopardized the public's health and safety, as well as economic development.[904]

Although federal legislation passed in the 1970s mandated the cleaning of America's air and water, Boston suffered from a classic case of the tragedy of the commons. City, state, and federal authorities were mired in a bureaucratic gridlock. No party was directly accountable for the worsening condition of Boston's waterfront and harbor—which, by then, was so bad that area beaches were frequently closed because of sewage runoff—so no one party was willing to bear the tremendous cost of cleanup and infrastructure modernization required. As a result, Boston's waste treatment facilities were hugely inadequate to the city's need. At one point in the early 1980s, the Smithsonian Institution asked the city of Boston if it could have for display the antique 1860 Corliss Steam Engine from an old Boston pump station. The city had to refuse because the engine was still in use.[905]

In 1982, the city of Quincy, Massachusetts filed suit against the regional agency responsible for sewage management in the forty-three cities and towns that make up the Boston metropolitan area.[906] This was the first of several lawsuits demanding that some relevant government body take responsibility for cleaning up the harbor and nearby waterfront. In 1983, the Conservation Law Foundation—a New England nonprofit dedicated to the protection of the region's environment—sued the state and federal government to the same end.[907] Thus began a complex series of parallel litigation that would—with the help of Boston's civic sector—ultimately result in sweeping changes in Boston's waste management and a massive public investment in the cleanup and revitalization of the city's harbor and waterfront areas.

Strategy. From very early on, the Boston Foundation (TBF), one of the nation's oldest and largest community foundations,[908] played a key supporting role in this legal maneuvering and the cleanup that has resulted from it. As Patricia Brady describes in her anthology of the Foundation's most significant grants, "the Boston Foundation provided funds to two organizations that played key roles in cleaning up Boston Harbor: the Conservation Law Foundation [CLF] and Save the Harbor/Save the Bay. The former fought the legal battle, the latter, the battle for hearts and minds."[909]

TBF grants in 1983 and 1985 to the Conservation Law Foundation, of $15,000 and $25,000 respectively, supported the latter organization's efforts to break in court the gridlock that had obstructed adequate appropriations for the processing of Boston's waste and the maintenance of its abundant water resources. The Boston Foundation continued helping to underwrite the legal fees, and, indeed, still supports CLF to this day.

At the same time, TBF has supported Save the Harbor/Save the Bay, an advocacy organization founded by Ian Menzes (a columnist for *The Boston Globe*), Paul Garrity (the judge who presided over the initial municipal-level lawsuit), and Bill Golden (the former Quincy solicitor general who, himself, had filed that suit). In 1986, the Boston Foundation gave the trio a $60,000 start-up grant "for initial staff and operating expenses."[910] Throughout the clean-up struggle, TBF continued to support Save the Harbor/Save the Bay. And now, in that struggle's aftermath, the Foundation and the advocacy group, in partnership with the City of Boston, have undertaken the Boston Harbor Indicators Project to research the state of the harbor and waterfront, and to measure progress toward making them more fully realized drivers of economic growth and recreational activity along the Massachusetts coast.

Outcomes. Since the mid-1980s, the Boston Harbor and its adjacent waterfront has been transformed. The three lawsuits brought into the public eye the extreme degradation of Boston's water resources, the resultant public health risks, and the public sector buck-passing that had theretofore stymied progress. A court order established that sludge discharge into the harbor must end by 1991. And legal action led to the creation in 1984, by the state legislature, of the Massachusetts Water Resource Authority, an entirely new government agency charged with the provision and monitoring of water and sewer services, one that as Haar recalls, "could take on the responsibility for the harbor's revitalization."[911] Haar calls this establishment "a major environmental triumph."

From 1986 to 2004, a massive public investment—over $21 billion, all told—changed the face of downtown Boston. The so-called "Big Dig" built a state-of-the-art ten-lane underground expressway, created a swath of parkland along the City's waterfront, and encompassed a range of other public investment. Public pressure, stoked by Save the Harbor/Save the Bay and rulings from city, state, and then federal courts—sought by the Conservation Law Foundation—were forceful enough that government officials could no longer ignore the worsening state of Boston's harbor and her beaches. Although in the mid-1980s it was thought that the clean up of Boston Harbor would take decades, the state and federal governments eventually committed to bearing the cost. Between 1989 and 1998, the city's pumping capacity increased from 700 million to 900 million gallons per day.[912] Secondary treatment, brought online in 1997, decreased significantly the pollutants running into the water. Far ahead of early projections, the main clean up was completed in 2000, when a new 9.5 mile ocean outfall opened, redirecting diluted effluent from the harbor out into Massachusetts Bay.

As a result of these and other improvements, bacteria levels in the waters around Boston are down significantly. Local beaches are now open all but a few days each summer, and Boston's waterfront, long a deserted blight on the city, has been reborn. The massive public investments of the '80s and '90s— encompassing sewage treatment, harbor clean up, and a host of other public works—opened the door to a surge of private investment along the waterfront. Between 1987 and 2004, for-profit investments in the area have exceeded $2.2 billion, including vast new developments of office, retail, residential, research, and industrial space.[913] According to a Harbor Indicators Project report, "the waterfront has [since the late 1980s] been at the leading edge of Boston's growth in population, jobs, and earnings."[914] In all three categories, growth along the waterfront has outpaced significantly the City's overall rate of increase.

Impact. The Boston Foundation did not, itself, underwrite the cleanup of the Boston Harbor, or the modernization of the City's waste treatment facilities. Those projects required an investment far beyond the Foundation's means. And the Boston Foundation did not, directly, undertake the legal or public advocacy campaigns that thrust this issue into the public consciousness. Rather, the Foundation's role was a supporting one. TBF lent credibility, convening power, and an ability to act autonomously, yet in the public interest, to the battles waged by a number of concerned citizens determined to achieve change.

The Boston Foundation grants to the Conservation Law Foundation, for example, helped CLF fight the critical, and highly successful, legal battles. But those grants were of a fairly modest scale, hardly enough to compel large-scale reform. Equally important, according to Douglas Foy, former head of CLF, was the legitimacy conferred on its efforts by the support of the venerable and respected Boston Foundation. As Foy recounts in Brady's retrospective:

> It [the litigation] was very expensive. . . . It was also extremely controversial. . . . [Nevertheless] the Boston Foundation helped fund our work from the start. And it lent us considerable support as a prestigious old Boston institution. I'm sure that people at the Foundation thought long and hard about whether to weigh in and be identified with such a contentious public battle. No one back then could have anticipated how ultimately successful it would be.

By supporting the efforts of CLF, Save the Harbor/Save the Bay, and other grantees, the Boston Foundation helped bring about a major reorganization of Boston's environmental resource administration, and a long-overdue modernization of the City's infrastructure. As a result, Boston's Harbor and waterfront, the city's great historic strengths, were transformed and given back to the public as vital centers of residential, commercial, and recreational activity. The Indicators Project report predicts that private investment in waterfront development over the next twenty years will top $8.4 billion, which "would directly create or accommodate approximately 47,000 jobs. . . ."[915] Civic sector initiative spurred responsible government action, which, in turn, opened the door to substantial private investment, and the residents of Boston, as well as the ecosystem of which the City is a part, are far better off today for the cleanup and revitalization of the City's Harbor, its beaches, and its waterfront districts.

Case 61

BIODIVERSITY PROTECTION

John D. and Catherine T. MacArthur Foundation, 1986

SCOTT KOHLER

Background. The enormous diversity of species, populations, and ecosystems found on Earth has been the subject of serious research for only a short time—about twenty years. Among the findings of this research has been an extremely high proportion of plant and animal species concentrated in a comparatively tiny fraction of the planet. Scientists now tell us that some two-thirds of all terrestrial species inhabit lowland humid tropical forests.[916] Indeed, biological hotspots, stretching over just 1.4 percent of the Earth's surface, contain 44 percent of all species of higher plants and 35 percent of all land vertebrate animals.[917] We also know that these hotspots are fragile ecosystems, many of which are constantly threatened by humans. Most of them lie in developing countries, where the pressures of poverty and rapidly expanding populations put them at especially high risk of degradation and destruction.

Strategy. One of the first organizations to begin working to preserve species diversity[918] was the John D. and Catherine T. MacArthur Foundation. In 1982, the Foundation had established the World Resources Institute, its first foray into environmental grantmaking. After making several grants for conservation in 1985, the Foundation decided in 1986 to establish the World Environment and Resources Program[919] as a major arm of its operations. Biodiversity protection was chosen as the Program's exclusive focus for several reasons. Unlike other environmental crises, such as pollution, ozone depletion, and global warming, the loss of biodiversity is a threat both fast-moving and irreversible.[920] It is also highly concentrated in a few hot, tropical regions and warm, shallow tropical waters.[921] So the Foundation would be able to focus its efforts and funds tightly,[922] and thereby, it was hoped, achieve significant impact.

The Foundation chose to work in nine biodiversity hotspots: the Southern Tropical Andes, the Northern Tropical Andes, the Insular Caribbean, the Eastern Himalayas, the Lower Mekong, Indo-Melanesia, Madagascar, the Lower Guinean Forest, and the Albertine Rift. Its grants were organized by four themes: conservation science, law and policy, sustainable economic development, and environmental economics. The Foundation employed a "moving spotlight" approach, whereby it focused on specific regions, from among the list of nine, in rotating years. So, while MacArthur support has been continuous, Foundation staff have not needed to keep up with grant requests for each separate area all at once. In a strategic review conducted by the Foundation in 2000, this approach was credited with lowering the program's administrative costs; enabling the Foundation to give its grantees the freedom they need to have impact; and, most importantly, producing a series of converging effects that would not have been possible with one linear approach to each hotspot.[923] By the time that review was conducted, the MacArthur Foundation had given 1,114 grants totaling over $207 million.

Outcomes. The MacArthur Foundation led the way in establishing biodiversity protection as a major field of activity. The range of outcomes it has produced is enormous. In Brazil, for example, MacArthur support brought significant attention—as well as funds from USAID and the World Bank—to the Atlantic Forest, which is threatened by the encroachment of several cities, but has generally received far less attention than its larger, less endangered neighbor, the Amazon. In Madagascar, the Foundation has supported the "training of local scientists and conservationists," to enable the country to better manage the flow of foreign capital that has resulted from increasing global attention to Madagascar's unique and fragile ecosystem, the most diverse in the world. Working across national lines, the Foundation has contributed to the development of civil societies. For instance, it has given major support to Fundacion Pro-Sierra Nevada, which has become "one of the most effective NGOs in Latin America" working for both conservation and peace.[924] In the United States, MacArthur planning and research helped establish the Florida Keys National Marine Sanctuary.[925]

Impact. The MacArthur Foundation was the first organization to protect biodiversity on a global scale. Until very recently, it was the only private funder to do so.[926] Along the way, MacArthur has been very successful in attracting other donors to support various biodiversity projects. These have included other foundations, NGOs and major international organizations. The Foundation was a major supporter, for instance, of the U.N. Conference on Environment and Development, which generated landmark global treaties on biodiversity and climate change. And in 2001, the Foundation, in partnership with the World Bank, Conservation International, and the

Global Environmental Facility, established the Critical Ecosystems Partnership Fund, a $100 million commitment to protect biodiversity.[927] By taking biodiversity as its cause long before it had received major support or recognition, the MacArthur Foundation has played a major role in building the field up to what it is today.

Case 62

SCHOOL CHOICE: VOUCHERS IN MILWAUKEE

Lynde and Harry Bradley Foundation and Joyce Foundation, 1986

STEVEN SCHINDLER

Background. School vouchers emerged as a conservative public policy issue when Milton and Rose Friedman, both prominent and influential free-market economists, proposed vouchers as a way to promote school choice and educational competition. Independently, many individuals in African American communities have promoted vouchers as a means to attain greater local control over public schools.[928] Public school system advocates largely oppose vouchers, fearing the public school system would lose funding to private schools. Other opponents believe vouchers supporting private parochial schools constitute a breach of the separation between church and state.

The Lynde and Harry Bradley Foundation emerged into the national spotlight as a financial supporter of conservative causes in 1985 when the sale of the Allen-Bradley Company, the firm Lynde founded and his younger brother Harry joined three years later, lifted the foundation's assets from $14 million to $290 million. Lynde died before the foundation could be created, but Harry provided the Foundation with direction, instilling a commitment to conservative and anti-communist causes. Upon the Foundation's tremendous increase in capital, the board recruited Michael Joyce from the conservative Olin Foundation to serve as president.[929] Joyce brought with him the approaches employed at the Olin Foundation as well as interests in conservative causes.

Strategy. Desiring to promote vouchers as a policy position consistent with its ideology, the Bradley Foundation first began funding research and stimulating intellectual interest in school vouchers before promoting more direct advocacy of school voucher policies and, eventually, offering direct support for voucher programs. In 1986, the Foundation initiated its school choice funding campaign with a grant of $75,000 to support the research and writing of John Chubb and Terry Moe's *Politics, Markets, and America's Schools*, a book supporting with empirical data the school choice ideas proposed by the Friedmans.[930] In 1990, at the time of the book's publication, the Foundation gave another $300,000 to help promote the book.[931]

In the late 1980s, the Foundation also helped to found the Wisconsin Policy Research Institute, a state-oriented conservative policy think tank. WPRI published a number of studies outlining educational problems in Milwaukee and throughout Wisconsin. Chubb and Moe participated in some of these Bradley-supported studies.

In response to a small pilot school choice program for Milwaukee, the State Superintendent of Public Instruction joined a teachers' union lawsuit challenging school choice as unconstitutional. The Bradley Foundation, in turn, provided $500,000 in grants to the Landmark Legal Foundation to support school choice in the courts.[932]

In 1992, Bradley granted $1.5 million to Partners Advancing Values in Education (PAVE) to run a privately-funded voucher program, helping to pay for the education of low-income children at the private schools of their choice, including religious schools. Local businesses gave an additional $2.5 million to the program.[933]

When the Wisconsin Supreme Court issued an injunction preventing a publicly-funded voucher program from proceeding, the Bradley Foundation responded to PAVE's appeal to fund the program temporarily with private dollars in what the *New York Times* called "the most dramatic show of support," giving $800,000 in a direct grant and $200,000 in a matching grant for the operation of the school.[934] Over two years, 1995 and 1996, PAVE raised roughly half of its funds for the program from the Bradley Foundation.[935]

In support of the voucher cause in the Wisconsin judicial system, the Bradley Foundation provided the financial support to enable Governor Tommy Thompson to hire Kenneth Starr, then of Kirkland & Ellis law firm, to represent the state in the litigation. The state attorney general had opposed school choice in his campaign and was therefore unlikely to defend the state's voucher policy. Bradley granted $350,000 to help pay for Starr's legal work.[936]

Following the Wisconsin Supreme Court's approval of the voucher legislation, the Joyce Foundation made a grant of $246,000 to the Public Policy Forum in Wisconsin to evaluate the results of its voucher program in hopes of promoting the program in other communities.[937]

In 2001, with many of Milwaukee's private schools operating at capacity, Bradley gave a $20 million grant to PAVE to help the city's best private schools expand their capacity. Bradley also funds studies of Milwaukee's students to support the potential of more wide-scale voucher programs.[938]

Impact. Almost three years after the PAVE program began, the legislature in Wisconsin passed a voucher program for as many as 7,000 students, allowing them to use the vouchers at private religious or secular schools. When the state supreme court prevented the public voucher program from proceeding, David McKinley, leader of PAVE, helped to raise enough money to fund the program for 4,650 students who had anticipated receiving state aid.[939]

After years of stalling in the state judicial system, the Wisconsin Supreme Court sustained the voucher legislation in 1998. In 2002, the U.S. Supreme Court sustained public voucher programs supporting student education at private, even religious, schools.[940] In assessing these victories for the voucher movement, one commentator called the financial support of the Bradley Foundation "crucial to the voucher coalition" in Milwaukee.[941]

Case 63

THE AARON DIAMOND AIDS RESEARCH CENTER

Aaron Diamond Foundation, 1987

SCOTT KOHLER

Background. The Aaron Diamond Foundation was set up in 1955 by Aaron Diamond and his wife Irene. Mr. Diamond had, by then, begun to accumulate what would become an impressive fortune by investing in New York real estate. His wife worked as a talent scout and script editor in the motion picture industry.[942] The Foundation was intended, from the start, to be the receiver of the bulk of Mr. Diamond's fortune. It was not until the mid-1980s, however, that the Diamonds began seriously to plot the course of their philanthropy. Together, they decided that, because the Foundation's resources were relatively modest—it ultimately disbursed about $220 million—it must maintain a tight focus if it were to have any significant impact. And the Diamonds were determined that it would. They decided that 40 percent of the Foundation's activities would be in the field of medical research; 40 percent would be for minority education, and 20 percent would go to support culture in the city of New York. The Diamonds' motivation was to give back, as much as they were able, to the city that had given them so much over the years, as well as to the world at large.

In 1984, Aaron Diamond died suddenly of a heart attack, and Mrs. Diamond was left to follow through on their philanthropic plan. She recruited the foundation's board and its executive director, Vincent McGee, and she, herself, took on its presidency. But Irene Diamond was determined that, although her voice would be the strongest within the foundation that bore her husband's name, it would not dominate. Looking back, Vincent McGee recalled that "Irene Diamond stated that one of our best board meetings was the occasion of her being outvoted 10-to-1 on three grants."[943] This, to her, indicated a vigorously engaged board of trustees. It was, as she herself insisted, "as it should be."[944] The Aaron Diamond Foundation became operational on January 1, 1987. From the start, it was understood that the Foundation must spend out its entire endowment and close its doors by December 31, 1996. Another principle upon which the Diamonds had agreed before Mr. Diamond's death was that the Foundation, rather than linger on to face the problems of later generations, would do all the good it was able to do in a short period of time—only ten years.

Strategy. The Diamond Foundation started out "by casting a broad net in each [of its program areas], making short-term grants."[945] One problem that drew Mrs. Diamond's attention was the emergent AIDS epidemic. By 1987, scientists had made advances in their understanding of what had originally been called "gay pneumonia," but federal funding for research of the virus was still very scarce. In the Foundation's Final Report, Vincent McGee describes the stigma still hindering efforts to fight the disease in the late '80s:

> . . . fear and homophobia still blocked concentrated, clear and focused efforts to meet the [AIDS] crisis nationally. The larger international dimensions were only beginning to be understood. . . . Most of the decision-makers felt that those dying of AIDS and closely related drug abuse were negligible elements in society—gays, racial minorities, the poor and drug addicts.[946]

The Diamond Foundation was conscious of its limited means and recognized that it would not be able to stop the epidemic alone. But its officers and trustees also saw that New York, which, along with Los Angeles, was an epicenter of new plague, was lagging far behind in its response to AIDS. Joining the effort against this little-understood, widely feared disease would allow the Foundation both to pursue its medical research program goals and to support its home city. As McGee explains, "this gradually led to a realization that there was an opportunity for a modest private foundation to jump-start basic and applied research in the face of lagging public support and institutional hesitancy to come to grips with an expanding epidemic of historic proportion."[947]

In late 1987, Irene Diamond was approached by Steven Joseph, the New York City Commissioner of Health. Joseph proposed that the Diamond Foundation assemble and coordinate a group of private foundations to partner with the city in establishing a cutting-edge AIDS research laboratory in the heart of New York. Mrs. Diamond liked the idea, but she was concerned that Joseph's plan would lead to a lot of bureaucratic hand-wringing and would proceed slowly. Mrs. Diamond, eager to assure that the plan would be carried out quickly and in accordance with her demanding specifications, responded that she would like her foundation to undertake the program by itself. Vincent McGee credits the Foundation's limited life span and its small staff (the Diamond Foundation had only twelve full-time employees) for its ability to respond so quickly to a challenge.[948]

Certainly, the determination of Irene Diamond was also a factor. From the start, she was very hands-on in the planning of the new facility. She was critical of the conditions in which scientists were forced to work and wanted the new research center to be different. And, to that end, it was she who selected the architectural firm that would design and build the lab.[949] Mrs. Diamond also had her own ideas about who should run the facility. She was the primary advocate of Dr. David Ho, a young virologist from UCLA. She later recalled, "I wanted somebody young who was really committed and had a drive to do good research. . . . Most of my search committee of eminent doctors and scientists did not agree with me at the time. They wanted me to take somebody who was already well known. . . ."[950] In the end, however, Irene's search committee, as she labels it, came to agree with her.

The Diamond Foundation contributed $8 million over the three years of the center's construction, while the city of New York added the remaining $3.4 million. In addition, the city provided, at no charge, the 20,000-square-foot site on which the Aaron Diamond AIDS Research Center would be built. Conscious of its niche, the center would determine to focus "on viral molecular biology and basic immunology as the most promising path toward understanding and controlling the virus."[951]

With this major investment, and the years of subsequent support, the Diamond Foundation became the largest private funder of AIDS research in the country. The Research Center was definitely the Foundation's most significant contribution, but not its only one. The Foundation also funded research fellowships for post-doctoral students studying HIV/AIDS. And it took a controversial stand for AIDS education and prevention when, in 1992, the Foundation contributed $450,000 to help the New York City Board of Education offer free condoms to public high school students.

Outcomes. The Diamond Center opened on April 16, 1991. At its opening ceremony, Mayor David Dinkins praised the facility's creation as "an act of faith in our ability to end this epidemic through creative, hard work." Dinkins remained an avid supporter of the Diamond Center and the Diamond Foundation. In fact, in 1994, he joined the Foundation's board. The new research center was very soon fully staffed, and, indeed, it was not long before it began to outgrow its space. The Foundation met this challenge head on—funding an expansion of the labs in 1995 that fully doubled the size of the center. By the time the Aaron Diamond Foundation closed its doors, it had contributed more than $25 million to the AIDS Research Center.

Led by Dr. Ho, the scientists working at the Aaron Diamond AIDS Research Center have ever since been on the forefront of the global effort to control and eradicate HIV/AIDS. Continually collaborating with fellow researchers around the world, the Diamond Center team has, in particular, been recognized for five major breakthroughs:[952]

1. They identified the CCR5 molecule, which is the "central gateway" through which the HIV virus enters the CD4 lymphocytes.

2. Following up on earlier work by Dr. Ho, they demonstrated that the HIV virus does not lie dormant within the body for several years after infection. Rather, the virus is, from the time of infection on, locked in a battle against the body's immune system. This advance was especially groundbreaking, since it contradicted the prevailing consensus among the medical establishment, and, in so doing, radically altered the treatment of HIV patients.[953]

3. Diamond Foundation researchers identified "an early HIV genome from a 1959 blood sample," shedding new light on the evolution of the virus.

4. A harmless gene defect, shared by approximately one in every hundred people of European descent, which confers immunity to HIV, was discovered at the Diamond Center.

5. The first combination drug therapy for AIDS was developed at the Diamond Center. Using new protease inhibitor drugs, as well as the existing treatment, AZT, these so-called drug "cocktails" have "helped reduce the death rate from AIDS in America to a fifth of what it once was. . . ."

The impact, in particular, of this last development, has been enormous. Such cocktails are expensive and can produce unpleasant side-effects, and it no longer appears that they will be able fully to eradicate the virus from an infected person's body, but they have, without a doubt, made AIDS a far cry from the sentence of imminent death that it once was—at least, they have in nations where such treatments are affordable.[954]

Impact. The Aaron Diamond AIDS Research Center has been widely credited for its leading role in these and other advances. Dr. Ho, on whom the Foundation took a chance in the late '80s, was selected by *Time* magazine as its Man of the Year for 1996, in recognition of his and his team's cutting-edge work in unraveling the mysteries of HIV/AIDS. Conceding that Ho, and his fellow AIDS researchers, are not exactly household names, the magazine declared, "[b]ut some people make headlines while others make history. And when the history of the era is written, it is likely that the men and women who turned the tide on AIDS will be seen as true heroes of the age."[955]

Without a doubt, David Ho is not the only such hero. Doctors like Michael Gottlieb, who first reported on the new virus, Luc Montaigne, who first isolated it, and many others, working for the Centers for Disease Control, the National Institutes of Health, pharmaceutical companies, and elsewhere, have contributed enormously. And the battle is still raging. Nor can the Diamond Foundation take all the credit for enabling David Ho to do his work. Young though he was, Dr. Ho had already chosen HIV/AIDS as his focus several years before the idea for the Diamond Center was born, and, as Irene Diamond readily acknowledged, "his talent is his talent."[956] But Dr. Ho has always credited Mrs. Diamond for her courage and commitment, in going where other leaders of foundations and government would not, at a time when the word "AIDS" was still spoken in hushed tones—when it was spoken at all. As Dr. Ho has said, Mrs. Diamond's "insight was truly profound and prescient. . . ." It was she and her foundation, after all, that gave, to what she called "a young, talented, but no name scientist," what he would later refer to as "a chance of a lifetime."[957]

Case 64

CLARE BOOTHE LUCE PROGRAM

Henry R. Luce Foundation, 1987

SCOTT KOHLER

Background. Born in 1904, Clare Boothe Luce never attended college. Yet she became a noted writer, actor, and playwright. She was also the U.S. Ambassador to Italy and the first woman from Connecticut elected to the

United States Congress. Throughout her life, Mrs. Luce was concerned about the challenges women face pursuing education and career aspirations. And upon her death, she created a major vehicle for the advancement of women in higher education.

Strategy. The Clare Boothe Luce Program was preceded, in 1987, by a fund given by the Henry R. Luce Foundation, named for Clare's late husband, the publisher of *Time*, *Life*, and *Fortune* magazines. The fund, itself named for Mrs. Luce, granted two-year visiting professorships to outstanding female scholars at four universities: Yale, Columbia, Brown, and NYU. The fund was created after the Luce Foundation in the mid-1980s conducted a study of women in higher education. The report showed a huge gender gap. Women at the time comprised more than half the nation's undergraduates and a third of its Ph.D.s, yet they held only 12 percent of all tenured positions at public and private universities.[958] At the most prestigious major research universities, the proportion of all tenured positions held by women was even lower—just 5 percent.[959]

The study and professorships were the Foundation's first steps, but when Clare Luce died, later that year, she expanded dramatically the Foundation's role. Mrs. Luce left $70 million for the Foundation to create—in perpetuity—funds for at least thirteen universities to give undergraduate scholarships, graduate fellowships, and "term support for tenure-track appointments at the assistant or associate professorship level."[960] The awards are made to promising women pursuing careers in the sciences, mathematics, and engineering. Mrs. Luce hoped "to encourage women to enter, study, graduate, and teach" in these, the fields where they are historically least represented.[961]

Outcomes. Over the past sixteen years, the Clare Boothe Luce Program has awarded fellowships for over 800 undergraduates and 390 graduate students, as well as 137 Clare Boothe Luce professorships.[962] These prestigious awards have benefited 114 four-year institutions, in addition to the thirteen original designates.

Impact. According to Robert E. Armstrong, then vice president and executive director of the Luce Foundation,[963] the Clare Boothe Luce Program was intended "to cause these [recipient] institutions to look harder for qualified women candidates than they have done in the past instead of settling for the first qualified male applicant."[964] Since its creation, the Clare Boothe Luce Program has been the single largest source "of private support for women in science, engineering, and mathematics."[965] It continues serving as the major source of private support for a gradual reduction in the long-standing disparity between the numbers of men and women in American higher education.

Case 65

BALANCING THE POWER IN COLLEGE SPORTS: THE KNIGHT COMMISSION ON INTERCOLLEGIATE ATHLETICS

John S. and James L. Knight Foundation, 1989

STEVEN SCHINDLER

Background. As the 1980s came to a close, the National Collegiate Athletic Association (NCAA) was facing a crisis. More than a decade of dramatic, highly visible scandals in intercollegiate athletics had shaken the public trust in college sports. Widespread recruiting violations, payments to players, student gambling, drug use and point-shaving incidents revealed a dark side of the college athletics world. An investigation following the drug overdose death of basketball superstar Len Bias at the University of Maryland in 1986 revealed substandard academic achievement among student athletes.[966] In 1987, repeated revelations of payments to Southern Methodist University football players, a scheme in which the governor of Texas was implicated, led the NCAA to impose the "death penalty" on the program, its harshest sanction ever.[967] The NCAA later dealt severe penalties to both the University of Florida's football program and the University of Nevada at Las Vegas's basketball program for numerous blatant violations of NCAA rules.[968]

A major element of the controversy stemmed from the tension between university athletics programs and the universities of which they are a part. Presidents of universities gathered to form a Presidents' Commission in 1983, in large part to address the difficulty they had in controlling their athletics departments.[969] A few presidents who attempted meaningful oversight and control over their athletic programs, however, were rebuffed or even pressured to resign by their governing boards and alumni.[970]

Public outcry over scandals in college sports rose to such a high level that Congress took notice. Over the history of college sports, the federal government had intervened only on rare occasions when the intercollegiate governance system proved incapable of addressing major issues of public concern.[971] While the NCAA struggled to gain control over what seemed to be a downward spiral of public trust in the integrity of college athletics, critics of the NCAA suggested that a body, whose members were the very college athletics programs which were guilty of rules violations, was inherently incapable of reform.[972] Because of the rapid downward spiral of public trust in the integrity of college athletics, Congress appeared ready to intervene.[973]

Strategy. The John S. and James L. Knight Foundation, created in 1950 by the brothers who founded Knight Newspapers, had a heritage rooted in education and educational values. The Foundation's inspiration for funding educational programs came from the founders' father, who provided financial assistance to college students unable to pay their education bills.[974] In the mid-1980s, the Foundation's assets increased by a factor of twenty, making it the twenty-first largest foundation in the United States. Then, in early 1988, Creed Black, a Knight-Ridder executive and former publisher of the *Lexington Herald-Leader*, became the Foundation's president.

Two years earlier, a journalist at Black's former paper, the *Herald-Leader*, was awarded a Pulitzer Prize for coverage of a basketball scandal at the University of Kentucky.[975] A year into his presidency, Black led the Knight Foundation to tackle problems plaguing college sports across the country. In March 1989, the Foundation commissioned a public survey which assessed public sentiment on the state of intercollegiate sports; about four-out-of-five respondents indicated that intercollegiate athletics were "out of control."[976] Six months later, the Knight Foundation created the Knight Commission on Intercollegiate Athletics, a panel of distinguished community leaders from the academic, business, and sports communities, to study and propose reforms for college sports.[977]

The Knight Foundation initially granted $2 million to the Commission, and the Commission was expected to study reform proposals for approximately two years.[978] The Commission's founding co-chairmen, former presidents Rev. Theodore M. Hesburgh of Notre Dame and William C. Friday of the University of North Carolina system, were highly respected higher education leaders whose universities had storied athletics programs.[979] After months of anticipation, the Commission released its first report, *Keeping Faith with the Student-Athlete*, in March 1991.[980] Reported to be the first comprehensive study of the state of college athletics since the Carnegie Foundation released a similar study in 1929, *Keeping Faith* condemned a system in which half of Division I-A schools had been sanctioned by the NCAA in the 1980s and set forth a reform agenda.[981] Central to the report's recommendations was the conclusion that college presidents must exert greater authority over their universities' athletic programs.[982]

After the release of the report, the Commission, and the Commission's co-chairmen in particular, embarked on an extensive lobbying effort with the NCAA members to see that its proposals were adopted. The very existence of the Knight Commission seems to have heartened the Presidents

Commission—many university presidents served on both bodies—to embark on an ambitious reform agenda.[983] Indeed, in March 1993, the Knight Commission was dissolved upon adoption of many of its major reforms.[984] Nineteen months later, however, proposals for minimum academic standards for freshman student athletes to compete in inter-collegiate athletics led the Commission to reconvene, with the Knight Foundation's support.[985] Again disbanding in 1996 and reconvening in 2000, the Knight Commission has since served as combination blue-ribbon panel and watchdog organization, weighing in against proposals that empower college athletics programs at the expense of the higher education system and in support of proposals that enhance academic standards and graduation rates for student athletes.[986] Most recently, in January 2006, the Knight Commission held a "Summit on the Collegiate Athletic Experience," an event that brought Commission members face-to-face with top high school and college prospects and professional athletes to hear firsthand the issues facing student athletes.[987] To enhance visibility of the Summit, the Knight Commission has made podcasts of the sessions available to the public on its website.[988]

Impact. While the public image of college sports still suffers from occasional revelations of rule-breaking, intercollegiate athletics has progressed far from its low in the 1980s. The Knight Commission has marshaled that progress at each stage, working to prevent regression in policy for the sake of academics and the student athletes. In 1996, the entire governance structure of the NCAA was changed to give college presidents greater authority; a *New York Times* editorial credited the Knight Commission's work for the presidents' reform victory, stating that the reform provisions were "lifted chapter and verse," from the Commission's proposals.[989] The Commission has certainly not prevailed in every battle; most recently, the football schedule was lengthened to a twelve-game season over its fervent protests.[990] Still, the Commission's efforts have been widely credited with counterbalancing the trend toward increasing commercialization in intercollegiate athletics and with representing educational values and the well-being of student-athletes in debates over the future of college sports.

Case 66

GOLDMAN ENVIRONMENTAL PRIZE

Richard and Rhoda Goldman Environmental Foundation, 1989

SCOTT KOHLER

I am greatly appreciative of the aims of the Goldman Environmental Prize and of the achievements of the Goldman Laureates. Efforts to protect the African environment will only succeed if such efforts render tangible benefits to the peoples of Africa through the sustainable use of the living and other natural resources on our continent. Recognition of the importance of this principle through the Goldman Environmental Prize will contribute to the world-wide promotion thereof and thus considerably enhance the status of this award amongst those countries burdened with large scale poverty.

—NELSON MANDELA

Background. Richard and Rhoda Goldman had a long philanthropic history by the time they started the Goldman Environmental Prize. Since 1951, the Richard and Rhoda Goldman Fund has quietly made charitable donations to a wide range of causes, including the environment, Jewish affairs, the arts, and social services in the Goldman's native California.[991] But in 1989, the Goldmans decided to break their habit of quiet giving in order to honor leadership in environmental protection.

Strategy. Inspired by the MacArthur Fellows "Genius Grants," and the Nobel Prize, the Goldmans created a distinct organization, the Goldman Environmental Foundation, to administer a new award, to be given annually to six "environmental heroes" from around the world. According to its website, the Goldman Environmental Prize is given "for sustained and important efforts to preserve the natural environment, including but not limited to protecting endangered ecosystems and species, combating destructive development projects, promoting sustainability, influencing environmental policies and striving for environmental justice."[992] Nominations are accepted from either of two sources: "a network of thirty-one internationally known environmental organizations, and a confidential panel of environmental experts from more than forty-five nations, including citizen activists and prominent policymakers."[993] Laureates are honored with a bronze sculpture and a monetary prize at an awards ceremony in San Francisco that is timed each year on or around Earth Day, and at a reception in Washington, D.C., at the National Geographic Society.[994]

Outcomes. The Goldman Environmental Prize is the largest award in the world honoring grassroots environmental activism.[995] The awards now receive significant media coverage, and Goldman Laureates are generally invited to address such groups as the U.S. Congress and the World Bank. Endorsed by more than 100 heads of state, the Goldman Environmental Prize is often referred to as "the Nobel Prize for Environmentalists."[996] And it is an appropriate moniker. The Goldman Prize has recognized and brought increased prominence to over one hundred champions of a host of environmental causes. In fact, in 2004, one of the earliest Goldman Laureates— Wangari Maathai of Kenya—was honored with the Nobel Peace Prize "for her contribution to sustainable development, democracy and peace."[997] Another member of the inaugural class of Laureates, Harrison Ngau Laing, used his prize money to finance a successful campaign for a seat in Malaysia's Parliament.[998]

Impact. The Goldman Environmental Prize has legitimated leadership in the field and continues to draw attention to a host of environmental challenges being tackled by grassroots activists around the world. According to President Clinton: "The Goldman Prize winners have raised awareness of important environmental issues and motivated people to preserve and protect natural treasures for future generations."[999] By honoring achievement in the protection of the Earth, the Goldman Environmental Prize benefits not only its recipients or those who may aspire to win it. Rather, it strengthens the environmental movement as a whole, and, by extension, benefits us all.

Case 67

COOPERATIVE SECURITY AND THE NUNN-LUGAR ACT

John D. and Catherine T. MacArthur Foundation and Carnegie Corporation of New York, 1989

SCOTT KOHLER

Background. Foreign affairs in the second half of the twentieth century were dominated by the specter of the Cold War. In the aftermath of victory in the Second World War, relations between the United States and the Soviet Union worsened rapidly, soon calcifying into a barely restrained hostility that cast its shadow across the earth. For decades, the two superpowers raced to develop and mass-produce weapons capable of enormous destruction, always wary of falling behind in the largest military buildup the world had ever seen. Converted into 2005 dollars, the United States, between 1950 and 1990, spent over $16.3 trillion "creating and maintaining a large peacetime military establishment, essentially for the first time in its history."[1000] This huge cost was justified by the need to deter and contain the seemingly imminent Soviet threat.

Yet in the mid-1980s, the character of the Cold War began to subtly change. While its two principals still had thousands of nuclear missiles pointed straight at each other's cities, the Soviet Union under Mikhail Gorbachev began to undertake a process of mild political and economic liberalization that awakened the hopes for a possible détente. Among those working to de-escalate tensions between the two superpowers were several major American foundations. Soon after Gorbachev became the Soviet president, the Carnegie Corporation of New York joined with the John D. and Catherine T. MacArthur Foundation and the W. Alton Jones Foundation, as Jane Wales, then a Carnegie program officer, recounts, "in supporting a group of U.S. and Soviet scientists that served as a brain trust to the Soviet president developing options for nuclear arms control and disarmament."[1001] This partnership marked the first time nuclear scientists from the two nations had had any sort of sanctioned collaboration.

Strategy. Throughout the 1980s, MacArthur and Carnegie in particular were major funders of research and exchange efforts aimed at bridging the Soviet-American divide. Much of this support was aimed at think tanks, particularly the Washington-based Brookings Institution.[1002] Meanwhile, the Soviet system was in fact crumbling, despite Gorbachev's best efforts to repair and save it. And as the Cold War came to a close, work funded by these foundations would play a critical role in shaping the United States' response to the collapse of its longtime rival.

In a 1989 grant proposal to the MacArthur Foundation, the Brookings Institution's foreign policy research staff contended that "a conjuncture of economic and political circumstances now provides a unique opportunity for the United States jointly with the Soviet Union to shape their foreign and defense policies and budgets in a way that would markedly improve . . . the international political climate. . . ."[1003] Brookings' proposal was approved, and in December of that year the MacArthur Foundation committed $5 million to the think tank over the next five years.

With that grant, as well as support from Carnegie and its own endowment, researchers at Brookings began to develop the framework for a collaborative approach to de-escalation and nuclear threat reduction. This approach, dubbed "cooperative security," called for transparency in securing nuclear technologies and reducing each nation's respective arsenal of weapons of mass destruction (WMD). Even considering Gorbachev's reforms, and the improving relations of the two superpowers, cooperative security still represented, at the time, a radical departure from decades of zero-sum politics and mutually assured destruction.

A number of scholars were involved in this work. Publications such as "Cooperative Security and the Political Economy of Non-Proliferation," by Wolfgang H. Reinecke, and *The Logic of Accidental War*, by Bruce G. Blair were funded in part by grants from these foundations. And with the support of the Carnegie Corporation and the MacArthur Foundation, Brookings "formed a consortium with the Center for Science and International Affairs at Harvard, the Center for International Security and Arms Control at Stanford, and the Carnegie Endowment for Peace in Washington."[1004] By 1991, the scholars collaborating through this partnership had concluded that "cooperative security principles appear to offer the most promising, perhaps even necessary, context for developing a redesigned and consolidated set of proliferation controls."[1005]

Especially significant was the collaboration of John Steinbruner, director of Brookings' Foreign Policy Studies Program, with Ashton Carter of the Kennedy School of Government at Harvard, and William Perry, then a professor at Stanford. With funding from MacArthur and Carnegie, the three laid out an approach to Soviet-American cooperative threat reduction in *A New Concept of Cooperative Security*, published in 1992.

Even before the work's publication, however, the three presented their innovative approach in a paper given at the 1991 Aspen Congressional Seminar. Hosted by former Senator Dick Clark, and partially underwritten by the two foundations, the seminar that year was attended by Senators Sam Nunn (D-GA), and Richard Lugar (R-IN). The presentation resonated strongly with the two senators, both of whom were concerned about the danger that unsecured Soviet nuclear weapons might fall into the wrong hands, or be deployed by accident as command and control mechanisms began to fail.

Senator Nunn, for his part, had recently failed to secure a vote on the Senate floor for a $1 billion relief package for the Soviet Union, and he understood well that many of his colleagues in Congress were strongly opposed to the idea of bailing the Soviet Union out of any trouble. Nonetheless, Ashton Carter's presentation "had an astounding effect"[1006] on both senators, and the two decided to spearhead a bipartisan effort to improve the security of the Soviet WMD arsenal. Briefed regularly by Steinbruner, Carter, and Perry, the two senators set about making the case to their fellow lawmakers that American assistance could, and should, help the Soviet states destroy their stockpiles of poorly secured nuclear, biological, and chemical weapons.

Outcomes. Only weeks later, in mid-December, Congress approved the Soviet Nuclear Threat Reduction Act of 1991. More commonly known as the Nunn-Lugar Act, the bill set up a fund to pay for the dismantling of Soviet weaponry, the secure storage of nuclear materials, and the cleanup of nuclear facilities.[1007] As detailed in S.313, a bill removing several restrictions upon the original act, the Nunn-Lugar Cooperative Threat Reduction Program has, "as of January 2005:

(A) Deactivated 6,564 nuclear warheads;

(B) Destroyed 568 intercontinental ballistic missiles;

(C) Eliminated 477 intercontinental ballistic missile silos;

(D) Destroyed 17 mobile intercontinental ballistic missile launchers;

(E) Eliminated 142 bombers;

(F) Destroyed 761 nuclear air-to-surface missiles;

(G) Eliminated 420 submarine-launched ballistic missile launchers;

(H) Eliminated 543 submarine-launched ballistic missiles;

(I) Destroyed 28 strategic nuclear submarines; and

(J) Sealed 194 nuclear test tunnels or holes."[1008]

In addition, the Nunn-Lugar Program, with over $5 billion spent to date, has funded work by thousands of scientists with WMD expertise from the former Soviet states.[1009] Nunn-Lugar has helped these scientists, whose knowledge, as Al Hunt points out in the *Wall Street Journal*, "would be a treasure trove for terrorists," transition into non-weapons research "such as environmental modeling and pollution cleanup."[1010]

Impact. William Perry, who became Secretary of Defense under President Clinton,[1011] has said that Nunn-Lugar "built a channel of trust and cooperation with the former Soviet Republics and in my mind (without any doubt) was the critical factor in leading . . . three of these nations, Ukraine, Belarus, and Kazakhstan, to agree to become non-nuclear states."[1012] And Senator Lugar believes that "Nunn-Lugar assistance helped encourage the Ukraine to sign the nuclear proliferation treaty (NPT) and as a result the START I treaty was finally entered into force. In effect, Nunn-Lugar helped to break the START I logjam."[1013]

Senator Nunn once referred to the Cooperative Threat Reduction Program as "a very solid success."[1014] It is safe to say he was being modest. Nunn-Lugar set the tone for Russo-American relations in the aftermath of the Cold War. And while that relationship is still not perfect, it is far better than it might have been. It is important to remember that many lawmakers were adamantly opposed to any cooperation with, let alone financial or technical assistance to, America's perceived Communist enemy. Even a few weeks before Senators Nunn and Lugar partnered to endorse the principles of cooperative security developed by Carter, Perry, Steinbruner, and their colleagues at Brookings, Harvard, Stanford, and the Carnegie Endowment, the idea seemed far-fetched. That this changed—and did so rapidly enough to keep pace with the sudden collapse of the Soviet empire—is a credit to the lawmakers who understood the urgency of the situation. Al Hunt is probably closer to the mark when he writes that Nunn-Lugar "may be the greatest international investment since the Marshall Plan."

To draw a straight line from the grants made by Carnegie and MacArthur to the passage of the Nunn-Lugar Act would be a gross oversimplification, and would probably exaggerate the foundations' role in a story that is far bigger than any one of its parts. But it is undeniable that, from at least the mid-1980s, those two foundations were promoting strategic collaboration between the U.S. and the U.S.S.R., particularly in the area of WMD control. The foundations helped shape the research agenda, as described in a Brookings report stating that "the purposes of the MacArthur Foundation effort have been made integral to our research planning. . . ." They organized and supported the consortium that produced a groundswell of research and analysis, culminating in the work of Cater, Perry, and Steinbruner to propose a cooperative threat reduction plan. The two foundations also helped to orchestrate the crucial meeting at which the arguments of the former were presented to Senators Nunn and Lugar. The resulting legislation has made enormous inroads in securing former Soviet WMD arsenals, and, while much remains to be done, much has already been accomplished thanks to the spirit of cooperation and détente that has developed between the one-time adversaries of the Cold War.

Case 68

CARE AT THE END OF LIFE

*Robert Wood Johnson Foundation and Open Society Institute,
1989 and 1994*

SCOTT KOHLER

Background. A century ago, most people died relatively quickly of sudden injury or disease. People usually died at home, with their families close at hand. Today, advances in medical technology and public health have greatly extended the average human lifespan, allowing more people to survive into old age. As a result, many people live for weeks, months, or years, with "chronic illness or serious disability."[1015] Motivated by his own experience with the deaths of his parents, George Soros in 1994 directed his Open Society Institute to begin the Project on Death in America (PDIA). The project's goal was to "transform the culture of dying"[1016] in the United States.

The Robert Wood Johnson Foundation's interest in care at the end-of-life had begun in 1989, when it funded a five-year study for $28 million. The Study to Understand Prognoses and Preferences for Outcomes and Risks of Treatment (SUPPORT) examined the experiences, in U.S. hospitals, of dying people and their families. Published in 1995, the study's results were unexpectedly bleak. SUPPORT showed that "most Americans die in hospitals, often alone and in pain, after days or weeks of futile treatment, with little advance planning, and at high cost to the institution and the family."[1017] Rapid progress in medicine over the twentieth century had not only increased health care costs dramatically, but it had also encouraged medical practitioners to always focus on trying to prolong a patient's life, even at the cost of the patient's well-being, and often against the patient's express wishes. A *Newsweek* article summed up the study's findings, after SUPPORT was published in 1995, explaining: "The larger problem . . . is that American medicine lacks any concept of death as a part of life."[1018]

Strategy. The Robert Wood Johnson Foundation sought to promote widespread adoption of palliative and end-of-life care by means of a three-part strategy:

1. Professional Education: changing medical and nursing school curricula and textbooks; offering workshops for practitioners; working to get palliative care added to licensure and certification exams; supporting journal articles (in, for example, the *Journal of the American Medical Association* and the *American Journal of Nursing*)

- Example: RWJ has funded a program of the American Medical Association, called "Education for Physicians on End-of-Life Care," which is designed to educate doctors on best-practices in caring for dying patients and their families.

- Example: $1.83 million was given to the Stanford and Massachusetts General Hospitals to train their faculties in end-of-life care.

2. Institutional Change: increasing the capacity of hospitals to deliver palliative care; working to develop pain management standards for hospital accreditation agencies

- Example: The "Promoting Excellence in End-of-Life Care" program funded twenty-two diverse projects aimed at changing institutions' responses to death. Some of such programs were directed specifically at underserved populations (minorities, the mentally ill, etc.), whereas others attempted to demonstrate the efficacy of new techniques at a single institution.

- Example: Last Acts, a coalition founded by the Foundation, which now comprises over 900 organizations (including the Department of Veteran's Affairs, the AMA, etc.) has drafted a set of best practice standards, "The Precepts," designed to guide hospitals and practitioners in the provision of care at the end of life.

3. Public Engagement: increasing public awareness of systemic factors determining patient/family experience with terminal illness and death; encouraging individual advocacy and the formation of community groups; using information and entertainment media to inform the public's perception of the issues

- Example: The Foundation spent $2.75 million to commission a four-part, six-hour documentary series by Bill Moyers. "On Our Own Terms" followed the stories of several people coping with impending death, and aired on PBS in September 2000.

Meanwhile, the Open Society Institute pursued a strategy of its own. PDIA collaborated frequently with the RWJF (such as by providing tech support and some content for the Bill Moyers documentary series). The primary focus of PDIA was on professional development: building human capital in order to help palliative and end-of-life care spread through hospitals and medical schools.

- Example: The OSI Faculty Scholars Program spent $13.4 million to provide two years of funding to eighty-seven medical school faculty members for research and training in care at the end of life.

Outcomes. Since 1989, the Robert Wood Johnson Foundation has given over $148 million to programs on care at the end of life, while the Open Society Institute gave $45 million between 1994 and 2003.[1019] Workshops conducted by the "Education for Physicians on End-of-Life Care" have been consistently oversubscribed, and the program's training materials are widely circulated.[1020] The "Promoting Excellence in End-of-Life Care" program received 678 responses to its Call for Proposal, of which twenty-two were funded. Each program is carefully evaluated (with RWJF assistance). Evaluation costs are funded by the Foundation (not out of the organization's grant money), and, while it is too early to trace the lasting impacts of most of the programs, some have already served as effective demonstrations. For example, one program's work with a native Alaskan tribe has been successful enough that it is being adopted by the Alaskan Native Tribal Health Consortium, and will soon be implemented across Alaska.[1021] Another success—Last Acts' "Precepts"—have been widely adopted and are "now quoted in medical literature as the most up-to-date and accepted summarization."[1022] The critically acclaimed Bill Moyers broadcast, "On Our Own Terms," was watched by over 20 million viewers, who were directed to additional information on the PBS website.[1023] And within a year after the publication of an RWJF-funded article in the *Journal of the American Medical Association*, over one-third of all medical textbooks had added, or were in the process of writing, a new section on end-of-life-care.

The PDIA Final Report concludes that the Faculty Scholars program "had a major impact on the field." One measure of its achievement is that the $13.4 million that the OSI spent on Faculty Scholars has been leveraged into a further $113 million in grants awarded by other funders to the eighty-seven Faculty Scholars "for research, education, and program development in hospice and palliative care."[1024] Another is that the eighty-seven scholars have collectively published more than 2,000 books and journal articles.

Over 500 hospitals now have palliative care programs. Virtually every one of these has developed since the two foundations became involved.[1025]

Impact. The RWJF was not the first institution to take an interest in care at the end of life. The best hospices, for example, have, for some twenty-five years, demonstrated the benefits of palliative care at the end of life. Still, only about 20 percent of Americans receive hospice care.[1026] A range of outside factors has spurred the increased awareness of end-of-life care. They include the highly publicized actions of Dr. Jack Kevorkian, legislative debates in the

'90s on euthanasia, the AIDS epidemic, and, perhaps, most significantly, the gradual aging of the massive baby boom generation, members of whom are increasingly grappling with their own, and their parents', mortality.

Steven Schroeder credits the RWJF's initial study with providing much of the stimulus, to both the Foundation and the larger medical community, saying, "SUPPORT's methods were so meticulous and its investigators so credible that our nation's medical leadership could not duck, deny, or dismiss its message: 'Care at the end of life is lousy.'"[1027]

According to Judith Miller of the *New York Times*, "the sharp increase in research on death demonstrates the growing power of philanthropy almost to create an academic field."[1028] Certainly, the Open Society Institute and the Robert Wood Johnson Foundation are not the only two foundations that have contributed to the surge in attention paid to care at the end of life. But they are widely credited with having led the charge.[1029] OSI recognized that its frequent collaborator, the RWJF, had done the most. In a letter in the PDIA's final report, its Director, Kathleen Foley, writes that "[OSI] could never equal the Robert Wood Johnson Foundation's impact on public education and community outreach." But both foundations were at the vanguard of what is still a growing movement.

Case 69

New Standards Project

Pew Charitable Trusts and John D. and Catherine T. MacArthur Foundation, 1990

Scott Kohler

Background. Education in the United States has, from the time of the nation's founding onward, been characterized by decentralization and local control. School boards and teachers, like early Anti-Federalists, have bridled at the thought of distant federal policymakers telling them how to do their jobs. Increasingly, however, the American system of education—specifically pre-college public education—has also been frequently characterized by a policy known as social promotion: moving students up to the next grade level, and, ultimately, to graduation, regardless of whether or not they are actually learning at a pace commensurate to their progress. This habit is one of the primary phenomena that have been blamed for the decline of public education in the United States.

Strategy. In 1990, the Pew Charitable Trusts and the John D. and Catherine T. MacArthur Foundation launched a new collaborative—the New Standards Project (NSP)—to promulgate a set of "best practices" and benchmarks of achievement that would help schools ensure that their students were, in fact, learning at grade level. The two foundations made initial grants to two not-for-profits dedicated to reform in American education: the National Center on Education and the Economy (NCEE), and the Learning Research and Development Center (LRDC), at the University of Pittsburgh. With these funds, the two organizations created New Standards, an education organization based in Washington, D.C.

New Standards set out to do research, examining education systems in countries with highly effective education and training systems, convening meetings of education experts, and collaborating with a wide range of stakeholders in public education. Based on its findings, the NSP then set out to design a set of national standards that could be tailored to guide teaching around the country. Final decisions on the standards were made by NSP's Governing Board, which was composed of governors, state legislators, school superintendents, teachers, school board members, and representatives of a number of other constituencies. Working in mathematics, literacy, science, and applied learning, NSP set out to provide, to willing school district partners standards, assessment techniques, professional development, technical assistance, and quality control.[1030]

Outcomes. Throughout the 1990s, the perceived decline in public education led more and more groups to favor common standards, of the sort promoted by New Standards. President Clinton, for example, advocated national standards with clear benchmarks that would enable parents to compare their child's progress to that of children in other school districts and states. This proposal foundered in Congress over concerns that such a move would threaten local authority. However, policymakers at the state and local levels were not all so ambivalent, and a number of communities began in the early and mid-1990s to work actively with New Standards on curricular reform. By 1995, New Standards had eighteen state and six district partners, collectively enrolling "nearly half the public school children in the United States."[1031] In July of that year, Pew appropriated an additional $6 million to LRDC, and the MacArthur Foundation a further $2.3 million to the NCEE, "to continue work on [NSP]."[1032]

In December 1996, the New York City Schools Chancellor, Dr. Rudy Crew, announced a plan to adopt gradually the national standards disseminated by NSP. Announcing the move, Dr. Crew said, "I am proposing adoption of the standards developed by the New Standards project because they are the best available national standards, because teachers can use them, because they are based on common sense as well as academic excellence, and because they are ready now."[1033] Crew's proposal was approved by the Board of Education, making New York "the largest district to embrace the standards."[1034] Crew's decision was largely welcomed within the New York educational community. Dianne Ravitch, a researcher at NYU, called it "a good strategy," and the president of the United Parents Association, Ayo Harrington, enthused, "I say hallelujah. . . . It's way past due."[1035] Just thirteen months later, an article in the New York Times would declare:

> Now, like skyscrapers being renovated using the same blueprint, hundreds of city schools like P.S. 158 are beginning to incorporate those academic standards—first in reading and writing, with math and science to follow—aligning their expectations of what students should learn and changing how that achievement is measured.[1036]

Transition to the standards would not occur overnight, and certainly required major adjustment on the part of teachers and administrators. NSP had anticipated the extensive need for technical assistance and professional training that would be necessary, however, and teachers were guided in the transition by a 200-page document helping them develop assignments, grade consistently, and use NSP guidelines as a jumping off point for their own individual lesson plans. In addition, the schools sponsored workshops for parents to learn about the new standards and offer feedback. Around the county, this process was repeated as NSP standards were picked up—in whole or in part—by a number of communities, including Milwaukee, Philadelphia, Denver, and Boston.[1037]

Impact. The debate over how much centralization is desirable in public education is still very much alive. But the need for some degree of uniformity, of expectations and evaluation, has gained significant traction in the public consciousness. The most visible sign of this is, of course, the No Child Left Behind Act. Passed by Congress with bipartisan support in 2001, the Act mandates common standards and rigorous measurement of progress toward specific educational goals. Both LRDC and NCEE continue to support education reform, and proponents of uniformity of education practices—of whom there are now many—continue to use and build on the work of the foundation-funded New Standards Project, an early leader in the movement.

Case 70

SUSTAINABLE ENVIRONMENT PROGRAMS

Pew Charitable Trusts, 1990

SCOTT KOHLER

Background. The Pew Charitable Trusts (PCT) has a long history of making grants to promote environmental protection and sustainability in a range of fields, from energy policy, to marine life, to forestry. Its environmental programs all fall under one of the Trusts' three main areas of activity: Advancing Policy Solutions. Pew's involvement in the field has both mirrored and contributed to the rise of environmental advocacy over the last twenty years, and has been particularly significant since 1990.

Strategy. The full range of Pew's activities is beyond the scope of this brief history, but a look at several of Pew's major initiatives provides a window into several of the diverse strategies by which the Trusts have achieved impact in promoting environmental protection and sustainability. Two of the main areas in which Pew has been significantly involved are global climate change and marine life protection.

Global Warming and Climate Change Program: In 1990, Joshua Reichert, director of the Policy Initiatives and the Environment Program of the Pew Charitable Trusts, recommended the initiation of a program to advance research on and analysis of global climate change and non-partisan policy solutions to the threat of global warming. Reichert's proposal was motivated by the almost complete lack of federal action despite ". . . mounting scientific evidence that global warming was under way and posed an unprecedented threat to Planet Earth."[1038] Inertia at the federal level convinced the Trusts to pursue a multi-tiered approach at the state level. Pew began with a core focus on California, New York, Connecticut, Rhode Island, Massachusetts, Vermont, New Hampshire, and Maine. In those eight states, and in thirteen other Tier 1 and Tier 2 target sites, the Trusts worked to increase awareness of global warming and to leverage state funds in support of more efficient, sustainable practices. In addition, PCT convened an advocacy coalition of groups around the country dedicated to curbing global warming. Between 1990 and 1998, the Trusts, along with its partner the Energy Foundation, made 261 grants totaling $39.8 million.[1039] In 1998, PCT launched the Pew Center on Global Climate Change, an independent, nonpartisan, not-for-profit institution designed to continue the foundation's work by "[depoliticizing] global climate change as a domestic issue and . . . [working] with 'the more constructive elements of the business community.'"[1040] The Center produces reports, works with members of Congress and the executive branch as well as the media, and convenes the Business Environmental Leadership Council (BELC), a consortium of thirty-eight major corporations (most of them in the FORTUNE 500) committed to finding better environmental solutions through ongoing dialogue. Eileen Claussen, former Assistant Secretary of State for Ocean and International Environmental and Scientific Affairs, heads the Center.[1041]

Protecting Ocean Life Program: The Pew Trusts' "marine work is aimed at preserving the biological integrity of marine ecosystems and primarily focuses on efforts to curb overfishing, reduce bycatch, and prevent the destruction of marine habitiat."[1042] As with climate change, Pew supports research and public education efforts to highlight the impact on species and ecosystems of human activities, such as industrial fishing. In addition, the Trusts in 1997 established the Ocean Law Project, a "marine litigation unit" to pursue court actions when necessary, and to protect the public interest in preserving marine life. More recently, PCT created the independent Pew Institute for Ocean Science to carry on the work. In addition, the Trusts convened the so-called "Pew Oceans Commission," a panel of experts that released, in 2003, "the first thorough review of [U.S.] ocean policy in thirty-four years."

Outcomes. The strategies pursued by the Trusts have produced a range of outcomes. Some, such as the Pew Oceans Commission, have been highly successful. Other efforts, such as those to scale up global warming changes from the core states to the rest of the nation have been less so. Even so, the Trusts' multi-pronged, multi-level approach to environmental protection has left a significant impression on the landscape.

In global warming and climate change, the Trusts hoped to encourage states to fund new renewable energy sources (such as wind, solar, and geothermal power) that would, by 2002, generate 6.5 million megawatt hours (mWh) of energy. In fact, as early as 2001, this goal had been exceeded by 1.5 million mWh.[1043] Similarly, the Trusts' work to secure state funding for energy efficiency was highly effective. Aiming for $700 million of new state funding by 2002, PCT actually helped bring about the appropriation— again, a year ahead of schedule—of more than $830 million.[1044] Every one of the ten states that, in the 1990s, adopted new energy efficiency and renewable energy use regulations were Pew target sites. Furthermore, an independent evaluation team headed by Roger R. Kasperson found that the majority of states that acted on these and other energy use issues were motivated, at least in part, by the work of Pew grantees.[1045] The Pew Center on Global Climate Change has produced forty-five reports, each of which been distributed to over 4,000 "opinion leaders" in the public and private sectors.[1046] The staff of the Center holds regular briefings for members of Congress and officials at relevant executive branch agencies. Furthermore, the Center's work, and the opinions of its staff, have been influential in shaping media coverage of global warming, which has since 1990 become a far more well-known issue, and which has recently been taken up in Congress by two influential senators: Joseph Lieberman and John McCain.[1047]

The Trusts' work to protect marine species and ecosystems is also continuing to yield significant rewards. One example of this work, the study released in 2003 by the Pew Oceans Commission, was hailed by the editorial board of the *New York Times* as a "landmark" that provided "stark evidence. . . [and] plausible road maps for recovery."[1048] Along with a subsequent Congressional Report, this Pew-funded study identified three major problems in U.S. marine management: pollution from agricultural and developmental runoff, industrial overfishing, and the "bureaucratic chaos" created by the current assortment of ad-hoc rules governing aspects of marine oversight. These two reports combined to spur the introduction of a number of measures, now before the House and Senate, which call for more coherent, conservation-oriented national policies governing marine ecosystem development and protection.

Impact. Environmental issues like global warming and the appropriate balance between conservation and development are some of the most controversial of the many questions facing public leaders. Over the last four decades, public-spirited individuals and institutions—many of them foundation-supported—have played a major role in helping to protect society's interest in clean air, clean water, species diversity, and a number of other areas, against countervailing voices that are often far more powerful. The Pew Trusts have been at the vanguard of this struggle. By working to influence state and federal legislators and other decision-makers, the Trusts have helped lead efforts to bring to the attention of the public and its elected leaders a number of environmental concerns. In so doing, the Trusts play a vital and public-spirited role in helping to ensure that future generations will not suffer for the mistakes of their short-sited predecessors.

Case 71

KIDS COUNT

Annie E. Casey Foundation, 1991

SCOTT KOHLER

Background. The Annie E. Casey Foundation was created in 1948 by Jim Casey, a founder of United Parcel Service (UPS), and his siblings, George, Harry, and Marguerite. The four named the Foundation in honor of their mother, and, from the start, directed it to support programs aimed at helping disadvantaged children.[1049] Its first grants were made to support a camp for underprivileged children in Seattle. After Mr. Casey's death in 1983, the Foundation's resources increased dramatically; its assets today are valued over $3.1 billion.[1050] By the late 1980s, the Casey Foundation's trustees had come to feel that real impact in improving children's lives on a large scale would require some lever to influence the public sector. As Douglas Nelson, the Foundation's president, has said, "anyone interested in children would have to be deliberately ignoring reality not to know that the real answers to these problems lie in the political realm and in public education."[1051]

Strategy. The Foundation's chosen lever was to be information. In the hope of improving public policy affecting children and families, the Annie E. Casey Foundation began the KIDS COUNT initiative in 1990 to track the well-being of children in the United States. The following year, KIDS COUNT released its first national data book, which included statistical measurements of a wide range of factors contributing to children's welfare. The national data, including such indicators as the percentage of children in single parent homes and the percentage of young adults who have dropped out of high school, were broken up state-by-state.

In addition, the Casey Foundation launched a network of state-level KIDS COUNT projects, to provide "a more detailed, county-by-county picture of the condition of children."[1052] These state-level programs seek to gather and disseminate data that will enable policymakers, nonprofits, academics, and the general public to observe trends in the social and economic well-being of children and young adults. The state projects also work to ensure that advocacy for children has a voice in the policymaking process that is data-driven. At both levels of operation—state and national—"KIDS COUNT exists to measure child outcomes and contribute to public accountability for those outcomes." Underlying the KIDS COUNT program is the Casey Foundation's belief that better information will lead to better outcomes. Policymakers, regardless of political affiliation, can find common ground on statistical fact, while hard data often bring to the fore critical questions of social justice and resource allocation.[1053]

Outcomes. Today, KIDS COUNT is, with the exception of the U.S. Census, the most widely used reference on the state of American children.[1054] According to Douglas Nelson, it is, among news media, the single most frequently cited data source for reporting on children and child poverty. It has now evolved into an integrated database that allows for an enormous amount of trend comparison, both nationally and at the state and local level. KIDS COUNT still publishes its annual data book, which now highlights ten core indicators. These are: "percent low birth-weight babies; infant mortality rate; child death rate; rate of teen deaths by accident, homicide, and suicide; teen birth rate; percent of children living with parents who do not have full-time, year-round employment; percent of teens who are high school dropouts; percent of teens not attending school and not working; percent of children in poverty; and percent of families with children headed by a single parent."[1055]

Impact. Thanks to KIDS COUNT, we now know that nine out of these ten indicators have improved since 1991.[1056] More importantly, "throughout the country, KIDS COUNT data are credited with influencing significant policy decisions to improve the condition of kids and families."[1057] While it is difficult to draw a line connecting KIDS COUNT to the improvement it has documented,[1058] it is fair to say at least that the Casey Foundation has created a valuable resource for those concerned with improving child welfare, and, in so doing, has succeeded in vastly improving the quantity and quality of data-driven advocacy for child policy at all levels of American society.

Case 72

THE TRANSFORMATION OF THE KAISER FAMILY FOUNDATION

Henry J. Kaiser Family Foundation, 1991

SCOTT KOHLER

Background. The Henry J. Kaiser Foundation was created to use for philanthropic purposes the fortune amassed by Henry Kaiser, a successful industrialist who founded the Kaiser Permanente health management organization.[1059] For most of its existence, the Foundation operated much like any other private family foundation, making grants in the field of health and health care, and overseen by a board of trustees. In the late 1980s, however, the Foundation's board—led by trustees Barbara Jordan (the first black woman to serve in the United States Congress), Hale Champion (of Harvard University's Kennedy School of Government), and Don Evans (formerly Governor of the State of Washington)—came to feel that its assets could be put to better use. In determining the Foundation's new direction, the trustees asked themselves only one question: "how can we best have an impact with (then) about $30-$40 million to spend each year in a rapidly changing, trillion-dollar health-care system?"[1060]

Looking at the landscape of American health care, the trustees came to feel that the Foundation's assets alone were insufficient to achieve real impact in such a large system. For-profit interests, on either side of any number of controversial health issues, would always be better funded. Similarly, the Kaiser Family Foundation, with holdings worth approximately $500 million, was too small to fund massive nationwide demonstration projects, of the sort that larger foundations have at times underwritten, aimed at proving some new program's large-scale efficacy. As they charted a new course for the Foundation, the trustees recruited Dr. Drew Altman to serve as its president. Altman had an admired track record at both the Pew Charitable Trusts and the Robert Wood Johnson Foundation.

Altman and the board came to perceive a very specific niche that was going unfilled in American health care. Despite the abundance of private and public interests opposing one another on a host of issues, there was no independent nonpartisan voice for the public as a whole. Kaiser's leadership came to feel that, by providing high-quality nonpartisan research and analysis and by using effective communications strategies to disseminate this information, the Foundation might be able to upgrade the quality of the many debates constantly unfolding across the health care system.

Strategy. To that end, the trustees voted to convert Kaiser into an operating foundation, which is to say it would design and operate its own programs internally, rather than making grants to outside nonprofits. As Altman recognized, "[y]ou can't operate in today's health care world effectively without quickly seeing that the main ballgame is government. Government policy and financing drives our health care system. And it's not doing it well enough."[1061] The Foundation's goal, therefore, was to improve the functioning of government in the health care arena. This was to be accomplished by playing the role of a disinterested entity, gathering the best available research on a range of important health care issues, conducting research of its own, and providing high-quality analysis in a form accessible to the general public.

The Foundation has also taken the unusual step of paying out well above the 5 percent mandated by law. Since the Kaiser Family Foundation's reorganization in 1991, its trustees have sought only to maintain the purchasing power of the Foundation's assets *at its 1991 level.* Most foundations, in contrast, seek not only to preserve the value of their assets, but indeed to increase it. As a result of this policy, the Kaiser Foundation is generally able to pay out between 9 and 10 percent of its assets each year.[1062] In fiscal year 2003, for example, the Foundation spent over $58 million on assets of $545 million.[1063]

Because the Kaiser Foundation operates its own programs, however, and because of its unique strategy, the Foundation is particularly reliant on its human capital over the value of its appropriations. According to Dr. Altman, the Foundation's primary resources are in fact its staff members, all of whom have relevant professional expertise, whether in polling, politics, broadcasting, statistical modeling, or elsewhere.[1064] Kaiser has no program officers, having abolished the traditional foundation job in favor of a system in which everyone is responsible both for the substantive work of research and analysis, and for helping to communicate its findings to the Foundation's target constituencies.

Today the Foundation operates twelve programs, ranging from partnerships with commercial media outlets to research and analysis aimed at educating physicians on the disparities in medical treatment among different racial and ethnic groups. At times these programs overlap, but all have in common a commitment to providing nonpartisan research and analysis to one of three constituencies: policymakers, the media, or the general public.[1065]

For the most part, the Kaiser Foundation's agenda mirrors the national health agenda. As a result, significant attention is given to such issues at Medicare, Medicaid, and prescription drug financing. However, the Foundation has also chosen to maintain a special focus on two particular issues: the spread of HIV/AIDS and the health care challenges unique to minority populations. Just over half of the Foundation's annual expenditures are targeted at these two foci.[1066] In this way, the Foundation both improves the quality of the dialogue, and also seeks to make sure that two particularly important, if often overlooked, health care challenges remain in the public eye.

The Kaiser Foundation's single largest initiative is the Kaiser Commission on Medicaid and the Uninsured. Staffed by foundation personnel, "under the guidance of a bipartisan group of national leaders and experts in health care and public policy," the Commission provides information and analysis to policymakers, journalists, and the general public on health care coverage in the United States.

The Foundation's second largest activity is its engagement in a range of partnerships with entertainment and news media organizations. The Kaiser

Family Foundation partners with *The Washington Post* to conduct polling on health care issues. And it has joined with Viacom in a joint initiative to promote HIV awareness, which Viacom has made a company-wide priority integrated into its networks' TV programming and online content. To date, Viacom has made media commitments of over $250 million to this partnership.[1067] And this is only one of the many partnerships the Foundation has forged to disseminate via news and entertainment outlets unbiased information on health and health policy in the United States.

The Foundation runs a multitude of other programs as well. It conducts studies of the media's impact on public health, and works to make physicians aware of the disparities in treatment—both its accessibility and quality—faced by minority patients. The Foundation takes advantage of California's role as a frequent incubator of innovative policy solutions to study which new developments in health care coverage and financing, once tried in that state, might be ripe for nationwide implementation.

Outcomes. The initiatives described above constitute a sample of Kaiser's operation, a sample intended to illustrate the Foundation's overall strategy. By improving the quality of information in the health care field—especially on issues of high public salience—and by disseminating information in an accessible form, whether to politicians, journalists, or sitcom-watching teenagers, the Kaiser Family Foundation is working to enable American citizens to reach more informed conclusions, and, by extension, to promote better outcomes for health care policy debates at the federal level.

The transformation of the Kaiser Family Foundation was announced in April 1991, and was greeted with acclaim from those in the philanthropic community who recognized what a big step it was. Steven A. Schroeder, then-president of the Robert Wood Johnson Foundation, called it "an adventuresome step," and Robert Blendon, chairman of the department of health policy and management at the Harvard School of Public Health predicted that "[i]t will have big symbolic importance. They [Kaiser] are trying to reverse the idea that philanthropic organizations should mirror the popular prejudice that it's hopeless" trying to reform health care policy.[1068]

Impact. The big issues in modern health care cut to the core of what kind of society the United States aspires to be. Rapid technological progress has enabled scientists and physicians to cure and prevent a host of diseases, to raise living standards in much of the world significantly, and indeed to extend considerably the average human lifespan. But the advance of health care technology has created countless issues that can, it seems, be answered only through government action. Will state-of-the-art treatments be extended to all? If so, how will society foot the bill? Should special protections be given to the old and infirm? Or should markets reign unchecked? These, and a great many other questions, are at the forefront of American public policy debates.

Not-for-profits, as well as foundations specifically, employ a multitude of strategies in the hope of improving our $1.6 trillion-per-year health care system, which consumes about 15 percent of the U.S. G.D.P. Recognizing its own inability to push government toward any meaningful reform, the Kaiser Family Foundation has instead carved out for itself a crucial niche between the people and the state. And $58 million per year is a drop in the bucket of federal health spending. But, targeted specifically to public outreach and education, it is enough to fund a tremendous flow of information. This information is enriching the national discourse on health care. It is equipping the public to perceive more clearly the tradeoffs implicit in public policy debate, and to understand more fully a discourse most often carried out in the language of doctors and policymakers.

Kaiser's work does not easily lend itself to specific outcome measurements or rigorous evaluations of impact. But as Dr. Altman says, "we aspire to play a special role, and have ample evidence that we are succeeding."[1069] Because the Kaiser Foundation is injecting itself into a number of highly contentious debates, it will not be universally loved. But one of its greatest strengths— conferred by its unique independence as a private operating foundation—is that the Foundation need not fear the political heat. Few organizations without skin in the game are similarly well placed. And among those that are— some other foundations, for instance—there is often great reluctance to appear to be taking sides. The Kaiser Foundation, in its new incarnation, recognizes that it is not the primary mover in its field, and it accepts the fact that by communicating information of any sort it will likely offend someone. But, motivated by a belief that its "special role" is a necessary one, the Kaiser Family Foundation is content to connect the decision-makers and regular people alike with objective information and then trust that over time they will act wisely.

Case 73

THE ENERGY FOUNDATION

MacArthur, Pew, Rockefeller, Hewlett, Packard, and McKnight Foundations, 1991

SCOTT KOHLER

Background. In January 1991, the Rockefeller and MacArthur Foundations, along with the Pew Charitable Trusts, announced the creation of a new partnership. The three large foundations committed $20 million, with a high likelihood of continuing support, to create the Energy Foundation, a nonpartisan grant-making institution dedicated to developing and disseminating technologies and practices to reduce America's dependence on non-renewable energy, and to boost energy efficiency. The idea for this new consortium was born, according to Adele Simmons, then-president of the MacArthur Foundation, in 1989, when the three foundations agreed "that there was growing public support for the concept of energy efficiency."[1070] At the time the announcement was made, progress in energy efficiency had stalled in the United States after the federal budget for energy conservation had been "cut drastically in the early 1980s."[1071]

Strategy. Since 1991, the Energy Foundation has worked to promote increased energy efficiency and sustainability, primarily through a "focus on technology and regulatory solutions."[1072] Three "strategic assumptions" underlie all the Foundation's work:

1. New technologies can grow the economy with far less pollution.

2. Policy shapes today's energy markets, determining which technologies thrive or wither.

3. Intelligent philanthropy can influence energy policy with multi-billion dollar payoffs.[1073]

The Energy Foundation works in five primary fields: "renewable energy, transportation, utility energy efficiency, appliance standards, and climate change." It makes grants to a wide range of nonprofits working at both the local and national levels. It works to convene interested parties, and, when one city or region is successful in using a new technique, or a new regulation, the Foundation works to export this innovation. Grant requests are assessed by the magnitude of impact they seek to achieve, as well as the likelihood (resulting from a combination of factors: political will, public awareness, leverage points, etc.) that the desired outcomes will be brought about.

The three original funders—MacArthur, Pew, and Rockefeller—did, indeed, renew their support of the Energy Foundation, although Pew and Rockefeller have since ended their involvement. Today, MacArthur supports the Energy Foundation in partnership with the Hewlett, Packard, and McKnight Foundations. The Energy Foundation's annual budget now stands at approximately $24 million.

Outcomes. That number is dwarfed, however, by the magnitude of the changes wrought over the last fourteen years on energy efficiency and sustainability in the United States[1074] as a result—sometimes direct, other times indirect—of the Energy Foundation and its many grantees. According to an independent evaluation of the Energy Foundation, released in May 1998, the Foundation "has been highly successful"[1075] in pursuing its goal of "a sustainable energy future."[1076]

There are many examples of this success. In the mid-1990s, for instance, the Foundation initiated six regional campaigns to promote the use of renewable energy. To date, sixteen states have adopted renewable portfolio standards mandating varying minimum levels of renewable energy use by power companies. In fifteen of these states, the standard can be traced directly to the Energy Foundation campaigns. Energy Foundation research, analysis, and education efforts contributed in the early '90s to the adoption in California of tough new regulations for low-emission vehicles. And in 2002, the California State Assembly passed AB 1493, the first bill to regulate, at the state level, air quality standards above and beyond the federal standards.[1077] The Energy Foundation has worked to keep standards tough in California, and has exported the California regulations to seven other states: New York, New Jersey, Massachusetts, Connecticut, Vermont, Maine, and Rhode Island.[1078] Energy Foundation grantees have worked to develop regulations making it more profitable for utilities to invest in energy efficiency, and, since 1992, utilities have spent over $13 billion "on efficiency programs that saved $45 billion worth of electricity. . . ."[1079] Federal appliance efficiency standards developed and enacted with Energy Foundation support "will cut projected electricity use in 2020 by 8 percent and will net consumers $186 billion in energy bill savings through 2030."[1080] And in its work to prevent global warming, the Energy Foundation convinced over thirty of the largest companies in the United States to commit publicly to reducing their carbon-based emissions. The reductions pledged by these firms total more than 100 million metric tons.[1081] Furthermore, according to the 1998 evaluation, the Energy Foundation probably deserves "credit for retaining

federal support for efficiency and renewable energy . . . [and] appliance standards" during the mid-1990s.

Impact. These examples bear out the success of the Energy Foundation's
tight focus on funding only those projects that seem likely to achieve substantial impact. The Energy Foundation's budget is not nearly large enough
to underwrite large-scale direct changes in energy use. But the Foundation
has used its grants to encourage action by state legislatures and energy con-
glomerates, themselves the keepers of resources far beyond those of any nonprofit. It has provided support for the advocates of tougher standards, and
has shown the way to efficiency gains. In so doing, the Energy Foundation
has leveraged the funds of its several grantor foundations to achieve ends far
beyond the value of the dollars it has had to spend.

Case 74

CENTRAL EUROPEAN UNIVERSITY

Open Society Institute, 1991

SCOTT KOHLER

Background. More than fifty years ago, George Soros fled his native Hungary's Communist regime. He went on to become a billionaire financier and
philanthropist, and has strongly supported the reconstruction of central and
eastern Europe since the end of the Cold War. In 1988, Soros and a group of
several dissidents came up with the idea of founding a university in Eastern
Europe that would serve as a beacon of the democratic values of openness
and freedom, but it was not until the revolutions two years later that he was
able to bring that idea to life.[1082]

Strategy. In 1991, Soros gave $25 million to create Central European Uni-
versity (CEU). The institution was to serve as a bridge connecting central
and eastern European college graduates to the opportunities of a western education. At the time of its foundation, Soros planned to continue his support
of CEU only "if the university proves itself in terms of academic quality and
wins acceptance in the region."[1083] One critical benchmark was whether CEU
would become a fully accredited university, which it succeeded very quickly
in doing. Satisfied with its progress, Soros pledged in 1993 to continue supporting the fledgling university with additional donations of at least $10 mil-
lion a year for the next twenty years.[1084] The new university signed contracts

with the Czech and Hungarian governments to establish the university in Prague and Budapest, with the national governments paying rent and local salaries and the Soros Foundation paying all other costs.[1085]

CEU was able to attract renowned scholars to teach, lecture, and serve as administrators. The first rector and president, for example, was Alfred Stepan, former dean of the School of International and Public Affairs at Columbia.[1086] Using lecturers on short appointments, the new university was able to get up and running very quickly. Its remarkable ability to cut through red tape owed, in large part, to Soros' willingness to bear its costs alone. Looking back, he said, "When I launched the university, I felt the region was in a critical period and things needed to happen quickly in order not to miss the great window of opportunity for change."[1087]

The university offered masters degrees in several social science and humanities subjects, and, at the outset, CEU was envisioned as a place where students from the region could do post-graduate study that would prepare them to pursue doctorates in western Europe and the United States.[1088] The university also hosted an array of "practical spin-offs"[1089] intended to make it an anchor of the open society[1090] in the heart of the former Soviet bloc. For instance, the CEU Press has worked to translate and publish classic texts of western philosophy, history, and law. These works, including many of the foundations upon which much of the western democratic tradition is based, had, for decades, been virtually impossible to find behind the Iron Curtain, where state run presses published only the works of "approved" authors.[1091]

Outcomes. Over the last fourteen years, CEU has grown into what the *Chronicle of Higher Education* has called "a regional intellectual powerhouse."[1092] Its academic programs have been so successful that its mission has changed from preparing students for western universities to offering them a full array of opportunities within their native region. CEU now has its own doctoral programs and over 900 students from sixty countries.[1093] The university employs some 100 professors, most from all over Europe (western, central, and eastern) and from the United States. In 2000, CEU began actively recruiting students from countries outside the region with developing democracies of their own. There have been challenges associated with growth—navigating the line, for example, between being too regional and too Anglo-Saxon. And CEU has needed to develop a donor base much faster than most universities do. George Soros has been adamant that it must be weaned from his funds. In 2001, he discontinued his annual contributions, but rather than leave CEU empty-handed, he endowed it with a $250 million gift: the largest ever to any European university. And he continues to chair CEU's board of trustees.

Impact. Central European University has become a beacon of academic

excellence, cultural tolerance, and advanced research in the service of democratic policymaking. As Soros has said, "[It] is now on sound footing with a
proven track record, producing excellent graduates and establishing itself as a
first rate graduate institution."[1094] It has grown rapidly and will face many of
the same challenges, and opportunities, that confront universities in the
United States and Great Britain. What university in its region could have
said as much twenty years ago?

Case 75

LIVING CITIES

The National Community Development Initiative, 1991

SCOTT KOHLER

Background. Foundations have played a lead role in the development of community development corporations (CDCs), as well as of the Local Initiatives
Support Coalition (LISC) and the Enterprise Foundation, two of the major
support organizations facilitating community investment.[1095] By the early
1990s, CDCs—led by local residents with a personal stake in the success of
their work—had shown a reliable track record of achieving progress in run-
down neighborhoods. As Peter Goldmark, then-president of the Rockefeller
Foundation said in 1991, "[f]amilies in these communities who borrow to
rebuild their lives and their neighborhoods are some of the toughest, most
determined performers around. . . . Even from a narrow business view, I'd
rather put my money in a neighborhood CDC than in Donald Trump's Taj
Mahal." [1096]

Strategy. So in 1991, a group of seven foundations partnered with the Prudential Insurance Company of America to do just that. Announcing the
largest ever private contribution to neighborhood renewal, the group committed $62.5 million in grants and loans in the hope of leveraging an addi-
tional $500 million from banks, investors, and government agencies.[1097] The
seven philanthropic partners were the Rockefeller Foundation, the Lilly Endowment, the Pew Charitable Trusts, the John D. and Catherine T.
MacArthur Foundation, the William and Flora Hewlett Foundation, the
Knight Foundation, and the Surdna Foundation. Prudential, Rockefeller, and
Lilly committed $15 million each; Lilly's contribution was an outright grant,
while Prudential and Rockefeller contributed a significant portion of their
shares in program-related investments (PRIs). The other partners contributed

smaller shares, all over a three-year period. A major target of the coalition was private banks. In year two, the foundation partners managed to convince J.P. Morgan to commit $10 million, its first foray into community development support. And in later rounds, additional for-profit funders, including NationsBank (now Bank of America) and MetLife, came on board.

The program was called the National Community Development Initiative (NCDI), and was to be managed by two leading intermediary nonprofits engaged in community development support: LISC and the Enterprise Foundation, which was founded in 1982 by real estate developer James Rouse. The funds would be directed to twenty cities.[1098] On the local level, LISC and Enterprise would work with CDCs on the ground to administer the funds. The strategies pursued were different in each of the twenty cities, but the focus in each was on building or rehabilitating low-cost housing and spurring neighborhood renewal in underprivileged communities.[1099] As Peter Goldmark recounts, however, NCDI was about more than just housing:

> The housing, (and that's not all there was) was a step toward a larger objective: the reintroduction of social standards in communities that no longer had them, and whose residents no longer enforced them. That's what successful community development really is all about.[1100]

A principal adviser to the coalition was Mitchell Sviridoff, a former Ford Foundation vice president who in 1979 had come up with the idea for LISC and gone on to be its founding president. [1101]

Outcomes. In the ensuing years, the NCDI has far exceeded its initial goal. The coalition has changed over time, growing to incorporate new foundations and other funding partners, including the Department of Housing and Urban Development (HUD), and the Office of Community Services (OCS), a division of the Department of Health and Human Services.[1102] Mindful that NCDI could be undermined if it were subjected to political pressures, the coalition won a major victory by securing the federal government's agreement to support the partnership without receiving any say in which groups get funded. This is a rare funding arrangement, to say the least, but also one that protects the grant-receiving CDCs from the hazards of politics.

The group made additional contributions in two subsequent rounds, bringing NCDI's total disbursements for the 1990s to over $250 million.[1103] And with this money, the NCDI has been able to leverage over $2 billion to support its mission of "investment in urban neighborhoods."[1104] With the help of over 300 CDCs, working in more than 350 neighborhoods, this money has been used for low interest loans and outright grants enabling local community developers to "build low-cost housing, clinics, child-care facilities and commercial properties such as shopping centers, creating jobs in the process."[1105] Police stations and public parks have also been opened. Thanks to the NCDI, over 20,000 homes have been built or rehabilitated, and CDCs have constructed over 2 million square feet of new commercial space and community facilities.[1106] Motivated by the success of the NCDI, its funding partners decided to renew it with an additional $250 million for a second decade of activity (2001–2010) under a new name: Living Cities: The National Community Development Initiative.

Impact. The CDC approach to urban renewal has a proven track record of success. Determined residents, committed to the revitalization of their own neighborhoods, have, again and again, proved far more effective in achieving positive change than heavy-handed top-down interventions from the outside. The National Community Development Initiative is a major undertaking designed to take community development to scale. Because CDCs have a history of success, and because the two intermediaries chosen to run NCDI—LICS and the Enterprise Foundation—both have extensive experience in re-granting and monitoring large scale community improvement efforts, the foundation, government, and corporate partners that underwrote NCDI were willing to take a more hands-off approach. Rather than micromanaging every decision, a sure temptation given the huge funds committed, the partners instead agreed to put their money behind CDCs, trusting that these home-grown institutions would know best what their own communities needed. It is a tribute to CDCs' history of getting results that such a large coalition of public, for-profit, and not-for-profit funders has assembled behind it. By creating this coalition, and securing for it federal assistance, while at the same time protecting it from the ever-shifting political winds, the NCDI partners have given means to thousands of altruistic people, working in communities around the country to improve their own neighborhoods using the proven tools of community development.

Case 76

THE TOBACCO USE PROGRAMS

Robert Wood Johnson Foundation, 1991

SCOTT KOHLER

Background. Tobacco use is the largest single cause of preventable deaths in the United States. Over 400,000 people each year die of tobacco-related health problems such as lung cancer and heart disease. And cigarettes are, of course, addictive. Over 65 percent of smokers say they want to quit. Over 50 percent, in any given year, make a serious effort to do so. Only 2.5 percent of them succeed.[1107] The addictive nature and health risks of smoking are universally acknowledged.[1108] But this was not always the case. As recently as 1994, the chief executives of the nation's seven largest tobacco companies each swore, in testimony before Congress, that he believed neither nicotine to be addictive, nor cigarettes to be harmful.[1109] The estimated annual burden of tobacco-related health problems, on the American health care system, is $80 billion in direct expenditures and an additional $50 billion in indirect costs.[1110]

In 1990, the Board of the Robert Wood Johnson Foundation selected Dr. Steven Schroeder to serve as the Foundation's president, understanding clearly that Dr. Schroeder was interested "in taking the Foundation in the direction of working on substance abuse problems."[1111] At the time, no American foundations were involved in the fields of tobacco policy or research.[1112] In fact, the loudest voice in the public health debate over tobacco was that of the Tobacco Institute, an organization created by the tobacco companies to communicate their message to the news media and the public.

There were many risks associated with entering the field, especially considering the enormous political heft of the tobacco industry, which has annual sales of over $45 billion.[1113] However, the magnitude of the health risks associated with tobacco made it a tough issue to ignore.[1114] The Foundation's Board was initially deadlocked on the issue, but, once the proposal was narrowed to focus the Foundation's efforts on underage tobacco use, the Board agreed, adopting as a primary goal, "[The reduction of] the harmful effects, and the irresponsible use, of tobacco, alcohol, and drugs."

Strategy. Between 1991 and 2003, the Robert Wood Johnson Foundation spent approximately $408 million on a wide range of tobacco-related programs. The Foundation's primary aims have been to reduce the incidence of youth smoking, to publicize the negative health effects of tobacco use, and to help addicted smokers quit using tobacco. These goals have been pursued through a wide range of programs, including:[1115]

- **SmokeLess States:** Started in 1993, SmokeLess States is a state-level initiative designed to assist local groups in educating their communities about tobacco and about the policy options available to regulate it. SmokeLess States coalitions also offer prevention and treatment programs targeted primarily at teenagers. To date, the Foundation has contributed approximately $92 million to the program, every dollar of which is matched by the local coalitions receiving support.[1116]

- **The Center for Tobacco-Free Kids:** The Center is the RWJF's largest national endeavor to curb smoking. The Center was created by the Foundation, in partnership with the American Cancer Society, and was intended to serve as a proactive counterweight to the Tobacco Institute. Since 1995, the Foundation has provided over $70 million to the Center.

- **The Tobacco and Substance Abuse Policy Research programs:** There is an enormous range of factors that influence a person's decision to smoke, and, likewise, a wide range of concerns in any tobacco policy discussion. Recognizing that no one field of inquiry can possibly encompass the multiplicity of angles from which tobacco can be viewed, the Foundation has funded research exploring such issues as the biological and societal factors that can lead to nicotine addiction, the relationship between cigarette prices and consumption, and many others. Particularly important has been the RWJ-funded research into the elasticity of demand with respect to the price of cigarettes. The Foundation has used its leverage as a funder and an acknowledged leader in tobacco policy discussion to convene experts from a range of fields to promote the sharing of insights and the undertaking of multidisciplinary research into tobacco issues.[1117]

- **The Sports Initiative:** Through this endeavor, the Foundation seeks to enlist professional athletes and sports leagues to publicly discourage young fans from using tobacco. Of particular note is the National Spit Tobacco Education Program (NSTEP), a partnership between the RWJF and Joe Garagiola, a former major-leaguer who for years has recruited fellow baseball stars to help break the stereotypical association between baseball players and spit tobacco.

- **Smoke-Free Families:** While the bulk of the Foundation's resources have been dedicated to research and prevention, funds have also been allocated to tobacco cessation programs. The flagship of these efforts is the Smoke-Free Families program, which targets pregnant women and single mothers, offering them information and cessation assistance in view of the serious health effects that smoking can have on their unborn children and infants.

Outcomes. Many of the programs supported by the Robert Wood Johnson Foundation have had a significant effect on the huge national debate over tobacco. SmokeLess States coalitions are active in thirty-one states and the District of Columbia. By publicizing such information as the public-health effects of second-hand smoke and the effect of excise taxes on tobacco consumption, the coalitions have contributed to the enactment of many local laws regulating the sale and consumption of tobacco products. Foundation-funded research showing that children's consumption of cigarettes declines as price increases has provided the impetus for passage of tobacco tax increases in states across the nation. The Center for Tobacco-Free Kids has received significant public attention. In the late 1990s, it was asked, by the Attorneys General of several states, to participate, as a disinterested and trustworthy party, in the states' negotiations with the tobacco industry over pending litigation. The Center received much criticism from its allies in the anti-tobacco movement when this was publicized, and a combination of interests from the far left (opposed to any deal with the tobacco companies) and the far right (opposed, for political reasons, to any regulation of cigarettes) narrowly defeated the agreed-upon settlement.[1118] The National Spit Tobacco Education Campaign has been publicly supported by such All-Stars as Alex Rodriguez, Lenny Dykstra, Hank Aaron, and the late Mickey Mantle. And a wide range of other outcomes have flowed from RWJF tobacco programs. Foundation-sponsored research, for example, was cited repeatedly by the FDA in its determination to seek jurisdiction over tobacco products, and RWJ-supported experts have advised Members of Congress and testified before Congressional committees.[1119]

Impact. The Robert Wood Johnson Foundation was certainly not the first nonprofit organization to involve itself in tobacco research and advocacy. But the RWJF brought to bear the enormous resources of a major funder, and had the courage to tackle a problem that, for political reasons, the federal government had been hesitant to touch. The Foundation was able to convene and support a wide spectrum of influential actors, and, in so doing, serve as a private center of power in the interest of the public—polyarchical in every way. The Foundation, along with partners like the American Cancer Society, blazed a trail that many others have followed.[1120]

Joe Garagiola, for example, had been working to spread awareness of the threat posed to young baseball players by spit tobacco for years before the RWJF sought him out. But with the Foundation's help, he was able to take his message much more powerfully to scale. Garagiola himself recalls, "[u]ntil Robert Wood Johnson came along, I was working with a broken bat—now I [have] a Louisville Slugger."[1121]

Despite the controversy surrounding its participation—and the eventual collapse of the settlement it negotiated—the Center for Tobacco-Free Kids has clearly been seen as a key fixture in discussions about tobacco control. This is demonstrated by the fact that its involvement was directly sought, first by the state Attorneys General, but also by the FDA and the White

House. And the Center has succeeded as a counterweight to the Tobacco Institute. In fact, so discredited has the tobacco companies' message been that they shut down the Institute several years ago.

Since 1995, smoking rates among adults have declined by 12.6 percent and among teens by 18 percent.[1122] With a problem so enormously complicated, the Foundation's influence cannot be called determinative. However, since 1991, the Foundation has been at the forefront of tobacco research, education, advocacy, and treatment. As Sidney F. Wentz, then-Chairman of the its Board of Trustees, wrote elegantly in the Robert Wood Johnson Foundation's 1992 Annual Report: "There's no sword to cut through this Gordian knot, but we, as a Foundation, are obliged to keep picking at the strands of it with unremitting determination if we are ever to achieve our goal of improved health care for all Americans."

Case 77

CHARTER SCHOOLS FUNDING

Walton Family Foundation, 1991

STEVEN SCHINDLER

Background. The Walton Family Foundation, funded from the fortune of Wal-Mart founder Sam Walton in the late 1980s, first became involved in the field of education in the early 1990s. John Walton, family trustee and son of Sam Walton, felt strongly that education, and K–12 education in particular, was the field in which the foundation could wield the strongest leverage.[1123] John Walton also became frustrated, however, with the Foundation's early grants in the field of education; as promising as the educational programs chosen for funding may have been, the programs yielded only transitory impact. Walton attributed this to the lack of strong entrepreneurial leadership at the grantee organizations. Backing away from funding specific programs, he led the Foundation to undertake a study of education to understand more clearly how it could achieve impact in the field. After the study, the Foundation concluded that power in the field of education, through financial control, should be transferred from political leaders to parents in the form of school choice and the ability to direct financial resources accordingly.[1124]

Strategy. The Foundation began funding individual charter schools in 1996. By the beginning of 2003, the Foundation had granted almost $30 million in start-up grants to individual charter schools. In what the Foundation calls "Phase 1" of its support for charter schools, the strategy was to get a core set of charter schools up and running, both to show that they could work in practice and to have a set of data to study for improvement and scalability.[1125] One of John Walton's priorities was that each school should be successful. Pressed by charter school organizations for more funding to build additional schools, Walton insisted on the improvement of existing charter schools first. He did not want poorly performing charter schools to drain the potential momentum the charter school movement might build.[1126]

In "Phase 2," the Foundation has aimed to build the support capacity of statewide charter school support organizations to stem the tide of opposition against the charter school movement. The Foundation perceived that a number of the original charter school supporters in the state legislatures were facing increasing pressure from charter school opponents to repeal legislation enabling the creation of charter schools in their states. The statewide organizations advocating for charter schools generally had fewer than two full-time staff members; the Foundation provided what it considered efficient investments in the form of operating grants to such organizations for research and media relations in the states. Similarly, the Foundation supported national organizations that in turn provided assistance to the state support organizations and facilitated a nationwide charter school network.[1127]

In addition, the Foundation has supported the financing of buildings to house charter schools, the lack of which is a frequent barrier to the more widespread establishment of charter schools. The Foundation's most significant contributions to that end have been grants totaling $18 million to the Local Initiatives Support Corporation, created by the Ford Foundation, to create a grant program, financing center, and loan pool for charter school facilities, aimed at providing financial resources for charter school entrepreneurs and intended to attract additional support from other donors for the cause.[1128]

Impact. Since 1991, when Minnesota adopted the first charter school enabling law, thirty-nine other states and the District of Columbia have enacted similar laws. Approximately 3,600 charter schools operate nationwide.[1129] In the fall of 2005, about one million students were enrolled in charter schools.[1130] The Walton Family Foundation, while certainly not the only private funder of charter schools, was one of the earliest and remains one of the biggest financial supporters of the movement.[1131] Perhaps more importantly, the Foundation serves as a stable source of support for the charter school movement while public support for charter schools sways with the latest research studies.[1132] The Foundation, committed to the conclusions in its education study and the convictions of John Walton, continues to make both planning and start-up grants to individual charter schools in targeted urban school districts to provide more charter school options to families in those districts.[1133]

Case 78

JSTOR

Andrew W. Mellon Foundation, 1992

SCOTT KOHLER

Background. Traditional libraries are burdened with ever-growing storage costs. Old books and academic journals, though rarely used, take up enormous amounts of stack space and can require continuous maintenance to preserve. This has been an unavoidable reality faced over hundreds of years by thousands of libraries. In the 1970s and especially the 1980s, academic journal collection became even more burdensome, as publishers, faced with higher up-front costs, increased drastically the price of many journals.[1134] Meanwhile, academic specialization continued giving rise to more and more scholarly literature. Libraries often could not keep up with the proliferation of expensive journals, leading many in the higher education community to feel that they were "being priced out of adequate library resources."[1135]

In 1992, William G. Bowen, president of the Mellon Foundation (also president emeritus of Princeton University) had the idea for a digital library of scholarly journals. Bowen conceived the idea just after a meeting of the board of trustees of Denison University (of which he was then a member), when it was announced that the Denison library needed a $5 million addition to house its ever-expanding stacks filled with back editions of journals.[1136] Dubbed JSTOR (for "Journal STORage"), Bowen's digital database was to serve two purposes: (1) increase access to older journal articles, and (2) reduce the storage and maintenance costs imposed on libraries by their many costly journal subscriptions.[1137]

Strategy. From the start, it was clear that the "the technological and organizational complexities [of the project] were too great" to develop the JSTOR database in-house. To that end, the foundation recruited Ira Fuchs from Princeton University to help manage "tech hurdles," and selected the University of Michigan to develop the new database along the lines of TULIP, an early small-scale journal database created in a pioneering collaboration among Michigan and eight other universities with Elsevier Science, a scientific journal publisher.[1138] The Foundation gave Michigan an initial grant of $700,000 for software development, followed, four months later, by $1.5 million for production costs.[1139]

The Foundation did not leave the implementation of its plan entirely to the grantee. From the start, Bowen had been directly involved in the JSTOR project, and he took it upon himself to convince publishers to participate in the database. Eschewing a solely market-based approach, the Foundation made decisions about which fields of study should be included based upon the needs of scholars, not the likelihood of selling the final product.[1140]

The goal for the JSTOR prototype was to scan the complete backfiles of ten journals of economics and history: approximately 750,000 pages of material.[1141] The decision only to include backfiles was important. Old academic journals tend to gather dust in library stacks. They are not a source of revenue for their publishers. Critical to Bowen's success in negotiating licensing rights with publishers was the promise that their business would not be harmed by cooperating with JSTOR. They continue to make money selling their current volumes, but JSTOR gives scholars easy access to an immense base of knowledge compiled in years past.[1142] The database was tested at five library sites while the system was still being refined at Michigan. Although there was only limited content available, and technical problems were common, the new resource was well-received; especially popular was its ability to search for a word or phrase throughout the full text of the documents stored.[1143]

In keeping with the Mellon Foundation's determination not to fund JSTOR indefinitely, the Foundation set up JSTOR as an independent not-for-profit organization in August 1995. The new organization had its own staff, offices, and board of trustees (chaired initially by Bowen). According to Hal Varian of MIT, once "the core journals," including such titles as the *Journal of Political Economy* and the *Journal of Modern History*, had "come on board . . . [Bowen] was able to persuade Kevin Guthrie to become CEO. Kevin, in turn, assembled the team that has led to JSTOR's great success."[1144] JSTOR became available to the public in 1997. By the end of that year the Mellon Foundation had spent $5.2 million developing it.[1145]

Outcomes. Today, the JSTOR digital archive includes 449 scholarly journals, covering a wide range of topics in the humanities, social and natural sciences, mathematics, business, and more. Over 2.6 million articles are available through JSTOR, representing a total of some 16.4 million pages.[1146] And JSTOR is widely used. 2,160 schools and libraries in eighty-six countries are fee-paying members. In the first ten months of 2004 alone, users viewed more than 56 million pages of content and printed over 15 million articles from the JSTOR archive.[1147] JSTOR has been fully self-supporting since 1999.[1148]

While JSTOR had considerable up-front costs (software development) and does have recurring costs (maintenance, updating technology, adding content, etc.), these costs are far outweighed by the savings it creates. Libraries are able to economize stack space, and require fewer librarians to manage their collections. Delivering the Romanes Lecture at Oxford University in October 2000, William Bowen (an economist before he was a foundation or university president) estimated the system-wide savings in library capital costs to be at least $140 million.[1149]

Impact. The Mellon Foundation—its staff and trustees—came up with the idea for JSTOR, searched for an adequate model on which to build it, and enlisted publishers to donate licensing rights. They recognized what the foundation was well-equipped to do—create and support, in every way possible, this new archive. And what it was ill-equipped to do—directly manage it. So the Foundation recruited people to run the institution and gave them the resources to make it work.

The libraries' projected savings thanks to JSTOR are enormous. And JSTOR's impact in giving millions of people access to such a huge mine of scholarly resources is impossible to quantify. JSTOR is also significant as an early and (still) leading practical application of the technological advances of digitization and the World Wide Web. And, as Hal Varian points out, the database is of special value to the developing world:

> JSTOR has not only had a huge impact on scholarship at major research universities in the United States, but it also offers even greater benefits for relatively impoverished institutions in developing nations. Literature that was totally inaccessible to these institutions in the past is now just a click of the mouse away.

JSTOR is also "likely to cause a great deal of intellectual history to be revised."[1150] Fred R. Shapiro, associate librarian at the Yale Law School has, for example, found the origins of many terms in surprising places. He feels that "[t]he history of language is being rewritten because of these electronic tools." Similarly, Professor Cathleen Synge Morawetz, a winner of the National Medal of Science, contends that "there are important [mathematical] ideas to be picked up from papers of 100 years ago." Without JSTOR, many of those ideas would probably still be gathering dust.

Case 79

INTERNATIONAL SCIENCE FOUNDATION

Soros Foundations/Open Society Institute, 1992

SCOTT KOHLER

Background. Under the Communist regime of the Soviet Union, funding for scientific research was provided almost entirely by the state. As the Soviet empire declined, so too did support for the large Soviet scientific community. Soon after the treaty formally disintegrating the U.S.S.R. was signed in Belovezhskaya Pushcha on December 8, 1991, this already wavering governmental support virtually disappeared. At the same time, however, the financier and philanthropist George Soros stepped in, and his philanthropy over the next three years played a major role in keeping afloat the scientific communities of Russia and the other former Soviet republics at a time when they were critically endangered.

Soros had become interested in the struggle of Soviet researchers through discussions with Alex Goldfarb, a Russian-born microbiologist who, with his family, had immigrated to the United States. Soros had met Goldfarb in 1986, when he recruited the scientist to work with his Moscow foundation. In 1990, Goldfarb began lamenting that a project he was running in Russia was having difficulty paying salaries, since its grant from the United States National Science Foundation covered only equipment and supply costs.[1151] Soros agreed in principle to support science in the Soviet Union, because, as he explains in his autobiography:

> Soviet science was rich in advanced human intellectual achievements in a vein that differed slightly from that in which Western science had developed and it was worthy of being preserved. Scientists were then and are now on the front line of the struggle for an open society [in the Soviet Union and around the world]. In addition, there was a high probability that our efforts would be successful, since reliable criteria existed for the assessment of merit. The services of the international scientific community could be enlisted to this end, which would exert an additional influence on the screening process.[1152]

When the Soviet Union collapsed, the time to act had come. Once his initial efforts to persuade the U.S. and other governments to undertake a new Marshall Plan for the former Soviet republics proved unsuccessful, Soros sought to spur outside funding by example. After September 16, 1992, when his speculation against the value of the British pound made Soros over $1 billion in a single day, the financier set aside $100 million "to support basic natural sciences in the countries of the former Soviet Union."[1153]

At the time, over half of all people working in science in those nations lived below the poverty level.[1154] Within Russia, the average civilian scientist's wage was between $15 and $25 per month, and, as inflation ran rampant, conditions were rapidly deteriorating. By mid-1993, scientists in Georgia were earning an average of just twenty cents a month.[1155] When Soros officially announced his gift of $100 million, to be paid out over the next two years, ". . . no private individual had to date provided charitable support to another nation in such proportions."[1156]

Strategy. The promised funds were used to set up the International Science Foundation (ISF), which worked out of Moscow and New York. Soros, who argues that "he who gives quickly gives twice,"[1157] believed that haste was especially important in the work of the ISF, since inflation would eat away at the value of funds given slowly. The Foundation's first undertaking was the Emergency Grants Program, which provided $500 to any scientist in the former Soviet Union who, in the past five years, had published at least three articles in any of the more reputable scientific journals. The $500, which represented over a full year's salary for many recipients, could be used for living costs, travel, research, or however else the beneficiary wished.

This was soon followed by the Long-Term Research Grants Program, which, unlike the Emergency Grants Program, was a competitive enterprise. Leading researchers applied for grants of between $9,000 and $32,000. In addition each grantee's home institution was given a grant to cover any overhead costs incurred for ISF-sponsored research. Over 50,000 specialists in various scientific fields from around the world served as judges for this program, which effectively "introduced Russia to an open system of soliciting proposals and their selection through peer review on the Western model. . . ." In contrast to research under the Soviet regime, long-term grantees were chosen on the basis of merit—not political connections.

ISF also sponsored a Conference Travel Grant Program, which paid the travel costs to send any scientist invited to present at an international conference. Flights, lodging, and daily expenses were all fully underwritten. In addition, the Foundation funded subscriptions to scientific periodicals for libraries that could not afford them, as well as a Telecommunications Program that built infrastructure and provided technical assistance to extend access to the Internet to Soviet research institutions. Mr. Soros oversaw this last program in particular, because he viewed it as an important contribution to the broader democratization of the region.[1158]

Throughout its four years of operation, the International Science Foundation operated in all the former Soviet republics, offering equal consideration to each. From the outset, the Foundation relinquished all copyright claims, and other intellectual property rights, to the research it supported. Although there was little or no tradition of a not-for-profit sector in many of the republics, the ISF was exempt from taxation and customs duties everywhere it operated.[1159]

Outcomes. Between 1993 and 1996, the International Science Foundation gave out nearly $130 million.[1160] The Emergency Grants Program gave out a total of 26,145 grants, which supported approximately 23 percent of all the scientists working in the laboratories and universities of the former Soviet Union.[1161] Even more remarkable, all of those grants were made in ISF's first four months of operation.[1162] The Long-Term Research Grants Program eventually supported some 15,000 scientists, and gave out more than $80 million: about 63 percent of ISF's total giving. As noted above, it also introduced Russia, and the other republics, for the first time, to the competitive Western-style mechanism of peer-reviewed grant application. According to a 1997 study of the ISF by Irina Dezhina, the Library Assistance Program "single-handedly closed the enormous gap in the state procurement of scientific periodicals. . . ." Furthermore, 98 percent of foreign science journal subscriptions now held by Russian libraries were initiated with ISF funding.[1163] All these programs brought to the former U.S.S.R. the resources and expertise of western science. The Travel Grant Program, on the other hand, brought to the West a cadre of Russian scientists, and, according to Dezhina, "had a great moral and psychological impact" in enabling these researchers to emerge from the Iron Curtain and begin collaborating with the rest of the global scientific community.

Impact. Although some (primarily pro-Communist) elements in Russia sought to portray the ISF as a front for the CIA, hearings in the Duma spurred a wave of over 100 letters, signed by over 400 Russian scientists, praising the work of the Foundation. Ultimately, the Russian parliament issued a formal expression of gratitude to George Soros and the ISF, just as President Boris Yeltsin did in 1992, when the $100 million gift was first announced. It began the process of integrating the former Soviet bloc into the international scientific community, and provided the most desperately needed stopgap support with astonishing quickness. Until 1992, over 80 percent of all funding for Soviet scientific research had come from the state. Much of that dried up in the chaotic aftermath of dissolution, and ISF helped mitigate the damage inflicted by this loss. In so doing, ISF played a crucial role in sustaining thousands of scientists and research institutions.

As one member of the presidium of the Russian Academy of Sciences explained in 1994, "[t]he Foundation has played a tremendous role in seeing that our science is still alive, not only in terms of money but first and foremost psychologically."[1164] According to a biography of Mr. Soros by Michael T. Kaufman, the donor "considers [the ISF] perhaps his greatest single philanthropic achievement." This claim is borne out in Soros' own reflections. Recalling his International Science Foundation, Soros has said, "I think it was a roaring success, particularly because it came to an end. The ISF did its job. It had clear objectives, transparent operations, and it delivered."[1165]

Case 80

SUPPORT FOR ASIAN STUDIES AND CULTURAL EXCHANGE

Freeman Foundation, 1993

SCOTT KOHLER

Background. The Freeman Foundation was born of a trust created in 1978 by Mansfield Freeman, one of the founders of American International Group (AIG). Mr. Freeman had, prior to starting AIG, been a teacher at Tsinghua University in Beijing. He lived in China from 1919 to 1941, had a deep interest in East Asia, and was a published scholar of Chinese philosophy.[1166] Over the course of his lifetime, Mr. Freeman became concerned that Americans and Asians knew little about each other, and he hoped through his philanthropy to help bridge the disparate cultures. Upon his death in 1992, Freeman's family created the Foundation in accordance with his wishes, that it work:

> ... to strengthen the bonds of friendship between this country and those of the Far East; to develop a greater appreciation of oriental cultures in this country and a better understanding of American institutions and purposes on the part of the peoples of East Asia, and to stimulate an exchange of ideas in economic and cultural fields which will help create mutual understanding and thus lessen the danger of such frictions and disagreements as lead to war.[1167]

It is worth noting that, of all American foundations, the Freeman Foundation spends the highest proportion of its resources on international grantmaking. In 2002, the most recent year for which these figures have been published, the Foundation spent $60.8 million, equivalent to 74.6 percent of its total appropriations, on overseas grants.

Strategy. Since its creation, the Freeman Foundation has undertaken a broad range of activities to promote in the United States increased awareness of Asian history and culture, and to enable students—from both regions—to study abroad in the other. Most of the Foundation's support has been targeted at education. As its mission statement explains: "Through education and educational institutes, the Foundation hopes to develop a greater appreciation of oriental cultures, histories, and economies in the United States and a better understanding of the American people and of American institutions and purposes by the peoples of East Asia."[1168] What follows, then, is a sample of the Foundation's more notable grants in supporting cross-cultural interaction and understanding through education.

- In 1994, the Freeman Foundation made a five-year grant of $10 million to Wesleyan University—Mansfield Freeman's alma mater—to fund full four-year scholarships for twenty-two students each year. The scholarships are given to promising students from eleven Asian countries, "who would not otherwise have the opportunity to study in the U.S."[1169]

- In 1997, the Foundation appropriated $7.75 million for an emergency loan program to support Asian students in the United States whose ability to continue their studies had been jeopardized by the Asian financial crises of that year. More recently, the Foundation carried over unused funds from that program, ASIA-HELP, to fund a similar relief effort. Freeman-EAS (Emergency Assistance for Students) now offers "educational allowances of up to $5,000 to undergraduates from Indonesia, Malaysia, and Thailand . . . who are facing serious financial difficulties" as a result of the catastrophic tsunami of December 2004.

- The Freeman Foundation has underwritten the addition of Asian studies faculty, course offerings, and study opportunities to eighty-four grantee institutions of higher education. The four-year, $100 million Freeman Foundation Undergraduate Asian Studies Initiative has sought to increase the number of students majoring in Asian Studies, and to encourage and enable more and more American students to study abroad in East Asia.

- In 2002, the Foundation commissioned nine children's museums around the country to create seven different exhibits—each highlighting some facet of oriental culture or history. According to an article in *The Washington Post*, "the gift . . . is the first time children's museums have received money as a group. . . . [And it] wants to take advantage of the strong attendance figures [at these museums] to expand interest in Asian culture."[1170]

- The Freeman Foundation is also the primary supporter of the National Consortium for Teaching About Asia, "a nationwide initiative [launched in 1998] to encourage and facilitate teaching and learning about Asian history, geography, culture, and social issues for K–12 schools nationwide."[1171] The Consortium, run by five partner institutions, offers seminars and travel grants to teachers, who, it is hoped, then incorporate the Asian Studies material into their lesson plans.

Outcomes. The Freeman Foundation's Asian Studies grantmaking has strengthened the field, and has exposed students of all ages—from both Asia and the United States—to languages, cultures, and experiences thoroughly unlike their own. The Wesleyan scholarships, for example, have so far enabled 204 Asian students to study at Mr. Freeman's alma mater. The Foundation's two emergency loan programs have provided crucial support for Asian students whose homes were struck by disaster. David Arnold, then acting president of the Institute of International Education—which administered the ASIA-HELP grants—rightly identified the donation's importance in labeling it a "rapid and generous response to [the] crisis."[1172] In that case, as in the more recent case of Freeman-EAS, the Foundation has employed a timely infusion of much-needed funds to preserve for over 1,000[1173] students the dream of an American education.

Meanwhile, the Freeman Foundation Undergraduate Asian Studies Initiative, which paid out the balance of its $100 million commitment in 2004, has funded rapid growth in the study of oriental cultures and languages at American colleges and universities. Since 2000, the initiative has paid for over 100 new full-time faculty hires at the eighty-four grantee institutions. It has also funded the creation of more than 1,000 new courses on Asian studies (including languages), and has led the participating schools to add Asia-related content to over 800 pre-existing undergraduate courses. The initiative has enabled some 2,500 students and 600 faculty members to travel or study in Asia. And it has been the driving force behind a 39 percent increase—at the eighty-four schools—in the number of students majoring in Asian studies.

Freeman efforts to reach a younger audience have also proved effective. The seven children's museum exhibits underwritten by the Foundation began a tour in 2004 that will take them to seventy museums around the country by the end of 2007.[1174] In the first half of 2004 alone, the initial seven host museums had more than 250,000 visitors.[1175] And the teacher seminars on Asian studies hosted by the Freeman-funded National Consortium for Teaching About Asia have enriched the curricula of more than 950,000 students so far.[1176]

Impact. All told, the Freeman Foundation has been the largest private backer of Asian studies and of cross-cultural exchange between East Asia and the United States. Certainly, much of the West remains under-informed about life in the Orient, and a vastly greater share of attention will likely continue to be paid in American education to the European affairs. But the Freeman Foundation, which made grants last year of over $55 million for these and other Asia-related initiatives, is working to lessen this imbalance year by year, and, in so doing, "to strengthen the bonds of friendship between this country and the countries of the Far East." By precisely targeting its grant-making, it has succeeded in achieving outcomes far beyond the measure of its limited resources.

Case 81

The Prostate Cancer Foundation

1993

Scott Kohler

Background. When Michael Milken was diagnosed with prostate cancer in 1993, the prognosis was not good. The disease, in a man as young as Milken, was practically a death sentence.[1177] And research in the field was moribund. "People were afraid to try anything," says Howard Scher, chief of genitourinary oncology at Memorial Sloan-Kettering Cancer Center, looking back to those bleak days. "There was such nihilism in the field." For a young doctor, to enter the field of prostate cancer research was practically to commit career suicide. So Milken had little reason to be optimistic.

Strategy. Nonetheless, he quickly set up CaP Cure, a private foundation to be devoted entirely "to [finding] better treatments and a cure for recurrent prostate cancer."[1178] The foundation, which has since changed its name to the Prostate Cancer Foundation (PCF) was the vehicle through which Milken would apply many of the same talents that in the 1980s had made him the king of junk bonds, and one of the most powerful men on Wall Street.[1179] The Foundation set about tearing down the structural barriers inhibiting research. For instance, to get a government research grant was a process that often took three years and required the filling out of hundreds of pages in application and supporting documents. PCF's approach was radically different: grant applications were limited to five pages and, for those whose requests were approved, the actual grant—of between $75,000 and $150,000— would be made within ninety days. This flood of quick cash came with one requirement: all PCF grantees were required to give a detailed update of their progress at a gathering of scientists, physicians, and private industry groups convened by the Foundation every year.[1180] In the territorial world of medical research, obsessed with patent rights, this was a discouraging prospect. In its first year, the PCF received only eighty-five grant applications. But the scarcity of funding, from government and other sources, made it a tough offer to pass up. In 1994, the Foundation received 200 applications, and by '95 the number was up to 600.[1181]

Outcomes. Even as Milken battled his own cancer into remission, his foundation invigorated progress in the once-hopeless field of prostate cancer research. In 1993, 34,900 American men died of the disease. In 2004, that was down to 29,900, a 24 percent decrease in the per capita death rate.[1182] According to a cover story in FORTUNE magazine, "virtually everyone [in the field] agrees that Milken deserves an enormous share of the credit for the progress made against this major killer." Dr. Patrick Walsh, the head of urology at Johns Hopkins, insists that "Mike's done more for prostate cancer research than anyone in America."[1183] Since its founding, the Prostate Cancer Foundation has raised over $230 million and made grants to more than 1,200 projects at more than 100 different institutions.[1184] If it were a for-profit corporation that owned the products developed by research it has funded, the Foundation would be the third largest biotech company in the world.[1185]

PCF has also worked to increase awareness of the disease. One of the first people Milken met with after founding CaP Cure was Kwesi Mfume, then head of the Congressional Black Caucus (and until recently of the NAACP), who helped to spread word of the disease among the African-American community, whose members tend to be far less informed about prostate cancer than their white counterparts, despite being at a 65 percent higher risk of dying from the disease.[1186] In late '93, the Foundation organized a gala at the U.S. Capitol Building attended by members of Congress, celebrities, and prostate cancer researchers that has become an annual tradition and, in 2003, raised over $5 million.[1187] It is reminiscent of Milken's old Predator's Ball, except, as the *Washington Post* pointed out in a 1994 article, "the talk was not investment or junk bonds or corporate raiding. . . . Instead, the word on everyone's lips was prostate."[1188]

Impact. The revolutionary strategy pursued by the Milken and the PCF has major implications for the broader medical research community. According to

Andrew von Eschenbach, director of the National Cancer Institute, "Michael Milken changed the culture of [medical] research." Organizations like the Juvenile Diabetes Research Foundation and the Cystic Fibrosis Foundation have consulted with Milken for advice. Others, like the ALS Foundation and the Michael J. Fox Foundation for Parkinson's Disease, have modeled their own grantmaking on the PCF. In 1995, the Prostate Cancer Foundation organized a consortium of five research universities to devise a common set of rules for gathering, categorizing, and storing human tissue specimens.[1189] This uniform standard will be of great use to researchers studying many diseases. And in 1998, Milken helped to conceive, organize and fund the nationwide cancer demonstrations in 200 cities (including a 150,000-person march in Washington, D.C.), that are credited with spurring Congress to increase funding for the National Cancer Institute by 70 percent.[1190] By breaking down barriers to cooperation and by clearing up structural bottlenecks inhibiting the flow of funds for research, Michael Milken and his Prostate Cancer Foundation may be turning the tide against a deadly disease that infects one in every six men. And they have pioneered a new approach to medical research that is a model for many groups fighting similar fights.

Case 82

PAUL B. BEESON CAREER DEVELOPMENT AWARDS IN AGING RESEARCH PROGRAM

The Commonwealth Fund, Hartford Foundation, Atlantic Philanthropies, and Starr Foundation, 1994

SCOTT KOHLER

Background. Americans over the age of sixty-five make up the nation's largest bloc of health care consumers. And although their numbers are increasing faster than at any time in history, senior citizens are still usually treated by physicians with little or no special training in the biological effects of aging. Of the 125 medical schools in the United States, only thirteen require any coursework in gerontology, and fewer than 4 percent of all physicians have ever taken an elective on geriatrics.[1191]

Between 1978 and 1993, three conferences of the Institute of Medicine (IOM) identified the paucity of geriatric specialists as a major problem in the American health care sector, and called for major new support of research and training in the field. Recognizing that "the greatest deterrent to physicians-in-training being exposed to geriatrics. . . is the shortage of research-based academic leaders and role models among medical school faculty,"[1192] three private foundations in the early '90s sought to provide needed support. Beginning with a 1991 paper published by The Commonwealth Fund, these foundations—The Commonwealth, as well as the Atlantic Philanthropies and the John A. Hartford Foundation—discussed how best to draw talented physician-researchers into the geriatrics field.

Strategy. In the spring of 1994, the foundations announced the creation of ten national fellowships for research, teaching, and practice in aging and geriatrics. With an initial commitment of approximately $14 million, they set up the Paul B. Beeson Physician Faculty Scholars in Aging Research Program.[1193] The Program provides about ten new fellowships each year to promising medical school junior faculty members committed to pursuing a career in gerontology. The Beeson scholars are picked by an Advisory Committee of leading physician-scientists in the field, and the size of the award, up to $450,000 over three years, ensures that it is a major incentive. Each Beeson scholar has at least 75 percent of his or her time protected for research. This is meant to drive progress in the scientific study of aging, and to free promising faculty from the demands of clinical practice. In addition, each scholar is assigned a mentor from his or her institution, who assists in career advising and networking. Named for Paul B. Beeson, M.D., the distinguished medical professor who chaired the original 1978 IOM conference on "Aging and Medical Education," the program is administered and overseen by two not-for-profit organizations: the American Federation for Aging Research (AFAR) and the Alliance for Aging Research.

Outcomes. To date, the Beeson Program's foundation sponsors have spent over $46 million to give out 104 Beeson Career Development Awards.[1194] Competition for the awards has been stiff, with up to eighty applicants vying for the ten fellowships in any given year.[1195] Of the first group of scholars, those selected in 1995, 96 percent have since been promoted to tenured positions. This average for all ten classes of scholars taken together is 50 percent. According to Judith Salerno, Deputy Director of the National Institute on Aging, "[b]ecoming a Beeson scholar is like getting a halo. It has been a distinguished and well-recognized achievement and it gives researchers a step up unlike any other award."[1196]

Impact. Many of the Beesons have gone on to receive significant acclaim. In 2003, for instance, not one, but two Beeson alums—Drs. Ashley Bush and David Holtzman—shared the American Academy of Neurology's highest honor, the Potemkin Prize.[1197] Now, 93 percent of the Beeson alumni train new researchers and practitioners in the field. Over the past ten years, "they have trained more than 700 students and faculty."[1198] So not only has the Beeson Awards Program served as a major boost to a cadre of young experts, but its effects have rippled outward,[1199] leading more and more young medical students to receive more and better training in a field of medicine of enormous concern—not only to the elderly—but rather to all Americans who will one day join their ranks.

In 2000, the Starr Foundation joined the program as a major funder, which cleared the way the following year for The Commonwealth Fund to phase out its involvement. And in 2004, the National Institute on Aging (NIA) assumed responsibility for much of the program's administration, committing additional funds that increased the size of the award to between $600,000 and $800,000 over a period of three-to-five years for each new scholar. As a result, the Program's "financial future [is now] assured." Atlantic Philanthropies, as well as the Hartford and Starr Foundations, continues to work with AFAR, the Alliance for Aging Research and NIA to ensure that the Beeson Program will continue to grow and enrich the field of gerontology for many years to come.[1200]

Case 83

PICKER INSTITUTE

The Commonwealth Fund, 1994

SCOTT KOHLER

Background. Dr. Harvey Picker was a pioneer of X-ray and ultrasound technology. In 1986, the small family foundation that he had founded with his wife Jean merged with The Commonwealth Fund.[1201] After Jean Picker was hospitalized with a life-threatening medical condition, the Pickers decided that the medical profession, despite its impressive technology and expertise, was insufficiently responsive to the concerns of its patients. To remedy the failing, they initiated the Picker/Commonwealth Program for Patient-Centered Care. It was to be a research organization seeking to determine what factors are most important to patients and whether health care providers are adequately responsive to patient preferences.

Strategy. Over the next seven years, the Commonwealth/Picker Program conducted extensive academic research, including over 8,000 interviews with patients and their families, as well as focus groups composed of dozens of caregivers.[1202] This research showed that patient's preferences were too-often neglected, and that amenities, such as hospital food and access to parking, were given far too much significance in existing patient surveys. The Program also led to the definition of the seven dimensions of care that are most important to patients:[1203]

- Patients' preferences are respected

- Coordination of care

- Information and education about their condition

- Physical comfort

- Emotional support

- Support for family and friends, and

- Continuity of care and transition to normal life

In 1994, the Commonwealth Program was chartered as an independent not-for-profit institution, supported by The Commonwealth Fund and overseen by Dr. Picker. It would provide research on the state of health care on the local, regional, and national level, and offer surveys which hospitals and HMOs could use to gauge their performance.

Outcomes. The Picker Institute developed a wide range of survey tools that quickly set the standard in performance measurement within the health care field. In addition to its own research, the Institute was a leading partner in the creation of the Consumer Assessment of Health Plans (CAHPS) surveys, developed in conjunction with Harvard Medical School, the Research Triangle Institute, and the RAND Corporation, that have been widely used to help Medicare recipients navigate the maze of options offered to them around the nation. As demand for Picker surveys increased, the Institute had difficulty running large-scale data collection, processing, and reporting, and so its survey instruments were acquired by the for-profit National Research Corporation.

Impact. The Picker Institute's early research had a huge impact on the development of patient-centered care in the United States. And the tools developed with Commonwealth funds continue to be widely used. The Picker+NRC Group conducts actionable performance measurement research for a wide range of clients, including hospitals, HMOs, and the U.S. Departments of Veterans Affairs[1204] and Defense, as well as the National Institutes of Health. And the Picker Institute Europe, which has remained an independent nonprofit, works to assist health care providers in improving patient-centered care internationally.

Case 84

COLLEGE AND BEYOND DATABASE

Andrew W. Mellon Foundation, 1994

SCOTT KOHLER

Background. The Andrew W. Mellon Foundation has a long history of "supporting research in higher education."[1205] Among the many manifestations of this interest is a long trail of Mellon-supported literature examining a host of higher education issues and challenges. However, according to the Foundation's president, William G. Bowen, "it is entirely possible that the creation of the College and Beyond database will prove to be the most lasting contribution of the Foundation to research in higher education."[1206]

Strategy. The Mellon Foundation created the database to which Bowen refers over a period of almost four years, stretching from late 1994 into 1997. According to Bowen, "it was created to serve a range of scholarly objectives since those of us who created it thought that we needed to know more about outcomes in higher education generally."[1207] To that end, the Foundation approached the presidents of more than two dozen academically selective colleges and universities to ask for their cooperation. Specifically, the Foundation asked each school to release a broad set of data about several classes of graduates. The database would collate such information as the students' high school grades, test scores, family background at the time they applied, as well as collegiate performance indicators, such as undergraduate grade point average, graduation status (whether the student graduated and, if so, in how long), major field of study, and whether each student had participated in varsity athletics, or any other time-intensive extracurricular activity.[1208]

The presidents agreed, and, in the initial phase, the Mellon Foundation assembled data sets on the classes that had matriculated in 1951, 1976, and 1989 at each college or university. One stipulation, however, was that the resulting database was to be "restricted access": no information could be released that would identify any individual students or which school any data point had attended. So the data were meant to be broad samples of three generations at a cohort representative of the most academically selective corner of the higher education market.

The Foundation also made a grant to the Mathematica Policy Research group to do a survey of its sample population. Mathematica gathered data from "many of these same matriculants" on their post-college experience.

This encompassed a range of questions, including subjects' salary and job field, as well as their perceptions of the time spent in college. This survey data encompassed the second component of the C & B database, supplementing the "in college" information released by the twenty-eight participating colleges and universities. The final component of the C & B database would be linked records from other databases. The Foundation obtained, for example, permission to include data from the Educational Testing Service (ETS)'s SAT student questionnaires, as well as surveys of "pre-collegiate aspirations" conducted in 1976 and 1989.[1209]

Outcomes. The College and Beyond database has been a major resource for scholars researching higher education. It now contains data from over 90,000 former students at thirty-four participating institutions. These include four of the best public universities in the nation, several women's colleges, and a number of the most selective private institutions in the United States.

The database was the basis on which Bowen, who is also the former president of Princeton University, along with former Harvard President Derek Bok, wrote their landmark defense of affirmative action, *The Shape of the River: Long-Term Consequences of Considering Race in College and University Admissions.* Published in 1998, *The Shape of the River* has had a major impact on the debate over race-based admission policies, and was hailed, even by a critical reviewer in the *Washington Times*, as "an important and controversial book that should be read by anyone interested in the affirmative-action debate."[1210] Bowen has since published two other highly influential studies using the database. *The Game of Life*, co-authored by James L. Shulman, and *Reclaiming the Game*, written with Sarah A. Levin, are studies of the consequences—for academically selective institutions—of the culture of sport pervasive on most college campuses, and, in particular, of the policy of athletic admissions.

Impact. But the College and Beyond database has been used by other researchers as well. It is a tremendous resource, facilitating a wide range of scholarship by providing data that no author would likely be able to collect on his own. Many works have been published studying higher education with the data gathered and assembled by the Mellon Foundation. By persuading colleges and universities to make available the data, and then funding follow-up surveys to track outcomes, the Foundation has given current and future researchers the ability to more comprehensively describe the higher education field. And the database will allow those who would change the field to learn from a substantial body of evidence that would not otherwise be available.

Case 85

NATIONAL VIOLENT DEATH
REPORTING SYSTEM

Joyce Foundation, 1994

STEVEN SCHINDLER

Background. In the early 1990s, the United States was in the midst of an "epidemic of gun violence."[1211] Although hospitals had become much better at treating gunshot victims, deaths caused by firearms increased from 28,000 in the early 1980s to nearly 40,000 in the early 1990s.[1212] Public sentiment demanded action to curb fatalities resulting from gun violence, but bitter division arose over proposed policy solutions. Tighter restrictions on gun ownership and regulations on gun manufacture garnered some support, but gun manufacturers and the National Rifle Association protested ardently that such restrictions would endanger the public rather than curb gun violence.[1213] Some municipalities and families of victims filed civil suits against gun manufacturers directly for complicity in the rise in gun violence, asking courts to take actions where legislators would not do so.[1214]

A lack of comprehensive information about the circumstances surrounding incidents of gun violence facilitated this disagreement over the underlying causes and appropriate policy responses to gun violence. In fact, when studies in 1996 suggested a decline in gun violence had occurred, experts could not agree on the causes of the decline, with some pointing to gun control measures and others to attitudinal changes among young people.[1215]

In stark contrast to the lack of information on the circumstances surrounding violent deaths and gun-related crimes, a comprehensive database of traffic fatalities, maintained by the National Highway Traffic Safety Administration, has long provided policy makers as well as the public with extensive data about each traffic fatality. [1216] Public health researchers have pointed to the importance of the database in helping to develop policies on safety belts and air bags that have indisputably resulted in the saving of lives.[1217] No such database had ever been available for gun violence, even at a local or regional level, prior to the Joyce Foundation's involvement.

Strategy. The Joyce Foundation's program on gun violence began with the arrival of Deborah Leff as president of the Foundation in 1992.[1218] Leff came to the Joyce Foundation after having served as producer to the news shows "ABC World News Tonight with Peter Jennings" and "20/20."[1219] She personally undertook a research initiative on gun violence and convinced her board to begin making grants in the area in early 1993; results of an initial poll commissioned by the Foundation received widespread media coverage.[1220] In the foundation world, Joyce was the first to address gun violence as a matter of grave public health.[1221]

The Foundation's early funding efforts in gun violence included a great deal of fact-finding through the commissioning of reports and public opinion polls. Through its study, the Foundation came to believe that policy makers needed accurate information to craft appropriate solutions to solve the problems of gun violence. A survey commissioned by the Foundation reported that, even at the state level, little was done to maintain data on gun related injuries.[1222] Without the answers to important questions about gun violence, such as what proportion of homicides are related to drug trafficking, or whether homicides at school are increasing or decreasing, public officials had little basis for instituting new policies to reduce the number of gun-related fatalities. With no records keeping track of such data, policy makers have instead had to rely on fragmented information, anecdotal evidence, and speculation. A study by the National Academy of Sciences years after the Foundation began its work in the field of gun violence confirmed that the utter lack of information about gun-related crime left policy scholars unable to judge the effectiveness of a wide variety of policies.[1223]

Among its other gun violence initiatives, the Foundation adopted a strategy of promoting a database for violent and gun related deaths the better to inform policy decisions and to correct misperceptions among the public about the nature and extent of gun violence.[1224] In 1994, the Foundation made an initial grant to Dr. Stephen Hargarten at the Medical College of Wisconsin to begin a pilot database of violent and gun-related deaths in an eight-county region in Wisconsin. Hargarten collected data from numerous sources, including medical examiners, state crime laboratories, and police reports.[1225] The database was designed to record about 200 details surrounding each gun-related fatality.[1226] Another Joyce Foundation grant partially funded a pilot program at the Harvard School of Public Health that worked to improve the design and streamline the data collection process for a national gun violence database.

Impact. The Joyce Foundation's efforts to promote a nationwide database on gun violence are near full realization. A number of health organizations, such as the American Public Health Association, the American College of Physicians, and the American Psychiatric Association have called for a nation-wide system of violent death reporting modeled after the system developed by Joyce grantees. With the support of such groups and a broader public sentiment favoring better data collection, President Bush in 2002 instructed the CDC to direct $1.5 million to begin building a National Violent Death Reporting System (NVDRS). The database methods developed by Joyce Foundation grantees in Wisconsin and at Harvard have served as models for the new NVDRS.[1227]

The head of the NVDRS anticipated that nationwide deployment of the program would take up to ten years.[1228] The CDC announced in September 2002 that six states would receive grants totaling $7.5 million over five years to begin developing the system at the state level.[1229] By early 2005, Congress had expanded the NVDRS to include seventeen states.[1230] At its current rate of expansion, the NVDRS is on pace to provide policy makers and the public with detailed information on every violent fatality in the United States within ten years of its creation and less than twenty years after the Joyce Foundation first instituted its program on gun violence.

Case 86

NATIONAL URBAN RECONSTRUCTION AND HOUSING AGENCY (NURCHA)

Open Society Institute, 1995

SCOTT KOHLER

Background. On May 10, 1994, Nelson Mandela was sworn in as South Africa's first black president, and its first president ever chosen in a fully open and democratic election. President Mandela immediately identified as one of the nation's greatest challenges the vast shortage of housing for its poor, that is to say, for its black citizens. The South African federal government estimated that some 1.5 million low-cost housing units would be needed to fill this shortage, but even this figure was little more than a guess, since vast numbers of South African blacks lived in informal settlements—legacies of apartheid marked by extreme poverty and deplorable living conditions.[1231] In the township of Soweto, outside Johannesburg, for example, government figures estimated a population of 750,000; "unofficially . . . [however, estimates ranged] from 2.5 million up."[1232]

Soon after the 1994 elections, Frederick Van Zyl Slabbert, chairman of the Open Society Foundation for South Africa, proposed to George Soros the creation of a loan guarantee fund "that could bridge the gap between the banks and the poor."[1233] According to the OSI-published *Building the New*

South Africa: One House, One Dream at a Time, "Soros embraced the idea, but insisted that he would only get involved if the South African government was willing to contribute."

Strategy. The South African government responded enthusiastically, and in December 1994 the new collaboration was formally announced.[1234] The National Urban Reconstruction and Housing Agency (NURCHA) was created with donations of $5 million each from the Open Society Institute (OSI) and the South African government. In addition OSI appropriated a further $50 million to guarantee bank loans for bridging finance. NURCHA's goal was to make available funding for real estate developers and contractors to build low-cost housing for South Africa's poor. Banks in South Africa (as elsewhere in the world) have traditionally been reluctant to make loans for such housing projects because the profit margins on low-cost development are very low. Furthermore, as cottage industry construction companies proliferated on the chaotic post-apartheid landscape, it was difficult for banks to assess which borrowers were skilled at, or even serious about, their new jobs.

This is where NURCHA came in. It would identify viable projects in need of finance, and find a way to make the required funds available. Most often this was accomplished by guaranteeing a bank loan to the developer or contractor. When necessary, however, NURCHA would also "raise the finance and lend it" itself.[1235] NURCHA also took advantage of a national housing subsidy program enacted by the federal government to promote home ownership. So, in addition to facilitating the construction of housing units, NURCHA would make loans to enable the poorest South Africans— its clients have an average gross income of approximately R1,500 ($240) per month[1236]—to use government subsidies to buy a home.

More recently, NURCHA has expanded its operations to include a wider range of financial instruments. It has also fostered personal savings, and entered the broader field of community development, by making and guaranteeing loans for the construction of schools, roads, street lighting, and other community development facility and infrastructure projects.[1237] Recognizing that home ownership is simply not yet a realistic goal for many South Africans, NURCHA also supports rental-housing programs.[1238] From its inception, NURCHA has worked with developers both small, as in the enterprising individual with some bricks and a wheelbarrow, and large, as when it guaranteed the loans financing construction of the All Africa Games Village and then, after the September 1999 Games, oversaw the conversion of the athletes' village into 1,800 low-cost housing units sold to the working poor.

Outcomes. To date, NURCHA has helped finance the construction of over 135,000 houses,[1239] with a combined worth of more than $257 million.[1240]

This success has been recognized by the U.S. government, which, in 2003 committed to NURCHA $15 million through the U.S. Overseas Private Investment Corporation (OPIC). Combined with another $5 million from OSI, this gift will, according to the U.S. Department of State, "facilitate construction of a further 90,000 homes, housing up to half a million low-income South Africans.[1241] In addition, more than 44,000 people have opened savings accounts through NURCHA's nationwide personal savings program.

Impact. Because its work has benefited exclusively the South African poor, NURCHA has been at the leading edge of the South African government's massive effort to solve its housing shortage. This effort has, according to a press release of the U.S. State Department, led to the construction or renovation of some 500,000 housing units since 1994, with NURCHA supporting the bridging finance of the bulk of the low-cost units from among this total.[1242] In fact, the estimates of the South African government are considerably more generous. Sankie Mthembi-Mahanyele, the former South African Minister of Housing writes that "NURCHA's intervention has enabled the Department of Housing, as well as the government of South Africa, to deliver over a short period of time more than one million houses in South Africa. This accomplishment has . . . dramatically improved the lives of more than four million people in the country."[1243] Ms. Mthembi-Mahanyele goes on to declare, "there is no question in my mind that without NURCHA . . . R1 billion [about $160 million] would not have been possible."[1244]

Finally, it is worth mentioning that NURCHA almost single-handedly fostered the emergence of "a new generation of developers and contractors."[1245] Perhaps most significantly, much of this new generation is composed of women and blacks—two groups for whom it is especially difficult in South Africa to secure access to credit. According to Nonhlanhla Mjoli-Mncube, who chairs NURCHA's board and is a former executive director, "[a]lmost every woman contractor and every black contractor in this country who has made it, has made it through NURCHA."

Case 87

Pew Research Center for the People and the Press

Pew Charitable Trusts, 1995

Scott Kohler

Background. In 1995, the Times Mirror publishing company, concerned about its ability to turn a profit, was forced to consider shutting down its opinion research group, the Times Mirror Center for the People and the Press. Run by Andrew Kohut, former president of the Gallup Organization, the Center was a source of high-quality, nonpartisan polling and research, yet the for-profit Times Mirror—constrained by its bottom line—was unable to justify its support on the grounds of serving the public interest. Yet serve the public interest the Center did, and still does thanks to the intervention of the Pew Charitable Trusts (PCT), which assumed sponsorship of the Center that same year. For Pew, a major philanthropy unburdened by the need to make a profit, the research and opinion polling conducted by Kohut and his associates, widely regarded to be among the most incisive and reliable available, was, in and of itself, valuable to the public interest.

Strategy. Since 1995, Pew has sponsored the Center, which became known as the Pew Research Center for the People and the Press. According to Don Kimelman, director of Information Initiatives for PCT, "[t]he Trusts were very fortunate to have Andy [Kohut] bring his well-established polling operation into our orbit in 1995."[1246] The Center conducts research in five primary areas:[1247]

- The People and the Press
- The People, the Press, and Politics
- The News Interest Index
- America's Place in the World
- Media Use

This research is nonpartisan and relies primarily on hard data, rather than expert opinion.[1248] The Center's polling and research are aimed primarily at policymakers and journalists, but they are available—free of charge—to the general public via the Center's website. In addition, the Trusts in May 2001 launched a major new research effort: the Pew Global Attitudes Project. Run through the Center for the People and the Press, the Project is funded by Pew and the William and Flora Hewlett Foundation, and is directed by Kohut and chaired by former Secretary of State Madeleine Albright. It seeks to measure opinions around the world toward the rise of globalization. In the wake of 9/11, the Global Attitudes Project has also conducted research on people's views of American hegemony, the spread of democracy, and tensions between Islam and the West. The Project began with a survey of 275 "opinion leaders (influential people in politics, media, business, culture, and government)."[1249]

Outcomes. The Pew Research Center for the People and the Press is one of the leading institutions of opinion research in the United States. Its polling is widely cited by major news outlets, such as the *New York Times, The Washington Post,* and *USA Today.*[1250] Its polling continues to throw into deeper relief those issues which are important to the American people. In this way, the Center helps to frame public discussion, inform leaders and the people, and thereby promotes the public interest. The Global Attitudes Project has, to date, released two major reports. So far it has surveyed nearly 75,000 people in fifty populations (forty-nine countries, plus the Palestinian Authority). Already, it is the largest survey of its kind ever conducted. In April 2004, PCT announced that it would consolidate the Center for the People and the Press and the Global Attitudes Project, as well as five other Pew-sponsored research operations,[1251] under one roof: a new independent organization to be known as the Pew Research Center.[1252] Headed by Andrew Kohut, the Center has a $15 million annual budget, and is able to provide a permanent home to a variety of polling and research activities until then funded on an ad hoc basis. It functions as both a resource for the news media, policymakers, and academics, but also as a "fact tank," disseminating its findings "in an understandable and analytic way."[1253]

Impact. Society has a clear interest in the gathering and dissemination of reliable opinion research, which can inform the work of the news media and government leaders. The Pew Charitable Trusts, a public charity not beholden to any political constituency or bottom line other than the public interest, are well-placed to support this sort of important work. In funding the far ranging research conducted within the Center, Pew keeps open a channel of nonpartisan information connecting public officials to the people they mean to serve. With the Center for People and the Press as its core, the new Pew Research Center is a guarantee that the high-quality, influential data collection the Trusts have supported since 1995 will not be threatened any time soon by an unsure balance sheet.

Case 88

Sloan Digital Sky Survey

Alfred P. Sloan Foundation, 1995

Scott Kohler

Background. Until the mid-1990s, the last comprehensive study of a large portion of the cosmos was one undertaken in the 1950s by researchers at the Mount Palomar Observatory.[1254] This study remained state-of-the-art for forty years, until the Alfred P. Sloan Foundation moved to fund a new astronomical survey unprecedented in its breadth and depth. This "intergalactic census" would be conducted by the nonprofit Astrophysical Research Consortium, a partnership of research universities and laboratories, including the University of Chicago, Johns Hopkins, Princeton, and teams of researchers from Japan, Germany, and elsewhere.[1255] Each would provide manpower and funds, as would the federal government. But the project was initiated with Sloan Foundation funding, and, as evidenced by its name, the Foundation would remain its leading supporter. Once planning and design had been completed, the construction phase of the Sloan Digital Sky Survey (SDSS) got underway in 1995. At the time, scientists had accurate measurements of distance "for only a few tens of thousands of galaxies."[1256] With powerful new equipment and advanced research and analytic techniques, SDSS scientists would soon surpass tremendously this and other measures of progress in the field of astronomy.

Strategy. To that end, state-of-the-art observation equipment—including a 2.5-meter telescope and twin spectrographs each measuring 8.5 feet in length—was built and installed at the Apache Point Observatory in New Mexico. In February 1998, the massive SDSS telescope first cast its eye skyward, and, by early 1999, data collection at Apache Point—which is managed by the University of New Mexico—was proceeding at full speed. With a view of one quarter of the night sky, the Sky Survey telescope contains one of the most technologically advanced cameras ever built.[1257]

Photons hit the telescope and are collected by light sensors known as charge coupled devices. Images are then recorded onto magnetic tape, which is shipped by express courier to the Fermi National Accelerator Laboratory (Fermilab), the most advanced high energy physics laboratory in the world. Information is sent through Fermilab's Feynman Computing Center through various data pipelines (such as the spectrographic, astrometric, and monitor pipelines), each of which was developed by one of the collaborating research institutions to process huge data sets into information about various celestial objects, such as stars, nebula, and quasars. This information is then collated in an Operations Database, run by Fermilab and the U.S. Naval Observatory. Eventually, data sets are passed on to scientists at Johns Hopkins, who make it available (via a digital search engine) to researchers working with SDSS.[1258] Beginning in 2003, SDSS also releases periodically huge sets of its data to the general public. The total volume of information to be collected is estimated to fill some 20- to 40-trillion bytes of hard disk space.[1259]

In this way, SDSS is constructing a digital map of a full quarter of the night sky. In effect, it is constructing a three-dimensional field guide to the visible universe, and one with a volume 100 times greater than any picture of space humans had previously constructed. All told, SDSS will obtain detailed data—such as position and absolute brightness—on over 100 million celestial objects. Unlike most astronomical observations, which are limited to one spectrum, the SDSS uses color filters to view these objects in five different colors, which reveals a broader range of characteristics than are visible in any one wavelength.[1260]

Outcomes. SDSS is "the most comprehensive mapping survey of the cosmos ever undertaken."[1261] It has already produced 15 terabytes of data— nearly the same amount of information stored by the Library of Congress.[1262] Two massive data releases have given to the public a detailed look at tens of millions of astronomical objects, including redshifts of more than half a million.[1263] In order to manage its findings, SDSS has also pioneered an early "universal 'sky partitioning' system," which, according to Dr. Alex Szalay, an astrophysicist at Johns Hopkins, "will become increasingly necessary as more massive sky surveys are produced."[1264] To date, the Sloan Digital Sky Survey has cost approximately $80 million, of which the Sloan Foundation has provided one quarter. Additional funding has come from the National Science Foundation, NASA, and the individual Consortium members. The Survey was planned to operate for five years (from 1999 to 2004). However, in 2004, the Board of Trustees of the Sloan Foundation approved an additional $5.4 million to fund partially a $15 million extension of the program to enable it to meet its original aim of encompassing "the entire northern galactic sector. . . "[1265]

Impact. The Sloan Survey is enabling breakthrough research to be undertaken. In 1999, for instance, SDSS astronomers "discovered that typical galaxies may be twice as large and contain twice as much mass as suggested by previous measurements."[1266] SDSS data already "contain more spectra than [had previously] been published in the history of science."[1267] Last year, SDSS data were used "to calculate an important confirmation of the discovery of dark energy, the negative gravitational force that accelerates matter re-pulsively."[1268] These and other advances have driven the formulation of new theories on the nature and origins of galaxies and the universe itself. Yet it may be that SDSS has yet to yield its greatest impacts. Dr. Anneilia Sargent, a Cal Tech astronomer who is president of the American Astronomical Soci-ety, has predicted that the Survey is going "to turn a great many astronomical theories on their heads and confirm others."[1269] And in fact SDSS is more than a leap forward in human understanding of the cosmos; for in creating a framework "sky partitioning system," SDSS has laid a foundation for the next generation of astronomical research.

Case 89

Computational Molecular Biology and Professional Science Degrees

Alfred P. Sloan Foundation, 1995

Steven Schindler

Background. In the mid-1990s, biotechnology as an industry was at a curious juncture. The decoding of the human DNA was imminent, promising rapid growth in the field of biotechnology and research. The demand for trained scientists in the field was high. America's universities, however, were not pro-ducing students with the kind of training the biotechnology sector would demand. Educational institutions with research programs in the field of computational molecular biology had only handfuls of graduate students, and those students were being snatched up quickly by the private sector to pursue commercially viable research. Many of the top university researchers themselves were being recruited to large corporate pharmaceutical research units.[1270] Also, students lured by lucrative opportunities in the corporate sec-tor were not inclined to enter rigorous and lengthy Ph.D. programs.[1271] Fur-ther, the training students were receiving in traditional Ph.D. programs was inconsistent with the needs of emerging biotechnology firms; employees would not need to have completed dissertations but would need more core science training than undergraduate science degrees provided.[1272]

Still, universities largely failed to entertain innovations to the traditional degree program offerings. Universities simply were not efficiently equipping their students to serve the demands of the emerging biotechnology industry.

Strategy. The Alfred P. Sloan Foundation, created in 1934 by the CEO of General Motors, had long been funding science and technology research. In 1995, the Sloan Foundation, acknowledging the need for more quantitative scientists trained for practical research, initiated a joint program with the U.S. Department of Energy to fund ten post-doctoral fellowships for students in the quantitative sciences to fund their transition into the field of computational molecular biology, or bioinformatics. The program's aim was to "to produce scientists who can link the powerful theoretical and practical tools of molecular biology with the power of modern computational techniques."[1273] The Foundation expected that these fellowship recipients would be able to apply cross-disciplinary skills toward cutting-edge biotechnology problems.

The same year the Foundation began funding individual fellowships in computational molecular biology, Sheila Tobias, a consultant in science education, proposed dramatic changes in the university paradigms of traditional academic disciplines and degree programs. In her book, *Rethinking Science as a Career: Perceptions and Realities in the Physical Sciences,*[1274] Tobias suggested that universities create new basic science master's degree programs modeled after similar degrees that had long been offered in the engineering disciplines. These programs would be short, flexible, and designed to attract students interested in careers in the private sector rather than the academy.[1275]

Inspired by Tobias's idea, the Sloan Foundation opted to embark on a more ambitious strategy than merely funding individual fellowships. In 1997, the Foundation hired Tobias to help coordinate a new program in developing "professional science master's degrees." The Foundation began by providing grants to universities to develop these new degree programs that would cross traditional disciplinary boundaries to meet the demands of the emerging technological trends. The Foundation, in its first round of grants, provided start-up funds to five universities to launch eighteen graduate degree programs that would bring science to bear on real world applications and that would merge increased computational capacity with the science disciplines.[1276] These programs thrust the Sloan Foundation to the cutting edge of developing degree programs to serve the needs of the corporate science and technology community.[1277] Subsequently, the Foundation initiated a program to provide funding specifically for the creation of new master's degree programs in computational molecular biology.[1278] The Foundation adopted the strategy of coordinating a "competitive awards program" in which universities were encouraged to design such programs and to compete for available implementation funds.

To support the momentum the creation of these programs had begun, the Foundation created a website, www.sciencemasters.com, to serve as a clear-

inghouse for information on all Sloan-supported professional masters programs and as a promotional tool for the programs. The site allows prospective students to research the various professional science master's degree
options supported by the Sloan Foundation, and it provides student and
alumni testimonials in support of the programs.[1279] The Foundation also
made a grant in December 2002 to the Commission on Professionals in Science and Technology to collect and compile data on the education, employment, and income of these professional master's degree recipients in an effort
to promote wider adoption of such programs.[1280]

Impact. Since the beginning of the Foundation's programs in computational molecular biology, it has supported the creation of about ninety professional master's degrees at about forty different universities.[1281] The
prominence of the programs continues to rise. Some have likened the innovation in the academy represented by the Sloan Foundation's support of
new professional science master's degrees to the innovations giving rise to
the master of business administration as a new degree in the early 1900s.[1282]
A group of fifteen business organizations in the United States led by the
Business Roundtable and including the U.S. Chamber of Commerce issued a report in 2005 in which it recommended the continued creation
and support of professional science master's programs promoted by Sloan
to meet the engineering, science, and technology needs of the nation's
economy.[1283]

Case 90

GRANTMAKERS FOR EFFECTIVE
ORGANIZATIONS

David and Lucile Packard Foundation, 1996

SCOTT KOHLER

Background. In the early 1990s, there were a handful of foundations providing significant support for the organizational—as opposed to programmatic—effectiveness of their grantees. One of these was the David and
Lucile Packard Foundation, which had, as one of its program areas, an interest in Management Assistance. When Barbara Kibbe was hired in 1996 to direct that program, she organized a gathering at the annual conference of the
Council on Foundations to discuss the role of funders in supporting the

organizational capacity of their grantees—making them stronger institutions in the hope that they could then achieve better and more lasting results in their fields. The roundtable discussion was a success, and Kibbe, along with her counterparts at the James Irvine Foundation and the Ewing Marion Kauffman Foundation, decided to take the lead in coordinating an effort to build something from that day's discussion.[1284]

Strategy. Those three foundations provided the initial funding—which totaled $710,000[1285]—for the inaugural conference of Grantmakers for Effective Organizations (GEO). A sixteen-member steering committee led the new institution, which aimed to promote dialogue among funders about how best to strengthen the organizations they support. This has been a growing movement in the foundation sector, which has traditionally been far more focused on program strategy and the achievement of demonstrable outcomes. The early supporters of GEO were concerned that a range of impending pressures—from the inevitable end of the economic boom of the 1990s to the aging of the baby boom generation—would soon strain the not-for-profit sector enormously. Strong institutions, with competent leadership and a clear sense of mission, would be those best able to survive these pressures.

To that end, GEO—which is now an affinity group of the Council on Foundations—engages in a variety of activities designed to build organizational capacity and strengthen the nonprofit sector as a whole.[1286] These include supporting research into what steps can promote institutional strength, and developing programs for grant-receiving organizations interested in building capacity, as well as the dissemination of information to help such organizations. GEO also works to bring together networks of people and institutions, creating a "community of practice" that can put into effect the knowledge gained through GEO research, scholarship, and discussion. One of its primary activities is the sponsorship, every other year, of a GEO Conference for foundation and nonprofit leaders concerned with increasing their organization's performance and resilience. GEO is not, however, focused solely on grantee organizations. As its executive director, Kathleen Enright, says, the group, composed entirely of grantmakers, "wisely realized that they didn't have a lot of credibility [with not-for-profits] if they didn't look at their own performance."[1287] So GEO research also looks for metrics of achievement and best practices that can be used to strengthen foundations.

Outcomes. GEO has grown rapidly. It now has over 600 dues-paying members, who represent more than 400 grantmaking organizations. Its last national conference, held in March 2004, was attended by some 500 people working in the not-for-profit sector and featured panels and lectures on issues of how to improve the work of grant making and grant receiving nonprofits. Since its founding, GEO has become one of the most important organizations working to strengthen organizational capacity in the nonprofit sector.

Impact. It will take years to observe and document the full measure of its impact, but its early results are very promising. Paul Light, Vice President of the Brookings Institution, has conducted extensive research, in collaboration with GEO, which "suggests that the increased emphasis on organizational effectiveness among grantmakers has already had an impact on the nonprofit sector."[1288] For instance, 78 percent of the 500 experts and nonprofit executive directors Light interviewed agree "that nonprofit organizations are better managed today than they were five years ago."[1289] Cole Wilbur, former president of the Packard Foundation, has said that he thought the Foundation's funding for organizational effectiveness was, "dollar for dollar," the best money the Foundation spent in his tenure.[1290] Grantmakers for Effective Organizations has received continuing support from Packard[1291] and other foundations, and widespread acclaim from the foundation, which is coming more and more to realize the importance of building strong grantees, not just strong programs.

The scope of the civic sector is enormous. It accounts for some 8 percent of the U.S. gross domestic product, and some 10 percent of all American jobs. With annual expenditures approaching $1 trillion, the not-for-profit sector clearly makes its influence felt throughout society in countless ways every single day. Without a doubt, it is very much in the public interest that this money be well spent. We know that the civic sector has served as the launching pad for some of the greatest successes in American history. Yet we must also concede that it has, at times, been the stage for bitter disappointments, cases where funding and good intentions simply were not enough. Grantmakers for Effective Organizations, by working to improve the performance of civic sector charities, is helping to maximize the successes and minimize the disappointments. Helping foundations and their grantees to do more and better, it continues to be a leader in a movement with impressive potential to improve the nonprofit sector and, thereby, society as a whole.

Case 91

UNITED NATIONS ARREARS CAMPAIGN

United Nations Foundation/Better World Fund, 1997

SCOTT KOHLER

Background.

The effectiveness of the United Nations depends upon the Member States' meeting all their obligations. Assurance that these obligations will be met depends in turn upon the will of the peoples of the Member States. The vigor of the United Nations stems therefore from a public opinion educated to understand its problems . . .

The [United Nations] is the hope of the world for lasting peace. It provides mankind today with the best opportunity to unite for the preservation of civilization and for the continuation of human progress. . . .

On behalf of the United States Government and of its people, I renew the pledge of our utmost efforts to insure the success of the United Nations. We shall do our part.

—HARRY S. TRUMAN
June 25, 1947

President Truman spoke these words on the second anniversary of the founding of the United Nations. He was speaking to a world that had been torn by war and still faced massive challenges of reconstruction and reconciliation. For forty years, the United States lived up to Truman's commitment, taking a leadership role in the activities of the United Nations and meeting faithfully its financial obligations to the organization. However, by the 1980s, support for the U.N. in the U.S. Congress had become much diminished. Conservative lawmakers alleged that the U.N. had become a bloated, inefficient bureaucracy, riddled with corruption and possessing very little capacity to do real good. Furthermore, Republicans alleged, the U.N. almost never served American interests. Rather, it had become a forum wherein nations could criticize and attack the United States, even while the U.S. hosted the U.N. and was its single largest contributor of dues.

Motivated by such sentiments, the U.S. government began to pull back from participation in the U.N., and in the mid-1980s, Congress began to hold back a portion of its U.N. dues.[1292] By the mid-1990s the U.N. was more than $2 billion in debt, and roughly half of that amount was owing to the arrears chargeable to the United States.

When Kofi Annan became Secretary-General of the U.N. in 1996, he instituted fiscal reforms that cut the U.N.'s bureaucratic budget by over $200 million and reduced staff levels to increase efficiency. A measure was introduced in Congress to repay the full U.S. debt to the U.N., but it soon foundered on partisan disagreement over an unrelated amendment that had been attached by Representative Chris Smith.

Strategy. In September 1997, the United Nations received an unexpected windfall when billionaire media mogul R.E. "Ted" Turner surprised the audience at a Washington awards banquet by pledging to donate $1 billion to the United Nations. Turner had long been a dedicated internationalist and an ardent supporter of the U.N. He had also been heavily involved for years in the United Nations Association of the U.S.A., a not-for-profit group "that supports the work of the United Nations and encourages active civic participation in the most important social and economic issues facing the world today."[1293] To administer his gift, Turner created the U.N. Foundation, and its affiliate, the Better World Fund. According to the Foundation's president, former Senator Timothy Wirth, "[w]e set four broad priority areas: Women and population stabilization, sustainable environment and climate change, children's health, and strengthening the U.N. system."[1294] In effect, the United Nations Foundation handles the first three of these priorities, and the Better World Fund pursues the fourth. To that end, the Better World Fund quickly took up the case for repayment of the U.S. arrears to the United Nations.

The Better World Fund adopted a strategy composed of seven primary elements in its campaign to bring about repayment of the U.S. debt. These components were: advertising, media outreach, direct lobbying of legislators, local "grasstops" lobbying,[1295] polling, strategic partnerships, and collaboration with the executive branch. The general theory of change was that these efforts would complement one another to increase local attention to the U.S.'s financial delinquency and thereby encourage Congress to act.

Outcomes. The year 1999 was the most significant year of the campaign. In this, its first full year of operation, the BWF spent about $790,000 on lobbying expenditures. The Fund is a 501(c)(3) organization, but these expenditures fell within the amounts allowed under tax law. Faced with the threat of having its General Assembly seat revoked, the U.S. Congress approved the Helms-Biden Act, which set out conditions under which the U.S. would repay its debts in a series of three payments. Again, in 2000, the timing of the debate may have been politically fortuitous for the Better World Fund. The Clinton White House, in its final months, was eager to see this dispute resolved.[1296] Throughout 2000, the United States Ambassador to the U.N., Richard Holbrooke, worked with the BWF and spent much of his time "bullying and cajoling other countries' representatives into reducing Washington's [U.N. dues] and, in many cases, increasing their own."[1297] In November 2000, at a board meeting of the U.N. Foundation and the Better World Fund, came the breakthrough alluded to above. At that meeting, Ambassador Holbrooke explained to the board that most of the U.N. member states had already budgeted for 2001. Therefore, they were unwilling retroactively to increase their own shares of the U.N. budget. However, Helms-Biden declared that unless the U.S. share of regular U.N. dues had dropped to 22 percent by the end of 2001, the second, and largest, payment—$582 million—would not be authorized by Congress. Turner recognized an opportunity. He told Holbrooke that, if doing so would help him negotiate, he, Turner, would make up the difference between 22 and 25 percent of the U.N. regular budget, approximately $31 million.[1298] This grant of opportunity would also allow the U.S. to stay on the schedule set by Helms-Biden, and it would allow other U.N. member states another year in which to appropriate their newly increased shares of the United Nations budget. With Turner's offer, Holbrooke was able to convince the U.N. General Assembly to enact a new formula for the calculation of assessed contributions, one that would lower the U.S. share of the U.N. budget to levels acceptable under the Helms-Biden legislation.[1299] In February 2001, Congress released the second portion of the U.S.'s back dues. But that was not the end of the saga; a host of political challenges continued to threaten Helms-Biden's fulfillment. Finally, however, years of advocacy, education, negotiation, and lobbying by the Better World Campaign and others paid off. In September 2002, Congress authorized, and President Bush released, the third and final tranche, fulfilling the promise of the Helms-Biden agreement to pay off the full $926 million owed by the United States to the United Nations.

Impact. One limitation of the strategy employed is that direct causation is difficult to establish, but this is not a problem for officials at the Better World Fund. According to Susan Myers, "[w]e have never tried to take credit for [the] issue . . . I believe we filled [a] specific void, but there were many organizations and individuals (both within and outside of government) that deserve credit for this."[1300] We know that opportunities to resolve this issue had been missed in the past. It may well be that without the climate of broad support, fostered, in part, by the Better World Fund, such opportunities would have been missed again. The deadlock of late 2000 appears to have been especially intractable. External factors played an unexpected role, but that will always be the case in large-scale long-run efforts of such enormous complexity. This does not absolve concerned citizens of the responsibility to strive for progress. Certainly, when the issue at hand is the relationship of the world's only superpower to the world's primary supranational institution, humankind cannot rely on luck alone.

Case 92

YOUTH DEVELOPMENT PROGRAM

Edna McConnell Clark Foundation, 1999

SCOTT KOHLER

Background. With assets valued slightly over $670 million, the Edna McConnell Clark Foundation (EMCF) ranks sixty-ninth on the list of the largest foundations in the United States.[1301] Its annual grant-making of $25–30 million makes the Foundation a significant philanthropy, but not one that can move mountains simply by moving funds. Founded in 1969 by the heirs of the Avon fortune, EMCF, for most of its history, was like many foundations: generalist in approach, with several discrete programs operating in a diverse range of fields. In the case of the Clark Foundation, these included tropical disease research, children's welfare, and criminal justice.

When Michael Bailin assumed the Foundation's presidency in 1996, he brought to the job an outsider's perspective and a willingness to innovate. The former head of Public/Private Ventures, Bailin wondered whether the Foundation, given its limited resources, might be spreading itself too thin, and whether an increased focus on doing good *well*, rather than simply doing good,[1302] might enable EMCF to achieve greater impact. With assistance from a few of the Foundation's officers, and gradually, the support of the Foundation's Board, Bailin sought the aid of outside consultants, including Peter Szanton, and the newly-created Bridgespan Group, a nonprofit consulting firm spun off from the for-profit Bain and Company, to consider how the Edna McConnell Clark Foundation might best position itself to achieve significant philanthropic impact given its limited resources.

What has ensued is one of the boldest, most innovative transformations in any foundation's history.[1303] And from it has sprung a new EMCF: one that is employing a rigorous, highly focused approach to grant-making in a single field of activity: Youth Development. Within that narrow focus, the Foundation now aims at building models or strong nonprofit organizations capable of going to scale and becoming self-sufficient. Though early outcomes and promising signs of impact can be observed, this case is not meant to herald the success of the Clark Foundation's Youth Development Program. Rather, it is intended to be a case study in strategic philanthropy—a look at one new approach that is so far as significant for how it is being carried out, and what it may yet yield, as for its concrete achievements to date.

Strategy. The Youth Development Program of the Edna McConnell Clark Foundation is guided by a rigorous strategy and theory of change.[1304] Developed with the help of the Bridgespan Group, this strategy cum logic chain entails a six-step process:[1305]

1. Identifying Organizations: The Foundation consults with youth development experts, other foundations, and local agencies to "identify youth serving organizations that have been successful in helping young people and that appear to have the potential to substantially grow [sic] and expand their work."[1306] These organizations must meet specific Foundation criteria, including that they promote one of three objectives: enhancing educational opportunities; aiding in the transition to self-sustaining work at a competitive wage; or helping young people avoid the high-risk behaviors (such as teenage pregnancy and incarceration as a juvenile) that are shown most frequently to derail a person's long-term prospects.

2. Pre-Screening: The Foundation then screens the nonprofits that have been identified to determine which ones offer a product (generally some form of youth intervention) compelling enough to warrant further consideration. EMCF is a mezzanine funder, collaborating only with established, successful organizations that demonstrate potential to grow. It does not work with start-ups, nor does it create new nonprofits.

3. Due-Diligence: The most promising organizations are then thoroughly assessed according to six categories: quality and efficacy of services offered; proven leadership with a vision; current financial health; organizational strength and growth potential; interest in tracking organizational performance; and compatibility with the culture and values of the Edna McConnell Clark Foundation. By the time this step has been completed, the Foundation and its consultants have invested 200 to 300 hours of research in each organization without the prospective grantee even knowing that it is being considered. Those that meet, to some substantial extent, all six of the due diligence requirements, are then offered initial support from EMCF.

4. Business Planning: This initial support takes the form of a $250,000 grant to cover business-planning expenses. In addition, the Foundation

spends a further $250,00 to $300,000 to engage the Bridgespan Group to work with each grantee to refine its theory of change and develop a full business plan including well-defined outcome goals and specific benchmarks of performance along the way. The Foundation believes it can best leverage its resources by building strong youth development institutions, not by trying itself to reform the system. The creation of an individually tailored business plan is a time-consuming but integral step in adding value by strengthening each grantee.

5. Investments: Once it has become involved with a grantee nonprofit, the Foundation has committed itself to long-term hands-on support. At this point in the process, the Foundation makes a large grant of several million dollars over a three-to-six year period. This is general operating support, and often covers 20 percent or more of the grantee's total budget.

6. Performance Tracking and Evaluation: All grantees are expected to track their own results, gathering participation and outcome data. The Foundation measures participation by active service slots, the number of people able fully to participate, rather than the more superficial measure of clients served (which does not specify whether the client participated for one day or several years). EMCF looks to see whether its grantees are reaching more youths, and whether they are growing stronger as institutions. Internal data, such as unrestricted revenue growth, are, therefore, considered important. And within three years of the grant investment, every grantee must be ready to undertake a full external evaluation. Generally, this is a randomized controlled trial, but quasi-scientific tests are sometimes accepted. The costs of this evaluation are built into the initial grant, and EMCF works with its grantees to ensure that they are able to achieve what they set out to do. In some cases, exceptional grantees may have their multi-year general support grant renewed for an additional three-to-six years. Ultimately, however, the Foundation will look to move on to new organizations once it has strengthened and helped grow a nonprofit over the course of several years.

The Foundation describes its approach as Institution and Field Building (IFB). So, on the one hand, it seeks to strengthen youth development organizations and to help them reach larger numbers of low-income children and teenagers. On the other hand, EMCF hopes to build and improve the youth development field. One way it does this is through its support—as described above—of excellent institutions, which can then serve as leaders and models to other youth supporting nonprofits. Another way is by disseminating the knowledge gained along the way. The data gathered, both by the Foundation and its grantees, is used to analyze success and failure and to distill lessons that can be shared with the youth development community, to the benefit of all. The Foundation recognizes that its resources are insufficient to reform youth development. But by supporting a corps of leading service providers, and by creating and sharing knowledge for the field at large, the Clark Foundation believes it can leverage limited resources to achieve major long-term impact.

Outcomes. The short-term results of the Edna McConnell Clark Foundation's youth development strategy are encouraging. It has provided major support to a small but growing corps of youth-supporting nonprofits. Among these is the Harlem Children's Zone (HCZ), which grew out of the Rheedlen Center, a longtime EMCF grantee that was able to reshape its programs, and grow substantially with significant involvement from the Foundation. HCZ now encompasses a twenty-four-square block area of Harlem, and serves 10,000 at risk children.[1307] With major growth underway, it is being hailed as one of the most promising social reform experiments in the nation.[1308] Other EMCF grantees include the Nurse-Family Partnership, and Youth Villages, a Tennessee-based organization that provides mental health counseling to troubled children and teenagers at thirty-three locations around the Southeast and Mid-Atlantic.

Impact. It is too early to judge how well the Clark Foundation's unique approach will succeed in increasing the number of youths who achieve positive outcomes after participating in youth development programs; developing meaningful knowledge for the field; and disseminating that knowledge effectively to enhance the work of it grantees and the larger youth development community.[1309] Dr. David Hunter, the Foundation's Director of Evaluation and Knowledge Development, contends that EMCF is still on the low-to-mid range of demonstrating its effectiveness. He believes it will be another ten years before reasoned, data based judgment can be passed on the Foundation's strategy and theory of change.[1310]

What is clear is that the Edna McConnell Clark Foundation is pioneering a new approach to strategic philanthropy. It is certainly not the only good approach, but it is one that will generate much-needed data on what does not work, and, we can hope, what does. Certainly, it is a scientific, rather than an artistic, approach to philanthropy. So far, it appears to be enhancing and expanding high-quality, results-oriented nonprofits. And it may yet achieve its goal of enhancing significantly the youth development field. If it does, a victory will have been won both for low-income youths and their families, and also for the philanthropic sector, which will have a new, scientifically tested guide which may work for leveraging resources in a wide range of fields.

Case 93

THE PLAN FOR TRANSFORMATION OF PUBLIC HOUSING IN CHICAGO

John D. and Catherine T. MacArthur Foundation, 1999

SCOTT KOHLER

Background. By the end of the 1980s, it was apparent in Chicago—as in many cities—that the existing public housing infrastructure was badly broken. As the Chicago Housing Authority (CHA)'s brochure recounts:

> What began in the 1930s as a noble and well-intentioned effort to provide "transitional housing for low-income families, expanded dramatically in the 1950s and 1960s and eventually evolved into the isolated islands of poverty and crime widely associated with public housing."[1311]

The CHA was, by that time, an unwieldy bureaucracy managed by the federal Department of Housing and Urban Development (HUD). Amid a series of legal challenges, the CHA tried in the '80s to begin reforming public housing in Chicago. But it was not until the late 1990s, with the launch of a major new effort, that the city appeared ready to confront its problems.

Strategy. In June 1999, the city of Chicago assumed full control of the CHA, and soon after, under the leadership of mayor Richard Daley, it initiated the Plan for Transformation of Public Housing. The Plan, which is scheduled to be complete at the end of this decade, has three components. First, it will "renew the physical structure of the CHA properties."[1312] To that end, some 25,000 units of housing will be constructed or renovated by the end of 2009. Second, it aims to "promote self-sufficiency for public housing residents."[1313] As Mayor Daley has said, "we must do more than simply build new homes. This is about building lives."[1314] So a wide range of public and private social service agencies and organizations are being engaged. Finally, the Plan includes reforming the administration of the Chicago Housing

Authority.[1315] Drafted with the support of HUD and the input of affected residents and community leaders, the $1.6 billion Plan is the largest public housing reform initiative in American history.

At each step along the way, one of its primary participants and supporters of the Plan for Transformation has been the Chicago-based John D. and Catherine T. MacArthur Foundation. Recognizing the Plan as an historic opportunity both to reform Chicago's decrepit housing infrastructure and to blaze a trail that other cities could follow, the Foundation has played two main roles since December 1999. The first is to be "a neutral place for problem-solving and conflict resolution."[1316] Given the diversity of interests involved in such a massive undertaking, it is a role that the Foundation, with its credibility as an altruistic and disinterested resource for the city, is well positioned to fill. The second is more traditional: that of a funder. In particular, the Foundation has targeted significant "resources to efforts that build confidence that public housing improvement [can] be accomplished in a way that [is] sensitive to current public housing residents and to the city's neighborhoods."[1317] The Foundation has already contributed $41 million to the Plan for Transformation, and has so far budgeted an additional $8 million in grants for 2005–2008.[1318]

Outcomes. The results so far have been enormously promising. The CHA has lowered its administrative costs, increased its budget for property management, and has managed to balance its budget for the past four years.[1319] It currently provides public housing to 38,000 people, and housing vouchers to an additional 97,000. Several run-down high-rise developments—each one a blight on the community and a haven for crime and poverty—have been torn down and are being replaced by newer low-rise mixed income housing.

The MacArthur Foundation has played a significant role in this progress. For instance, the Foundation provided neutral meeting space, gave logistical support, and mediated the discussions that led to the adoption of a Relocation Rights Contract specifying the rights and responsibilities of the city and the affected tenants as the construction and relocation moved forward. This contract cleared a major roadblock that could have kept the Plan held up in court for many years to come. Furthermore, MacArthur has recruited and funded an independent monitor to ensure that both sides comply with the contract. The Foundation also conceived an innovative "gap financing" system that enabled CHA and the City "to cover anticipated gaps in the cost of building market-rate, for-sale housing in the new mixed-income communities."[1320] The Foundation put up $15 million to guarantee the City's loans. This was the risk capital that convinced Fannie Mae to lend out the money needed for construction. MacArthur funds have supported social science research in order to understand better the successes and failures of the project.

They have been used to streamline the relocation process and convene partnerships of private community organizations.

Impact. The Chicago Housing Authority's Plan for Transformation of Public Housing is the largest and most complicated urban renewal project in American history. Now early in its second phase, the Plan may yet succeed in improving dramatically the lives of Chicago's poor. If it does, it will be a beacon of hope and an example for other cities to follow. Throughout its planning and implementation, the MacArthur Foundation has supported it vigorously. As Kathryn Greenberg, a spokeswoman for the CHA said in April 2003, "since the housing rebuilding job began, we have had an especially deep partnership with the MacArthur Foundation."[1321] In fact, the city official who authored the plan is now a vice president of the Foundation.[1322] Clearly, MacArthur will continue to work for progress as the Plan for Transformation continues to effect positive change in the Foundation's own back yard.

Case 94

CHINA SUSTAINABLE ENERGY PROGRAM

David and Lucile Packard Foundation and William and Flora Hewlett Foundation, 1999

SCOTT KOHLER

Background. At the dawn of the twenty-first century, the Chinese economy is expanding at an incredible pace. Throughout most of the 1990s, China experienced 8 percent annual GDP growth. This rapid modernization has created enormous opportunity for millions of Chinese, but it also carries with it significant hazards. Curbing this economic boom is not a viable option; indeed, the Chinese government, hoping to keep up with the needs of its massive population, is committed to quadrupling its GDP over the next twenty years.[1323] Among the risks posed by this ambitious goal is the very real possibility that China could destroy its natural environment for the sake of continued industrialization and economic growth. Such an environmental disaster could have environmental implications on a global scale—rapidly accelerated global warming, for instance. But it could also cause political and economic turmoil. As more and more nations require ever larger shares of a limited pie of energy resources, geopolitical stability will inevitably be undermined.

Strategy. As part of its Conservation and Science Program, the David and Lucile Packard Foundation in 1999 convened "a series of meetings and consultations with scientists, policy-makers, business leaders, and analysts in China and the United States"[1324] in an effort to understand the nature of this problem on the horizon. In March of that year, the Packard Foundation committed $22.2 million, over the next five years, for the China Sustainable Energy Program (CSEP). The program was to be managed by the Energy Foundation, and would aim "[t]o assist in China's transition to a sustainable energy future by promoting energy efficiency and renewable energy."[1325]

Its strategy in seeking to do so is multi-pronged; it matches Chinese government officials, academic researchers, and NGOs to the "best practices" of international energy experts in an effort "to spot and pursue energy savings."[1326] The CSEP makes direct grants to organizations in China; conducts workshops to tackle risks associated with China's continuing economic growth; and collaborates with local and national government officials, proposing policies and bringing to the fore problems of energy efficiency. Its six target areas are low-carbon development paths, appliance standards and buildings, industry, electric utilities, renewable energy, and transportation. In 2002, the William and Flora Hewlett Foundation joined the program with a grant of $2 million for the program's transportation work.[1327] Still, with a budget of approximately $7 million per year, the China Sustainable Energy Program is small, compared to other international efforts—those of the U.N. Development Program, World Bank, and European Union, for example. However, those organizations are not significantly involved in policy development. This has allowed the CSEP—through a combination of political connections, a sterling reputation (thanks both to the competence of its staff and the good names of the Packard and Hewlett Foundations), and an ability to harness international expertise—to carve out a niche that affords it great leverage in promoting energy sustainability.[1328]

Outcomes. The CSEP has been highly effective in pursuing its mission.[1329] Much of this is owed to its excellent relations with many top Chinese government officials. Because of this working relationship, the CSEP has been able to propose new policy on such issues as Chinese auto emissions and the energy efficiency of appliances in a nation of 1.3 billion consumers of energy. Among the principal successes of the China Sustainable Energy Program was its pivotal role in developing and winning support for the six mandatory energy efficiency standards adopted in China between 1999 and 2003. These standards will produce savings over the next fifteen years of 300 million tons of coal and will prevent the emission, by China, of some 798 million tons of CO_2.[1330] The CSEP also played a leading role in supporting the adoption of labeling laws and efficiency requirements for lighting, washing machines,

TVs and other appliances, "which by 2010 are expected to save [China] enough energy to avoid the need for at least ten large new power plants."[1331] And CSEP research and analysis helped shape the Chinese government's fuel economy standard—the first by a developing nation—which "could save 6 billion barrels of oil and reduce carbon emissions by over 800 million tons between now and 2030."[1332]

Impact. Certainly, CSEP does not deserve all the credit for these and other promising developments. The Chinese government would, no matter what, be dealing with many—if not all—of the same issues that CSEP works on. No nation China's size could undergo anything like its degree of development and industrialization in this era of globalization and interdependence without being forced to consider the broad effects—environmental, economic, and political—of its policies. And the Chinese government has already managed, between 1980 and 2000, to quadruple its growth while only doubling its energy consumption.[1333] But, according to an evaluation of CSEP carried out by Energy Resources International (ERI), the efforts of the Packard, Hewlett, and Energy Foundations have definitely added value. In fact, the ERI evaluators were unanimous in their belief "that the CSEP has been exceptionally valuable to Chinese stakeholders," and "has both accelerated the development of policies and improved their substance."[1334] As China continues to modernize, there will be a growing need for such acceleration of action and improvement of policy outcomes.

Case 95

SMART GROWTH INITIATIVE

Surdna Foundation et al, 1999

SCOTT KOHLER

Background. The late twentieth century saw an explosion in urban sprawl. As cities crept farther and farther outward, residents complained of a range of worsening conditions. Increased air pollution and runoff, disappearing parklands, rising infrastructure costs, and ever more obesity: these are just a few consequences of urban sprawl.[1335] By the mid and late '90s, many state and local governments were experimenting with ways of slowing—if not stopping outright—the proliferation of vast suburban landscapes.[1336] States such as Oregon, New Jersey, and California struggled with the appropriate balance between development, on the one hand, and, on the other, environmental protection and economic efficiency. In Maryland, Governor Parris N. Glendening pioneered a multi-pronged strategy called by some "the most promising new tool for managing growth in a generation."[1337] Glendening's approach followed a set of precepts known as "Smart Growth," which encourage town-centered development, availability of multiple transportation options, and environmental protection. As Glendening has said, "the goal of smart growth is not no growth or even slow growth. Rather, the overall goal is sensible growth that balances our need for jobs and economic development with our desire to save our natural environment."[1338]

Strategy. In 1999, the New York-based Surdna Foundation launched the Smart Growth Initiative to promote smart growth development and demonstration in four states: New Jersey, Maryland, New Mexico, and Utah. The Foundation chose to operate in four very different states so as to develop a broad range of workable Smart Growth strategies that could be adapted to varying environments. With funding of approximately $1 million per year, over a projected 3–5 years, the Initiative focused on "reducing vehicle miles traveled," so as to mitigate air pollution, while at the same time spurring controlled growth, job creation, and economic prosperity.[1339] In the spring of '99, Surdna invited six other foundations—the Turner, Irvine, Ford, MacArthur, Packard, and Energy Foundations—to join it in creating the Funders' Network for Smart Growth and Livable Communities, a consortium "established to inform and strengthen philanthropic funders' individual and collective abilities to support and connect organizations working to . . . create better economies, build livable communities, and protect and preserve natural resources."[1340]

Impact. According to Michael Barrette, of the journal *Planning*, "foundations across the country have [now] made smart growth and regionalism an explicit part of their mission."[1341] Private funders frequently collaborate with state governments to fund bricks and mortar projects, and to promote shared policy aims. According to Hooper Brooks, the Surdna Foundation's Environment Program Director, the Foundation's work in four dissimilar states has enabled it to gather data on which approaches work best in which circumstances. One major finding has been that broad coalitions of support—including many relevant public sector actors—are necessary to get things done. This has been the case, for instance, in both Maryland and New Jersey, where Governor James McGreevey in 2002 declared a "war on sprawl" featuring incentives for smart growth development. McGreevey's initiatives brought in "nearly every state agency in . . . 'the war on sprawl.'"[1342] The Funders' Network now has over 100 dues-paying members, and has grown far beyond a membership interested only in environmental protection to a diverse consortium of interested nonprofits. With Foundation support, replicable models of Smart Growth have been endorsed by the Environmental Protection Agency (in 2002),[1343] and are being tried out in a number of states, including Minnesota, Wisconsin, and Tennessee.[1344]

Case 96

INTERNATIONAL FELLOWSHIPS PROGRAM

Ford Foundation, 2000

SCOTT KOHLER

Background. Time and again, private foundations have sought to achieve impact by supporting the development of human capital. Emerging fields of medical practice have been opened, and human knowledge carried forward and built upon by talented recipients of philanthropic educational support. the *New York Times* has noted, for example, that "[g]raduate fellowships are a mainstay of philanthropy, an area in which there is consensus that an investment produces a social return. . . "[1345] The Ford Foundation once supported a number of such fellowship programs around the world. Most, however, were terminated in the 1970s, when economic concerns forced the Foundation to scale back its grant-making. According to Susan Berresford, Ford Foundation's president, hindsight has since persuaded many Ford officials that these earlier graduate fellowships—which supported such future leaders as the young Kofi Annan—had, in fact, been highly successful and were worthy of reconstitution.[1346] The focus of the Ford Foundation's major new investment in global human capital would be easing the disparity between those who—by reason of wealth, geography, connections, or whatever else—are benefiting from today's knowledge-based economy, and those who, through no fault of their own, are at highest risk of being left behind.

Strategy. To that end, the Foundation in November 2000 announced the largest grant in its history: a $330 million appropriation, to be paid out in one year and spent over a period of ten, for the Ford Foundation International Fellowships Program (IFP).[1347] The Program provides full support for up to three years of graduate study at any university of the individual fellow's choosing. Fellows are chosen on the basis of three criteria: academic excellence, leadership potential, and commitment to a career of service at the local or national level.[1348] They are free to pursue a Masters, Ph.D., or professional degree in any field, so long as it relates to work conducted in one of the Ford Foundation's three broad grant-making areas: Asset Building and Community

Development; Knowledge, Creativity, and Freedom; or Peace and Social Justice. IFP recruits fellows from twenty-one countries and territories in Africa, Asia, Latin America, the Middle East, and Russia.

But living in one of these places and meeting the three criteria mentioned above are not enough. IFP Fellows must be people who, despite their evident potential, would otherwise be least likely to ever have the opportunity for international study and membership in the governing class. This means different things in different countries. In one place, for example, IFP might seek out female grantees; in another, members of a persecuted ethnic minority. So, while the particulars vary according to local conditions, Fellows are always drawn from the most at-risk, deprived elements of local society. As Ms. Berresford explained at the November 2000 announcement of IFP, this will "broaden the talent pool from which decision makers will be drawn so that people who normally would not be at the table have a chance to be there."[1349] The program, which will run until 2012, seeks to support at least 3,500 fellows, each of whom is encouraged to apply his or her talents to achieving progress back home by means of a $1,500 stipend given for work within his or her home community at the Fellowship's conclusion.[1350] $280 million of the Ford Foundation's grant defrays the costs of the fellowships, and $50 million supports the development of pipelines within universities in the developing world to enable them to prepare qualified students for IFP fellowship.

Outcomes. To date, over 1,500 Fellows have been selected, and have studied, or are currently studying, at some 300 universities worldwide. As of the end of 2003, 51 percent of the IFP Fellows were women, 61 percent were from outside the capital cities of their respective countries, and 5 percent were physically disabled.[1351] More than half of all IFP Fellows have fathers who did not advance beyond primary school.[1352] Each of these metrics describes a group that, in much of the developing world, is usually at an acute disadvantage in seeking higher education or any significant voice in government. At the same time, more than 85 percent of the Fellows who had completed their studies had, as intended, returned to work in their home country, while the remaining 15 percent were pursuing further study at their host university.[1353]

Impact. It is, of course, still too early to determine the role of the Ford Foundation International Fellowships Program in developing a network of change agents who can uplift their own communities and bring to local and national governance the perspective of those whom globalization tends to leave behind. The outcomes described above suggest, however, that the Program is, at least, living up to Ford's high expectations. As Senator Richard Lugar said at the official launch of the IFP, "the scope of this new program is breathtaking but it must be to meet a challenge that is truly awesome."[1354] The

International Fellowships Program is certainly one of the largest such efforts history. It is not nearly large enough to change the course of globalization or third-world development directly. However, the leaders it supports, and the engagement it fosters, may yet move mountains. As Susan Berresford declared at the Program's outset, "[p]eople matter, even in this time of globalized forces that can seem beyond the control of individuals. . . . And widening the talent pool also matters if we hope to build stable and just societies."[1355] With this massive ongoing initiative, the Ford Foundation is helping to uplift a sizable corps of leaders whose prospects would otherwise be circumscribed by the conditions of their birth. In so doing, Ford, like many foundations, is aiming squarely at the fulfillment of that hope.

Case 97

SUSTAINABLE DEVELOPMENT IN THE GREAT BEAR RAINFOREST

David and Lucile Packard Foundation, Rockefeller Brothers Fund et al, 2000

SCOTT KOHLER

Background. Over the course of the last few centuries, humankind has wrought enormous change on ecosystems of every imaginable kind and in virtually every corner of the world. The so-called "human footprint," as viewed from space, is enormous, and shows clearly that there remain very few large places where human development has not yet had a major impact. Among the largest of these rare reservoirs of pristine habitat is the Canadian Boreal region, and in particular the Great Bear Rainforest.[1356] Stretching over some 21 million acres, the Great Bear Rainforest is composed largely of huge old growth trees—many of them over 2,000 years of age. Nearly 60 percent of the world's coastal temperate rainforests have already been logged, and the Great Bear Rainforest composes fully one quarter of all that remains.[1357] With more biomass per acre than any other ecosystem on Earth, the Great Bear Rainforest contains an abundance of natural resources, in- cluding vast but diminishing salmon reserves, millions of migratory birds, and the world's last significant population of white Kermode, or Spirit Bears. It is also home to about 10,000 indigenous peoples, known in Canada as First Nations.

Local Canadian environmental groups began, in the early 1980s, to become concerned, as Merran Smith of ForestEthics recalls, "that our little postage-stamp sized parks were just not protecting wildlife."[1358] By the early 1990s, this concern had matured into organized resistance to the logging industry's massive clear-cutting operations in the Boreal. In 1993, an announcement by the provincial government of British Columbia that it planned "to allow logging in two-thirds of the ancient hemlock, fir and cedar forests of Clayoquot Sound, on the western coast of Vancouver Island," touched off the largest civil disobedience episode in Canadian history—a massive protest in which 800 people were arrested.[1359] According to Merran Smith, the Clayoquot Sound protest convinced local environmental groups that they could "protect an entire ecosystem, rare on the planet, on [a] large enough scale so it wouldn't be eroded over time."[1360] The Great Bear Rainforest "became an icon for people in the United States and Europe who don't have that kind of biodiversity jewel."[1361]

Environmentalists soon decided, however, that they could not use the same protest tactics in the far less accessible northern British Columbia as they had further south. To that end, they launched a major consumer awareness campaign to pressure buyers of timber and timber products not to purchase wood from old-growth trees. This aggressive advocacy campaign produced startling results, most notably in December 1999, when Home Depot announced it would phase out purchases of old growth timber. Because fully 10 percent of all wood sold in the United States goes through Home Depot, this decision sent shockwaves through the logging industry. Facing enormous economic pressure from Home Depot and such groups as the European Pulp and Paper Manufacturer's Association, the six timber companies active in British Columbia soon called for negotiations with the environmentalist groups, the First Nations, and the provincial government.

It must be said that this remarkable development did not result solely from the environmentalists' advocacy campaign. For years, the First Nations—who were generally skeptical at best of the crusading environmental groups—had contested in court that all the land in question and more was, in fact, theirs by right. In 1997, they won a major court victory holding that the First Nations' rights and title to this vast region—96 percent of which was claimed by the Crown—had never been extinguished. That ruling threw into flux all development plans, and this uncertainty, combined with the old growth timber boycott described above, combined to bring the logging companies to the negotiating table. In any event, there was in early 2000 an unprecedented opportunity for all the relevant stakeholders to work together for a broadly acceptable sustainable development plan in the Boreal. Recognizing that the most important work was just about to begin, the environmental groups at this point sought the aid of the David and Lucile Packard Foundation.

Strategy. The Packard Foundation saw in the Cascadia negotiations a chance to think several steps in advance of development, and to help create a sustainable development plan that would enable humans—both the First Nation residents and the interested timber companies—to utilize the region's abundant resources, while still preserving irreplaceable habitats for salmon, eagles, bears, and the vast host of other organisms sharing the Great Bear Rainforest. The negotiation offered the chance to explore sustainable development on an unprecedented scale, and with more or less willing partners, so the Packard Foundation acted quickly to get involved.

The Foundation's trustees approved almost immediately an out-of-cycle grant of $2 million. The environmental groups would put half of this up immediately as capital to show their timber industry counterparts that they were serious about finding a workable solution. The second half would help the Foundation's grantee organizations—which after all were composed of passionate campaigners, not savvy negotiators—to develop internally. This initial grant was seen by the Foundation as a high-risk, high-reward investment. As the negotiations proceeded—and began to bear fruit—the Foundation continued appropriating funds to facilitate crucial discussions feeding into the larger government-sanctioned negotiation, dubbed the Joint Solutions Project.[1362] In addition, the Packard Foundation has engaged other funders—including the William and Flora Hewlett Foundation and the Gordon and Betty Moore Foundation—in building a coalition to protect the Great Bear Rainforest.

Outcomes. On April 4, 2001, the timber companies, environmental groups, and First Nations leadership reached an historic compromise. Under the terms of the agreement, forty-two valleys, covering an area of some 1.5 million acres—twice the size of Yosemite National Park—were set aside permanently for conservation, and logging was suspended across another 2 million acres while negotiations continued. Depending on the outcome of those continuing talks, annual logging along the coast of British Columbia will fall by at least 15 percent, and possibly as much as 60 percent. Most importantly, the April 4 agreement declared the Joint Solutions Project's goal to be "ecosystem-based management." An explicit commitment to this approach was a major breakthrough. As a Packard Foundation memo explains: "Nowhere else in the world, not even in the threatened Amazon rainforest, is an experiment like this being carried out on such a large scale."[1363] With the agreement of three key stakeholder groups a fait accompli, the provincial government was essentially forced to endorse the plan.

Very soon afterward, however, shifting political winds threw a wrench into the ongoing work of the Joint Solutions Project. In May 2001, provincial elections brought to power in British Columbia a new regional government. The newly elected Liberal Party leaders were far more conservative and opposed to regulation of business activities than their predecessors had been. This created a major sticking point, because without the engagement and consent of the provincial authority, no agreement would actually be implemented. In response, the Rockefeller Brothers Fund—which had been making modest grants in the region for several years preceding the formation of the Joint Solutions Project—convened a meeting of eight private foundations, including the Ford, Hewlett, Moore, and Packard Foundations, with Gordon Campbell, the new Premier of British Columbia. In this and subsequent talks, the foundations were able to overcome the new government's early opposition to the effort, and secure an agreement to continue collaborative negotiations through the Joint Solutions Project.

Those negotiations are still going on. Although the four major groups have not yet reached full consensus, they are continuing to craft a sustainable development plan combining the best international research and theory with the local realities of British Columbia. To ensure that the solution is workable when it is finally reached, the environmental groups—with the aid of their foundation allies—have embarked on an ambitious fund-raising plan. Their goal is to raise $100 million, half of which will be committed by the local government. To the small regional NGOs that have up to now led the charge to protect the Great Bear Rainforest, this is an unapproachable sum. Recognizing this, the foundations brought in The Nature Conservancy (TNC) to manage this private fundraising drive. In addition, the foundations have played the key role of broker between TNC and the smaller nonprofits, seeking to ensure that the full resources of The Nature Conservancy are brought to bear without TNC trampling the existing coalition of smaller groups that have been working in the region for years. In partnership with these local environmental NGOs, The Nature Conservancy has taken on the Great Bear Rainforest fundraising effort as a project of high global priority.

Impact. What was once an outright battle has now become a collaborative effort to preserve the Great Bear Rainforest. This transition alone is tremendously significant in breaking the traditional cycle of antagonism between environmental and industry groups, and in clearing a path for lasting progress. That it came about at all is a tribute to the tireless efforts of the First Nations, who have refused to give up a land to which they have deep attachment, and to a network of local environmental activists, including ForestEthics, the Rainforest Action Network, and Greenpeace–British Columbia, that brought the threatened Boreal into the public eye and thereby pressured logging companies to accept the necessity of compromise.

Foundations have not been the central actors in this ongoing drama, but their role has been very important. With a timely infusion of funds, the Packard Foundation helped to legitimate the environmental groups working on the Joint Solutions Project. The Rockefeller Brothers Fund built on years of involvement in and understanding of the region, using to full effect its local contacts in brokering the meeting between Premier Campbell and the eight foundations. These efforts cleared a major roadblock—the initial skepticism of the new government—that might otherwise have derailed the larger negotiations ongoing since 2000. These and other foundations secured the support of The Nature Conservancy in a large-scale fundraising effort that none of the smaller nonprofits could have managed, and then worked to ensure that TNC and the local network of NGOs worked as partners, not competitors, in a turf war. In facilitating the Joint Solutions Project, the Packard, Rockefeller Brothers, Moore, Hewlett, Ford, and other foundations have employed a range of resources—from money to convening power to access to the international research community. These resources have served to guide and support a negotiation process that is one of the bright lights of conservation and sustainable development in the history of the environmental movement.

Case 98

TALENTED STUDENTS IN THE ARTS INITIATIVE

Surdna Foundation and Doris Duke Charitable Foundation, 2000

SCOTT KOHLER

Background. The Arts Programs of the Doris Duke Charitable Foundation (DDCF) and the Surdna Foundation have different, if overlapping, missions. The Duke Foundation aims "to support performing artists with the creation and public performance of their work."[1364] Surdna, on the other hand, seeks to "contribute to the ability of young people to explore their own identity and their relationship to the world through high-impact, long-term experiences creating art with accomplished professional artists," and to "deepen the ability of artists and arts organizations to contribute to the artistic expression of young people."[1365] So it is not surprising that the Doris Duke Charitable Foundation has extensive relationships with arts professionals, or that Surdna has a history of collaboration with arts educators. In

2000, however, the two foundations combined their respective expertise to support high-quality arts institutions engaged in "the training of young people with demonstrated talent in the performing arts." The Talented Students in the Arts Initiative came at a critical time for many such institutions, as public support for the arts—at both the local and national levels—was being cut around the nation.[1366]

Strategy. Having resolved to collaborate on an arts initiative of mutual interest, the two foundations began in 2000 by conducting field research to inform the program's design. By 2001, they had decided to focus on offering promising teenagers the opportunity to work with established artists. The Talented Students in the Arts Initiative was, therefore, to be a three-year project offering grants both to performing arts high schools and to national arts institutions working with professionals and young people. Pledging a combined total of $16 million, the foundations then issued a request for proposal to leading institutions around the country. Invited applicants were required to demonstrate the excellence of their program, its commitment to developing young artists, and an ability to raise additional funds.

The Surdna Foundation provided three-to-five-year program support grants "to fund scholarships, internships, artistic programs, and faculty resources during the grant period." DDCF, meanwhile, would pledge endowment support to ensure the sustainability of the initiatives undertaken by grantee organizations, which were required to raise matching endowment funds at a 1:1 ratio. The project had three phases. In the first round, announced in April 2001, four training institutions and five performing arts high schools received between $975,000 and $1.6 million. A year later, four more professional training institutions were given a total of more than $3.5 million, and in late 2002, another two training institutions were chosen to receive similar grants. All told, DDCF gave out $11.75 million over the grant period, while Surdna added a further $4.5 million.

Outcomes and Impact. With government support of the arts in a state of seemingly perpetual decline, the Surdna and Duke Foundations created the Talented Students in the Arts Initiative to serve as a bulwark of support for those institutions fostering the arts in their communities, and, especially, among the most promising artists of the next generation. The program strengthened institutions, such as the Jacob's Pillow Dance Festival—the oldest in the United States. Jacob's Pillow, which in 2003 was certified as a National Landmark, receives support for its three-month festival from a number of foundations and other funders. Yet the actual organization relied heavily of the funding it receives under TSAI.[1367] The Initiative also offered hundreds of young performers the opportunity to purse their interests alongside established professionals. The Cleveland School for the Arts, for example, used its grant "to send about twenty more school of the arts students to summer enrichment camps and internships" each year.[1368]

As Edward Skloot, executive director of the Surdna Foundation, said in 2002, the Talented Students in the Arts Initiative enabled both foundations "to leverage [their] program and financial heft . . . [And] virtually [guarantee] that the programs we nurture today will continue."

Case 99

A MODEL FOR THE NEW INNER-CITY SCHOOL: KIPP ACADEMIES

Pisces Foundation, 2000

STEVEN SCHINDLER

Background. Public education reform has been the object of a great deal of private foundation grantmaking, particularly in the last couple of decades. Much of the activity has arisen from the progress of the school choice movement, fueled in large part by conservative foundations. Charter schools, schools typically run by entrepreneurial leaders as alternatives to traditional public schools, have been among the favorite grantees of private foundations.

KIPP, or Knowledge is Power Program, now perhaps the most distinguished name in the charter, started as a single school in Houston in 1995.[1369] David Levin and Michael Feinberg, roommates and fellow Teach for America corps members in Houston, developed the KIPP model out of frustration with the lack of discipline and motivation in their students. Their school, they decided, would operate on the premise that students would attend KIPP on a voluntary basis. Students opting for KIPP rather than a traditional public school, however, would have to make a number of commitments, including attending school for a few extra hours each day (7:30 a.m.-to-5:00 p.m.) and for forty days more than their public school counterparts each school year. KIPP would demand a lot from its students and their parents, but it would also offer them an escape from the low achievement to which they might otherwise be destined.[1370]

Levin and Feinberg recruited a few low-achieving students in the first year, and those students' test scores rose dramatically. Levin then sought to open a school in his home town, New York City. A former school official working at the Manhattan Institute, a conservative policy organization funded in large part by conservative foundations, was able to secure a few classrooms, and Levin returned to New York City's South Bronx to open KIPP's second school. Despite the Houston school's success, the KIPP model faced some opposition. Only after New York enabled Levin to open a school there did Houston Superintendent Rod Paige, later the Secretary of Education, prevent a revocation of the original KIPP charter and classroom space. [1371]

Strategy. The Pisces Foundation, a supporting organization based in San Francisco, was created in 1997 by Donald and Doris Fisher, cofounders of Gap, Inc. It has endeavored to "leverage change in public education—especially in schools serving disadvantaged students—through large strategic investments in a small number of initiatives that bolster student achievement."[1372] The Foundation, noting the acclaim KIPP was earning for its success in educating disadvantaged students in New York and in Houston, made a grant of $15 million in 2000 to enable KIPP founders to expand their charter school model nationwide.[1373] By 2004, the Pisces Foundation and the Fishers individually had given a total of $34.5 million to KIPP.[1374]

When approached by the Fishers, the leaders of KIPP considered how they might best utilize the funds to expand the KIPP model. One option the Fishers and the KIPP leaders considered was to create new schools that KIPP would own and operate uniformly and centrally, similar to the model the Fishers adopted for Gap stores in shopping centers nationwide. Neither Levin nor Feinberg, however, had any experience in business or administration other than their brief service as heads of their schools, and neither was interested in mimicking the for-profit Edison Schools network. Both also feared that centralized control would deter entrepreneurial and creative individuals like themselves from becoming principals of future KIPP schools.[1375]

Instead of funding the creation of new schools, the KIPP leaders decided to use the grants from the Pisces Foundation to fund a training program at the KIPP national office for prospective KIPP principals.[1376] KIPP would use the money to recruit the best and most ambitious teachers to be trained according to the principles Levin and Feinberg developed in their own schools.[1377] KIPP would then assist these individuals in creating their own charter schools across the country, employing the KIPP model guidelines but also adapting to the unique challenges of each school setting. KIPP-trained individuals have the privilege of using the KIPP name in the title of their charter schools, a mark of certification that is a valuable asset in light of the strong goodwill that KIPP has fostered. But for continued enjoyment of that privilege, schools must continue to uphold the core principles of KIPP and must permit KIPP officials to inspect the schools. A handful of schools have been stripped of the right to use the KIPP name.[1378]

Impact. Some charter schools have endured criticism for failing to demonstrate evidence of an ability to raise test scores at a relatively higher rate than their public school counterparts. Even KIPP's success has been challenged by claims that students in KIPP schools are ahead of their low-income peers because of selection bias. Nevertheless, KIPP Academies instill a sense of responsibility that, independent of KIPP schools' success in attaining high levels of achievement, has made KIPP the premier brand in the charter school movement for addressing the problem of low student achievement. *Washington Post* columnist Jay Matthews has called KIPP "the nation's most interesting and most successful response so far to the problem of low achievement in inner city and rural public schools."[1379] Reading and math scores of students at KIPP schools have increased dramatically.[1380] Early figures suggest that students attending KIPP schools will be much more likely to attend college than the national average.[1381] With the support of the Pisces Foundation in training new KIPP principals, there are now fifty-two KIPP schools operating in sixteen states and the District of Columbia, serving over 11,000 students.[1382]

Case 100

CONNECTING FOR HEALTH: A PUBLIC-PRIVATE COLLABORATIVE

John and Mary R. Markle Foundation, 2002

SCOTT KOHLER

Background. Since 1969, when Lloyd Morrisett assumed its presidency, the Markle Foundation has focused on "mass communications in a democratic society" as a means "to promote the advancement and diffusion of knowledge . . . and the general good of mankind."[1383] In 1988, under the leadership of current president Zoë Baird, the Foundation narrowed its focus to "information and communication technology." Today, this remains the lever by which Markle seeks to leverage it modest resources—about $140 million in assets—to achieve sustainable impact in two program areas: Health and National Security.

In its Health program, the Foundation seeks to ensure that the enormous potential of information technology (IT) is realized in the health and healthcare fields, and that the primary beneficiary of this realization is the patient.[1384] To that end, the Foundation in 2002 launched Connecting for Health: A Public-Private Collaborative. The initiative draws together all the relevant stakeholders in the field, including physicians, hospitals, patients' advocates, IT professionals, and government, in an effort to guide the spread of IT into healthcare.[1385] To understand the significance of this effort, it is necessary to consider how antiquated are most American health systems. In a field characterized by ever-shifting boundaries of possibility, enormous resources, and rapid technological advancement, paper records remain almost universal, and physicians often have little or no way of knowing their patients' full medical histories. The system is reliant upon patient visits even for minor services: a dynamic that benefits healthcare providers, but inconveniences, and often overcharges, the mass of healthcare consumers.

Strategy. Through the Connecting for Health initiative, the Markle Foundation plays the role of a neutral, disinterested convener. It is a role that no other stakeholder in the system could play. In 2002, the Foundation committed $2 million to the project, much of which has gone for research, small demonstration projects, and other ways of building the evidence base to encourage the development of personal, portable, electronic health records. Such records can improve the quality of care received by enabling a doctor to know exactly what the patient's medical history is (allergies, possible drug interactions, tests already received etc.). They also offer the promise of increased security, as patients have both ownership of and access to their full medical histories. Personal electronic health records can enable patients not to be the passive consumers of healthcare they all too often are.

Still, the money spent by Markle has been primarily for the "glue" that binds together the project's more significant efforts. The real meat of Connecting for Health is its steering committee and its working groups. The steering committee, now composed of over sixty members, includes an enormous range of stakeholders all working though their many differences toward shared goals—the improvement of health care provision, the increased accessibility of health care to all Americans, and the maintenance of high standards of privacy in medicine. The committee meets to develop standards for the use of IT in health care. Markle also convenes several working groups, which gather to research and make recommendations about thorny issues of IT development. The members of the steering committee and the working groups freely donate their time, and the Foundation's calculations show that the value of time donated exceeds—by several orders of magnitude—the money spent on the initiative. Concerned that IT was developing ever more, and ever better discrete silos of information, where knowledge lived and died, the Markle Foundation convened this collaborative to promote the sharing of knowledge and the airing of concerns in the hope that the benefits of IT could accrue to all—not just to those with market power. One major interest of the Foundation—openly espoused—has been *interoperability*, or open standards. In effect, the Foundation has sought to guide the steering committee's discussions toward a realization that health records must be portable—and therefore transferable among systems (like e-mail)—or else the patient will be held hostage by his or her current health plan or provider. Recognizing the potential of Connecting for Health, the Robert Wood Johnson Foundation in 2004 joined Markle as a funding partner. To date, the two foundations have spent a total of approximately $3 million on the project.[1386]

Outcomes. The outcomes achieved by the collaborative have been impressive. In March 2003, Secretary Thompson, of the U.S. Department of Health and Human Services, announced that the Connecting for Health standards would be adopted by the federal government as it moved toward the goal of personal electronic health records.[1387] In his announcement, Secretary Thompson explicitly thanked the Markle Foundation for enabling the conversation about IT in healthcare to take place at all, and to include such a wide range of stakeholders. This inclusive approach, which rejected no one who wanted to participate, made it easy for the federal government to accept the Connecting for Health standards without fear of some special-interest backlash. All the special interests had already been at the table negotiating. Such dissimilar leaders as President Bush and Sen. Hillary Clinton have both embraced the idea of portable personal electronic health records for all Americans.[1388] Dr. David Brailer, the federal government's national health information technology coordinator was, until his appointment by President Bush, the chair of a Connecting for Health working group.[1389]

Impact. The value added by Markle's participation has been widely recognized. As a private foundation, Markle was able to fill a key niche: that of the convener. No other entity, public or private, would have been able to conduct the discussions that led to the Connecting for Health standards. A recent article, in the online version of the journal *Health Affairs*, estimates "that $78 billion a year could be saved by moving to electronic patient records in a network with open communications standards, or interoperability, in computing terms."[1390] To be sure, plenty of roadblocks remain. Privacy issues continue to be contentious, and the costs of maintaining electronic health records—about $25,000 per year—remain prohibitive for many doctors' offices. Market penetration is still only about 5 percent.[1391] But the promise of IT for healthcare is now well understood. And patient welfare is now the guiding light for future progress. Before the Markle Foundation got involved, the conversation was barely taking place. Now, it is being conducted among all the relevant actors, and has won approval from key leaders in the private and public sectors. The Foundation secured a place for open standards and convened a discussion that continues to work through technical and financial roadblocks in the American healthcare field.

NOTES

Introduction

1. Recent books on foundations which are particularly good are the following: Marion Fremont-Smith, *Governing Nonprofit Organizations: Federal and State Law and Regulation* (Cambridge: Harvard University Press, 2004); Ellen Condliffe Lagemann, *The Politics of Knowledge: The Carnegie Corporation, Philanthropy, and Public Policy* (Middletown: Wesleyan University Press, 1989); Lagemann, *Private Power for the Public Good: A History of the Carniege Foundation for the Advancement of Teaching* (Middletown: Wesleyan University Press, 1983); Stephen C. Wheatley, *The Politics of Philanthropy: Abraham Flexner and Medical Education* (Madison: University of Wisconsin Press, 1988); and Gerald Freund, *Narcissism and Philanthropy: Ideas and Talent Denied* (New York: Viking, 1996. Warren Weaver's *U.S. Philanthropic Foundations; Their History, Structure, Management, and Record* (New York: Viking, 1967) is an older book that has stood the test of time.

2. From 1993–2000, I was president of the Atlantic Philanthropic Service Company, which served as the program staff in the United States for Atlantic Philanthropies, a world-wide foundation whose president was Harvey P. Dale. Atlantic Philanthropic Service Company formulated philanthropic program strategies within the geographical areas for which it was responsible and recommended to Atlantic Philanthropic grants pursuant to those strategies.

Cases 1–100

1. Howard S. Berliner, *A System of Scientific Medicine: Philanthropic Foundations in the Flexner Era* (New York: Tavistock Publications, 1985).

2. Martin Morse Wooster, "The Donors are In: What Gates Can Learn from Rockefeller about Global Health." *Philanthropy*, August/September 2001.

3. Ron Chernow, *Titan: The Life of John D. Rockefeller, Sr.* (Random House: New York, 1998).

4. Ibid.

5. "The Rockefeller University: History," available from http://www.rockefeller.edu.

6. Berliner, *A System of Scientific Medicine*.

7. Ibid.

8. Ibid.

9. Ibid.

10. Ibid. See also the case study of the Diamond Foundation's creation of the Aaron Diamond AIDS Research Center.

11. "About the Rockefeller University: Quick Facts," available from http://www.rockefeller.edu.

12. Ibid.

13. Ibid.

14. Available from http://www.rockefeller.edu. See also Wooster, "The Donors are In: What Gates Can Learn from Rockefeller about Global Health."

15. Chernow, *Titan: The Life of John D. Rockefeller, Sr.*

16. Ibid.

17. Raymond B. Fosdick, *Adventure in Giving: The Story of the General Education Board* (New York: Harper & Row, Publishers, 1962), 4.

18. Ibid., 4–10.

19. Ibid., 4–10.

20. Ibid., 4–10.

21. "Rockefeller Board to Enter New Field," *New York Times*, 6/15/1915, 5.

22. Fosdick, *Adventure in Giving*, 25.

23. Ibid., 26.

24. Ibid.

25. Ibid., 27.

26. Ibid., 30–32.

27. Ibid., 35–36.

28. Charles D. Biebel, "Private Foundations and Public Policy: The Case for Secondary Education During the Great Depression," *History of Education Quarterly*, Vol. 16, No. 1 (Spring 1976), 4.

29. Fosdick, *Adventure in Giving*, 22.

30. Ibid., 32–33.

31. Ibid., 34.

32. Ron Chernow, "Mystery of the Generous Monopolist," *New York Times*, 11/18/1998, G18.

33. "Carnegie Funds Millions for College Pension Fund," *New York Times*, 4/28/1905, 1.

34. Andrew Carnegie, "The Best Fields for Philanthropy," *North American Review*, 149 (1889), 691.

35. Ibid.

36. Stephen C. Wheatley, *The Politics of Philanthropy: Abraham Flexner and Medical Education* (Madison: University of Wisconsin Press, 1988), 22.

37. Ibid., 14–15.

38. Ibid., 27–28.

39. Ibid.

40. Henry Pritchett, Introduction, *Medical Education in the United States and Canada*, Abraham Flexner (New York: Carnegie Foundation for the Advancement of Teaching, 1910, Reprint 1972), vii.

41. Nicholas Murray Butler, "The Carnegie Foundation as an Educational Factor," *New York Times*, 1910.

42. Kenneth M. Ludmerer, *Learning to Heal* (New York: Basic Books, 1985), 170.

43. Wheatley, *Politics of Philanthropy*, 47–49.

44. "The Making of Doctors," *New York Times*, 6/12/1910, 12.

45. Flexner, *Medical Education in the United States*.

46. Wheatley, *Politics of Philanthropy*, 49.

47. Ibid., 50–51.

48. Howard J. Savage, *Fruit of an Impulse: Forty-Five Years of the Carnegie Foundation, 1905–1950* (New York: Harcourt, Brace, 1953), 104–108.

49. Ibid.

50. Ibid.

51. Raymond B. Fosdick, *The Story of the Rockefeller Foundation* (New York: Harper & Brothers, 1952), 96.

52. Wheatley, *Politics of Philanthropy*, 83.

53. Fosdick, *Story of the Rockefeller Foundation*, 97.

54. Ibid., 99.

55. Ibid., 98.

56. Robert P. Hudson, "Abraham Flexner in Perspective" *Bulletin of the History of Medicine* 46 (1972), 561.

57. Ludmerer, *Learning to Heal*, 192.

58. Ibid., 180.

59. Ibid., 208.

60. Raymond B. Fosdick, *The Story of the Rockefeller Foundation* (New York: Harper & Brothers, 1952), 6.

61. John Farley, *To Cast Out Disease: A History of the International Health Division of the Rockefeller Foundation, 1913–1951* (Oxford: Oxford University Press, 2004), 3.

62. Fosdick, *Rockefeller Foundation*, 10.

63. Farley, *To Cast Out Disease*, 3.

64. Fosdick, *Rockefeller Foundation*, 10.

65. Ibid., 24.

66. Farley, *To Cast Out Disease*, 19–20.

67. Fosdick, *Rockefeller Foundation*, 32–34.

68. "Expect to Prevent Malaria Entirely," *New York Times*, 6/25/1919, 10.

69. "Yellow Fever Banished," *New York Times*, 12/15/1921, 5; "Says Medicine Must Take the Offensive," *New York Times*, 8/7/1924, 17; "Rockefeller Fight on Disease Gaining," *New York Times*, 9/7/1924, E5; "Succeeds in Fight on Yellow Fever,"

New York Times, 6/3/1926, 14; "Yellow Fever Conquered," *New York Times*, 6/17/1927, 23.

70. Fosdick, *Rockefeller Foundation*, 32–36.

71. Ibid., 32–35.

72. Ibid., 32–40.

73. Farley, *To Cast Out Disease*, 84.

74. Hoyt Bleakley, "Disease and Development: Evidence from Hookworm Eradication in the American South," *Job Market Paper*, 10/4/2002, 4–5.

75. Fosdick, *Rockefeller Foundation*, 32–57.

76. "Yellow Fever—An Opportunity," *New York Times*, 3/24/1938, 22.

77. "Nobel Prize Won by New Yorker for Work on Yellow Fever Virus," *New York Times*, 10/19/1951, 1.

78. Ibid.

79. George S. Bobinski, *Carnegie Libraries: Their History and Impact on American Public Library Development* (Chicago: American Library Association, 1969), 11.

80. Ibid., 12.

81. Ibid., 13.

82. Ibid., 12.

83. Andrew Carnegie, "Wealth," *North American Review* 148 (1889), 663.

84. Stephen C. Wheatley, *The Politics of Philanthropy: Abraham Flexner and Medical Education* (Madison: University of Wisconsin Press, 1988).

85. Bobinski, *Carnegie Libraries*, 196.

86. Wheatley, *Politics of Philanthropy*.

87. Bobinski, *Carnegie Libraries*, 98.

88. Ibid., 98–99.

89. Ibid., 143–44.

90. Ibid., 146.

91. Ibid., 156.

92. Ibid., 156–57.

93. Ibid., 158–59.

94. Robert M. Lester, *A Thirty Year Catalog of Grants* (New York: Carnegie Corporation, 1942), 146.

95. Bobinski, *Carnegie Libraries*, 3.

96. Ibid., 7.

97. Ibid., 191.

98. Diana Tittle, *Rebuilding Cleveland: The Cleveland Foundation and its Evolving Urban Strategy* (Ohio State University Press: 1992), 27–33.

99. Ibid., 45–46.

100. Ibid., 46.

101. Ibid., 49.

102. Ibid., 50.

103. Ibid., 50–51.

104. Ibid., 51.

105. Ibid.

106. Ibid., 51–52.

107. Ibid., 53–54.

108. Ibid., 54.

109. Ibid., 54.

110. Michael Bliss, *The Discovery of Insulin* (Chicago: University of Chicago Press, 1982), 11.

111. The Carnegie Corporation of New York: Report of the Acting President, For the Year Ended September 30, 1922, 51.

112. Ibid.

113. Ibid., 52.

114. "History of Sansum Diabetes Research Institute," http://www.sansum.org/history.htm.

115. Bliss, *Discovery of Insulin*, 31.

116. Seale Harris, *Banting's Miracle: The Story of the Discoverer of Insulin* (Philadelphia: J.B. Lippincott, 1946), 49–57.

117. Ibid., 57–59.

118. Ibid., 68–69.

119. Ibid., 87–88.

120. Bliss, *Discovery of Insulin*, 140.

121. "History of Sansum Diabetes Research Institute," http://www.sansum.org/history.htm.

122. The Carnegie Corporation of New York: Report of the Acting President, For the Year Ended September 30, 1922, 54.

123. Bliss, *Discovery of Insulin*, 141.

124. The Carnegie Corporation of New York: Report of the Acting President, For the Year Ended September 30, 1922, 22.

125. Harris, *Banting's Miracle*, 200.

126. The Carnegie Corporation of New York: Report of the Acting President, For the Year Ended September 30, 1922, 55.

127. The Carnegie Corporation of New York: Report of the Acting President, For the Year Ended September 30, 1923, 30.

128. Harris, *Banting's Miracle*, 94.

129. "Organization of the National Research Council," http://www7.nationalacademies.org/archives/nrcorganization.html.

130. Ibid.

131. Ellen Condliffe Lagemann, *The Politics of Knowledge: The Carnegie Corporation, Philanthropy, and Public Policy* (Middletown: Wesleyan University Press, 1989), 35–37.

132. Ibid., 41–42.

133. Alice M. Rivlin, *The Role of the Federal Government in Financing Higher Education* (Washington: Brookings Institution, 1961), 29.

134. Lagemann, *Politics of Knowledge*, 43.

135. Ibid., 44–47.

136. "Organization of the National Research Council," http://www7.nationala-cademies.org/archives/nrcorganization.html.

137. Ibid., 47–49.

138. Ibid., 43.

139. A. Hunter Dupree, *Science in the Federal Government: A History of Policies and Activities* (Baltimore: Johns Hopkins University Press, 1957), 311–12.

140. Ann Shola Orloff, *The Politics of Pensions: A Comparative Analysis of Britain, Canada and the United States, 1880–1940* (Madison: University of Wisconsin Press, 1993), 3–10.

141. Orloff, *Politics of Pensions*, 13.

142. Stephen C. Wheatley, *The Politics of Philanthropy: Abraham Flexner and Medical Education* (Madison: University of Wisconsin Press, 1988), 43.

143. "Carnegie Millions for College Pensions," *New York Times*, 4/28/1905, 1.

144. Theron F. Schlabach, *Pensions for Professors* (Madison: State Historical Society for Wisconsin, 1963), 19.

145. Ibid.

146. Ibid., 15.

147. Ibid.

148. Howard J. Savage, *Fruit of an Impulse: Forty-Five Years of the Carnegie Foundation, 1905–1950* (New York: Harcourt, Brace, 1953), 114.

149. Ibid.

150. Robert M. Lester, *A Thirty Year Catalog of Grants* (New York: Carnegie Corporation, 1942), 144–45.

151. "Company History," *TIAA-CREF Web Center*, http://www.tiaa-cref.org/newsroom/history.html.

152. "Company History," *TIAA-CREF Web Center*, http://www.tiaa-cref.org/newsroom/history.html.

153. "Facts and Figures," TIAA-CREF, *Annual Report*, 2004, 57.

154. Roberts, Alicia S., "Julius Rosenwald," *Learning to Give*, http://www.learn-ingtogive.com/papers/people/julius_rosenwald.html.

155. Ibid.

156. Julius Rosenwald, "The Burden of Wealth," *Saturday Evening Post*, 1/5/1929, 136.

157. George Brown Tindall, *The Emergence of the New South, 1913–1945* (Baton Rouge: Louisiana State University Press, 1967), 271.

158. "History," *The Rosenwald Schools Initiative*, http://www.rosenwald schools.com/history.html#5.

159. S. L. Smith, *Builders of Goodwill: The Story of the State Agents of Negro Education in the South, 1910 to 1950* (Nashville: Tennessee Book Company, 1950), 72–74.

160. Tindall, *The Emergence of the New South*, 271.

161. Ellen Condliffe Lagemann, *The Politics of Knowledge: The Carnegie Corporation, Philanthropy, and Public Policy* (Middletown: Wesleyan University Press, 1989), 53–54.

162. Ibid.

163. Ibid., 54.

164. Ibid., 55.

165. Ibid., 56.

166. Ibid., 57.

167. Ibid., 58–59.

168. Ibid., 59.

169. Ibid.

170. Ibid., 60.

171. Ibid., 61.

172. Ibid., 62.

173. Ibid.

174. Ibid., 63–64.

175. Ibid., 65.

176. Ibid., 69.

177. "NBER Information," *National Bureau of Economic Research*, http://www.nber.org/info.html.

178. Ellen Condliffe Lagemann, *The Politics of Knowledge: The Carnegie Corporation, Philanthropy, and Public Policy* (Middletown: Wesleyan University Press, 1989), 71.

179. Ibid., 72.

180. Ibid, 72.

181. Ibid., 73.

182. Ellen Condliffe Lagemann, *Private Power for the Public Good: A History of the Carnegie Foundation for the Advancement of Teaching* (Middletown: Wesleyan University Press, 1983), 76–77.

183. Ibid., 75–76.

184. Ibid., 79–81.

185. Lagemann, *Politics of Knowledge*, 79.

186. Lagemann, *Private Power*, 81.

187. "For Court Control of Bar Admission," *New York Times*, 4/13/1931, 27.

188. Lagemann, *Politics of Knowledge*, 73–74.

189. Ibid., 77.

190. Ibid., 80.

191. Ibid., 91.

192. Ibid., 71.

193. Ibid., 91.

194. "This is ALI," *The American Law Institute*, http://www.ali.org/ali/thisALI.pdf.

195. A. McGehee Harvey and Susan L. Abrams, *For the Welfare of Mankind: The Commonwealth Fund and American Medicine* (Baltimore: Johns Hopkins University Press, 1986).

196. Ibid.

197. Ibid.

198. Ibid.

199. This is not broken out, except by year. In addition to hospital construction, the Division funded postgraduate fellowships for aspiring rural doctors.

200. Harvey, *For the Welfare of Mankind: The Commonwealth Fund and American Medicine.*

201. Mary Lou Russell, Robert Oksner, and Anne MacKinnon, *For the Common Good: The Commonwealth Fund 1918–1993* (New York: The Commonwealth Fund, 1994).

202. Department of the Treasury, Internal Revenue Service Form 990 of Southside Community Hospital, Inc., available from http://www.guidestar.org.

203. Harvey, *For the Welfare of Mankind.* Harvey and Abrams describe the Rural Hospitals Program as "an important example for the framers of the Hill-Burton Hospital Survey and Construction Act."

204. In fact, the Hill-Burton Act required communities to raise two-thirds of the money, as opposed to the one-third requirement of the Commonwealth Fund.

205. Available from http://www.hrsa.gov/osp/dfcr/about/aboutdiv.htm.

206. Available from http://www.hao.ucar.edu/public/education/sp/images/hale.html.

207. This body was soon absorbed into Rockefeller's General Education Board.

208. National Park Service website, Astronomy and Astrophysics: Palomar Observatory 200-inch Reflector, available from http://www.cr.nps.gov/history/online_books/butowsky5/astro4e.htm.

209. In fact, the Telescope eventually cost $6.55 million (after a supplemental appropriation in 1946), a sum equivalent to approximately $71.6 million in 2004 dollars. Waldemar Kaempffert, "The Supreme Task of Science," *New York Times*, 10/24/1948.

210. National Park Service website, Astronomy and Astrophysics: Palomar Observatory 200-inch Reflector, available from http://www.cr.nps.gov/history/online_books/butowsky5/astro4e.htm.

211. Kaempffert, "The Supreme Task of Science."

212. RedNova Reference Library website, available from http://www.rednova.com/education/reference_library/?article_id=5.

213. National Park Service website, Astronomy and Astrophysics: Palomar Observatory 200-inch Reflector, available from http://www.cr.nps.gov/history/online_books/butowsky5/astro4e.htm.

214. Ibid.

215. Raymond B. Fosdick, *The Story of the Rockefeller Foundation* (New York: Harper & Brothers, 1952), 137–39.

216. Ibid., 156–58.

217. Ibid., 159.

218. George W. Beadle, "The Role of Foundations in the Development of Modern Biology," *U.S. Philanthropic Foundations: Their History, Structure, Management, and Record*, Warren Weaver (New York: Harper & Row, 1967) 226, 232; "M.I.T. Gets $500,000 for Biology Study," *New York Times*, 1/22/1953, 21.

219. Ibid., 228–30.

220. Ditta Bartels, "The Rockefeller Foundatin's Funding Policy for Molecular Biology: Success or Failure?" *Social Studies of Science*, Vol. 14 (1984), 238–43, for example, outlines some of the contours of the early debate.

221. Fosdick, *Story of the Rockefeller Foundation*, 161.

222. Beadle, "The Role of Foundations," 234.

223. Ibid.

224. Lucille Fidler, "Fifty and Forward," (Chapel Hill: Blue Cross Blue Shield, 1983), 3.

225. Robert F. Durden, *Lasting Legacy to the Carolinas: The Duke Endowment, 1924–1999* (Durham: Duke University Press, 1998), 57.

226. Durden, *Lasting Legacy*, 58.

227. Fidler, "Fifty and Forward," 3.

228. Eugene B. Crawford, "History of Hospital Saving Association of North Carolina, Inc." (Chapel Hill: Blue Cross Blue Shield, 1968).

229. Ibid.

230. Durden, *Lasting Legacy*, 59.

231. William G. Anlyan, "The Evolution of American Medicine and The Duke Endowment Health Care (Hospital) Division Since 1924," *North Carolina Medical Journal*, Vol. 63, No. 2 (March/April 2002), 69.

232. Adam Searing, "Blue Cross Blue Shield History," *NC Justice Center*, http://www.ncjustice.org/cms/index.php?pid=100.

233. Anlyan, "The Evolution of American Medicine," 69.

234. Adam Searing, "Blue Cross Blue Shield History," *NC Justice Center*, http://www.ncjustice.org/cms/index.php?pid=100.

235. Crawford, "History of Hospital Saving Association."

236. Ibid.

237. Fidler, "Fifty and Forward," 4.

238. Crawford, "History of Hospital Saving Association."

239. Ibid.

240. "About Us: History and Facts," *BlueCross BlueShield of North Carolina*, http://www.bcbsnc.com/inside/company.

241. Ellen Condliffe Lagemann, *The Politics of Knowledge: The Carnegie Corporation, Philanthropy, and Public Policy* (Middletown: Wesleyan University Press, 1989), 124.

242. Ibid., 123.

243. Ibid., 127–29.

244. Ibid., 132–33.

245. Ibid., 134–35.

246. Ibid., 136.

247. Ibid., 139.

248. Ibid., 140.

249. Ibid.

250. Ibid., 142–45.

251. Ibid., 124.

252. David W. Southern, *Gunnar Myrdal and Black-White Relations: The Use and Abuse of* An American Dilemma, *1944–1969* (Baton Rouge: Louisiana State University Press, 1987), 294.

253. Jack Greenberg, *Crusaders in the Court: How a Dedicated Band of Lawyers Fought for the Civil Rights Revolution* (New York: Basic Books, 1994), 197–98.

254. *McClesky v. Kemp*, 481 U.S. 279, 303 (1987); *United Steelworkers of America v. Weber*, 443 U.S. 193, 199 (1979); *Frontiero v. Richardson*, 411 U.S. 677, 685 (1973); *Brown v. Board of Education*, 346 U.S. 483, 495 (1954); *Hughes v. Superior Court of California*, 339 U.S. 460, 463 (1950).

255. Laughlin McDonald, *A Voting Rights Odyssey: Black Enfranchisement in Georgia* (Cambridge: Cambridge University Press, 2003), 58.

256. John H. Stanfield, *Philanthropy and Jim Crow in American Social Science* (Westport: Greenwood Press, 1985) 174.

257. Stanfield, *Philanthropy and Jim Crow*, 174.

258. Lagemann, *Politics of Knowledge*, 146.

259. While Dr. Papanicolaou's most significant medical achievement was the development of the Pap Smear Test, his earlier work on measuring female sex cycles contributed to the first isolation—by Willard Allen—of a hormone: estrogen.

260. Exfoliative cytology is the practice of using cells shed from some part of the body, or from a tumor, to identify cancer or hormonal irregularities. http://www.medicinenet.com/pap_smear/page7.htm.

261. Mary Lou Russell, Robert Oksner, and Anne Mackinnon, *For the Common Good: The Commonwealth Fund 1918–1993* (New York: The Commonwealth Fund, 1994).

262. Erskine Carmichael, *The Pap Smear: Life of George N. Papanicolaou* (Springfield: Charles C. Thomas, 1973).

263. Available from http://www.questdiagnostics.com.

264. Available from http://www.medicinenet.com/pap_smear/page7.htm.

265. Ibid.

266. Ibid.

267. Carmichael, *The Pap Smear: Life of George N. Papanicolaou*.

268. Harvey McGehee, *For the Welfare of Mankind: The Commonwealth Fund and American Medicine* (Baltimore: Johns Hopkins University Press, 1986).

269. Available from: http://www.laskerfoundation.org.

270. Claudia Levy, "Philanthropist Mary Lasker Dies at 93," *Washington Post*, 2/23/1994.

271. Sana Siwolop and Jerry Brazda, "The Fairy Godmother of Medical Research," *Business Week*, 7/14/1985.

272. Nadine Brozan, "Woman in the News: Mary Lasker; Lobbyist of a National Scale," *New York Times*, 11/21/1985.

273. Siwolop, "The Fairy Godmother of Medical Research."

274. Ibid.

275. Available from: http://www.nih.gov/news/budgetfy2004/fy2004presidents-budget.pdf.

276. Eric Pace, "Mary W. Lasker, Philanthropist for Medical Research, Dies at 93," *New York Times*, 2/23/1994.

277. Mary Lasker, "The Lasker Foundation: We're Not That Rich," *Business Week*, 8/11/1985.

278. Martin Weil, "Florence Mahoney Dies at 103; Helped to Establish NIH," *Washington Post*, 11/30/2002.

279. Ibid.

280. Elizabeth Weise, "The Man Who Fed the World," *USA Today*, 10/21/2003, 9D.

281. Norman Borlaug, "Nobel Lecture: The Green Revolution, Peace, and Humanity," 12/11/1970, http://nobelprize.org/nobel_prizes/peace/laureates/1970/borlaug-lecture.html.

282. John C. Culver and John Hyde, *American Dreamer: The Life and Times of Henry A. Wallace* (New York: Norton, 2000).

283. Rockefeller Foundation, *Annual Report*, 1962.

284. Gordon Conway, *The Doubly Green Revolution: Food for All in the Twentieth Century*. (New York: Comstock, 1997), 47.

285. Norman Borlaug, "Nobel Lecture."

286. Conway, *Doubly Green Revolution*, 47.

287. Norman Borlaug, "Nobel Lecture."

288. Ibid.

289. Conway, *Doubly Green Revolution*, 54.

290. Deborah Fitzgerald, "Exporting American Agriculture," in *Missionaries of Science: The Rockefeller Foundation and Latin America*, Marcos Cueto, ed. (Bloomington: Indiana University Press, 1994), 72.

291. Furthermore, Fitzgerald argues, the Americans had not done enough to bring small farmers in at the planning stages of the MAP. Therefore, tactics to promote widespread adoption of new practices were initially geared toward a farming community, like that of the United States, which was based on the land-grant system.

292. It was important to develop crops that could flourish regardless of the length of the days, because such crops would grow in dissimilar regions of the world and could be planted twice a year, thereby doubling the potential yield per hectare.

293. Dwarf wheat has two major advantages over taller varieties. First, wheat evolved to compete for sunlight (that is, to grow very tall) has a tendency to fall down once it is laden too heavily with kernels. Second, shorter wheat hybrids do not expend as much energy growing inedible stalks, so they are more efficient producers of grain.

294. William Paddock and Paul Paddock, *Famine—1975! America's Decision: Who Will Survive?* (Boston: Little, Brown, 1967).

295. The Paddocks do acknowledge the advances that had theretofore been made by Dr. Borlaug and the Rockefeller Foundation. However, they argue that the spread of new agricultural technologies, like Mexican dwarf wheat, will be limited by the

availability of qualified scientific personnel to adapt them to new (especially tropical) environments. Ultimately, they conclude that "The Population-Food Collision is Inevitable: It Is Foredoomed."

296. Ambassador David C. Mulford, "U.S.-India Partnership: Creating Economic Opportunities in Agriculture," remarks given on 4/16/2004, http://newdelhi.usembassy.gov/ambapr162004a.html.

297. Norman Borlaug, "Nobel Lecture."

298. Conway, *Doubly Green Revolution*, 55.

299. Rockefeller Foundation, *Annual Report*, 1968.

300. Pakistan and India had gone to war with one another while the first shipment of dwarf wheat seed to the region was on its way from Mexico.

301. Gregg Easterbrook, "Forgotten Benefactor of Humanity," *Atlantic Monthly*, Vol. 279, No. 1, January 1997, 74.

302. The Paddocks wrote of the Philippines, "no matter how miraculously the new research programs may improve agriculture the gains will be washed out by [a] tidal wave of new births." This has not proved to be the case.

303. The Nobel Committee awarded Borlaug its Peace Prize, as he explains in his acceptance speech, in recognition of "the actual and potential contributions of agricultural production to prosperity and peace among the nations and peoples of the world."

304. Elizabeth Weise, "The Man Who Fed the World."

305. Ibid.

306. Rockefeller Foundation, *Annual Report*, 1968.

307. Norman Borlaug, "The Green Revolution Revisited and The Road Ahead," remarks given on 9/8/2000, http://nobelprize.org/nobel_prizes/peace/articles/borlaug/borlaug-lecture.pdf.

308. Once the centers proved promising, the U.S. government provided funds. Over $1 million was allocated between 1966 and 1968, for example.

309. Norman Borlaug, "The Green Revolution Revisited and The Road Ahead."

310. In the 1970 *Annual Report* of the Rockefeller Foundation, president George Harrar lays out an in-depth assessment of the various critiques leveled at the Green Revolution. Ultimately, he concludes that the problems will be mitigated by further research and that, in any event, they are outweighed by the benefits.

311. Elizabeth Weise, "The Man Who Fed the World."

312. Leonard S. Rosenfeld and Henry B. Makover, *The Rochester Regional Hospital Council* (Cambridge, Massachusetts: Harvard University Press, 1956).

313. Ibid.

314. A. McGehee Harvey and Susan L. Abrams, *For the Welfare of Mankind: The Commonwealth Fund and American Medicine* (Baltimore: Johns Hopkins University Press, 1986).

315. Ibid.

316. Ibid.

317. Ibid.

318. Ibid.

319. Ibid.

320. Andrew Rich, *Think Tanks, Public Policy, and the Politics of Expertise* (Cambridge: Cambridge University Press, 2004).

321. These five are by no means the only such organizations set up or supported by the Ford Foundation. They are discussed because they are especially noteworthy. In addition, several other similarly successful policy research institutions—that can be considered "think/test tanks"—were created with significant help from the Foundation and are discussed in separate case studies. These include the Manpower Demonstrations Research Corporation (MDRC), Public/Private Ventures (P/PV), the Vera Institute of Justice, and the Police Foundation. Though discussed separately, these various organizations are, in fact, a related set. Taken together, they advanced considerably the Ford Foundation's goal of supporting on-the-ground, evidence-based policy research.

322. Available from http://www.rand.org/.

323. Ibid.

324. Ford Foundation, Office of Resources and the Environment. "Resources for the Future: A Review." September 1976.

325. Ibid.

326. Available from http://www.brookings.edu/.

327. Ibid.

328. Ibid.

329. Spencer Rich, "Think Tank Survives Lean Times: Foundations Help Fund 'Liberal' Urban Institute During Reagan Era," *Washington Post*, 5/16/1988.

330. Frederick O'R. Hayes and Anthony F. Japha. "The Urban Institute: An Evaluation," Ford Foundation.

331. Rich, *Think Tanks, Public Policy, and the Politics of Expertise*.

332. Rushworth M. Kidder, "From Left to Center: Jockeying for Thinkers, Funds, and Influence, Brookings Puts Scholarship Over Partisanship," *Christian Science Monitor*, 10/2/1984.

333. Available from http://www.rand.org/.

334. Ford Foundation, Office of Resources and the Environment. "Resources for the Future: A Review."

335. Jonathan Rauch, "Ideas Change the World—And One Think Tank Quietly Did," *National Journal*, 10/5/2002.

336. Ford Foundation, Office of Resources and the Environment. "Resources for the Future: A Review."

337. Jeff Shear, "Tightfisted Liberals," *National Journal*, 9/3/1994.

338. Available from http://www.cbpp.org/.

339. Shear, "Tightfisted Liberals."

340. Available from http://www.cbpp.org/.

341. Ibid.

342. Spencer Rich, "Think Tank Survives Lean Times: Foundations Help Fund 'Liberal' Urban Institute During Reagan Era," *Washington Post*, 5/16/1988.

343. "John Van Nostrand Dorr Dies; Metallurgist, 90, Was Inventor," *New York Times*, 7/1/1962, 57.

344. *The Dorr Foundation Report: December 28, 1940 to December 31, 1957* (New York: Dorr Foundation), 5.

345. Ibid.

346. Joseph C. Ingraham, "Line on Road's Edge is Cutting Accidents," *New York Times*, 1/5/1955, 1.

347. Cliff Ridley, "The Case for the Right Shoulder Line," *Fairfield County Fair*, 8/18/1955, 10.

348. Dorothy Fagerstrom, "Another Line for Safety: The Story of a Man and His Idea," *Law and Order*, June 1958, 5.

349. Fagerstrom, "Another Line," 5; Ridley, "Case for the Right Shoulder Line," 7.

350. Ridley, "Case for the Right Shoulder Line," 7.

351. "Right Shoulder Guides Gain as Road Safeguards," *Fleet Owner*, July 1955, 128.

352. Fagerstrom, "Another Line," 5; Ridley, "Case for the Right Shoulder Line," 7.

353. Ingraham, "Line on Road's Edge," 1, 18; Ridley, "Case for the Right Shoulder Line," 7.

354. "Right Shoulder Guides," 128.

355. Ingraham, "Line on Road's Edge," 18.

356. Ibid.

357. Ridley, "Case for the Right Shoulder Line," 10.

358. Joseph C. Ingraham, "Automobiles: Edges," *New York Times*, 9/22/1957, 165.

359. Ingraham, "Automobiles," 165.

360. Fagerstron, "Another Line," 5.

361. Ingraham, "Automobiles," 165.

362. "Now That White Paint Is Saving Lives," *Mt. Vernon Argus* (New York), 10/7/1954; Arthur D. Camp, letter to the editor, *Daily Times* (Mamaroneck, NY), 12/20/1954; "White Line on the Right," *Daily Times* (Mamaroneck, NY), 12/20/1954; H.P. Hawes, letter to the editor, *Farmingdale Post* (NY), 2/16/1955; W.N. Seymour, Jr., letter to the editor, *Adirondack Daily Enterprise*, 4/11/1955; Helen S. Nason, "They Are So Right!" *Adirondack Daily Enterprise*, 4/13/1955; "Why Neglect Safety on Bronx Parkway?" *Mt. Vernon Argus* (NY), 5/11/1955.

363. *Dorr Foundation Report*, 14.

364. *Bulletin 266: Pavement Edge Markings, Shoulders and Medians*, (Washington: Highway Research Board, 1960), 1.

365. *Bulletin 266*, 2.

366. *Bulletin 266*, 6.

367. *Dorr Foundation Report*, 13.

368. *Dorr Foundation Report*, 14.

369. Steven W. Sinding, "The Great Population Debates: How Relevant Are They for the 21st Century?" *American Journal of Public Health*, Vol. 90, No. 12 (December 2000), 1841.

370. "About the Population Council: History," *Population Council*, http://www.popcouncil.org/about/history.html, February 2005.

371. *The Population Council: A Chronicle of the First Twenty-Five Years, 1952–1977* (New York: Population Council, 1978), 12–13.

372. Michael S. Teitelbaum, "The Population Threat," *Foreign Affairs*, Vol. 71, No. 5 (Winter 1992), 63.

373. *The Population Council: A Chronicle*, 14.

374. Ibid., 23.

375. "About the Population Council: Highlights in Council History," *Population Council*, http://www.popcouncil.org/about/timeline.html.

376. "About the Population Council: History," *Population Council*, http://www.popcouncil.org/about/history.html, February 2005.

377. *The Population Council: A Chronicle*, 25–26.

378. Ibid., 27.

379. Teitelbaum, "The Population Threat," 63.

380. *The Population Council: A Chronicle*, 28.

381. Ibid., 60–62.

382. Ibid., 62.

383. "About the Population Council: Highlights in Council History," *Population Council*, http://www.popcouncil.org/about/timeline.html.

384. Kathleen Teltsch, "U.N. Officials See Birth-Control Project as Important Step Forward," *New York Times*, 3/11/1970, 8.

385. "About the Population Council: History," *Population Council*, http://www.popcouncil.org/about/history.html, February 2005.

386. Sinding, "Great Population Debates," 1841.

387. Richard Magat, *The Ford Foundation at Work: Philanthropic Choices, Methods, and Styles* (New York: Plenum Press, 1979), 103.

388. Edward H. Berman, *The Ideology of Philanthropy: The Influence of the Carnegie, Ford, and Rockefeller Foundations on American Foreign Policy* (Albany: State University of New York Press, 1983), 99.

389. Ibid., 100.

390. Ibid., 101.

391. Magat, *Ford Foundation at Work*, 178–79.

392. Ibid.

393. Ford Foundation, *Annual Report: To Advance Human Welfare*, 1960, 67.

394. Ford Foundation, *Annual Report: To Advance Human Welfare*, 1961, 20.

395. Ibid., 21.

396. Berman, *Ideology of Philanthropy*, 100–01.

397. Ibid., 99.

398. Ibid., 102.

399. Ibid., 102.

400. Ibid., 103.

401. Available from http://www.hhmi.org.

402. Ibid.

403. Ibid. In fact, the MRO exception to the 1969 Tax Reform Act had been in-cluded by Congress primarily to enable HHMI to retain full ownership of the Hughes Aircraft Company.

404. Ibid.

405. Ibid.

406. Ibid.

407. Ibid.

408. Ibid.

409. James E. Howell, "The Ford Foundation and the Revolution in Business Education: A Case Study in Philanthropy," September 1966.

410. Ibid.

411. Ibid.

412. In 1967, "Carnegie Tech" merged with the Mellon Institute to create Carnegie-Mellon University.

413. James E. Howell, "The Ford Foundation and the Revolution in Business Education: A Case Study in Philanthropy."

414. Ibid.

415. John Wheeler, "Report to Ford Foundation on Changes in Collegiate Business Education in the United States 1954–64 and the Role of the Ford Foundation in these Changes," September 1965.

416. James E. Howell, "The Ford Foundation and the Revolution in Business Education: A Case Study in Philanthropy."

417. The Gordon-Howell report was often referenced alongside another influential study, by Franklin Pierson, funded by the Carnegie Corporation of New York.

418. John Wheeler, "Report to Ford Foundation on Changes in Collegiate Business Education in the United States 1954–64 and the Role of the Ford Foundation in these Changes," September 1965.

419. James E. Howell, "The Ford Foundation and the Revolution in Business Education: A Case Study in Philanthropy."

420. Benjamin Fine, "Ford Foundation Gives $20,000,000 for Scholarships," *New York Times*, 9/7/1955, 1.

421. Carnegie Corporation of New York, *Annual Report*, 1955, 28–29, 33.

422. Ford Foundation, *Annual Report: To Advance Human Welfare*, 1955, 14.

423. Ibid., 153.

424. Carnegie Corporation of New York, *Annual Report*, 1955, 33–34.

425. Joan Cook, "John Stalmaker, Ex-Administrator of Merit Scholarships, Dies at 87," *New York Times*, 8/22/1990, D21.

426. "About Us: National Merit Scholarship Corporation," http://www.nationalmerit.org/about.php.

427. "Merit Student Plan Reports Successes," *New York Times*, 11/23/1961, 25.

428. "1,900 Are Named Merit Scholars," *New York Times*, 4/29/1965, 24.

429. "About Us: National Merit Scholarship Corporation," http://www.nationalmerit.org/about.php.

430. Peter Applebome, "The Eyes of Texas on Star Students," *New York Times*, 4/15/1984, ES21.

431. "$20,000,000 Talent Search," *New York Times*, 9/8/1955, 30.

432. Benjamin Fine, "Ford Foundation Gives $20,000,000 for Scholarships," *New York Times*, 9/7/1955, 1.

433. "10 Standard Oil Scholarships," *New York Times*, 1/20/1957, 31; "200 Scholarships Planned by I.B.M.," *New York Times*, 2/13/1957, 33.

434. "Labor Gives Six Grants," *New York Times*, 4/30/1959, 21.

435. "1,900 Are Named Merit Scholars," *New York Times*, 4/29/1965, 24.

436. National Merit Scholarship Corporation, *Annual Report: 2003–04*, available at http://www.nationalmerit.org/04_annual%20report.pdf, 6.

437. This figure is am improvement over the 3 percent of defendants who have paid bail yet intentionally miss their trial dates.

438. This may be because free men are better able to mount a defense, but it probably stems in large part from the simple fact that the same factors leading to a positive Vera recommendation correlate strongly to a high probability of innocence.

439. Patricia M Wald, "To Feel the Great Forces: The Times of Burke Marshall," *Yale Law Journal*, Vol. 105, Issue 3 (1995).

440. Available from http://www.presidency.ucsb.edu/ws/index.php?pid=27931&st=bail+reform&st1=johnson.

441. Jon O. Newman, "The Art of the Practical: An Evaluation of the Vera Institute of Justice," Robert B. Goldman, ed., available from http://www.vera.org.

442. Herbert Sturz, interview with Joel L. Fleishman, 9/6/2004.

443. Newman, "The Art of the Practical."

444. Available from http://www.vera.org/about/about_2.asp.

445. Richard Magat, *The Ford Foundation at Work: Philanthropic Choices, Methods, and Styles* (New York: Plenum Press, 1979).

446. Carnegie Corporation of New York, *Annual Report*, 1964, 65.

447. Carnegie Corporation of New York, *Annual Report*, 1965, 28–29, 78.

448. Carnegie Corporation of New York, *Annual Report*, 1967, 29–30, 83.

449. Carnegie Corporation of New York, *Annual Report*, 1969, 37–38.

450. "How Did NAEP Evolve," National Assessment Governing Board, http://www.nagb.org/about/evolve.html.

451. "How Did NAEP Evolve," National Assessment Governing Board, http://www.nagb.org/about/evolve.html.

452. "What is NAEP," National Center for Education Statistics, http://nces.ed.gov/nationsreportcard/about/.

453. Alain Jehlen, "Another Intriguing History," *NEA Today*, Vol. 22, No. 8 (May 2004), 29.

454. Gail Russell Chaddock, "US Report Card: Young Readers Make Big Gains," *Christian Science Monitor*, 7/15/2005, 1.

455. Teresa Mendez, "Public Schools: Do They Outperform Private Ones?" *Christian Science Monitor*, 5/11/2005, 11.

456. Caroline Hendrie, "NAEP Study Fuels Debate Over Charter Schools," *Education Week*, Vol. 24, No. 16, 1/5/2005, 5.

457. Joyce Pulcini and Mary Wagner, "Nurse Practitioner Education in the United States: A Success Story," *Clinical Excellence for Nurse Practitioners*, Vol. 6, No. 2 (2002).

458. A. McGehee Harvey and Susan L. Abrams, *"For the Welfare of Mankind": The Commonwealth Fund and American Medicine* (Baltimore: Johns Hopkins University Press, 1986).

459. Ibid.

460. Pulcini, "Nurse Practitioner Education in the United States."

461. Ibid.

462. R.D. Carter and J. Strand, "Physician Assistants: A Young Profession Celebrates the 35th Anniversary of Its Birth in North Carolina," *North Carolina Medical Journal*, Vol. 61, No. 5 (2000).

463. Ibid.

464. Ibid.

465. Ibid.

466. Terrance Keenan, "Support of Nurse Practitioners and Physician Assistants," *To Improve Health and Health Care: The Robert Wood Johnson Foundation Anthology 1998–1999*, Stephen L. Isaacs and James R. Knickman. eds., (San Francisco: Jossey-Bass: 1999).

467. Carter, "Physician Assistants: A Young Profession Celebrates the 35th Anniversary of Its Birth in North Carolina."

468. Ibid.

469. Keenan, "Support of Nurse Practitioners and Physician Assistants."

470. Pulcini, "Nurse Practitioner Education in the United States."

471. Ibid.

472. Harvey, *"For the Welfare of Mankind": The Commonwealth Fund and American Medicine.*

473. Ibid.

474. Pulcini, "Nurse Practitioner Education in the United States."

475. Carter, "Physician Assistants: A Young Profession Celebrates the 35th Anniversary of Its Birth in North Carolina."

476. Ibid.

477. Harvey, *"For the Welfare of Mankind": The Commonwealth Fund and American Medicine.*

478. Ibid.

479. Ibid.

480. Keenan, "Support of Nurse Practitioners and Physician Assistants."

481. Harvey, *"For the Welfare of Mankind": The Commonwealth Fund and American Medicine.*

482. John Burke, *An Historical-Analytical Study of the Legislative and Political Origins of the Public Broadcasting Act of 1967* (New York: Arno Press, 1979, reprinted from original, 1972), 76–77.

483. Ibid., 90.

484. Interview with Arthur Singer, 1/6/2005.

485. Ibid.

486. Burke, *An Historical-Analytical Study*, 90.

487. Ibid., 93.

488. Ellen Condliffe Lagemann, *The Politics of Knowledge: The Carnegie Corporation, Philanthropy, and Public Policy* (Middletown: Wesleyan University Press, 1989), 224.

489. Burke, *An Historical-Analytical Study*, 102–03.

490. Lagemann, *Politics of Knowledge*, 224.

491. Carnegie Corporation, *Annual Report*, 1965, 45.

492. John Witherspoon and Roselle Kovitz, *The History of Public Broadcasting* (Washington: Current, 1989), 19.

493. Interview with Art Singer, 1/6/2005.

494. Lagemann, *Politics of Knowledge*, 224.

495. Jack Gould, "New Guides for Educational TV," *New York Times*, 11/21/1965, X21.

496. Lagemann, *Politics of Knowledge*, 225.

497. Witherspoon, *History of Public Broadcasting*, 13.

498. Interview with Arthur Singer, 1/6/2005.

499. Witherspoon, *History of Public Broadcasting*, 14.

500. Witherspoon, *History of Public Broadcasting*, 13.

501. James Reston, "A Base for a Milestone," *New York Times*, 1/26/1967, 27.

502. Lagemann, *Politics of Knowledge*, 225.

503. James Ledbetter, *Made Possible By . . . The Death of Public Broadcasting in the United States* (London: Verso, 1997), 22.

504. Ledbetter, *Made Possible By*, 22.

505. Ledbetter, *Made Possible By*, 22.

506. Jack Gould, "Pace and 12 Others Named by President to Public TV Board," *New York Times*, 2/18/1968, 79.

507. Legislative History of PL 90–129 Public Broadcasting Act of 1967, USC-CAN 1967 Vol. 1, Senate Report No. 222, Department of Health, Education, and Welfare, 3/24/1967, 1782–86.

508. Legislative History of PL 90–129 Public Broadcasting Act of 1967, USC-CAN 1967 Vol. 1, House Report No. 572, 1811, 1827.

509. Ledbetter, *Made Possible By*, 22–23.

510. Mitchell Sviridoff, ed., *Inventing Community Renewal: The Trials and Errors that Shaped the Modern Community Development Corporation* (New York: Community Development Research Center: 2004).

511. Ibid.

512. Ibid.

513. Adjusted for inflation, $1500 in 1966 is equivalent to over $9000 in 2005. "Inflation Calculator" available at http://www.bls.gov/.

514. This meant, for example, that although Bedford-Stuyvesant was in many

ways the poorest neighborhood in any city on the East Coast, it received virtually none of the $380 million given to New York City under the National Housing Act of 1949.

515. In a nutshell, the Gray Areas program set up demonstration projects in five cities: Oakland, CA; New Haven, CT; Philadelphia, PA; Boston, MA; and Washington, D.C. In each city the Ford Foundation established an independent community agency that would develop a plan to revitalize the city, and then work to "[enlist and redirect] the efforts of city government, schools, social welfare agencies, and neighborhood leaders." The plan, and an allocation of seed money from the Foundation, would be used "to induce financial commitments from other agencies—public and private, local and national." Throughout the process, the poor themselves would be directly involved in setting up and carrying out the renewal of their communities. See Sviridoff, *Inventing Community Renewal.*

516. Ibid.

517. Ibid.

518. Ibid.

519. In fact, the Corporation's original name was the Bedford-Stuyvesant Restoration and Renewal Corporation, but it splintered after an early power struggle among its trustees, and the victorious faction—which was the progressive group—was known as the Bedford-Stuyvesant Restoration Corporation. Ibid.

520. Ibid.

521. Ibid.

522. Ibid.

523. Ibid.

524. Ibid.

525. Ibid.

526. Ibid.

527. James Day, *The Vanishing Vision: The Inside Story of Public Television* (Berkeley: University of California Press, 1995), 146–47.

528. Ford Foundation, *Annual Report,* 1969, 3; Carnegie Corporation, *Annual Report,* 1968, 20.

529. Carnegie Corporation, *Annual Report,* 1968, 20.

530. Day, *Vanishing Vision,* 145–46.

531. Richard M. Polsky, *Getting to Sesame Street: Origins of the Children's Television Workshop,* (Praeger Publishers: 1974), 2.

532. Polsky, *Getting to Sesame Street,* 9.

533. Ellen Condliffe Lagemann, *The Politics of Knowledge: The Carnegie Corporation, Philanthropy, and Public Policy* (Middletown: Wesleyan University Press, 1989), 232.

534. Polsky, *Getting to Sesame Street,* 25–26.

535. Ibid., 26.

536. Ibid., 64–65.

537. Lagemann, *Politics of Knowledge,* 232.

538. Day, *Vanishing Vision,* 152.

539. Ibid., 152–53.

540. *Sesame Street Research: A 20ᵗʰ Anniversary Symposium* (Children's Television Workshop, 1990), 5.

541. Lagemann, *Politics of Knowledge*, 234.

542. Day, *Vanishing Vision*, 160.

543. *Sesame Street Research: A 20ᵗʰ Anniversary Symposium*, 15.

544. Ibid.

545. Lagemann, *Politics of Knowledge*, 235–36.

546. "The World's Longest Street," *Sesame Workshop*, http://www.sesameworkshop.org/aboutus/around_longest.php.

547. "Sesame Street Tops Guinness World Record with Most Emmys of All Time," Press Release, 3/23/2005, http://www.sesameworkshop.org/aboutus/inside_press.php?contentId=14325318.

548. Ellen Condliffe Lagemann, *The Politics of Knowledge: The Carnegie Corporation, Philanthropy, and Public Policy* (Middletown: Wesleyan University Press, 1989), 216–21.

549. Ibid., 227–28.

550. Ibid., *229*.

551. Fred M. Hechinger, "Carnegie Panel Asks U.S. to Send Poor to College," *New York Times*, 12/13/1968, 1.

552. William K. Stevens, "College Opportunity for All Urged in Carnegie Report," *New York Times*, 3/3/1970, 1.

553. Stevens, "College Opportunity," 24.

554. Fred M. Hechinger, "Colleges: How Much and What Kind of Federal Aid?" *New York Times*, 6/13/1971, E9.

555. Fred M. Hechinger, "Congress Gives it the Old College Try," *New York Times*, 8/1/1971, E7.

556. David E. Rosenbaum, "New Hope for College Aid," *New York Times*, 1/10/1972, E28.

557. David E. Rosenbaum, "No-strings Funds for Colleges Are Backed by House Committee," *New York Times*, 10/1/1971, 20.

558. David E. Rosenbaum, "General-Purpose Aid to Colleges Is Withheld in a Strategic Move," *New York Times*, 1/25/1972, 17.

559. Fred M. Hechinger, "Some Badly Needed Money for Colleges," *New York Times*, 6/11/1972, E9.

560. Evan Jenkins, "U.S. Agency Prepares to Aid Students," *New York Times*, 2/18/1973, 30.

561. Richard Magat, *The Ford Foundation at Work: Philanthropic Choices, Methods, and Styles* (New York: Plenum Press, 1979), 154.

562. Ibid.

563. Ibid., 155.

564. Ibid.

565. Ibid.

566. Ibid, 156.

567. Ford Foundation, *Annual Report*, 1968 (New York: Ford Foundation, 1968), 6.

568. Robert B. McKay, *Nine for Equality Under Law: Civil Rights Litigation* (New York: Ford Foundation, 1977) 17.

569. Ford Foundation, *Annual Report*, 1970 (New York: Ford Foundation, 1970), 16, 18.

570. Ford Foundation, *Annual Report*, 1971 (New York: Ford Foundation, 1971), 22, 26; Ford Foundation, *Annual Report*, 1968 (New York: Ford Foundation, 1972), 21.

571. A. James Lee and Burton A. Weisbrod, "Public Interest Law Activities in Education," *Public Interest Law: An Economic and Institutional Analysis*, Burton A. Weisbrod, ed. (Berkeley: University of California Press, 1978), 317.

572. Ford Foundation, *Annual Report*, 1973 (New York: Ford Foundation, 1973), 40; Ford Foundation, *Annual Report*, 1974 (New York: Ford Foundation, 1974), 7.

573. McKay, *Nine for Equality Under Law*, 33.

574. McKay, *Nine for Equality Under Law*, 22.

575. Gary M. Stern, "Can the Puerto Rican Legal Defense and Education Fund Be Saved?" *The Hispanic Outlook in Higher Education*, Vol. 14, No. 9 (2/9/2004), 22.

576. Andrew H. Maclcolm, "New Police Chiefs Put New Ideas on the Force," *New York Times*, 4/23/1990.

577. Ibid.

578. William Grinker, "The Police Foundation: An Assessment of the Last Five Years and a Look to the Future," prepared for the Ford Foundation, 1983.

579. Susan V. Berresford, letter to Joel L. Fleishman and J. Scott Kohler. I am extremely grateful to Susan Berresford for her comments on this and several other case studies. Any shortcomings or errors within the text are, of course, my own.

580. Available from http://www.policefoundation.org/.

581. Ibid.

582. Ibid.

583. Ibid.

584. Maclcolm, "New Police Chiefs Put New Ideas on the Force."

585. Joel R. Gardner, Julius Krevans, and Margaret Mahoney, "A Conversation About the Clinical Scholars Program," *Medical Care*, Vol. 40, No. 4 (2002), Supplement, pp. II–25 to II–31.

586. Jonathan Showstack, et. al., "The Robert Wood Johnson Clinical Scholars Program," *The Robert Wood Johnson Foundation Anthology: To Improve Health and Health Care, Vol. VII*, Stephen L. Isaacs and James R. Knickman, eds. (San Francisco: Jossey-Bass, 2004).

587. Available from http://rwjcsp.stanford.edu/NPO/index.html.

588. "National Program Report: The Robert Wood Johnson Clinical Scholars Program," available from http://www.rwjf.org/reports/nreports/scholarse.htm.

589. Annie Lea Schuster, et. al., "An Innovation in Physician Training: The Clinical Scholars Program," *Journal of Medical Education*, Vol. 58 (February 1983).

590. Rashi Fein and John W. Rowe, A Review of the Robert Wood Johnson Clinical Scholars Program, 6/1/1992.

591. Gardner, "A Conversation About the Clinical Scholars Program."

592. Jonathan Showstack, Arlyss Anderson Rothman, Laura C. Leviton, and Nyonneweh Greene (2002). *Final Report: Survey of the Market for the Clinical Scholars Program*, June 7.

593. Ford Foundation, *Annual Report: To Advance Human Welfare*, 1952, 32.

594. *Annual Report*, 1952, 32.

595. Ibid.

596. Richard Magat, *The Ford Foundation at Work: Philanthropic Choices, Methods, and Styles* (New York: Plenum Press, 1979), 186–87.

597. *Annual Report*, 1965, 31.

598. Robert Cameron Mitchell, "From Conservation to Environmental Movement: The Development of the Modern Environmental Lobbies," chapter in *Government and Environmental Politics: Essays on Historical Developments Since World War Two*, Michael J. Lacey, ed. (Washington: Wilson Center Press, 1989), 84–86.

599. Ibid., 88–89.

600. Ibid., 89.

601. Ibid.

602. *Annual Report*, 1970, 18.

603. Mitchell Sviridoff, *Natural Resources Defense Council, Inc.*, inter-office memorandum, 2/23/1971, 1; *Annual Report*, 1973, 20.

604. Ibid., 2.

605. Ibid., 1.

606. Ibid., 2.

607. Ibid., 7.

608. Ibid., 8.

609. Mitchell, "From Conservation to Environmental Movement," 102.

610. John H. Adams, "Responsible Militancy—The Anatomy of a Public Interest Law Firm," *Record of the Association of the Bar of New York*, 631 (1974), 631–32.

611. Mitchell, "From Conservation to Environmental Movement," 102–03.

612. Adams, "Responsible Militancy," 632.

613. Mitchell, "From Conservation to Environmental Movement," 102–03.

614. "About Us," *Natural Resources Defense Council*, available at http://www.nrdc.org/about.

615. "About Us: Victories," *Natural Resources Defense Council*, available at http://www.nrdc.org/about/victories.asp.

616. "Origin & History," *Environmental Defense*, http://www.environmentaldefense.org/aboutus.cfm?tagID=362.

617. Phil McCombs, "ACLU Unit Winning Fight for Reforms in Nation's Prisons," *Washington Post*, 5/24/1982.

618. Ibid.

619. Margo Schlanger, "Beyond the Hero Judge: Institutional Reform Litigation as Litigation," *Michigan Law Review*, Vol. 97 (1994).

620. Available from http://www.aclu.org/Prisons/.

621. Ibid.

622. Ibid.

623. Phil McCombs, "ACLU Unit Winning Fight for Reforms in Nation's Prisons," *Washington Post*, 5/24/1982.

624. Ibid.

625. Ibid.

626. Elsa Walsh, "D.C. Told to Change Juvenile System; Judge Says Population in 3 Detention Centers Must Be Halved," *Washington Post*, 10/10/1987.

627. So, for example, it would be illegal to transfer a prisoner into maximum security simply because of his or her political beliefs. Associated Press, "Judge Bars U.S. from Isolating Prisoners for Political Beliefs," *New York Times*, 7/17/1988.

628. David Margolick, "From a Lonely Prison Cell, an Inmate Wins an Important Victory for Civil Liberties," *New York Times*, 3/6/1992.

629. Available from http://www.aclu.org/Prisons/.

630. Ibid.

631. The Prison Litigation Reform Act of 1996, for example, restricts the ability of federal courts to regulate prison conditions.

632. Ford Foundation, Discussion Paper: "Women's Programs: Past, Present, and Future," 1986.

633. Ibid.

634. Ibid.

635. Ibid.

636. Ibid.

637. Ibid.

638. These included *Reed v. Reed*, the landmark challenge to the automatic primacy of men, under law, in the administration of estates. Argued by Ginsburg in 1971, *Reed* marked "the first time [that] the Court held that a classification based on sex was unconstitutional, in violation of the equal protection clause." See http://www.aclu.org.

639. Available from http://www.aclu/org.

640. Ford Foundation, Discussion Paper: "Women's Programs: Past, Present, and Future," 1986.

641. Ibid.

642. Ibid.

643. Ibid.

644. Ibid.

645. John Sawyer, "Ginsburg Chosen for Court: Women's Champion a Surprise," *St. Louis Post-Dispatch*, 6/15/1993.

646. Cited at http://www.aclu.org/news/NewsPrint.cfm?ID=9072&c=33.

647. Ford Foundation, Discussion Paper: "Women's Programs: Past, Present, and Future," 1986.

648. Ibid.

649. Digby Diehl, "The Emergency Medical Services Program." *To Improve Health and Health Care 2000: The Robert Wood Johnson Foundation Anthology*, Stephen L. Isaacs & James R. Knickman, eds., (San Francisco: Josey Bass Publishers, 2000).

650. Ibid.

651. Ibid.

652. Ibid.

653. Ibid.

654. M. A. Farber, "$1-Billion Legacy Makes Foundation the Second Biggest," *New York Times*, 12/6/1971.

655. Diehl, "The Emergency Medical Services Program."

656. Ibid.

657. Ibid.

658. Ibid.

659. Ibid.

660. Ibid.

661. Ibid.

662. Ibid.

663. Ibid.

664. Ibid.

665. Ibid.

666. Robert Wood Johnson Foundation, *Annual Report*, 1972.

667. Diehl, "The Emergency Medical Services Program."

668. Ibid.

669. Ibid.

670. Ibid.

671. Cathy Siebold, *The Hospice Movement: Easing Death's Pains* (New York: Twayne Publishers, 1992).

672. Harvey and Abrams, *"For the Welfare of Mankind": The Commonwealth Fund and American Medicine* (Baltimore: Johns Hopkins University Press, 1986).

673. Ibid.

674. Siebold, *The Hospice Movement.*

675. Ibid.

676. Bert Hayslip, Jr. and Joel Leon, *Hospice Care* (Newbury Park: Sage Publications, 1992).

677. Siebold, *The Hospice Movement.*

678. Hospice of Lake Sumter website, available from http://www.hospicels.com/faq.htm.

679. Harvey, *For the Welfare of Mankind.*

680. Ibid.

681. Siebold, *The Hospice Movement.*

682. The Foundation considered alternative fields, such as disaster relief, but Dr. Donald Hoffman, the officer in charge of international programming and science and technology, and James Henry, the Foundation's president, agreed during a return

flight from Nicaragua in 1973 that tropical disease might be an appropriate niche. "The Edna McConnell Clark Foundation's Tropical Disease Research Program: A 25-Year Retrospective Review 1976–1999."

683. Ibid.

684. The examples of the foundation-supported innovations of the Green Revolution, and, in particular, the National Foundation for Infantile Paralysis' development of the Salk vaccine for polio, suggested to the EMCF that it should focus on vaccine development.

685. The Clark family did not feel it would be appropriate for the Foundation to engage in such public advocacy. Ibid.

686. Ibid.

687. Joseph Cook, e-mail to Scott Kohler, 11/16/2004. Dr. Cook offered clarification and additional detail that aided in the writing of this case. Any errors are, of course, my own.

688. EMCF convened Pfizer, the National Eye Institute, and NIAID "to develop plans for assessing prospects for [Zithromax's] use in trachoma control." The use of Zithromax, as a part of SAFE, has greatly enhanced the effectiveness of that strategy. The pre-existing antibiotic treatment was an ointment that required constant reapplication and was, therefore, used inconsistently. Ibid.

689. Cook, e-mail to Scott Kohler.

690. This was a marked contrast from the Foundation's decision, in oncho research, to eschew collaboration with the pharmaceutical industry, focusing on prevention at the expense of control.

691. "The Edna McConnell Clark Foundation's Tropical Disease Research Program: A 25-Year Retrospective Review 1976–1999."

692. Pfizer also preferred to work through an independent, rather than WHO-controlled, institution.

693. "The Edna McConnell Clark Foundation's Tropical Disease Research Program: A 25-Year Retrospective Review 1976–1999."

694. Ibid.

695. Ibid.

696. Available from http://www.trachoma.org/support.asp.

697. "The Edna McConnell Clark Foundation's Tropical Disease Research Program: A 25-Year Retrospective Review 1976–1999."

698. For example, EMCF funded research demonstrated that face-washing can prevent trachoma infection, and EMCF worked with Pfizer to demonstrate the efficacy of Zithromax.

699. Ford Foundation, *Annual Report*, 1984.

700. Richard Magat, *The Ford Foundation at Work: Philanthropic Choices, Methods, and Styles* (Plenum Press: New York, 1979).

701. William Serrin, Information Bank Abstracts, *New York Times*, 2/28/1980.

702. Congressman Clay Shaw, Jr. (D-FL) says, for instance, "In an area often dominated by politics and emotion, MDRC is a beacon of rigorous research and reliable analysis," available from http://www.mdrc.org.

703. Ford Foundation, *Annual Report*, 1989.

704. Available from http://www.mdrc.org.

705. John J. Miller, *Strategic Investment in Ideas: How Two Foundations Reshaped America.* (Washington: The Philanthropy Roundtable, 2003), 10.

706. Michael A. Fletcher, "What the Federalist Society Stands For," *Washington Post*, 7/29/2005, A21.

707. Miller, *Strategic Investment in Ideas*, 28.

708. Ibid., 28–29.

709. Ibid., 29.

710. Ibid.

711. Ibid., 32.

712. Ibid., 30.

713. Thomas B. Edsall, "Federalist Society Becomes a Force in Washington," *Washington Post*, 4/18/01, A4.

714. Fletcher, "What the Federalist Society Stands For."

715. John M. Olin Programs in Higher Education, Books on Public Affairs and Litigation, Internal Memo, Spring 2002, 8.

716. Ibid., 7.

717. Ibid., 8.

718. Rone Tempest, "Breaks Many Rules Bangladesh: A Bank Just for the Poor," *Los Angeles Times*, 11/28/1987.

719. See http://www.state.gov/r/pa/ei/bgn/3452.htm.

720. Alan Jolis, "The Good Banker," *Independent*. 5/5/1996.

721. Grameen Bank, *Annual Report*, 2003., available from http://www.grameen-info.org.

722. Tempest, "Breaks Many Rules Bangladesh."

723. Jolis, "The Good Banker."

724. Grameen borrowers have used their Grameen loans for diverse enterprises, from manufacturing musical conch shells to processing animal entrails and more. Ibid.

725. Today, "Grameen Bank finances 100 percent of its outstanding loan from its own fund and the savings from its depositors. Over 68 percent of its deposits come from bank's own borrowers," available from http://www.grameen-info.org.

726. M. Kabir Hassan and Luis Renteria-Guerrero, "The Experience of the Grameen Bank of Bangladesh in Community Development," *International Journal of Social Economics*; Vol. 24, Issue 12 (1997).

727. Remarks by Susan V. Berresford at the University of Southern California's Center on Philanthropy and Public Policy, 2/13/2003, available from http://www.fordfound.org.

728. Mohammed Yunus, *Banker to the Poor: Micro-Lending and the Battle Against World Poverty* (New York: PublicAffairs, 1999).

729. http://www.grameen-info.org.

730. Ibid.

731. Grameen borrowers also commit to a set of "16 Decisions" for a healthy and

productive life, including such promises as "We shall educate our children and ensure that they can earn to pay for their education," and "We shall not take any dowry at our sons' weddings, neither shall we give any dowry at our daughters wedding. We shall keep our centre free from the curse of dowry. We shall not practice child marriage."

732. Statement by Mr. Anwarul K. Chowdhury, United Nations Under-Secretary-General and High Representative for the Least Developed Countries, Landlocked Developing Countries and Small Island Developing States in the Second Committee of the Fifty-ninth Session of the General Assembly. 11/15/2004.

733. Jolis, "The Good Banker."

734. Bruce Shenitz, "What Poor Bangladesh Can Teach Rich America: A $100 Loan May Not Sound Like Much, but if You're an Ambitious Entrepreneur, It Can be a Ladder to Economic Success," *Los Angeles Times*, 5/9/1993. The Foundation has given further support to the spread of microfinance, including a Chinese replica: the Yixian Grameen Bank. Jasper Becker, "Bank Plants Seeds of Independence," *South China Morning Post*, 8/14/1995.

735. Statement by Mr. Anwarul K. Chowdhury.

736. http://nobelprize.org/nobel_prizes/peace/laureates/2006/press.html

737. Ibid.

738. David Perlman, "A Celebration of the Ocean: Monterey Bay Aquarium's Mission to 'Inspire, Engage, Empower' Marks Twentieth Year," *San Francisco Chronicle*, 10/18/2004.

739. Ibid.

740. Marcia McNutt, "How One Man Made a Difference: David Packard," paper presented at the symposium "Oceanography: The Making of a Science," 2/8/2000, available from http://www.mbari.org.

741. Ibid.

742. Ibid. McNutt, the executive director of MBARI, identifies these four elements—science, engineering, operations, and information dissemination—as the four pillars of the Institute.

743. David Perlman, "Deep-Sea Robot Reports on Life in Monterey Bay," *San Francisco Chronicle*, 8/9/1993.

744. Perlman, "A Celebration of the Ocean."

745. Robert Lindsey, "Huge Ocean-Front Aquarium to Open in Steinbeck's Monterey," *New York Times*, 10/20/1984.

746. Form 990 of The Monterey Bay Aquarium Research Institute, 2003.

747. In 2003, for example, the Packard Foundation gave $32 million to the Institute, which, unlike the aquarium, cannot support itself by fees.

748. Available from http://www.mbari.org/.

749. Ibid.

750. "'History' of the International Criminal Court," available from http://www.icc.org.

751. "Background on MacArthur Human Rights Grantmaking" memo, from the John D. and Catherine T. MacArthur Foundation.

752. Ibid.

753. "Background on MacArthur Support for the International Criminal Court" memo, from the John D. and Catherine T. MacArthur Foundation.

754. The Canadian Foreign Minister referred to the Coalition's approach as "the mobilization of shame." Ibid.

755. David Davenport, "The New Diplomacy," *Policy Review*, No. 116 (2002).

756. On December 31, 2000, President Clinton signed the Rome Statute. At the time, however, he reaffirmed the position of the United States government that the treaty was flawed and would not be sent to the Senate for ratification in its present form. The Bush administration has been even less willing to contemplate joining the ICC. Nonetheless, the Court is now operational, although its relationship to the United States remains problematic at best.

757. http://www.justiceinitiative.org/.

758. Ibid.

759. Ibid.

760. http://www.fordfound.org/.

761. Ford Foundation, *Annual Report*, 1998, available from http://www.ford-found.org/.

762. "Background on MacArthur Support for the International Criminal Court" memo, from the John D. and Catherine T. MacArthur Foundation.

763. Ford Foundation, *Annual Report*, 1988, available from http://www.ford-found.org/.

764. "International Justice: An Emerging Global System," newsletter from the John D. and Catherine T. MacArthur Foundation, Vol. 2 (Summer 2005).

765. Joseph Alper, "The Nurse Home Visitation Program," *The Robert Wood Johnson Foundation Anthology, Vol. V*, Stephen L. Isaacs and James R. Knickman, eds. (San Francisco: Jossey-Bass, 2002).

766. Ibid.

767. RWJF-sponsored studies have shown that home visitation by nurses works better than by other professionals and that deviating from the program's curriculum tends to decrease its effectiveness. Ibid.

768. Mothers are eligible for the program if they meet two or more of the following criteria: unmarried, unemployed, or no high school diploma. Ibid.

769. http://www.nccfc.org/research_publications.cfm.

770. RWJF News Release. "Families, Nurses, Members of Congress Salute Model Program's Success in Preventing Abuse, Promoting Health."

771. Alper, "The Nurse Home Visitation Program."

772. Ibid.

773. http://www.nccfc.org/research_publications.cfm.

774. David Olds, Peggy Hill, and Elissa Rumsy, "Prenatal and Early Childhood Nurse Home Visitation," *Juvenile Justice Bulletin*. U.S. Department of Justice. November 1998.

775. Ibid. According to the Robert Wood Johnson Foundation, the cost to society

each time a juvenile "leaves high school for a life of crime and drug use" is between $1.7 million and $2.3 million.

776. John J. Miller, *Strategic Investment in Ideas: How Two Foundations Reshaped America* (Washington: The Philanthropy Roundtable, 2003), 9.

777. Ibid.

778. Ibid., 10.

779. Ibid.

780. "Simon: Preaching the Word for Olin," *New York Times*, 7/16/1978, F1.

781. Ibid.

782. Miller, *Strategic Investment in Ideas*, 11–12.

783. William E. Simon, *A Time for Truth* (New York: Reader's Digest Press, 1978), 218–21.

784. "Simon: Preaching the Word for Olin."

785. Miller, *Strategic Investment in Ideas*, 23–25.

786. Ibid.

787. "Overview of John M. Olin Foundation Grants in Law," Internal Memo, John M. Olin Foundation, Spring 2002.

788. "Simon: Preaching the Word for Olin."

789. Kathleen Teltsch, "Conservative Unit Gains from Legacy," *New York Times*, 10/2/1983.

790. "Overview of John M. Olin Foundation Grants in Law," Internal Memo, John M. Olin Foundation, Spring 2002.

791. Miller, *Strategic Investment in Ideas*, 26.

792. Ibid., 28.

793. Alexander Von Hoffman, *House by House, Block by Block: The Rebirth of America's Urban Neighborhoods* (New York: Oxford, 2003).

794. Harry Edward Berndt, *New Rulers in the Ghetto: The Community Development Corporation and Urban Poverty* (Westport: Greenwood, 1977).

795. Von Hoffman, *House by House, Block by Block*.

796. Kathleen Teltsch, "Funds Are Packaged To Aid Communities," *New York Times*, 6/7/1981.

797. Ford's partners in founding LISC were Aetna Life & Casualty Foundation, Atlantic Richfield Foundation, Continental Illinois National Bank and Trust Company of Chicago, International Harvester Company, Levi Strauss & Co., and the Prudential Insurance Company of America.

798. Ford Foundation, *Annual Report*, 1980.

799. This three part strategy is described in greater detail on LISC's website: http://www.lisc.org.

800. Alan S. Oser, "Nonprofit Realty Groups Getting More Private Help," *New York Times*, 3/18/1984.

801. Local Initiatives Support Corporation, *Annual Report*, 2002, available from http://www.lisc.org.

802. Oser, "Nonprofit Realty Groups Getting More Private Help."

803. Ibid.

804. Kathleen Teltsch, "Foundation Helps Renew City Areas," *New York Times*, 12/7/1986.

805. Ibid.

806. *Local Initiatives Support Corporation Site*, available from http://www.lisc.org.

807. Teltsch, "Foundation Helps Renew City Areas."

808. Von Hoffman, *House by House, Block by Block*.

809. Available from http://www.foundationcenter.org.

810. Available from http://www.soros.org.

811. Available from http://www.foundationcenter.org.

812. Michael T. Kaufman, *Soros: The Life and Times of a Messianic Billionaire* (New York: Alfred A Knopf, 2002), 185.

813. Karen Pallarito, "Soros' New Mission," *Journal of Mental Health Counseling*, Vol. 27, Issue 44 (11/3/1997), 20.

814. "Giving it Away," *Economist*, 10/25/1997, 77.

815. "Opening Russian Society," editorial, *New York Times*, 6/12/2003, 34.

816. Kaufman, *Soros*, 196–200.

817. Ibid, 199.

818. Ibid, 177.

819. Soros' Ukraine Foundation pursued a similar program, which trained some 70,000 former soldiers before Soros' feud with Ukraine's president, Leonid Kuchma, brought operations to a halt.

820. Pallarito, "Soros' New Mission."

821. Kaufman, *Soros*, 178.

822. Ibid, 281.

823. Ibid, 262–63.

824. Katie Jamieson e-mail to Scott Kohler, 4/6/2005, on file with the author.

825. "Opening Russian Society," *New York Times*.

826. "The MacArthur Fellows Program: Frequently Asked Questions," available from http://www.macfound.org.

827. Ibid.

828. Ibid.

829. The identities of the nominators and the selection committee members are kept secret, as are all inquiries (such as interviews with friends or colleagues) made as part of the process of review. There are several reasons for this. One is to free nominators and selectors from the burden of fielding the many requests for support that would inevitably flood in were their identities known. The other is to ensure candid, forthright evaluation of all nominees. People are far more likely to say what they really think if they are not concerned that it will get back to the person in question.

830. There are two reasons for this as well. One is that the very nature of the program is such that it seeks to identify innovators who work off the beaten path, escaping the notice of most funders. The second reason is more concrete: it was a condition imposed for IRS approval of the program.

831. A complete list of the MacArthur Fellows is available on the Foundation's website, at http://www.macfound.org.

832. Elizabeth Venant, "MacArthur's Award for Genius Fellowship: The Big Honor Bestowed on Scientists, Humanists, and Artists is Prestigious and Comes with No Strings Attached," *Los Angeles Times*, 12/25/1989.

833. There have, for instance, been stories of MacArthur fellows facing resentment from their peers and having difficulty convincing other funders to support them after having received such a generous grant. But these are the exceptions, not the rule.

834. Ibid.

835. Liz McMillen, "MacArthur Foundation Is Expected to Review, and Perhaps Revise, Its Fellows Program," *Chronicle of Higher Education*, 3/8/1989.

836. Venant, "MacArthur's Award for Genius Fellowship."

837. Paul Goldberger, "James W. Rouse, 81, Dies: Socially Conscious Developer Built New Towns and Malls," *New York Times*, 4/10/1996.

838. Available from http://www.enterprisefoundation.org.

839. Paul Goldberger, "James W. Rouse, 81, Dies: Socially Conscious Developer Built New Towns and Malls," *New York Times*, 4/10/1996.

840. Available from http://www.enterprisefoundation.org.

841. Ibid.

842. Edward Skloot, interview with Joel L. Fleishman.

843. Enterprise Foundation, *Annual Report*, 2003, available from http://www.enterprisefoundation.org.

844. Ibid.

845. Ibid.

846. James W. Rouse, "The American City Award Acceptance Speech; New York," November 1993.

847. Keith Sinzinger, "North Carolina's Self-Help Credit Union Seeks to be a 'Resource for Change'; Community Development Innovations Gain Attention on Capitol Hill," *Washington Post*, 4/25/1993.

848. The Credit Union now offers slightly above-market returns.

849. Ibid.

850. Mary Mountcastle, interview by the author, 12/14/2004. I have relied, for an overall picture of Self-Help, and for much detail, on Mary Mountcastle, whom I interviewed for this case study and who has been very helpful to me in researching Self-Help. Any errors are, of course, my own.

851. Gary M. Pomerantz, "Credit Union Founder's Generosity Pays: People Deemed Loan Risks are Exactly Those Whose Business One New MacArthur Fellow Aims to Attract," *Atlanta Journal-Constitution*, 7/19/1996.

852. Mountcastle, interview by the author.

853. Martin Eakes, interview by Lynn Adler and Jim Mayer, for the PBS special, "Faith, Hope and Capital." March 2000.

854. Fannie Mae cannot purchase a mortgage directly from a bank unless a down payment of at least 20 percent has been paid by the homebuyer. Because these were loans to low-income buyers, the loans allowed for lower down payments; so Self-

Help served as the necessary middleman between Fannie Mae and the banks, and the Ford Foundation's risk capital enabled it to do so.

855. The original loans were to be made primarily by five national banks, through their extensive network of offices. They were: BankAmerica Corp., Chase Manhattan Corp., NationsBank Corp., Banc One Corp., and Norwest Corp. Judith Havemann, "A Hand Up, Via Homeownership: North Carolina Group Given $50 Million to Aid Working Poor," *Washington Post*. 7/24/1998.

856. Remarks by Susan V. Berresford, 10/28/2003, available from http://www.fordfound.org.

857. Press Release, "Self-Help, Ford Foundation, Bank of America, Chevy Chase Bank and Fannie Mae Announce Successful Completion of $2 Billion Homeownership Initiative," 10/28/2003, available from http://www.fordfound.org.

858. This means that it is allowed to spend up to 20 percent of its annual budget, to a maximum of $1 million, on lobbying activities. This ceiling applies to the cumulative activities of entire Center for Community Self-Help, which functions as a holding company for the Credit Union, the Ventures Fund, and the Center for Responsible Lending.

859. Julie Kosterlitz, "Bleeding Heart Conservatives," *National Journal*, 6/19/2004.

860. Available from http://www.responsiblelending.org.

861. Ibid.

862. Mountcastle, interview by the author.

863. From remarks by Susan V. Berresford at a Fannie Mae/Ford Foundation/Self-Help Event in Washington, D.C., 10/28/2003.

864. David Kovick, *The Hewlett Foundation's Conflict Resolution Program: Twenty Years of Field-Building, 1984–2004* (May 2005), 5, available at http://www.hewlett.org/NR/rdonlyres/12265FA6–95F8–45F9-B786–2B729423B910/0/HewlettConflictResolutionProgram.pdf.

865. Susan Carpenter, "Assessment of the William and Flora Hewlett Foundation's Conflict Resolution Program," June 2000, 1.

866. Roger W. Heyns, "President's Statement," *Annual Statement: The William & Flora Hewlett Foundation*, 1992, 2.

867. Ibid.

868. Carpenter, "Assessment," 1.

869. Kovick, *Hewlett Foundation's Conflict Resolution Program*, 10.

870. Jerome T. Barrett, *A History of Alternative Dispute Resolution: The Story of a Political, Cultural, and Social Movement*, (San Francisco: Jossey-Bass, 2004), 222–23.

871. Carpenter, "Assessment," 2.

872. Kovick, *Hewlett Foundation's Conflict Resolution Program*, 19.

873. Carpenter, "Assessment," 2–3.

874. Kovick, *Hewlett Foundation's Conflict Resolution Program*, 30.

875. Ibid., 37.

876. Barrett, *History of Alternative Dispute Resolution*, 222–23.

877. "Frequently Asked Questions about Conflict Resolution," *Association for Conflict Resolution*, http://www.acrnet.org/about/CR-FAQ.htm, 2003.

878. Marshall A. Ledger, "Stopping By," *Trust*, January 2000, available from http://www.pewtrusts.com/ideas/ideas_item.cfm?content_item_id=253&content_type_id=17&page=17&issue=13&issue_name=Misc&name=Pew-produced%20Publications. In all likelihood, the large discrepancy between these figures results from the distinction between the occasional homeless (those who are forced onto the streets but will find new jobs and housing) and the chronic homeless (those who, over a long period of time, are unable to house or support themselves).

879. "About HCH," *U.S. Department of Health and Human Services*, http://bphc.hrsa.gov/hchirc/about/face_homelessness.htm.

880. Available from http://bphc.hrsa.gov/Hchirc/.

881. Ledger, "Stopping By."

882. Ibid.

883. Available from http://bphc.hrsa.gov/Hchirc/.

884. Ledger, "Stopping By."

885. Ibid.

886. "About HCH."

887. Available from http://bphc.hrsa.gov/Hchirc/.

888. "About NBPTS: History & Facts," National Board for Professional Teaching Standards, http://www.nbpts.org/about/hist.cfm.

889. Carnegie Corporation of New York, *Annual Report*, 1984, 37.

890. Carnegie Corporation of New York, *Annual Report*, 1985, 30.

891. Carnegie Corporation of New York, *Annual Report*, 1986, 27.

892. "About NBPTS: History & Facts," National Board for Professional Teaching Standards, http://www.nbpts.org/about/hist.cfm.

893. Carnegie Corporation of New York, *Annual Report*, 1985, 27.

894. Carnegie Corporation of New York, *Annual Report*, 1987, 31.

895. "Looking Back at Our Roots: Early Days, Critical Players," National Board for Professional Teaching Standards, http://www.nbpts.org/about/lookingback.cfm.

896. Carnegie Corporation of New York, *Annual Report*, 1988, 27.

897. Carnegie Corporation of New York, *Annual Report*, 1989, 21; Carnegie Corporation of New York, *Annual Report*, 1990, 37; Carnegie Corporation of New York, *Annual Report*, 1988–98.

898. "About NBPTS: History & Facts," National Board for Professional Teaching Standards, http://www.nbpts.org/about/hist.cfm.

899. "About NBPTS: State & Local Support & Initiatives," National Board for Professional Teaching Standards, http://www.nbpts.org/about/state.cfm.

900. Jay Matthews, "For Elite U.S. Teachers, Cachet and More Cash," *Washington Post*, 2/8/2005, A10.

901. Christine L. Compston, "Teacher Preparation and Certification: Who, What, Why, and How?" *The History Teacher*, Vol. 31, No. 4 (August 1998), 521.

902. Compston, "Teacher Preparation," 527.

903. Jay Matthews, "For Elite U.S. Teachers, Cachet and More Cash," *Washington Post*, 2/8/2005, A10.

904. Charles M. Haar, *Mastering Boston Harbor* (Cambridge: Harvard University Press: 2005).

905. Margot Hornblower, "Boston Harbor Sewers Back Up Into Litigation; Judge Blasts 'Cesspool,' Halts Hookups," *Washington Post*, 12/9/1984.

906. Haar, *Mastering Boston Harbor*.

907. See the Conservation Law Foundation website at http://www.clf.org.

908. TBF was founded in 1915 and has assets worth approximately $650 million.

909. Patricia Brady, "The Boston Foundation's 'Greatest Hits,'" December 2001.

910. Ibid.

911. Haar, *Mastering Boston Harbor*.

912. Available from the MWRA website: http://www.mwra.com.

913. Save the Harbor/Save the Bay. "The Leading Edge: Boston Harbor's New Role in the City's Economy," 2004, available from http://www.savetheharbor.org.

914. Ibid.

915. Ibid.

916. *Environmental Literacy Council*, http://www.enviroliteracy.org/subcategory.php/202.html.

917. Ibid.

918. Species diversity—the variety of individual species—is one of three facets of biodiversity. The other two are genetic diversity (within an individual species) and ecosystem diversity, the range of community types. The MacArthur Foundation chose to focus on species diversity because its concentration—in a few tropical areas—would enable the Foundation to "rank locations and make sharp choices about concentrating [its] resources along the basic dimension of geography." Ecosystem diversity would have been too big a focus, while genetic diversity "would have led to a focus on the variations in [a] very small number of plants and animals" and would offered the Foundation "no comparative advantage" or niche. "Strategic Review of Conservation Grantmaking," John D. and Catherine T. MacArthur Foundation, 2000.

919. This is now the Conservation and Sustainable Development arm of the Foundation's Global Security and Sustainability Program. It remains a major part of the MacArthur Foundation's grantmaking. In 2004, the Foundation spent $18 million on biodiversity protection. Ibid.

920. Ibid.

921. Ibid.

922. The total area of the Foundation's nine program sites amounts to less than 3 percent of the Earth's land surface, an area roughly one-third the size of the United States. Ibid.

923. Ibid.

924. Ibid.

925. Ibid.

926. The Gordon and Betty Moore Foundation, created in 2000, is now the world's largest private supporter of biodiversity protection.

927. This collaboration was joined in 2004 by the government of Japan.

928. John J. Miller, *Strategic Investment in Ideas: How Two Foundations Reshaped America* (Washington: The Philanthropy Roundtable, 2003), 41.

929. Ibid., 34–35.

930. John Chubb and Terry Moe, *Politics, Markets, and America's Schools*. (Washington: Brookings Institution, 1990).

931. Miller, *Strategic Investment in Ideas*, 41.

932. Ibid., 44.

933. Ibid., 44–45.

934. Peter Applebome, "Milwaukee Forces Debate on Vouchers," *New York Times*, 9/1/95, A12.

935. Frederick M. Hess, "Hints of the Pick-Axe: Competition and Public Schooling in Milwaukee," chapter in *Charters, Vouchers, and Public Education*, Paul E. Peterson and David E. Campbell, eds. (Washington: Brookings Institution, 2001), 175.

936. Miller, *Strategic Investment in Ideas*, 46.

937. "Evaluating School Reform," *Works in Progress: Newsletter of the Joyce Foundation*, January 1999.

938. Miller, *Strategic Investment in Ideas*, 47.

939. Ibid., 44–45.

940. Ibid., 40.

941. Frederick M. Hess, "Hints of the Pick-Axe," 168.

942. Over the years, Mrs. Diamond helped to launch the careers of such actors as Burt Lancaster, Kirk Douglass, and Robert Redford. And, in 1941, she had been impressed by an oft-rejected, never published play called "Everybody Comes to Rick's," and pushed for its adaptation into film. That proved to be a wise move. In 1941, thanks to Mrs. Diamond's strong backing, the play was released as a movie under a new title—*Casablanca*.

943. Aaron Diamond Foundation, *Final Report*, 1997.

944. Allan R. Clyde, "A Conversation with Irene Diamond," *Foundation News and Commentary*, March/April, 1998.

945. Aaron Diamond Foundation, *Final Report*, 1997.

946. Ibid.

947. Ibid.

948. Kenneth C. Danforth, "Out With a Bang," *Foundation News and Commentary*, January/February, 1993.

949. Laurie Garrett, "Cutting-Edge AIDS Lab to Open in City" *Newsday*, 4/14/1991.

950. Clyde, "A Conversation with Irene Diamond."

951. Danforth, "Out With a Bang."

952. The following list is adapted from descriptions of these scientific advances available on the web site of the Aaron Diamond AIDS Research Center at

http://www.adarc.org. Quotations, unless otherwise indicated, are drawn from that web site.

953. Christine Gorman, "The Disease Detective," *Time*, 12/30/1997. This finding was published in a 1995 article in *Nature* in conjunction with an article by Dr. George Shaw of the University of Alabama at Birmingham, who had simultaneously reached the same conclusion.

954. At a cost of up to $20,000 per year, such remedies remain far beyond the reach of the vast proportion of HIV/AIDS sufferers in areas like sub-Saharan Africa, which currently has some 25 million people living with the disease. To its credit, the Diamond Center today is working to extend the benefits of AIDS research to the developing world, especially China, where a full 20 percent of the population has never even heard of the AIDS virus.

955. Philip Elmer-Dewitt, "Turning the Tide," *Time*, 12/30/1997.

956. Clyde, "A Conversation with Irene Diamond."

957. David Da-I Ho, "Tribute to Irene Diamond," *Aaron Diamond AIDS Research Center*, http://www.adarc.org/news/Irene%20Diamond/memorial%20service.html.

958. Kathleen Teltsch, "Luce Fund Offering Aid to Scholarly Women," *New York Times*, 1/31/1987.

959. Ibid.

960. Available from http://www.hluce.org.

961. Kathleen Teltsch, "Mrs. Luce Left $70 Million for Women's Science Education," *New York Times*, 7/2/1989.

962. Available from http://www.hluce.org.

963. Mr. Armstrong is still a member of the Foundation's Board of Directors.

964. Teltsch, "Mrs. Luce Left $70 Million for Women's Science Education."

965. Available from http://www.hluce.org.

966. William C. Rhoden, "College Presidents Prepare to Police Sports," *New York Times*, 11/5/1989, D4.

967. Kerry Luft, "The High Price of Winning at All Cost," *Chicago Tribune*, 10/19/1989, C3.

968. "NCAA Chief Laments 'View' of College Sport," *Chicago Tribune*, 10/25/1989, C9.

969. William C. Rhoden, "Who's in Charge Here?" *New York Times*, 2/4/1990, Sports, 1.

970. Ibid.

971. Tom McMillen, "NCAA Heal Thyself, or Expect Congress to Issue Prescription," *USA Today*, 1/3/1991, 8C.

972. Len Hochberg, "Congress as Reform Medium: A Question of Timing," *Washington Post*, 5/8/1990, D7.

973. Len Hochberg, "Congress as Reform Medium: A Question of Timing," *Washington Post*, 5/8/1990, D7.

974. "Knight Foundation History," *John S. and James L. Knight Foundation*, http://www.knightfdn.org/annual/2005/history.asp.

975. Hochberg, "Congress as Reform Medium."

976. "Do You Feel that Intercollegiate Athletics Have Gotten Out of Control?" State of Intercollegiate Athletics, *Public Opinion Online*, March 1989, 002.

977. "About," *Knight Commission on Intercollegiate Athletics*, http://www.knight-commission.org/about/.

978. Debbie Becker, "Sports-Academics Study Has Support of Schools," *USA Today*, 2/1/1990, 4C.

979. Ibid.

980. Gerald Eskenazi, "Panel Tells College Heads to Take Control of Athletics," *New York Times*, 3/20/1991, D25.

981. Ibid.

982. Ibid.

983. Danny Robbins, "Presidents Oil Their Political Machine," *Los Angeles Times*, 1/6/1992, C2.

984. Mark Asher, "Knight Commission Issues Last Words," *Washington Post*, 3/19/1993, B5.

985. Mark Asher, "Eligibility Standards Stir Increasing Debate," *Washington Post*, 10/26/1994, D6.

986. Josh Barr, "Panel Eyes Money Issues," *Washington Post*, 8/29/2000, D7.

987. "Knight Commission Summit Information," Knight Commission on Intercollegiate Athletics, http://www.knightcommission.org/students/item/summit1/.

988. Ibid.

989. "The N.C.A.A. Gets it Right," editorial, *New York Times*, 1/23/1996, A14.

990. Liz Clarke, "College Football Gets Twelfth Game," *Washington Post*, 4/29/2005, D1.

991. In 2002, for example (the most recent year for which data were available), the Goldman Fund gave out $46.9 million. Available from the Foundation Center website at http://fdncenter.org/research/trends_analysis/top100giving.html.

992. http://www.goldmanprize.org.

993. Ibid.

994. Ibid.

995. When it was first given in 1990, the Goldman Prize gave out six awards of $75,000. That amount has been raised over the years, and now stands at $125,000, with no-strings-attached, given to each of the six winners.

996. Teresa Moore, "Rhoda Hass Goldman, Philanthropist, Dies at 71," *San Francisco Chronicle*, 2/19/1996.

997. Available from http://www.nobelprize.org.

998. Available from http://www.goldmanprize.org.

999. Available from http://www.goldmanprize.org.

1000. John Steinbruner. "Memorandum to 2050 Project Steering Committee," 12/30/1993.

1001. Jane Wales, *Advancing Stability in an Era of Change*. (New York: Rockefeller Brothers Fund, 2000).

1002. Between December 1984 and December 1989, for example, the

MacArthur Foundation made seven grants to Brookings. The last of these, a $5 million investment over five years, funded much of the policy research described later in this case.

1003. "Proposal to The MacArthur Foundation from the Brookings Institution," 6/22/1989, 2.

1004. MacArthur Foundation, *Annual Report*, 1991.

1005. Ibid.

1006. Sam Nunn, *White House Forum on the Role of Science and Technology in Promoting National Security and Global Stability*, March 29–30, 1995.

1007. Rich Kelley, "The Nunn-Lugar Act: A Wasteful and Dangerous Illusion." Foreign Policy Briefing No. 39, 3/18/1996, available from http://www.cato.org.

1008. "The Nunn-Lugar Cooperative Threat Reduction Act of 2005," S.313, 109th Congress, 1st Session. 2/8/2005.

1009. Albert R Hunt, "Take the Cuffs Off Nunn-Lugar," *Wall Street Journal*, 7/25/2002.

1010. Kathy Read, "Nobel Peace Prize: Nunn, Lugar More Deserving," *Milwaukee Journal Sentinel*, 10/15/2002.

1011. Ashton Carter became Assistant Secretary of Defense for International Security Policy.

1012. William Perry, *White House Forum on the Role of Science and Technology in Promoting National Security and Global Stability*, March 29–30, 1995.

1013. Richard Lugar, *White House Forum on the Role of Science and Technology in Promoting National Security and Global Stability*, March 29–30, 1995.

1014. Sam Nunn, *White House Forum on the Role of Science and Technology in Promoting National Security and Global Stability*, March 29–30, 1995.

1015. "Transforming the Culture of Dying: The Project on Death in America October 1994 to December 2003," available from http://www.soros.org.

1016. Ibid.

1017. Ethan Bronner, "The Foundation's End-of-Life Programs: Changing the American Way of Death." *The Robert Wood Johnson Foundation Anthology: To Improve Health and Health Care, Vol. VI*, Stephen L. Isaacs and James R. Knickman, eds. (San Francisco: Jossey-Bass, 2003).

1018. Ibid.

1019. The Project on Death in America ended as a result of George Soros' decision to reorganize his philanthropic giving. The project's final report emphasizes that the program was not discontinued either because it was failing *or* because it had fully succeeded, leaving nothing more to be done.

1020. Steven A. Schroeder, "Dying Patients and their Families," *Vital Speeches of the Day*, Vol. 66 (2000).

1021. Bronner, "The Foundation's End-of-Life Programs." The program has increased from 33 to 77 the percentage of elderly natives who die in their own villages. Previously, elders near death would be airlifted to far-away hospitals, where they would live out their final days far from all family and friends. Enabling tribesmen and women to receive palliative care at home has increased family satisfaction and reduced the cost, to the hospitals, of airlifting and admitting these patients.

1022. Frank Karel, "Getting the Word Out: A Foundation Memoir and Personal Journey," *The Robert Wood Johnson Foundation Anthology: To Improve Health and Health Care 2001*, Stephen L. Isaacs and James R. Knickman, eds. (San Francisco: Jossey-Bass: 2001).

1023. Bronner, "The Foundation's End-of-Life Programs."

1024. "Transforming the Culture of Dying: The Project on Death in America October 1994 to December 2003," available from http://www.soros.org.

1025. Bronner, "The Foundation's End-of-Life Programs."

1026. "Gathering the Pieces," from http://www.promotingexcellence.org.

1027. Schroeder, "Dying Patients and their Families."

1028. Judith Miller, "When Foundation's Chime In, The Issue of Dying Comes to Life," *New York Times*, 11/22/1997.

1029. Carey Goldberg, "After 10 Years, $200M Effort on Dying Reaches its Own End," *Boston Globe*, 11/9/2003.

1030. Robert L. Linn, et. al., "Technical Report: Generalizability of New Standards Project 1193 Pilot Study Tasks in Mathematics," National Center for Research on Evaluation, Standards, and Student Testing, January 1995.

1031. Ibid.

1032. "$6 Million Awarded to LRDC to Continue Skill Assessment Project." *Pittsburgh University Times*, 7/20/1995.

1033. Pam Belluck, "Crew Wants National Standards to be Used in New York Schools," *New York Times*, 12/5/1996.

1034. Ibid.

1035. Ibid.

1036. Jacques Steinberg, "New Standards Finding Way Into Schools," *New York Times*, 1/25/1998.

1037. Ibid.

1038. Roger E. Kasperson et al., "Cluster Review of the Global Warming and Climate Change Program of the Pew Charitable Trusts: Summary Report," May 1999.

1039. The creation of the Energy Foundation, which was accomplished jointly in 1991 by Pew, along with the Rockefeller and MacArthur Foundations, is discussed in a separate case study. Since 1991, the Energy Foundation has been a major partner to the Trusts in the field of global warming and climate change. Of the $39.8 million disbursed, the Energy Foundation contributed some $19.2 million. Ibid.

1040. Ibid.

1041. Ibid.

1042. Available from http://www.pewtrusts.org.

1043. Pew Charitable Trusts, "Report to the Board: Progress on Promoting Energy Efficiency and Renewable Energy Technologies in the Electric Sector," December 2003.

1044. Ibid.

1045. Roger E. Kasperson et al. "Cluster Review of the Global Warming and Climate Change Program of the Pew Charitable Trusts: Summary Report," May 1999.

1046. These reports have also been accessed by thousands more from the Center's website, where they are freely available. Ibid.

1047. "New Players on Global Warming," editorial, *New York Times*, 1/15/2003.

1048. "Ocean Rescue," editorial, *New York Times*, 8/6/2004.

1049. Available from http://www.aecf.org/.

1050. Available from http://www.foundationcenter.org/.

1051. Paul Taylor, "Nonprofits Boost Advocacy in the Interest of Children; Changes in Policy, Attitudes Seen Necessary," *Washington Post*, 1/13/1992.

1052. Deborah Morgan, "KIDS COUNT Self-Assessment: Bridging Evaluation with Strategic Communication of Data on Children & Families," Harvard Family Research Project, 2005, available from http://www.gse.harvard.edu/hfrp/eval/issue16/kidscount.html.

1053. Douglas Nelson, Casey Foundation president, presentation to the Foundation Impact Research Group (FIRG) at Duke University, 3/9/2005.

1054. Ibid.

1055. Available from http://www.caseyfoundation.org/kidscount.

1056. The lone exception is the percentage of low birth-weight babies born each year, which has remained more or less static. This may, however, be the result of advances in fertility medicine, rather than an indicator that infant health is not improving. Douglas Nelson, FIRG presentation, 3/9/2005.

1057. Morgan, "KIDS COUNT Self-Assessment: Bridging Evaluation with Strategic Communication of Data on Children & Families."

1058. The Casey Foundation, nonetheless, is attempting to study this connection by means of an ongoing Self-Assessment, being conducted jointly with an outside evaluation firm, which is seeking to evaluate KIDS COUNT's data collection process, and the external outcomes achieved by the national KIDS COUNT network. See Ibid.

1059. The Foundation is, however, an entirely separate entity, fully independent of Kaiser Permanente.

1060. Drew E Altman, "President's Message: The Kaiser Family Foundation's Role in Today's Health Care System," available from http://www.kff.org/.

1061. Staff, "Kaiser Foundation to Seek U.S. health Care Overhaul," *Los Angeles Times*, 4/13/1991.

1062. Drew Altman, interview with Joel L. Fleishman, 1/7/2004.

1063. IRS Form 990 of the Henry J. Kaiser Family Foundation, FY 2003, available from http://www.guidestar.org/.

1064. Ibid.

1065. Drew E Altman, "President's Message: The Kaiser Family Foundation's Role in Today's Health Care System," available from http://www.kff.org/.

1066. Altman, interview with Joel L. Fleishman.

1067. Altman, "President's Message."

1068. Staff, "Kaiser Foundation to Seek U.S. health Care Overhaul."

1069. Altman, interview with Joel L. Fleishman.

1070. Kathleen Teltsch, "In Rare Move, Big Donors Push Energy Efficiency," *New York Times*, 1/11/1991.

1071. Ibid.

1072. Julia Parzen, "Evaluation of the Energy Foundation," 5/18/1998.

1073. "Investing For Change: The World's Energy Problem and the Role for Philanthropy," The Energy Foundation, 2004.

1074. The Energy Foundation's focus is split between the United States—the largest energy market in the world—and China—the fastest growing. This case, discussing the impact of the creation and support of the Energy Foundation, does not go into the Foundation's work in China primarily because that is discussed in a separate case on the Packard-led China Sustainable Energy Program, which is administered by the Energy Foundation.

1075. Parzen, "Evaluation of the Energy Foundation."

1076. From the Energy Foundation Mission Statement; see http://www.energyfoundation.org.

1077. This bill is currently being challenged in court by U.S. auto manufacturers, who claim it pre-empts federal authority. Whatever the outcome of that action, however, AB 1493 is clearly another example of California leading the national debate about issues the federal government has yet to resolve. JSK notes—see sources.

1078. "Investing For Change: The World's Energy Problem and the Role for Philanthropy," The Energy Foundation, 2004.

1079. Ibid.

1080. Ibid.

1081. Ibid.

1082. John O'Leary, "Lessons in Freedom," *The Times*, 2/24/1992.

1083. Ibid.

1084. He also donated $30 million at the time of the pledge. Colin Woodard, "$230-Million Gift to Central European U. Expected to Enlarge Its Role in the Region," *Chronicle of Higher Education*, 10/13/1993.

1085. Because of a dispute with the Czech government following the breakup of Czechoslovakia, CEU closed its Prague campus and made Budapest its central location. Today, however, some programs of the University are also conducted at a CEU campus in Warsaw.

1086. Woodard, "$230-Million Gift to Central European U. Expected to Enlarge Its Role in the Region."

1087. Theresa Agovino, "Central European U. Faces Dilemma as its Benefactor Limits his Support," *Chronicle of Higher Education*, 10/16/1998.

1088. Ibid.

1089. Susan Greenberg, "Billionaire Santa Snubbed by Klaus," *The Guardian*, 1/12/1993.

1090. The concept of promoting "open societies" is a unifying theme that runs through most of George Soros' diverse philanthropic endeavors. The term "open society" was popularized by Karl Popper in his 1945 book, *Open Society and its Ene-*

mies. It is taken by Soros to refer to a culture "characterized by reliance on the rule of law, the existence of a democratically elected government, a diverse and vigorous civil society, and respect for minorities and minority opinions," available from http://www.ceu.hu.

1091. This effort, the CEU Press Translation Project, was actually an outgrowth of several smaller such efforts being conducted at the time by various Soros philanthropies around central and eastern Europe. Frances Pinter, "Books Across Borders," *Washington Post*, 7/28/1996.

1092. Agovino, Theresa, "Central European U. Faces Dilemma as its Benefactor Limits his Support," *Chronicle of Higher Education*, 10/16/1998.

1093. Available from http://www.ceu.hu.

1094. Agovino, "Central European U. Faces Dilemma as its Benefactor Limits his Support."

1095. See the case studies in this volume on LISC and the Enterprise Foundation.

1096. Kathleen Teltsch, "New Alliance Plans Housing in 20 Cities," *New York Times*, 3/1/1991.

1097. Ibid.

1098. That number has since increased to twenty-three. They are: Atlanta, Baltimore, Boston, Chicago, Cleveland, Columbus, Dallas, Denver, Detroit, Indianapolis, Kansas City, Los Angeles, Miami, Minneapolis-St. Paul, Newark, New York, Philadelphia, Phoenix, Portland, San Antonio, the San Francisco Bay Area, Seattle, and Washington, D.C. Available from http://www.livingcities.org.

1099. The NCDI has also supported research into the state and potential of urban communities through partnerships with the Brookings Institution, the Urban Institute, and New School University, available from http://www.livingcities.org.

1100. Peter Goldmark, email to Scott Kohler, on file with the author. I am very grateful to Mr. Goldmark for sharing with me some of his insight on the Initiative. Any errors that may remain, are, of course, entirely my own.

1101. Teltsch, "New Alliance Plans Housing in 20 Cities."

1102. The current investors in Living Cities: NCDI are as follows: AXA Community Investment Program, Bank of America, the Annie E. Casey Foundation, J.P. Morgan Chase & Company, Deutsche Bank, the Fannie Mae Foundation, the Robert Wood Johnson Foundation, the John S. and James L. Knight Foundation, the John D. and Catherine T. MacArthur Foundation, the McKnight Foundation, Metropolitan Life Insurance Company, the Office of Community Services (OCS), Prudential Financial, the Rockefeller Foundation, and the Department of Housing and Urban Development (HUD).

1103. See http://www.livingcities.org.

1104. Ibid.

1105. "Group of Companies, Foundations Gives $97 Million to Project," *Wall Street Journal*, 6/18/1997.

1106. "Unique Public-Private Partnership Commits a Half Billion Dollars Over

Next Decade to Spark Inner-City Revitalization," Living Cities press release, 8/5/2002, available from http://www.livingcities.org.

1107. C. Tracy Orleans and Joseph Alper, "Helping Addicted Smokers Quit: The Foundation's Tobacco-Cessation Programs," *The Robert Wood Johnson Foundation Anthology: To Improve Health and Health Care, Vol. VI*, Stephen L. Isaacs and James R. Knickman, eds. (San Francisco: Jossey-Bass, 2003), 125–48.

1108. Philip Morris, the nation's largest cigarette manufacturer, proclaims on its website, that "Philip Morris USA (PM USA) agrees with the overwhelming medical and scientific consensus that cigarette smoking causes lung cancer, heart disease, emphysema and other serious diseases in smokers. Smokers are far more likely to develop serious diseases, like lung cancer, than non-smokers. There is no safe cigarette." See http://www.philipmorrisusa.com/.

1109. "Nicotine and Cigarettes," Frontline: Inside the Tobacco Deal, http://www.pbs.org/wgbh/pages/frontline/shows/settlement/timelines/april94.html.

1110. Orleans, "Helping Addicted Smokers Quit," 125–49.

1111. Robert G. Hughes, "Adopting the Substance Abuse Goal: A Story of Philanthropic Decision Making." In *The Robert Wood Johnson Foundation Anthology: To Improve Health and Health Care 1998–1999*, Vol. II, Stephen L. Isaacs and James R. Knickman, eds. (San Francisco: Josey-Bass, 1998), 3–18.

1112. Steven Schroeder, interview with Joel Fleishman, 1/9/2004.

1113. http://www.cnn.com/US/9705/tobacco/business/.

1114. The estimated 435,000 people per year killed by tobacco was more than four times the number estimated to die as a result of alcohol (100,000) and more than twenty times the number estimated to be killed by illegal drugs (20,000). See Hughes, "Adopting the Substance Abuse Goal: A Story of Philanthropic Decision Making."

1115. These five programs are only a sample of the Foundation's many undertakings in tobacco and substance abuse-related areas. I believe they are indicative of the breadth and depth of the Foundation's involvement in tobacco issues, and they include the most significant examples of RWJ efforts on several fronts of the effort.

1116. C. Tracy Orleans, "Challenges and Opportunities for Tobacco Control: the Robert Wood Johnson Foundation Agenda." *Tobacco Control Online*, 1998, http://tc.bmjjournals.com/cgi/content/full/7/suppl_1/S8.

1117. Nancy J. Kaufman and Karyn L. Feiden, "Linking Biomedical and Behavioral Research for Tobacco Use Prevention: Sundance and Beyond." In *The Robert Wood Johnson Foundation Anthology: To Improve Health and Health Care 2000, Vol. III*, Stephen L. Isaacs and James R. Knickman, eds. (San Francisco: Josey-Bass, 1999), 161–85.

1118. This story has been extensively chronicled by the news media. Sheryl Gay Stolberg, "Beleaguered Tobacco Foe Holds Key to Talks," *New York Times*, 6/4/1997; Digby Diehl, "The Center for Tobacco-Free Kids and the Tobacco-Settlement Negotiations." In *The Robert Wood Johnson Anthology: To Improve Health and Health Care, Vol. VI*, Stephen L. Isaacs and James R. Knickman, eds. (San Francisco: Jossey-Bass,

2003), 101–24; Michael Pertschuk, *Smoke in Their Eyes: Lessons in Movement Leadership from the Tobacco Wars* (Nashville: Vanderbilt University, 2001).

1119. Kaufman, "Linking Biomedical and Behavioral Research for Tobacco Use Prevention: Sundance and Beyond."

1120. Other private foundations now involved in tobacco research, advocacy, and control include the Commonwealth Fund, the Ford Foundation, the Annie E. Casey Foundation, the Joyce Foundation, the Kaiser Family Foundation, and others.

1121. Leonard Koppett, "The National Spit Tobacco Education Program," *The Robert Wood Johnson Foundation Anthology: To Improve Health and Health Care 1998–1999, Vol. II*, Stephen L. Isaacs and James R. Knickman, eds. (San Francisco: Jossey-Bass, 1998), 43–56.

1122. "Q & A with Risa Lavizzo-Mourey, M.D., M.B.A.: Tobacco Strategy," available from http://www.rwjf.org/news/special/tobaccoStrategy.jhtml.

1123. Andy Serwer, "The Waltons: Inside America's Richest Family," *Forbes*, 11/15/2004, 86.

1124. "Salute to Effective Education Philanthropy," *Philanthropy Magazine*, January/February 2003.

1125. "Charter Schools: Challenges and Opportunities," *Philanthropy Magazine*, January/February 2003.

1126. Jonathan Schorr, *Hard Lessons: The Promise of an Inner City Charter School* (New York: Ballantine Books, 2002), 224–25.

1127. "Charter Schools," 2003.

1128. Ibid.

1129. "All About Charter Schools," *Center for Education Reform*, http://www.edreform.com/index.cfm?fuseAction=document&documentID=1964.

1130. Sam Dillon, "Backer of Charter Schools Finds They Trail in Financing," *New York Times*, 8/23/2005, A14.

1131. Jim Hopkins, "Wal-Mart Heirs Pour Riches into Reforming Education," *USA Today*, 3/11/2004, 1B.

1132. V. Dion Haynes, "Applications Halted; Hearing Set on Shifting Authority," *Washington Post*, 6/2/2006, B4.

1133. "Program Focus," *The Walton Family Foundation*, http://www.wffhome.com/program_focus.htm#A.%20Charter%20School%20Initiative.

1134. For a far more in-depth look at the development of JSTOR, written from an insider's perspective, see Roger C. Schonfeld, *JSTOR: A History* (Princeton: Princeton University Press, 2003). According to Schonfeld, a variety of changes—including in exchange rates, paper costs, publishers' profit margins, and postage costs—combined to force the price increases.

1135. Ibid. In fact, a Mellon Foundation study showed that academic libraries were able to collect each year a smaller and smaller portion of the total scholarly output.

1136. Ethan Bronner, "You Can Look It Up, Hopefully," *New York Times*, 1/10/1999.

1137. William G. Bowen, "At a Slight Angle to the Universe: The University in a Digitized, Commercialized Age," Romanes Lecture for 2000, 10/17/2000.

1138. The University of Michigan was selected after the Foundation concluded that it was best equipped, among the TULIP participants, to launch JSTOR. According to Karen Hunter, senior vice president of Elsevier, Michigan was "the outstanding player" among the group that had established TULIP. Schonfeld, *JSTOR: A History*.

1139. Ibid.

1140. Bowen, "At a Slight Angle to the Universe."

1141. Kevin M. Guthrie, "JSTOR and the University of Michigan: An Evolving Collaboration," *Library Hi Tech*, Vol. 16 (1998), 9–17. The TULIP program had not stored more than 50,000 pages.

1142. In fact, users of JSTOR have come to realize that much of the scholarship in those old journals is still very relevant, but had been lost to most researchers as a result of its inaccessibility. See Bronner, "You Can Look It Up, Hopefully."

1143. Guthrie, "JSTOR and the University of Michigan."

1144. Introduction to Schonfeld, *JSTOR: A History*.

1145. The Foundation had also contributed $1 million in March 1997 to provide access to JSTOR to several private, historically black colleges and universities. Mellon would continue providing funds to JSTOR, even after it had become financially self-sustaining. These grants have ranged in purpose from adding of new journals to the database to spreading access to JSTOR to universities in Eastern Europe.

1146. Available from http://www.jstor.org/about/facts.html.

1147. Ibid.

1148. JSTOR charges membership fees from participating institutions. These fees are on a sliding scale based on an institution's projected usage and its ability to pay. Fees are set so as not to discourage small, relatively underfunded libraries from joining.

1149. It is important to keep in mind that when this estimate was made, JSTOR was less than 30 percent of its current size. The savings may be much higher now. Bowen, "At a Slight Angle to the Universe."

1150. Bronner, "You Can Look It Up, Hopefully."

1151. Michael T. Kaufman, *Soros: The Life and Times of a Messianic Billionaire* (New York: Alfred A. Knopf, 2002).

1152. George Soros, *Soros on Soros* (New York: John Wiley & Sons, 1995).

1153. Irina Dezhina, *The International Science Foundation: The Preservation of Basic Science in the Former Soviet Union* (New York: International Science Foundation, 1997).

1154. Ibid.

1155. Ibid.

1156. Ibid.

1157. Ibid.

1158. Ibid. See also the case study of Soros/OSI programs to foster democracy and civil societies in Central and Eastern Europe.

1159. In some countries, such as Russia, this was accomplished by means of specific governmental recognition. In others, such as Tajikistan, Turkmenistan, and Azerbaijan, ISF was simply exempt, de facto, in the absence of any formal regulation, from taxes and customs duties. And in at least one of the republics—Estonia—the International Science Foundation set the precedent for the tax exemption of the country's emerging not-for-profit sector. See Dezhina, *The International Science Foundation*.

1160. Ibid.

1161. Kaufman writes that the 20,763 Russian scientists receiving grants made up 18.5 percent of all Soviet scientists. But the total number of scientists who received emergency grants, across all the republics, is 26,145 (Dezhina). Accepting Kaufman's figures, therefore, tells us that this totaled just over 23 percent of Soviet scientist population.

1162. Dezhina, *The International Science Foundation*.

1163. Ibid.

1164. Lee Hockstader, "U.S. Bureaucratic Battle Threatens Private Funds for Russian Scientists," *Washington Post*, 11/29/1994.

1165. Kaufman, *Soros*.

1166. Available from http://www.macalester.edu/freemangrant/about_Freeman.html.

1167. Freeman Foundation, *Annual Report*, 2004.

1168. Ibid.

1169. Available from http://www.iie.org.

1170. Jacqueline Trescott, "Asian Shows Funded at Youth Museums," *Washington Post*, 6/29/2002.

1171. Freeman Foundation, *Annual Report*, 2004

1172. Paul Desruisseaux, "Emergency-Loan Plan Established to help Asian Students Remain in U.S. Colleges," *Chronicle of Higher Education*, 5/8/1998.

1173. Ibid.

1174. Trescott, "Asian Shows Funded at Youth Museums;" see also Freeman Foundation, *Annual Report*, 2004.

1175. Freeman Foundation, *Annual Report*, 2004.

1176. Ibid.

1177. Prostate cancer spreads much more quickly in young victims than older ones. So, while a seventy-year-old man diagnosed with the cancer is likely to die of other causes before it has spread enough to kill him, a forty-six-year-old diagnosed with prostate cancer—like Milken in 1993—often has only a few months to live.

1178. Prostate Cancer Foundation website, http://www.prostatecancerfoundation.org/.

1179. Milken's one-time nemesis, Rudolph Giuliani, says of him that he "took the tremendous talent he had in business and is using it to fight prostate cancer. What more could you ask for?" Cora Daniels, "The Man Who Changed Medicine," *Fortune*, 11/29/2004, 91–112.

1180. Ibid.

1181. Ibid.

1182. Over the same period, the U.S. population has grown by 11 percent, and, in fact, the National Cancer Institute's estimate of this per capita drop is an even higher 26 percent.

1183. Daniels, "The Man Who Changed Medicine."

1184. Prostate Cancer Foundation website, http://www.prostatecancerfoundation.org/.

1185. Daniels, "The Man Who Changed Medicine."

1186. Ibid.

1187. Ibid.

1188. Rebecca Fowler, "Michael Milken's Riskiest Deal; He's Investing Heavily in Battling Cancer. But Will His Stock Go Up?" *Washington Post*, 9/29/1994.

1189. Cora Daniels, "The Man Who Changed Medicine," *Fortune*, 11/29/2004, 91–112.

1190. Ibid.

1191. Available from http://www.beeson.org.

1192. Ibid.

1193. The program's name has since changed to the Paul B. Beeson Career Development Awards in Aging Research Program.

1194. "Leading Science: 10th Anniversary Report, Paul B. Beeson Career Development Awards in Aging Research Program 1994–2004," American Federation for Aging Research, 2004, available from http://www.beeson.org/tenth_anniversary_beeson.pdf.

1195. Available from http://www.beeson.org.

1196. "Leading Science: 10th Anniversary Report."

1197. Ibid.

1198. Ibid.

1199. As Brian Hofland, MD, director of the Aging Program of the Atlantic Philanthropies, has said, "This program captures talented physician-scientists at a crucial point in their careers and encourages them to think of themselves as aging researchers. Since they are such high quality researchers, they have a ripple effect on other faculty and staff they train. As they take on leadership roles, they are having a tremendous influence on the field." Ibid.

1200. Ibid.

1201. Having decided that their $15 million could do more good as part of a larger pool of grantmaking funds, the Pickers chose the Commonwealth Fund because it was "an institution with a common interest in improving health care and a record of effective grantmaking, management, and leadership." See http://www.cmwf.org/.

1202. Available from http://thenrcpickergroup.com.

1203. Ibid. Since this early research, an eighth dimension—access to care—has been added to the list.

1204. Picker surveys are, for example, the standard used to evaluate and improve care at all of the VHA's 163 hospitals and 800 clinics around the nation.

1205. William G. Bowen and Derek Bok, *The Shape of the River* (Princeton: Princeton University Press, 2000).

1206. William G. Bowen, "President's Statement," Andrew W. Mellon Foundation, *Annual Report*, 1997.

1207. Interview with William G. Bowen, *Frontline*. Available from http://www.pbs.org/wgbh/pages/frontline/shows/sats/interviews/.

1208. Bowen, *Shape of the River*.

1209. William G. Bowen, "President's Statement," Andrew W. Mellon Foundation, *Annual Report*, 1997.

1210. Martin Morse Wooster, "Sustenance for the Affirmative," *Washington Times*, 1/1/2000.

1211. Warren E. Leary, "More Gun Violence, and Better Care for Victims," *New York Times*, 10/23/1994, A32.

1212. Ibid.

1213. B. Drummond Ayres Jr., "Gun Maker on Mayhem: That Is Not Our Doing," *New York Times*, 3/19/1994, A8.

1214. Pam Belluck, "Weary of Gun Violence, Chicago Considers Suit," *New York Times*, 6/12/1998, A12.

1215. Fox Butterfield, "Gun Violence May Be Subsiding, Studies Find," *New York Times*, 10/14/1996, A10.

1216. Abigail Trafford, "Measuring Violence," *Washington Post*, 6/25/2002, F01.

1217. David Tuller, "Combining the Scattered Data from Violent Deaths," *New York Times*, 1/14/2003, F7.

1218. Charles Storch, "TV-Journalist-Turned-Foundation-President Now Seeks to Solve Society's Problems," *Chicago Tribune*, 6/24/1993, T1.

1219. Ibid.

1220. Ibid.

1221. David B. Ottaway, "Legal Assault on Firms Is Armed by Foundations," *Washington Post*, 5/19/1999, A1.

1222. "Needed: Better Data on Firearm Injuries," *Works in Progress: Newsletter of the Joyce Foundation*, May 1997.

1223. Fox Butterfield, "Poor Data Hampers Gun Policies, Study Says," *New York Times*, 12/17/2004, A25.

1224. "Tracking the Problem," *Works in Progress: Newsletter of the Joyce Foundation*, May 1998.

1225. Ibid.

1226. Marilynn Marchione, "Suicides Rank High in Gun Study," *Milwaukee Journal Sentinel*, 12/10/1998, A1.

1227. Abigail Trafford, "Measuring Violence," *Washington Post*, 6/25/2002, F01.

1228. Marilyn Marchione, "System to Track Firearm Injuries to Be Expanded Nationwide," *Milwaukee Journal Sentinel*, 1/23/2002.

1229. David Tuller, "Combining the Scattered Data from Violent Deaths," *New York Times*, 1/14/2003, F7.

1230. "Just the Facts," *Works in Progress: Newsletter of the Joyce Foundation*, February 2005.

1231. Ari Korpivaara, *Building the New South Africa: One House, One Dream at a Time* (Connecticut: Herlin Press, 2001).

1232. Ibid.

1233. Ibid.

1234. Staff, "Soros Pledges Dollars 55M to S Africa," *Financial Times*, 12/15/1994.

1235. Korpivaara, *Building the New South Africa.*

1236. Available from http://www.nurcha.co.za/.

1237. NURCHA, *Annual Report*, 2004.

1238. Ibid.

1239. Ibid.

1240. Available from http://www.nurcha.co.za/.

1241. "U.S. and Southern African National Plan for Upcoming FTA Negotiations," Press Release, U.S. Department of State, 1/13/2003.

1242. Ibid.

1243. Korpivaara, *Building the New South Africa.*

1244. Ibid.

1245. Ibid.

1246. Pew Press Release, "Pew Charitable Trusts Establishes New Nonprofit Research Organization to Help Better Inform Public & Policymakers on Issues & Trends," Available from http://www.pewtrusts.com.

1247. Available from http://people-press.org.

1248. Brian Faler, "Pew Trusts to Open Research Center in D.C.," *Washington Post*, 4/27/2004.

1249. Available from http://people-press.org.

1250. A glance at the Center's website, for example, shows that in the first six weeks of 2005, these three papers featured at least ten articles citing data gathered by the Pew Research Center. See http://people-press.org.

1251. The other five are the Project for Excellence in Journalism, Stateline.org, the Pew Internet & American Life Project, the Pew Forum on Religion and Public Life, and the Pew Hispanic Center.

1252. The creation of the Pew Research Center is the first major reorganization undertaken by the Trusts in the wake of its conversion in early 2004 from a private foundation to a public charity. In addition to institutionalizing support for the Center's composite research operations, the move allows the Trusts to forego about $1 million per year in administrative costs now that Pew need not pay outside nonprofits to administer its programs. Stephanie Strom, "New Pew Trusts Merging Works Into One Body," *New York Times*, 4/27/2004.

1253. Faler, "Pew Trusts to Open Research Center in D.C."

1254. In fact, this study was also made possible by a charitable foundation. See case study on the Rockefeller Foundation's underwriting of the construction of Mt. Palomar's 200-inch Hale Telescope.

1255. Staff, "A Million Galaxies to be Tracked," *Johns Hopkins Gazette*, 2/9/1998.

1256. Ibid.

1257. Available from http://www.sdss.org.

1258. The preceding description is available from http://www.sdss.org.

1259. "A Million Galaxies to be Tracked," *Johns Hopkins Gazette*.

1260. Ibid.

1261. John Noble Wilford, "Survey Offers a Look Deep Into Cosmos," *New York Times*, 6/6/2001.

1262. Available from http://www.sdss.org.

1263. Ibid.

1264. "A Million Galaxies to be Tracked," *Johns Hopkins Gazette*.

1265. Available from http://www.sloan.org.

1266. James Glanz, "Survey Reveals Massive Galaxies," *New York Times*, 12/14/1999.

1267. "A Million Galaxies to be Tracked," *Johns Hopkins Gazette*.

1268. Available from http://www.sloan.org.

1269. Wilford, "Survey Offers a Look Deep Into Cosmos."

1270. Eliot Marshall, "Demand Outstrips Supply," *Science*, Vol. 272, No. 5269 (6/21/1996), 1731.

1271. Mari N. Jensen, "Reinventing the Science Master's Degree," *Science*, Vol. 284, No. 5420 (6/4/1999), 1610.

1272. Kenneth R. Weiss, "Stirring Things Up," *Los Angeles Times*, 10/24/1999, T2.

1273. "General Information," Alfred P. Sloan Foundation, 2003, 6–7.

1274. Shelia Tobias, Daryl E. Chubin, and Kevin Aylesworth, *Rethinking Science as a Career: Perceptions and Realities in the Physical Sciences* (Tuscon: Research Corporation, 1995).

1275. Janice Rosenberg, "Professional Master's Degrees a Growing Trend; Students Exhibit a Blend of Skills," *Chicago Tribune*, 9/21/2003, C5.

1276. Kenneth R. Weiss, "Stirring Things Up," *Los Angeles Times*, 10/24/99, T2.

1277. Nishad H. Majmudar, "Science Master's for Business Draws Critics," *Wall Street Journal*, 8/3/2004, B1.

1278. "General Information," Alfred P. Sloan Foundation, 2004, 7.

1279. "General Information," Alfred P. Sloan Foundation, 2000, 20; "Professional Science Masters," http://www.sciencemasters.com/.

1280. "General Information," Alfred P. Sloan Foundation, 2004, 20.

1281. "General Information," Alfred P. Sloan Foundation, 2004, 19.

1282. Donald N. Langenberg, "Time for Innovation in Math, Science Education," *Baltimore Sun*, 8/26/2005, 11A.

1283. *Tapping America's Potential: The Education for Innovation Initiative*, Business Roundtable, July 2005, available at http://www.businessroundtable.com/publications/publication.aspx?qs=2AF6BF807822B0F1AD1478E, 11.

1284. This history is based on an interview of Ms. Kibbe conducted in 2002 by

Mitch Nauffts of the *Philanthropy News Digest*. Available from http://fdncenter.org/pnd/newsmaker/nwsmkr.jhtml?id=5600108.

1285. The David and Lucile Packard Foundation: Program Profiles, "Grantmakers for Effective Organizations," available from http://www.packard.org.

1286. GEO's activities are described on its website at http://www.geofunders.org.

1287. Jon Christensen, "Exploring New Ideas for Making Finances Clearer and Scandals Rarer," *New York Times*, 11/17/2003.

1288. The David and Lucile Packard Foundation: Program Profiles, "Grantmakers for Effective Organizations," available from http://www.packard.org.

1289. These findings were presented by Light at the 2002 national conference of GEO. Ibid.

1290. Interview with Barbara Kibbe. *Philanthropy News Digest*, available from http://fdncenter.org/pnd/ newsmaker/nwsmkr.jhtml?id=5600108.

1291. Each of the three initial foundations—Packard, Kauffman, and Irvine—still support GEO, as do a host of other foundations. Packard and Kauffman, along with the W.K. Kellogg Foundation, are the three largest supporters, each providing over $75,000 per year. Available from http://www.geofunders.org.

1292. The original aim of withholding U.N. dues was to force budgetary reforms upon the world body. However, in subsequent years, a range of issues arose to impede progress toward full repayment of the U.S. debt.

1293. Available from http://www.unausa.org.

1294. Barbara Crossette, "U.N. Gives its First Grants from Big Ted Turner Gift," *New York Times*, 5/20/1998.

1295. This term refers to a strategy undertaken instead of a more traditional, numbers-oriented, "grassroots" approach. The Better World campaign recognized that, given the limited resources it could use, maximum impact would be achieved by building a groundswell of support among community leaders and prominent local organizations. These local bodies, in turn, could get the word out to the general public in their districts. To this end, the Better World campaign educated and lobbied prominent citizens within local communities. These included people with connections to the congressional representatives from their district, such as significant political donors and fundraisers, as well as local business owners who had a history of collaboration with their congressman or woman, or who simply had a significant voice in the community.

1296. It is likely that President Clinton saw, in arrears negotiations, an effort to shore up his legacy as an internationalist leader, and, to set a tone of international engagement for the incoming administration. For instance, Clinton also decided, in the last days of his presidency, to sign the controversial Rome Treaty, which created the International Criminal Court.

1297. Colum Lynch, "Turner Offers $35 Million to Help U.S. Pay U.N. Dues," *Washington Post*, 12/22/2002.

1298. As described above, the U.N. is prohibited from accepting a direct payment from Turner, or any other would-be donor. However, at the 11/00 BWF board meeting, Turner offered to pay his $31 million directly to the U.S. government, which would, in turn, pay that amount to the United Nations.

1299. For decades, contributions to the U.N. had been assessed on the basis of a country's average GDP over the past six years. Under the new agreement, contributions are determined by GDP averaged over only 4.5 years. This change had the effect of increasing the contribution of nations, such as Brazil, Singapore, and India, which have rapidly developing economies. And it has, consequently, lowered the relative contributions of more established economies, particularly the United States.

1300. Susan Myers, e-mail to Scott Kohler, 4/23/2004.

1301. Available from http://www.foundationcenter.org/.

1302. Joel L. Fleishman, "Simply Doing Good or Doing Good Well: Stewardship, Hubris, and Foundation Governance," *Just Money: A Critique of Contemporary American Philanthropy*, H. Peter Karoff, ed., (Boston: The Philanthropic Initiative, 2004).

1303. For a more detailed account of this transformation, see Daniel Curran and Allen Grossman, "EMCF: A New Approach at an Old Foundation," case study, Harvard Business School, 2002.

1304. "EMCF's Youth Development Fund: Strategy and Theory of Change," 6/10/2003, available from http://www.emcf.org.

1305. My discussion of this process draws on two sources. The first is the Edna McConnell Clark Foundation's website at http://www.emcf.org. The second is a presentation given on 2/23/2005 by Dr. David Hunter, Director of Evaluation and Knowledge Development at the Foundation, to the Foundation Impact Research Group at Duke University.

1306. Available from http://www.emcf.org.

1307. Ibid.

1308. Paul Tough, "The Harlem Project," *New York Times Magazine*, 6/10/2004.

1309. "EMCF's Youth Development Fund: Strategy and Theory of Change," 6/10/2003, available from http://www.emcf.org.

1310. Hunter, FIRG presentation, 2005.

1311. "Building New Communities: Building New Lives," brochure, The Chicago Housing Authority Plan for Transformation, 2002.

1312. Available from CHA website, http://www.thecha.org.

1313. Ibid.

1314. "Building New Communities: Building New Lives," brochure.

1315. Available from CHA website, http://www.thecha.org.

1316. Memorandum from Susan Lloyd, of the John D. and Catherine T. MacArthur Foundation, to Scott Kohler, 1/7/2005.

1317. Available from http://www.thecha.org.

1318. Ibid.

1319. Ibid.

1320. Memorandum from Susan Lloyd, of the John D. and Catherine T. MacArthur Foundation, to Scott Kohler.

1321. It should be noted that Greenberg, in this statement, went on to acknowledge "several other foundations and corporations." The Project for Transformation has been, and continues to be, a massive undertaking requiring the committed support of a host of groups in public and private sectors. Joe Ruklick, "CHA's Private-Public Partnership Continues as MacArthur Foundation Awards Planning Grant," *Chicago Defender*, 4/19/2003.

1322. Cheryl L. Reed, "Chicago's 100 Most Powerful Women: From Life in Hut to Giving Millions Away," *Chicago Sun-Times*, 4/14/2004.

1323. The David and Lucile Packard Foundation, Program Profiles: China Sustainable Energy Program, available from http://www.packard.org/index.cgi?page=consci-profile&id=0003.

1324. Ibid.

1325. Available from http://www.efchina.org/home.cfm.

1326. The David and Lucile Packard Foundation, Program Profiles: China Sustainable Energy Program.

1327. This was renewed the following year with an additional $2 million grant. The William and Flora Hewlett Foundation, *Annual Report*, 2003.

1328. Final Report: Evaluation of China Sustainable Energy Program, Prepared by Energy Resources International, Inc., 7/5/2003.

1329. Ibid.

1330. Ibid.

1331. The David and Lucile Packard Foundation, Program Profiles: China Sustainable Energy Program, available from http://www.packard.org/index.cgi?page=consci-profile&id=0003.

1332. Final Report: Evaluation of China Sustainable Energy Program, Prepared by Energy Resources International, Inc., 7/5/2003. The Hewlett Foundation's projection, in its 2003 Annual Report, is the considerably lower figure of 1.6 billion barrels (and over $100 billion in energy import savings). Both estimates, however, project significant savings, even in the context of China's massive economy.

1333. The David and Lucile Packard Foundation, Program Profiles: China Sustainable Energy Program, available from http://www.packard.org/index.cgi?page=consci-profile&id=0003.

1334. Final Report: Evaluation of China Sustainable Energy Program, Prepared by Energy Resources International, Inc., 7/5/2003.

1335. Linda A Long, "Infrastructure: Playing it Smart," *Foundation News and Commentary*, March/April 2003.

1336. In fact, some places began to take counter-measures even earlier. In the U.S., Oregon was first off the block with a set of tough zoning laws that "limited sprawl while protecting farmland and open space." Clark Williams-Derry, "Who is the Smart Growth Leader?" Elm Street Writers Group, 2002, available from Michigan Land Use Institute website at http://www.mlui.org/.

1337. Peter S. Goodman, "Glendening vs. Suburban Sprawl: Governor Banks on 'Smart Growth,' but Even Supporters Have Doubts," *Washington Post*, 10/6/1998.

1338. "What is Smart Growth," Fact Sheet, United States Environmental Protection Agency, available from http://www.epa.gov.

1339. Available from http://www.surdna.org/programs/environment.html.

1340. Available from http://www.fundersnetwork.org.

1341. Michael Barrette, "Smart Money," *Planning*, November 2001.

1342. Andrew Jacobs, "McGreevey, Focusing on Environment, Enlists in 'War on Sprawl,'" *New York Times*, 1/2/2003.

1343. Terry Rodgers and David E. Graham, "Smart Growth Supported by EPA Chief Whitman," *San Diego Union-Tribune*. 1/25/2002.

1344. Barrette, "Smart Money."

1345. Tamar Lewin, "$330 Million in Ford Grants Will Aid Foreign Students," *New York Times*, 11/29/2000.

1346. Remarks by Susan V. Berresford at the Launch of the Ford Foundation International Fellowships Program, 11/29/2000, available from http://www.fordifp.net.

1347. It is worth noting that this huge commitment drove Ford's payout rate for 2001 to 7.2 percent, significantly higher than the minimum payout required by law.

1348. Available from http://www.fordifp.net.

1349. Remarks by Susan V. Berresford at the Launch of the Ford Foundation International Fellowships Program, 11/29/2000.

1350. Joan Dassin, "Promoting Access and Equity in International Higher Education," *International Educator*, Summer 2004.

1351. Ibid.

1352. Ibid.

1353. Ibid.

1354. Remarks by Senator Richard Lugar at the Launch of the Ford Foundation International Fellowships Program, 11/29/2000, available from http://www.fordifp.net.

1355. Remarks by Susan V. Berresford at the Launch of the Ford Foundation International Fellowships Program, 11/29/2000.

1356. Much of this case study's substance was gleaned from a phone interview, conducted by the author on 4/19/2005, of Scott Rehmus, Program Officer for the Packard Foundation's Conservation and Science Program.

1357. Available from The Nature Conservancy website at http://www.tnc.org.

1358. "Cascadia: Great Bear Rainforest, British Columbia," memo from the David and Lucile Packard Foundation.

1359. Ibid.

1360. Ibid.

1361. Ibid.

1362. To date, the Packard Foundation has spent over $6 million in support of the Joint Solutions Project. Ibid.

1363. Ibid.

1364. Available from http://www.ddcf.org.

1365. Available from http://www.surdna.org.

1366. The director and dean of the Eastman School at the University of Rochester, a TSAI grantee, lauded the program for going against the local and national trend. See http://www.rochester.edu/Eastman/news/print.php?id=32.

1367. "Jacob's Pillow Named a National Historic Landmark," Press Release,

6/6/2003, available from http://williamstown.iberkshires.com/community/story10945.html.

1368. Julie E. Washington, "$1.1 Million in Grants for School of the Arts," *Plain Dealer*, 4/4/2001.

1369. Kathleen Kennedy Manzo, "Scholar Advocates 'Brand Name' Charter School Networks," *Education Week*, Vol. 23, No. 37 (5/19/2004), 11.

1370. Jonathan Schorr, *Hard Lessons: The Promise of an Inner City Charter School* (New York: Ballantine Books, 2002), 49–51.

1371. Schorr, *Hard Lessons*, 51.

1372. Michael T. Hartney, "A Powerhouse Charter-funder Aims for the Next Level," *Philanthropy Magazine*, Sept/Oct 2004, available from http://www.philanthropyroundtable.org/magazines/2004/SeptOct/Powerhouse.htm.

1373. Kelly Pedersen, "Hard Work Pays Off," *Houston Chronicle*, 8/5/2000, A35.

1374. Hartney, "A Powerhouse Charter-funder Aims for the Next Level."

1375. Jay Mathews, "Marketing the Best Schools," *Washingtonpost.com*, 8/15/2006.

1376. Ibid.

1377. Ibid.

1378. Ibid.

1379. Jay Mathews, "Expert Takes a New Look at KIPP Schools," *Washington Post*, 5/12/2005, T3.

1380. Mathews, "Marketing the Best Schools."

1381. "KIPP: Results," http://www.kipp.org/press/KIPP_Overview.pdf.

1382. "About KIPP," *KIPP: Knowledge Is Power Program*, http://www.kipp.org/aboutkipp.cfm?pageid=nav6.

1383. The latter phrase is part of the mission statement of the Markle Foundation, which was founded in 1927 by John and Mary Markle, http://www.markle.org.

1384. Ibid.

1385. Carol Diamond, Managing Director of the Markle Foundation's Health Program, Presentation to the Duke University Foundation Impact Research Group (FIRG); 1/19/2005. The presentation, for which the author was present, informs this case study throughout.

1386. Diamond, FIRG presentation, 1/19/2005.

1387. "Federal Government Announces First Federal eGOV Health Information Exchange Standards," Press Release, United States Department of Health and Human Services, 3/21/2003.

1388. Diamond, FIRG presentation, 1/19/2005.

1389. Ibid.

1390. Steve Lohr, "Road Map to a Digital System of Health Records," *New York Times*, 1/19/2005.

1391. Diamond, FIRG presentation, 1/19/2005.

PublicAffairs is a publishing house founded in 1997. It is a tribute to the standards, values, and flair of three persons who have served as mentors to countless reporters, writers, editors, and book people of all kinds, including me.

I.F. STONE, proprietor of *I. F. Stone's Weekly*, combined a commitment to the First Amendment with entrepreneurial zeal and reporting skill and became one of the great independent journalists in American history. At the age of eighty, Izzy published *The Trial of Socrates*, which was a national bestseller. He wrote the book after he taught himself ancient Greek.

BENJAMIN C. BRADLEE was for nearly thirty years the charismatic editorial leader of *The Washington Post*. It was Ben who gave the *Post* the range and courage to pursue such historic issues as Watergate. He supported his reporters with a tenacity that made them fearless and it is no accident that so many became authors of influential, best-selling books.

ROBERT L. BERNSTEIN, the chief executive of Random House for more than a quarter century, guided one of the nation's premier publishing houses. Bob was personally responsible for many books of political dissent and argument that challenged tyranny around the globe. He is also the founder and longtime chair of Human Rights Watch, one of the most respected human rights organizations in the world.

For fifty years, the banner of PublicAffairs Press was carried by its owner Morris B. Schnapper, who published Gandhi, Nasser, Toynbee, Truman, and about 1,500 other authors. In 1983, Schnapper was described by *The Washington Post* as "a redoubtable gadfly." His legacy will endure in the books to come.

Peter Osnos, *Founder and Editor-at-Large*

Printed in the United States
93187LV00008B/75/A